the
cult of the
amateur

the
cult of the
amateur

how blogs, MySpace, YouTube,
and the rest of today's user-generated
media are destroying our economy,
our culture, and our values

andrew keen

Doubleday
New York London Toronto Sydney Auckland

DD

DOUBLEDAY

Published in the United States by Doubleday, an imprint of The Doubleday
Publishing Group, a division of Random House, Inc., New York.
www.doubleday.com

A hardcover edition of this book was originally published in 2007 by Currency.

DOUBLEDAY is a registered trademark and the DD colophon
is a trademark of Random House, Inc.

Book design by Chris Welch

Library of Congress Cataloging-in-Publication Data
Keen, Andrew.
The cult of the amateur : how blogs, MySpace, YouTube, and the rest of today's
user-generated media are destroying our economy, our culture, and our values /
Andrew Keen.
p. cm.
Includes bibliographical references and index.
1. Blogs—Social aspects. 2. Online social networks. 3. MySpace.com.
4. YouTube (Electronic resource) 5. Internet—Social aspects. 6. Internet—
Economic aspects. 7. Information society. 8. Self-publishing. I. Title.

HM851.K43 2007
303.48'33—dc22

2007048058

ISBN 978-0-385-52081-2

PRINTED IN THE UNITED STATES OF AMERICA

1 3 5 7 9 10 8 6 4 2

First Paperback Edition

For Elias, Zara, and Betsy

contents

foreword

The woman who came up to me after the lecture seemed traumatized. "How could it have happened," she asked me numbly. "Such a thing has never occurred before."

It was late November last year and we were standing together in the auditorium of a Berlin hotel trying to make sense of a senseless massacre that had just occurred at a small high school in Southern Finland. I had just given a lecture about why the Web 2.0 revolution is corrupting young people across the world. My speech had presented the same arguments that are laid out in this book: that MySpace and Facebook are creating a youth culture of digital narcissism; open-source knowledge-sharing sites like Wikipedia are undermining the authority of teachers in the classroom; the YouTube generation are more interested in self-expression than in learning about the outside world; the cacophony of anonymous blogs and user-generated content are deafening today's youth to the voices of informed experts and professional journalists; today's kids are so busy self-broadcasting on social networks that they no longer consume the creative work of professional musicians, novelists, or filmmakers.

The woman was a school teacher from Finland, a country distinguished not only for the exceedingly wired and interconnected lifestyle of its citizens (especially of its young people), but also for its exceptionally low rates of crime and violence. That blissful peace was shattered last November, however, soon after Pekka Eric Auvinen, an eighteen-year-old schoolboy from a small town just north of Helsinki, posted some content on YouTube. His video, authored under the name of "sturmgeist89" (which means "storm spirit" in German) and titled "Jokela High School Massacre—11/7/2007," featured the gun-toting Auvinen dressed in a "Humanity Is Overrated" T-shirt, predicting a massacre at his high school. Yet nobody—neither the YouTube administrators nor the site's millions of viewers—flagged this video or reported it to the police. As promised, two weeks later, on 11/7/2007, Auvinen walked into Jokela High School and shot dead two girls, five boys, and the headmistress.

The woman standing opposite me in the auditorium of the Berlin hotel was right. Such a *thing* has never occurred before in peaceful, enlightened Finland. I stared back at her in silence, not knowing what to say or how to comfort her. I couldn't blame user-generated media for this crime; YouTube wasn't the cause of Auvinen's murderous psychosis, it was merely the vehicle for his expression. And yet one can't deny that this tragic senseless story—the self-broadcasting teenager, the anonymous used-generated video, the absence of regulation or accountability on YouTube, the breakdown of cultural authority, the ultimate bloodbath—was, if not directly caused by the Web 2.0 revolution, at least facilitated by it.

"Anyway," she said, sticking out her hand out toward me, "I want to thank you."

"*Thank* me?" I replied, grabbing her cold hand. "I'm not sure I've been very helpful in explaining what happened."

"Nobody can explain such a thing," she said quietly. "But I want to thank you for your book and for your speech today. I certainly don't agree with everything you say, but finally somebody is raising serious cultural and ethical questions about this YouTube generation. You are starting a really important conversation. We all need to talk about this before it's too late."

A few months earlier, I'd had an entirely different response to the conversation this book has generated. It was the day before the publication of this book and a journalist friend was predicting its reception. "When your book comes out," she said, forewarning my impending infamy, "you'll instantly become one of the most hated people on the Internet."

"But it's just a book that is critical of user-generated media," I countered. "It's not exactly about life or death. Why would strangers hate me for writing a book?"

But my journalist friend had been right. As soon as the book hit the shelves, I was instantaneously attacked from all directions. For the digital utopians, *Cult of the Amateur* was more than just a book—it was a violent assault on their very lifestyle. The bloggers, the YouTubers, the Wikipedians, they not only all took my criticism seriously, but they also took it personally. I was subverting their original subversion, questioning their unquestioned faith in digital democracy, revolting against the very user-generated media revolution that had come to define their community.

So it was only fair, I suppose, that their attacks on me were also personal—bloggers called me and my book Luddite, error-ridden, simplistic, inaccurate, shameless, wrongheaded, beneath criticism, and worse—unprintably worse—the French newspaper *Libération* summed up my new infamy by calling me "L'Antichrist de la Silicon Valley," and an American reporter for CNet coined the book a "latter day 'J'accuse.'" The English newspaper *The Guardian* even dressed me up in religious garb, describing me as the "Martin Luther of the Internet counterreformation."

Were my critics correct?

I'm not sure about being either the Antichrist or Martin Luther 2.0, but they were certainly correct about one thing. Last summer, Stephen Colbert invited me onto his Comedy Central show, *The Colbert Report*. "You, sir," Colbert shouted, leaning forward and jabbing his finger under my nose. "You, sir, are an elitist!"

"Yes, I am," I admitted, backing away from Colbert's finger. "What's wrong with that?"

So, yes, I confess. It doesn't embarrass me to admit that I trust information about the Iraq war from accountable, well-trained *New York Times* reporters more than I trust it from anonymous bloggers, or that I put more stock in election coverage from NPR commentators than from poorly prepared podcasters. Nor am I ashamed to acknowledge that I prefer the professional wit of Stephen Colbert to any raw YouTube comic, and the refined music of Bob Dylan to that of an amateur self-broadcasting artist. Talent always has been, and will always be, scarce. So just as I want my doctor to have gone to a credible medical school and my lawyer to have passed the bar exam, so I want to be informed and entertained by trained, talented professionals.

That said, as for the other criticisms of the book, a handful are valid. Yes, I do at times put traditional mainstream media on a pedestal, ignoring the often dreadful quality of both network and cable television, particularly their so-called "news" shows and inane reality programming and *American Idol*–style popularity contests. Yes, I do fail to acknowledge that there is some very worthwhile and high quality content to be found on YouTube and on the blogosphere—if you know where to look. And, yes, I neglect to recognize that user-generated content has forced mainstream media to become more competitive and accountable. My detractors have helped me see the truth on these points, and for that I am grateful.

But most of the online criticisms of the book reflect the myopia of the digital mob. Like the claims that I hate technology, that I'm anti-progress, or a "Luddite"? I wish my critics could see me now. I am writing this foreword on one laptop while browsing the Internet on another. In one pocket is my BlackBerry device and in the other my iPod loaded with hundreds of podcasts.

If I'm as wired as a Finnish teenager, then why have I written a polemic against the Internet? The school teacher I met in Berlin put it best. I may not be Martin Luther, but I do want to start a conversation. While I concede that not all user-generated amateur content is worthless, talentless, or without merit, and while I admit that mainstream media is certainly far from perfect, I still believe that we need to talk about the consequences of today's user-generated media before it's too late. Blogs, MySpace, YouTube, and their ilk may not directly lead to the corruption of our culture—or to tragic events like the "Jokela High School Massacre—11/7/2007"— but the anonymous, unfettered nature of user-generated media is contributing to it by misinforming our young people, corroding our tradition of physical civic participation, endangering our individual rights to privacy, and corrupting our sense of personal responsibility and accountability.

This is the conversation I set out to start by writing this book—and I think I have succeeded, both in America and all over the world. Since this book came out last summer, I've been fortunate to talk with many thousands of people who, like me, are deeply worried and confused about the economic, cultural, and ethical consequences of our user-generated media revolution. The digital mob might hate me, but many others—teachers, recording engineers, politicians, musicians, librarians, parents, publishers, graphic artists, intellectual property lawyers, filmmakers, media entrepreneurs, and other professionals—are on my side. Like the school teacher from Finland, they want to talk about all this before it's too late.

I don't expect anyone to agree with every single one of my arguments. I'm not the head of the Internet counter-reformation and there's no "here I stand I can do no other" theology here. All I politely request that the reader bring to this book is an open mind toward both the benefits and problems of user-generated media. Such open-mindedness will create conversation about the digital revolution. And then this little book will have accomplished its purpose.

—Berkeley, January 5, 2008

the
cult of the
amateur

introduction

I f I didn't know better, I'd think it was 1999 all over again. The boom has returned to Silicon Valley, and the mad utopians are once again running wild. I bumped into one such evangelist at a recent San Francisco mixer.

Over glasses of fruity local Chardonnay, we swapped notes about our newest new things. He told me his current gig involved a new software for publishing music, text, and video on the Internet.

"It's MySpace meets YouTube meets Wikipedia meets Google," he said. "On steroids."

In reply, I explained I was working on a polemic about the destructive impact of the digital revolution on our culture, economy, and values.

"It's ignorance meets egoism meets bad taste meets mob rule," I said, unable to resist a smile. "On steroids."

He smiled uneasily in return. "So it's Huxley meets the digital age," he said. "You're rewriting Huxley for the twenty-first century." He raised his wine glass in my honor. "To *Brave New World 2.0!*"

We clinked wine glasses. But I knew we were toasting the wrong Huxley. Rather than Aldous, the inspiration behind this book comes from his grandfather, T. H. Huxley, the nineteenth-century evolutionary biologist and author of the "infinite monkey theorem." Huxley's theory says that if you provide infinite monkeys with infinite typewriters, some monkey somewhere will eventually create a masterpiece—a play by Shakespeare, a Platonic dialogue, or an economic treatise by Adam Smith.[1]

In the pre-Internet age, T. H. Huxley's scenario of infinite monkeys empowered with infinite technology seemed more like a mathematical jest than a dystopian vision. But what had once appeared as a joke now seems to foretell the consequences of a flattening of culture that is blurring the lines between traditional audience and author, creator and consumer, expert and amateur. This is no laughing matter.

Today's technology hooks all those monkeys up with all those typewriters. Except in our Web 2.0 world, the typewriters aren't quite typewriters, but rather networked personal computers, and the monkeys aren't quite monkeys, but rather Internet users. And instead of creating masterpieces, these millions and millions of exuberant monkeys—many with no more talent in the creative arts than our primate cousins—are creating an endless digital forest of mediocrity. For today's amateur monkeys can use their networked computers to publish everything from uninformed political commentary, to unseemly home videos, to embarrassingly amateurish music, to unreadable poems, reviews, essays, and novels.

At the heart of this infinite monkey experiment in self-publishing is the Internet diary, the ubiquitous blog. Blogging has become such a mania that a new blog is being created every second of every minute of every hour of every day. We are blogging with monkeylike shamelessness about our private lives, our sex lives, our dream lives, our lack of lives, our Second Lives. At the time of writing there are fifty-three million blogs on the Internet, and this number is doubling every six months. In the time it took you to read this paragraph, ten new blogs were launched.

If we keep up this pace, there will be over five hundred million blogs by 2010, collectively corrupting and confusing popular opinion about everything from politics, to commerce, to arts and culture. Blogs have become so dizzyingly infinite that they've undermined our sense of what is true and what is false, what is real and what is imaginary. These days, kids can't tell the difference between credible news by objective professional journalists and what they read on joeshmoe.blogspot.com. For these Generation Y utopians, every posting is just another person's version of the truth; every fiction is just another person's version of the facts.

Then there is Wikipedia, an online encyclopedia where anyone with opposable thumbs and a fifth-grade education can publish anything on any topic from AC/DC to Zoroastrianism. Since Wikipedia's birth, more than fifteen thousand contributors have created nearly three million entries in over a hundred different languages—none of them edited or vetted for accuracy. With hundreds of thousands of visitors a day, Wikipedia has become the third most visited site for information and current events; a more trusted source for news than the CNN or BBC Web sites, even though Wikipedia has no reporters, no editorial staff, and no experience in newsgathering. It's the blind leading the blind—infinite monkeys providing infinite information for infinite readers, perpetuating the cycle of misinformation and ignorance.

On Wikipedia, everyone with an agenda can rewrite an entry to their liking—and contributors frequently do. *Forbes* recently reported, for example, a story of anonymous McDonald and Wal-Mart employees furtively using Wikipedia entries as a medium for deceptively spreading corporate propaganda. On the McDonald's entry, a link to Eric Schlosser's *Fast Food Nation* conveniently disappeared; on Wal-Mart's somebody eliminated a line about underpaid employees making less than 20 percent of the competition.[2]

But the Internet's infinite monkey experiment is not limited to the written word. T. H. Huxley's nineteenth-century typewriter has evolved into not only the computer, but also the camcorder, turning the Internet into a vast library for user-generated video content. One site, YouTube, is a portal of amateur videos that, at the time of writing, was the world's fastest-growing site,[3] attracting sixty-five thousand new videos daily and boasting sixty million clips being watched each day; that adds up to over twenty-five million new videos a year,[4] and some twenty-five billion hits. In the fall of 2006, this overnight sensation was bought by Google for over a billion and a half dollars.

YouTube eclipses even the blogs in the inanity and absurdity of its content. Nothing seems too prosaic or narcissistic for these videographer monkeys. The site is an infinite gallery of amateur movies showing poor fools dancing, singing, eating, washing, shopping, driving, cleaning, sleeping, or just staring into their computers. In August 2006, one hugely popular video called "The Easter Bunny Hates You" showed a man in a bunny suit harassing and attacking people on the streets; according to *Forbes* magazine, this video was viewed more than three million times in two weeks. A few other favorite subjects include a young woman watching another YouTube user who is watching yet another user—a virtual hall of mirrors that eventually leads to a woman making a peanut butter and jelly sandwich in front of the television; a Malaysian dancer in absurdly short skirts grooving to Ricky Martin and Britney Spears; a dog chasing its tail; an Englishwoman instructing her viewers how to eat a chocolate and marmalade cookie; and, in a highly appropriate addition to the YouTube library, a video of dancing stuffed monkeys.

What's more disturbing than the fact that millions of us willingly tune in to such nonsense each day is that some Web sites are making monkeys out of us without our even knowing it. By entering words into Google's search engine, we are actually creating something called "collective intelligence," the sum wisdom of all Google users. The logic of Google's search engine, what technologists call its algorithm, reflects the "wisdom" of the crowd. In other words, the more people click on a link that results from a search, the more likely that link will come up in subsequent searches. The search engine is an aggregation of the ninety million questions we collectively ask Google each day; in other words, it just tells us what we already know.

This same "wisdom" of the crowd is manifested on editor-free news-aggregation sites such as Digg and Reddit. The ordering of the headlines on these sites reflects what other users have been reading rather than the expert judgment of news editors. As I write, there is a brutal war going on in Lebanon between Israel and Hezbollah. But the Reddit user wouldn't know this because there is nothing about Israel, Lebanon, or Hezbollah on the site's top twenty "hot" stories. Instead, subscribers can read about a flat-chested English actress, the walking habits of elephants, a spoof of the latest Mac commercial, and underground tunnels in Japan. Reddit is a mirror of our most banal interests. It makes a mockery of traditional news media and turns current events into a childish game of Trivial Pursuit.

The *New York Times* reports that 50 percent of all bloggers blog for the sole purpose of reporting and sharing experiences about their personal lives. The tagline for YouTube is "Broadcast Yourself." And broadcast ourselves we do, with all the shameless self-admiration of the mythical Narcissus. As traditional mainstream media is replaced by a personalized one, the Internet has become a mirror to ourselves. Rather than using it to seek news, information, or culture, we use it to actually BE the news, the information, the culture.

This infinite desire for personal attention is driving the hottest part of the new Internet economy—social-networking sites like MySpace, Facebook, and Bebo. As shrines for the cult of self-broadcasting, these sites have become tabula rasas of our individual desires and identities. They claim to be all about "social networking" with others, but in reality they exist so that we can advertise ourselves: everything from our favorite books and movies, to photos from our summer vacations, to "testimonials" praising our more winsome qualities or recapping our latest drunken exploits. It's hardly surprising that the increasingly tasteless nature of such self-advertisements has led to an infestation of anonymous sexual predators and pedophiles.

But our cultural standards and moral values are not all that are at stake. Gravest of all, the very traditional institutions that have helped to foster and create our news, our music, our literature, our television shows, and our movies are under assault as well. Newspapers and newsmagazines, one of the most reliable sources of information about the world we live in, are flailing, thanks to the proliferation of free blogs and sites like Craigslist that offer free classifieds, undermining paid ad placements. In the first quarter of 2006, profits plummeted dramatically at all the major newspaper companies—down 69 percent at the New York Times Company, 28 percent at the Tribune Company, and 11 percent at Gannett, the nation's largest newspaper company. Circulation is down, too. At the *San Francisco Chronicle,* ironically one of the newspapers of record for Silicon Valley, readership was down a dizzying 16 percent in the middle two quarters of 2005 alone.[5] And in 2007, Time, Inc., laid off almost 300 people, primarily from editorial, from such magazines as *Time, People,* and *Sports Illustrated.*

Those of us who still read the newspaper and magazines know that people are buying less music, too. Thanks to the rampant digital piracy spawned by file-sharing technology, sales of recorded music dropped over 20 percent between 2000 and 2006.[6]

In parallel with the rise of YouTube, Hollywood is experiencing its own financial troubles. Domestic box office sales now represent less than 20 percent of Hollywood's revenue and, with the levelling off of DVD sales and the rampant global piracy, the industry is desperately searching for a new business model that will enable it to profitably distribute movies on the Internet. According to *The New Yorker* film critic David Denby, many studio executives in Hollywood are now in a "panic" over declining revenue. One bleak consequence is cuts. Disney, for example, announced 650 job cuts in 2006, and an almost 50 percent drop in the number of animated movies produced annually.[7]

Old media is facing extinction. But if so, what will take its place? Apparently, it will be Silicon Valley's hot new search engines, social media sites, and video portals. Every new page on MySpace, every new blog post, every new YouTube video adds up to another potential source of advertising revenue lost to mainstream media. Thus, Rupert Murdoch's canny—or desperate—decision in July 2005 to buy MySpace for five hundred and eighty million dollars. Thus, the $1.65 billion sale of YouTube and the explosion of venture capital funding YouTube copycat sites. And, thus, the seemingly unstoppable growth at Google where, in the second quarter of 2006, revenue surged to almost two and a half billion dollars.

What happens, you might ask, when ignorance meets egoism meets bad taste meets mob rule?

The monkeys take over. Say good-bye to today's experts and cultural gatekeepers—our reporters, news anchors, editors, music companies, and Hollywood movie studios. In today's cult of the amateur,[8] the monkeys are running the show. With their infinite typewriters, they are authoring the future. And we may not like how it reads.

1

the great seduction

First a confession. Back in the Nineties, I was a pioneer in the first Internet gold rush. With the dream of making the world a more musical place, I founded Audiocafe.com, one of the earliest digital music sites. Once, when asked by a San Francisco Bay area newspaper reporter how I wanted to change the world, I replied, half seriously, that my fantasy was to have music playing from "every orifice," to hear the whole Bob Dylan oeuvre from my laptop computer, to be able to download Johann Sebastian Bach's Brandenburg Concertos from my cellular phone.

So yes, I peddled the original Internet dream. I seduced investors and I almost became rich. This, therefore, is no ordinary critique of Silicon Valley. It's the work of an apostate, an insider now on the outside who has poured out his cup of Kool-Aid and resigned his membership in the cult.

My metamorphosis from believer into skeptic lacks cinematic drama. I didn't break down while reading an incorrect Wikipedia entry about T. H. Huxley or get struck by lightning while doing a search for myself on Google. My epiphany didn't involve a dancing coyote, so it probably wouldn't be a hit on YouTube.

It took place over forty-eight hours, in September 2004, on a two-day camping trip with a couple of hundred Silicon Valley utopians. Sleeping bag under my arm, rucksack on my back, I marched into camp a member of the cult; two days later, feeling queasy, I left an unbeliever.

The camping trip took place in Sebastopol, a small farming town in northern California's Sonoma Valley, about fifty miles north of the infamous Silicon Valley— the narrow peninsula of land between San Francisco and San Jose. Sebastopol is the headquarters of O'Reilly Media, one of the world's leading traffickers of books, magazines, and trade shows about information technology, an evangelizer of innovation to a worldwide congregation of technophiles. It is both Silicon Valley's most fervent preacher and its noisiest chorus.

Each Fall, O'Reilly Media hosts an exclusive, invitation-only event called FOO (Friends of O'Reilly) Camp. These friends of multi-millionaire founder Tim O'Reilly are not only unconventionally rich and richly unconventional but also harbor a messianic faith in the economic and cultural benefits of technology. O'Reilly and his Silicon Valley acolytes are a mix of graying hippies, new media entrepreneurs, and technology geeks. What unites them is a shared hostility toward traditional media and entertainment. Part Woodstock, part Burning Man (the contemporary festival of self-expression held in a desert in Nevada), and part Stanford Business School retreat, FOO Camp is where the countercultural Sixties meets the free-market Eighties meets the technophile Nineties.

Silicon Valley conferences weren't new to me. I had even organized one myself at the tail end of the last Internet boom. But FOO Camp was radically different. Its only rule was an unrule: "no spectators, only participants." The camp was run on open-source, Wikipedia-style participatory principles—which meant that everyone talked a lot, and there was no one in charge.

So there we were, two hundred of us, Silicon Valley's antiestablishment establishment, collectively worth hundreds of millions of dollars, gazing at the stars from the lawn of O'Reilly Media's corporate headquarters. For two full days, we camped together, roasted marshmallows together, and celebrated the revival of our cult together.

The Internet was back! And unlike the Gold Rush Nineties, this time around our exuberance wasn't irrational. This shiny new version of the Internet, what Tim O'Reilly called Web 2.0, really was going to change everything. Now that most Americans had broadband access to the Internet, the dream of a fully networked, always-connected society was finally going to be realized.

There was one word on every FOO Camper's lips in September 2004. That word was "democratization."

I never realized democracy has so many possibilities, so much revolutionary potential. Media, information, knowledge, content, audience, author—all were going to be *democratized* by Web 2.0. The Internet would *democratize* Big Media, Big Business, Big Government. It would even *democratize* Big Experts, transforming them into what one friend of O'Reilly called, in a hushed, reverent tone, "noble amateurs."

Although Sebastopol was miles from the ocean, by the second morning of camp, I had begun to feel seasick. At first I thought it was the greasy camp food or perhaps the hot northern California weather. But I soon realized that even my gut was reacting to the emptiness at the heart of our conversation.

I had come to FOO Camp to imagine the future of media. I wanted to know how the Internet could help me "bring more music to more orifices." But my dream of making the world a more musical place had fallen on deaf ears; the promise of using technology to bring *more* culture to the masses had been drowned out by FOO Campers' collective cry for a democratized media.

The new Internet was about self-made music, not Bob Dylan or the Brandenburg Concertos. Audience and author had become one, and we were transforming culture into cacophony.

FOO Camp, I realized, was a sneak preview. We weren't there just to talk about new media; we *were* the new media. The event was a beta version of the Web 2.0 revolution, where Wikipedia met MySpace met YouTube. Everyone was simultaneously broadcasting themselves, but nobody was listening. Out of this anarchy, it suddenly became clear that what was governing the infinite monkeys now inputting away on the Internet was the law of digital Darwinism, the survival of the loudest and most opinionated. Under these rules, the only way to intellectually prevail is by infinite filibustering.

The more that was said that weekend, the less I wanted to express myself. As the din of narcissism swelled, I became increasingly silent. And thus began my rebellion against Silicon Valley. Instead of adding to the noise, I broke the one law of FOO Camp 2004. I stopped participating and sat back and watched.

I haven't stopped watching since. I've spent the last two years observing the Web 2.0 revolution, and I'm dismayed by what I've seen.

I've seen the infinite monkeys, of course, typing away. And I've seen many other strange sights as well, including a video of marching penguins selling a lie, a supposedly infinite Long Tail, and dogs chatting to each other online. But what I've been watching is more like Hitchcock's *The Birds* than *Doctor Doolittle:* a horror movie about the consequences of the digital revolution.

Because democratization, despite its lofty idealization, is undermining truth, souring civic discourse, and belittling expertise, experience, and talent. As I noted earlier, it is threatening the very future of our cultural institutions.

I call it the great seduction. The Web 2.0 revolution has peddled the promise of bringing more truth to more people—more depth of information, more global perspective, more unbiased opinion from dispassionate observers. But this is all a smokescreen. What the Web 2.0 revolution is really delivering is superficial observations of the world around us rather than deep analysis, shrill opinion rather than considered judgment. The information business is being transformed by the Internet into the sheer noise of a hundred million bloggers all simultaneously talking about themselves.

Moreover, the free, user-generated content spawned and extolled by the Web 2.0 revolution is decimating the ranks of our cultural gatekeepers, as professional critics, journalists, editors, musicians, moviemakers, and other purveyors of expert information are being replaced ("disintermediated," to use a FOO Camp term) by amateur bloggers, hack reviewers, homespun moviemakers, and attic recording artists. Meanwhile, the radically new business models based on user-generated material suck the economic value out of traditional media and cultural content.

We—those of us who want to know more about the world, those of us who are the consumers of mainstream culture—are being seduced by the empty promise of the "democratized" media. For the real consequence of the Web 2.0 revolution is less culture, less reliable news, and a chaos of useless information. One chilling reality in this brave new digital epoch is the blurring, obfuscation, and even disappearance of truth.

Truth, to paraphrase Tom Friedman, is being "flat-tened," as we create an on-demand, personalized version that reflects our own individual myopia. One person's truth becomes as "true" as anyone else's. Today's media is shattering the world into a billion personalized truths, each seemingly equally valid and worthwhile. To quote Richard Edelman, the founder, president, and CEO of Edelman PR, the world's largest privately owned public relations company:

> In this era of exploding media technologies there
> is no truth except the truth you create for yourself.[1]

This undermining of truth is threatening the quality of civil public discourse, encouraging plagiarism and intellectual property theft, and stifling creativity. When advertising and public relations are disguised as news, the line between fact and fiction becomes blurred. Instead of more community, knowledge, or culture, all that Web 2.0 really delivers is more dubious content from anonymous sources, hijacking our time and playing to our gullibility.

Need proof? Let's look at that army of perjurious penguins—"Al Gore's Army of Penguins" to be exact. Featured on YouTube, the film, a crude "self-made" satire of Gore's pro-environment movie *An Inconvenient Truth*, belittles the seriousness of Al Gore's message by depicting a penguin version of Al Gore preaching to other penguins about global warning.

But "Al Gore's Army of Penguins" is not just another homemade example of YouTube inanity. Though many of the 120,000 people who viewed this video undoubtedly assumed it was the work of some SUV-driving amateur with an aversion to recycling, in reality, the *Wall Street Journal* traced the real authorship of this neocon satire to DCI Group, a conservative Washington, D.C., public relationships and lobbying firm whose clients include Exxon-Mobil.[2] The video is nothing more than political spin, enabled and perpetuated by the anonymity of Web 2.0, masquerading as independent art. In short, it is a big lie.

Blogs too, can be vehicles for veiled corporate propaganda and deception. In March 2006, the *New York Times* reported about a blogger whose laudatory postings about Wal-Mart were "identical" to press releases written by a senior account supervisor at the Arkansas retailer's PR company.[3] Perhaps this is the same team behind the mysterious elimination of unflattering remarks about Wal-Mart's treatment of its employees on the retailer's Wikipedia entry.

Blogs are increasingly becoming the battlefield on which public relations spin doctors are waging their propaganda war. In 2005, before launching a major investment, General Electric executives met with environmental bloggers to woo them over the greenness of a new energy-efficient technology. Meanwhile, multinationals like IBM, Maytag, and General Motors all have blogs that, under an objective guise, peddle their versions of corporate truth to the outside world.

But the anticorporate blogs are equally loose with the truth. In 2005, when the famous and fictitious finger-in-the-chili story broke, every anti-Wendy's blogger jumped on it as evidence of fast-food malfeasance. The bogus story cost Wendy's $2.5 million in lost sales as well as job losses and a decline in the price of the company's stock.

As former British Prime Minister James Callaghan said, "A lie can make its way around the world before the truth has the chance to put its boots on." That has never been more true than with the speeding, freewheeling, unchecked culture of today's blogosphere.

It doesn't require the gravitas of a world leader to appreciate the implications of this democratized media. In a flattened, editor-free world where independent videographers, podcasters, and bloggers can post their amateurish creations at will, and no one is being paid to check their credentials or evaluate their material, media is vulnerable to untrustworthy content of every stripe—whether from duplicitous PR companies, multinational corporations like Wal-Mart and McDonald's, anonymous bloggers, or sexual predators with sophisticated invented identities.

Who is to say, for example, that a Malaysian prostitution ring didn't sponsor the famous YouTube video of the sexy Malaysian dancer? Or that the Englishwoman in the YouTube video eating the chocolate and marmalade cookie isn't really being paid by United Biscuits Incorporated?

Who is to say that the glowing review of *The Cult of the Amateur* on Amazon.com that might have led you to purchase this "brilliantly original" book wasn't authored by me, posing as an enthusiastic third party?

As I'll discuss in more detail in Chapter 3, truth and trust are the whipping boys of the Web 2.0 revolution. In a world with fewer and fewer professional editors or reviewers, how are we to know what and whom to believe? Because much of the user-generated content on the Internet is posted anonymously or under a pseudonym, nobody knows who the real author of much of this self-generated content actually is. It could be a monkey. It could be a penguin. It could even be Al Gore.

Look at Wikipedia, the Internet's largest cathedral of knowledge. Unlike editors at a professional encyclopedia like the *Britannica*, the identity of the volunteer editors on Wikipedia is unknown. These citizen editors out-edit other citizen editors in defining, redefining, then rededefining truth, sometimes hundreds of times a day. Take, for example, July 5, 2006, the day Enron embezzler Ken Lay died. At 10:06 A.M. that day, the Wikipedia entry about Lay said he died of an "apparent suicide." Two minutes later, it said that the cause of death was an "apparent heart attack." Then at 10:11 A.M., Wikipedia reported that the "guilt of ruining so many lives finally led him to his suicide."[4] At 10:12, we were back to the massive coronary causing Lay's demise. And in February 2007, just minutes after ex-*Playboy* Playmate Anna Nicole Smith died in Florida, her Wikipedia page was flooded with conflicting, speculative versions of the cause of death. As Marshall Poe observed in the September 2006 issue of the *Atlantic:*

> We tend to think of truth as something that resides in the world. The fact that two plus two equals four is written in the stars. . . . But Wikipedia suggests a different *theory of truth.* Just think about the way we learn what words mean. . . . The community decides that two plus two equals four the same way it decides what an apple is: by consensus. Yes, that means that if the community changes its mind and decides that two plus two equals five, then *two plus two does equal five.* The community isn't likely to do such an absurd or useless thing, but it has the ability.[5]

In Orwell's *Nineteen Eighty-Four,* Big Brother insisted that two plus two equaled five, transforming a patently incorrect statement into the state-sanctioned, official truth. Today, as I discuss in Chapter 7, there is potentially an even more threatening Big Brother lurking in the shadows: the search engine. We pour our innermost secrets into the all-powerful search engine through the tens of millions of questions we enter daily. Search engines like Google know more about our habits, our interests, our desires than our friends, our loved ones, and our shrink combined. But unlike in *Nineteen Eighty-Four,* this Big Brother is very much for real. We have to trust it not to spill our secrets—a trust, as we will see, that has repeatedly been betrayed.

Paradoxically enough, the holy grail of advertisers in the flattened world of the Web 2.0 is to achieve the trust of others. And it is turning the conventional advertising industry upside down. MySpace, according to the *Wall Street Journal* and other papers, now runs profiles of fictional characters in an attempt to market certain products by creating "personal relationships with millions of young people." News Corp. (which owns MySpace) has bought the right to include profiles of fictional characters such as Ricky Bobby (played by Will Ferrell) from the 2006 blockbuster *Talladega Nights*. Other recent members of the MySpace community include advertising vehicles like Gil, the crab from the Honda Element commercials; Burger King's royal mascot; and a character called "Miss Irresistible," the gleaming-toothed spokesperson for a new version of Crest toothpaste. But are Gil, the Burger King king, and Miss Irresistible really our friends? No. They are fictional characters whose only purpose is to sell our impressionable kids more toothpaste and hamburgers.

Our trust in conventional advertising is being further compromised by the spoof advertisements proliferating on the Internet. For example, the *New York Times* reported on August 15, 2006, that at the time, over 100 videos mocking an ad campaign launched by the Internet phone provider Vonage were posted on YouTube, and that many had been viewed at least 5,000 times. These amateurish, unauthorized send-ups of popular commercials are rarely flattering, and typically invent or expose flaws in a brand or a product. However, to the chagrin of ad executives (the interactive creative director for Crispin, Porter & Bogusky likens the phenomenon to "brand terrorism on the internet"), the homemade videos are often cobbled together from clips of actual advertisements, making the knockoffs often indistinguishable from the real commercials.

Our attitudes about "authorship," too, are undergoing a radical change as a result of today's democratized Internet culture. In a world in which audience and author are increasingly indistinguishable, and where authenticity is almost impossible to verify, the idea of original authorship and intellectual property has been seriously compromised. Who "owns" the content created by the fictional movie characters on MySpace? Who "owns" the content created by an anonymous hive of Wikipedia editors? Who "owns" the content posted by bloggers, whether it originates from corporate spin doctors or from articles in the *New York Times*? This nebulous definition of ownership, compounded by the ease in which we can now cut and paste other people's work to make it appear as if it's ours, has resulted in a troubling new permissiveness about intellectual property.

Cutting and pasting, of course, is child's play on the Web 2.0, enabling a younger generation of intellectual kleptomaniacs, who think their ability to cut and paste a well-phrased thought or opinion makes it their own. Original file-sharing technologies like Napster and Kazaa, which gained so much attention during the first Web boom, pale in comparison to the latest Web 2.0 "remixing" of content and "mashing up" of software and music. In a twisted kind of Alice in Wonderland, down-the-rabbit-hole logic, Silicon Valley visionaries such as Stanford law professor and Creative Commons founder Lawrence Lessig and cyberpunk author William Gibson laud the appropriation of intellectual property. As Gibson wrote in the July 2005 issue of *Wired* magazine:

> Our culture no longer bothers to use words like *appropriation* or *borrowing* to describe those very activities. Today's audience isn't listening at all— it's participating. Indeed, *audience* is as antique a term as *record,* the one archaically passive, the other archaically physical. The record, not the remix, is the anomaly today. The remix is the very nature of the digital.

Top students at Britain's Oxford University are heeding Gibson's advice; in June 2006, the *Guardian* newspaper reported that the university's reputation was "under threat as students increasingly copied slabs of work from the Internet and submitted it as their own." A survey published in *Education Week* found that 54 percent of students admitted to plagiarizing from the Internet. And who is to know if the other 46 percent are telling the truth? Copyright and authorship begin to lose all meaning to those posting their mash-ups and remixings on the

Web. They are, as Professor Sally Brown at Leeds Metropolitan University notes, "Postmodern, eclectic, Google-generationists, Wikipediasts, who don't necessarily recognize the concepts of authorships/ownerships."

The intellectual consequences of such theft are profoundly disturbing. Gibson's culture of the ubiquitous remix is not only destroying the sanctity of authorship but also undermining our traditional safeguards of individual creativity. The value once placed on a book by a great author is being challenged by the dream of a collective hyperlinked community of authors who endlessly annotate and revise it, forever conversing with each other in a never-ending loop of self-references.

Kevin Kelly, in a May 2006 *New York Times Magazine* article,[6] rhapsodizes over the death of the traditional stand-alone text—what centuries of civilization have known as the book. What Kelly envisions instead is an infinitely interconnected media in which all the world's books are digitally scanned and linked together: what he calls the "liquid version" of the book. In Kelly's view, the act of cutting and pasting and linking and annotating a text is as or more important than the writing of the book in the first place. It is the literary version of Wikipedia. Instead of traditional books by the Norman Mailers, Alice Walkers, and John Updikes, we should embrace, according to Kelly, a single, hyperlinked, communal, digital text that is edited and annotated by amateurs.

So what happens when you combine Kelly's liquid version of the book with a wiki? You get a million penguins.

That's actually the title of De Montford University's January 2007 "wiki-novel,"[7] a democratic literary experiment sponsored by the British publisher Penguin, which invites anyone to contribute to a collective online novel. But can a collaboration of amateur voices create an authoritative, coherent fictional narrative? I doubt it. As Penguin blogger and literary critic Jon Elek wrote, "I'll be happy so long as it manages to avoid becoming some sort of robotic-zombie-assassins-against-African-ninjas-in-space-narrated-by-a-Papal-Tiara type of thing."[8]

It is not just our aesthetic sensibilities that are under assault. The Internet has become the medium of choice for distorting the truth about politics and politicians on both sides of the fence. The 2004 attack on John Kerry's Swift Boat record in Vietnam, for example, was orchestrated by hundreds of conservative bloggers who painted a patriotic American public servant as a patsy for Vietcong propaganda. And what about the left-wing blogosphere's assault, in the summer and fall of 2006, on Joe Lieberman, the centrist Democratic Connecticut senator, who attackers dressed up as a right-wing, Bush-loving, warmongering Republican, costing him the 2006 primary (he, of course, went on to win the general election, vindicating himself in the end). None of these blogs, from MoveOn.org to Swiftvets.com, seriously debate the issues or address the ambiguities and complexity of politics. Instead, they cater to an increasingly partisan minority that uses "democratized" digital media to obfuscate truth and manipulate public opinion.

The Cost of Democratization

This blurring of lines between the audience and the author, between fact and fiction, between invention and reality further obscures objectivity. The cult of the amateur has made it increasingly difficult to determine the difference between reader and writer, between artist and spin doctor, between art and advertisement, between amateur and expert. The result? The decline of the quality and reliability of the information we receive, thereby distorting, if not outrightly corrupting, our national civic conversation.

But perhaps the biggest casualties of the Web 2.0 revolution are real businesses with real products, real employees, and real shareholders, as I'll discuss in Chapters 4 and 5. Every defunct record label, or laid-off newspaper reporter, or bankrupt independent bookstore is a consequence of "free" user-generated Internet content—from Craigslist's free advertising, to YouTube's free music videos, to Wikipedia's free information.

What you may not realize is that what is free is actually costing us a fortune. The new winners—Google, YouTube, MySpace, Craigslist, and the hundreds of start-ups all hungry for a piece of the Web 2.0 pie—are unlikely to fill the shoes of the industries they are helping to undermine, in terms of products produced, jobs created, revenue generated, or benefits conferred. By stealing away our eyeballs, the blogs and wikis are decimating the publishing, music, and news-gathering industries that created the original content those Web sites "aggregate." Our culture is essentially cannibalizing its young, destroying the very sources of the content they crave. Can that be the new business model of the twenty-first century?

A *Business 2.0* July 2006 cover story asked who are the fifty people "who matter most" in the new economy. Leading the list was not Steve Jobs or Rupert Murdoch or Sergey Brin and Larry Page, the two founders of Google. It was "YOU! The Consumer as Creator":

> You—or rather, the collaborative intelligence of tens of millions of people, the networked you— continually create and filter new forms of content, anointing the useful, the relevant, and the amusing and rejecting the rest. . . . In every case, you've become an integral part of the action as a member of the aggregated, interactive, self-organizing, auto-entertaining audience.

Who was *Time* magazine's 2006 Person of the Year? Was it George W. Bush, or Pope Benedict XVI, or Bill Gates and Warren Buffett, who together contributed more than $70 billion of their wealth to improving life on earth? None of the above. *Time* gave the award to YOU:

> Yes, you. You control the Information Age. Welcome to your world.

This same YOU! rules Wikipedia, where the knowledge consumer is also the knowledge creator. YOU! defines YouTube, where the tens of thousands of daily videos are both produced and watched by one and the same. YOU! are both ordering and reviewing books on Amazon.com, bidding and auctioning goods on eBay, buying and designing video games on Microsoft's Xbox platform, and listing and responding to advertisements on Craigslist.

Of course, every free listing on Craigslist means one less paid listing in a local newspaper. Every visit to Wikipedia's free information hive means one less customer for a professionally researched and edited encyclopedia such as *Britannica*. Every free music or video upload is one less sale of a CD or DVD, meaning one less royalty for the artist who created it.

In his recent bestselling book *The Long Tail*,[9] *Wired* magazine editor Chris Anderson celebrates this flattening of culture, which he describes as the end of the hit parade. In Anderson's brave new world, there will be infinite shelf space for infinite products, thus giving everyone infinite choice. *The Long Tail* virtually redefines the word "economics"—shifting it from the science of scarcity to the science of abundancy, and promising an infinite market in which we cycle and recycle our cultural production to our hearts' content. It's a seductive notion. But even if one accepts Anderson's dubious economic arguments, the Long Tail theory has a glaring hole. Anderson assumes that raw talent is as infinite as the shelf space at Amazon or eBay. But while there may be infinite typewriters, there is a scarcity of talent, expertise, experience, and mastery in any given field. Finding and nurturing true talent in a sea of amateurs may be the real challenge in today's Web 2.0 world. The fact is, Anderson's vision of a hitless, flattened media is a self-fulfilling prophecy. Without the nurturing of talent, there will, indeed, be no more hits, as the talent that creates them is never nourished or permitted to shine.

Today, on a Web where everyone has an equal voice, the words of the wise man count for no more than the mutterings of a fool. Sure, all of us have opinions; but as I discuss more fully in Chapter 2, few of us have special training, knowledge, or hands-on experience to generate any kind of real perspective. Thomas Friedman, the *New York Times* columnist, and Robert Fisk, the Middle Eastern correspondent of the *Independent* newspaper, for example, didn't hatch from some obscure blog—they acquired their in-depth knowledge of the Middle East by spending years in the region. This involved considerable investments of time and resources, for which both the journalists themselves, and the newspapers they work for, deserve to be remunerated.

Talent, as ever, is a limited resource, the needle in today's digital haystack. You won't find the talented, trained individual shipwrecked in his pajamas behind a computer, churning out inane blog postings or anonymous movie reviews. Nurturing talent requires work, capital, expertise, investment. It requires the complex infrastructure of traditional media—the scouts, the agents, the editors, the publicists, the technicians, the marketers. Talent is built by the intermediaries. If you "disintermediate" these layers, then you do away with the development of talent, too.

The economics of *The Long Tail* are dead wrong. Technology utopians like Anderson suggest that self-created content will somehow result in an endless village of buyers and sellers, each buying a little and choosing from an extraordinary number of things. But the more self-created content that gets dumped onto the Internet, the harder it becomes to distinguish the good from the bad—and to make money on any of it. As Trevor Butterworth reported in the *Financial Times*, nobody is getting rich from blogging, not even Markos Moulitsas Zuniga, the founder of the Daily Kos, the most popular of all the political blogs.

Take the case of GoFugYourself.com, a celebrity parody site attracting a huge audience of 100,000 visitors a day. According to Butterworth, the site is only generating "beer money" for its founders. Above-average sites like JazzHouston.com, which attracts 12,000 visitors a day, bring in peanuts—around $1,000 a year in ad revenue from Google.[10] Then there's Guy Kawasaki, author of one of the fifty most popular blogs on the Internet, whose pages were viewed almost two and a half million times in 2006. And how much did Kawasaki earn in ad revenue in 2006 off this hot media property? Just $3,350.[11] If this is Anderson's long tail, it is a tail that offers no one a job.

At best, it will provide the monkeys with peanuts and beer.

The real challenge in Anderson's long tail market of infinite shelf space is finding what to read, listen to, or watch. If you think the choice in your local record store is daunting, then just wait till the long tail uncoils its infinite length. Trawling through the blogosphere, or the millions of bands on MySpace, or the tens of millions of videos on YouTube for the one or two blogs or songs or videos with real value isn't viable for those of us with a life or a full-time job. The one resource that is challenged all the more by this long tail of amateur content is our time—the most limited and precious resource of all.

Yes, a number of Web 2.0 start-ups such as Pandora.com, Goombah.com, and Moodlogic.com are building artificially intelligent engines that supposedly can automatically tell us what music or movies we will like. But artificial intelligence is a poor substitute for taste. No software can replace the implicit trust we place in a movie review by Nigel Andrews (*Financial Times*), A. O. Scott (*New York Times*), Anthony Lane (*New Yorker*), or Roger Ebert (*Chicago Sun-Times*)—a thoughtfully crafted review, informed by decades of education, training, and movie-reviewing experience. No algorithm can match the literary analysis of the reviewers at the *London* or the *New York Review of Books,* nor the wealth of musical knowledge espoused by reviewers at magazines like *Rolling Stone, Jazziz,* or *Gramophone.*

Chris Anderson is right to say the infinite space of the Internet will afford more and more opportunities for niche programming, but the downside is that this will ensure that such niches generate less and less revenue. The more specialized the niche, the narrower the market. The narrower the market, the more shoestring the production budget, which compromises the quality of the programming, further reducing the audience and alienating the advertisers.

One example of this dark cycle is NBC's attempt in 2006 to create exclusive interactive Internet mini-episodes of the sitcom *The Office*. The mini-episodes were so underfunded that NBC couldn't even afford to cast Steve Carell, the star of the show. As one TV critic said, it looked like "outtakes swept up from the remainder bin."[12]

Network television is already grappling with the fragmentation of the audience into thinner and thinner slices. In 2006, NBC developed video sites for gay men and TV junkies, and CBS introduced an interactive Web channel for teenagers and another (Showbuzz.com) dedicated to entertainment news and gossip. The Scripps Network, in a desperate attempt to expand its total viewership, also introduced video channels for increasingly narrow subjects, from woodworking to quilting to healthy eating.

Where does it end? With a channel for every one of us, in which we are the solitary broadcaster and the sole audience? This would be democratization on the most fundamental level. Such an absurd conclusion is not pure fantasy. In the short time since FOO Camp 2004, Web 2.0's narcissistic, self-congratulatory, self-generated content revolution has exploded. Before September 2004, there was no YouTube, and author-generated sites like Wikipedia and MySpace were well-kept Silicon Valley secrets. Today, we are watching a hundred million clips a day on YouTube, and MySpace, founded in July 2003, has over ninety-eight million profiles. There are now almost infinite social media sites for teens, pre-teens, post-teens, and, as we will see, even fake teens.

The bloggers and the podcasters have taken over our computers, our Internet-enabled cell phones, our iPods. What was once just a weird Silicon Valley cult is now transforming America.

In a cartoon that appeared in *The New Yorker* in 1993, two dogs sit beside a computer. One has his paw on the keyboard; the other is looking up at him quizzically.

"On the Internet," the dog using the keyboard reassures his canine friend, "nobody knows you're a Dog."

That is more true than ever. On today's self-publishing Internet, nobody knows if you're a dog, a monkey, or the Easter Bunny. That's because everyone else is too busy ego-casting, too immersed in the Darwinian struggle for mind-share, to listen to anyone else.

But we can't blame this sad state of affairs on some other species. We human beings hog the limelight on this new stage of democratized media. We are simultaneously its amateur writers, its amateur producers, its amateur technicians, and, yes, its amateur audience.

Amateur hour has arrived, and the audience is now running the show.

2

the noble amateur

Every revolution is celebrated on behalf of some seemingly noble abstraction. And the Web 2.0 revolution is no different. The noble abstraction behind the digital revolution is that of the *noble amateur*.

I first heard this phrase in 2004, over breakfast with a Friend of O'Reilly. He had told me that these "noble amateurs" would democratize what, with a wave of his coffee cup, he called "the dictatorship of expertise." The Web 2.0 was the most "awesomely" democratic consequence of the digital revolution, he said. It would change the world forever.

"So instead of a dictatorship of experts, we'll have a dictatorship of idiots," I might have responded. His ideal of the "noble amateur" seemed like more Silicon Valley chatter, just more irrationally exuberant nonsense.

But the ideal of the noble amateur is no laughing matter. I believe it lies at the heart of Web 2.0's cultural revolution and threatens to turn our intellectual traditions and institutions upside down. In one sense, it is a digitalized version of Rousseau's noble savage, representing the triumph of innocence over experience, of romanticism over the commonsense wisdom of the Enlightenment.

So let me begin this journey to the center of the digital world with a definition. The traditional meaning of the word "amateur" is very clear. An amateur is a hobbyist, knowledgeable or otherwise, someone who does not make a living from his or her field of interest, a layperson, lacking credentials, a dabbler. George Bernard Shaw once said, "Hell is full of amateur musicians," but that was before Web 2.0. Today, Shaw's hell would have broadband access and would be overrun with bloggers and podcasters.

For a more empirical and objective definition, the *Shorter Oxford English Dictionary (OED)* defines "amateur" as:

> 1. A person who is fond of something; a person who has a taste for something 2. A person who practices something, esp. an art or game, only as a pastime; an unpaid player, performer (opp. *professional*), also (*depreciative*) a dabbler

The *Shorter OED*, of course, epitomizes what the Friend of O'Reilly would call the "dictatorship of expertise." Published by Oxford University Press and currently in its fifth edition, the *Shorter OED* is a two-volume, four-thousand-page dictionary edited by a team of sixteen professional lexicographers and an expert cohort of other researchers and advisors. It is a book in which two plus two always adds up to four.

On today's Internet, however, amateurism, rather than expertise, is celebrated, even revered. Today, the *OED* and the *Encyclopaedia Britannica*, two trusted reference volumes upon which we have long relied for information, are being replaced by Wikipedia and other user-generated resources. The professional is being replaced by the amateur, the lexicographer by the layperson, the Harvard professor by the unschooled populace.

Wikipedia describes itself as "the free encyclopedia that anyone can edit." The site claims to run on "democratic" principles, as its two hundred thousand anonymous editors are all unpaid volunteers. Unlike the *OED*, which was crafted by a carefully vetted and selected team of experienced professionals, Wikipedia, as I discussed earlier, allows absolutely anyone to add and edit entries on its Web site.

So what is wrong with such a "democratized" system? Isn't the ideal of democracy that everyone has a voice? Isn't that what makes America so attractive? (While not born in the United States myself, I've lived here since the early 1980s, am married to a woman from Alabama, and have raised my family in California. I'm a classic example of the immigrant entrepreneur who came to America seeking more economic and cultural freedom.)

While this is true in terms of elections, a radically democratic culture is hardly conducive to scholarship or to the creation of wisdom. The reality is that we now live in a highly specialized society, where excellence is rewarded and where professionals receive years of training to properly do their jobs, whether as doctors or journalists, environmental scientists or clothing designers. In *The Wealth of Nations*, economist Adam Smith reminds us that specialization and division of labor is, in fact, the most revolutionary achievement of capitalism:

> The greatest improvement in the productive powers
> of labour, and the greater part of the skill, dexterity,
> and judgment with which it is any where directed,
> or applied, seem to have been the effects of labour.

In the twenty-first century, this division of labor does not just refer to the breakdown of jobs in a manufacturing plant or on an assembly line. It includes the labor of those who choose a trade or a field, acquire education or training, gain experience, and develop their abilities within a complex meritocracy. They all have the same goal: to acquire expertise.

In a notorious section from *The German Ideology*, Karl Marx tried to seduce his reader with an idyllic post-capitalist world where everyone can "hunt in the morning, fish in the afternoon, rear cattle in the evening, criticize after dinner." But if we can all simultaneously be hunters, fishers, cattle herders, and critics, can any of us actually excel at anything, whether hunting, fishing, herding, or criticizing? In a world in which we are all amateurs, there are no experts.

On the Web 2.0, one senses that is perhaps the ideal. Wikipedia's entry for the word "amateur"—which has been amended by other editors more than fifty times since June 2001—defines one as both a "virtuoso" and a "connoisseur":

> In the areas of computer programming and open source, as well as astronomy and ornithology, many amateurs make very meaningful contributions equivalent to or exceeding those of the professionals. To many, description as an amateur is losing its negative meaning, and actually carries a badge of honor.

While the Wikipedia entry doesn't use the word "noble," you don't need to be a scholar to read between the lines. The editors at Wikipedia wear their amateur badge with pride. The problem? As Marshall Poe put it in a recent conversation:

> It's not exactly expert knowledge; it's common knowledge . . . when you go to nuclear reactor on Wikipedia you're not getting an encyclopedia entry, so much as you're getting what people who know a little about nuclear reactors know about nuclear reactors and what they think common people can understand. [Wikipedia] constantly throws

people off and they think, well, if it's an encyclopedia why can't I cite it; why can't I . . . rely on it? And you can't; you just can't rely on it like that.[1]

Wikipedia's editors embrace and revel in the commonness of their knowledge. But as the adage goes, a little knowledge is a dangerous thing. Because on Wikipedia, two plus two sometimes *does* equal five.

In the July 2006 issue of *The New Yorker*, Stacy Schiff wrote, "Wikipedia may be the world's most ambitious vanity press."[2] But it is a press with a peculiar sort of vanity, raising up the amateur to a position of prominence exceeding that of the salaried experts who do what they do for money. Wikipedia claims to be amassing the world's largest real estate of knowledge, and yet Wikipedia's readers seem to revel in its very lack of authority.

This vanity of the innocent was underscored by founder Jimmy Wales, who, commenting about the identity of Wikipedian editors, said, "To me, the key thing is getting it right. I don't care if they're a high school kid or a Harvard professor." Or, it seems, a high school kid *posing* as a Harvard professor. In fact, in March 2007, *The New Yorker* magazine discovered that "Essjay," an avid Wikipedia contributor interviewed for a recent article by the magazine's Stacey Schiff, had edited thousands of Wikipedia articles under a false identity. It turned out that "Essjay" was not a tenured professor of theology with four academic degrees, as his profile claimed, but was in fact a twenty-four-year-old high school graduate from Kentucky named Ryan Jordan with no academic or professional credentials. What's worse is that when confronted with the blatant deception perpetrated by one of his star contributors ("Essjay" was not only a frequent editor of articles but also had administrative privileges on Wikipedia and had recently been given a job at the for-profit company Wikia, which Wales also helped to found), Wales was less than apologetic. "I regard it as a pseudonym and I don't really have a problem with it," he told *The New Yorker*.

Wales is himself a graduate school drop-out from both the University of Alabama and Indiana University.[3] The problem is, how does Wales know who's right? Often, you need an expert to help you figure it out.

Wales told *The New Yorker*'s Schiff, "I'm actually quite an enlightenment kind of guy." But the reverse is actually true—he's a *counter*-enlightenment guy, a wide-eyed romantic, seducing us with the ideal of the noble amateur. So who is Jimmy Wales? Educated in a one-room school in Huntsville, Alabama, Wales first discovered the Internet as a teenager playing Multi-User Dungeon (MUD) fantasy games such as Zork, Myst, and the Scepter of Goth. Then, as an undergraduate at the University of Alabama, Wales was converted by the libertarian idealism espoused by Ayn Rand, a philosophy of rugged self-realization, which stands against tradition and established authority.

In the Wild West–style Internet economy of the mid-Nineties, Wales co-founded a Web directory called Bomis. Described by *The Atlantic* magazine as "The *Playboy* of the Internet," Bomis provided the peer-to-peer technology to link together sites about Pamela Anderson and Anna Kournikova. What Wales had learned as an adolescent playing video games, and relearned from his experience with Bomis, was the power of the network, the value of what has become known as "distributed" technology. In January 2000, he hired Larry Sanger, a doctoral student in philosophy, with the instruction of building an open-source encyclopedia project. This blossomed into Nupedia, a free encyclopedia consisting of peer-reviewed articles by experts and scholars. However, while many experts embraced Nupedia, the site was rejected by digital utopians because its strict editorial standards went against their "democratic" principles. So, a year later, Wales and Sanger added wiki technology, which allows anyone to add content to a communal Web site without the approval of a central authority.[4] The hubris behind this experiment would later grow into the idea that a collective of anonymous, volunteer enthusiasts could aggregate their knowledge into the sum total of human wisdom.

As a result, in the not-so-hidden ideology of the collective Wikipedia experiment, the voice of a high school kid has equal value to that of an Ivy League scholar or a trained professional. This became Jimmy Wales' big idea. Wales, who was lauded on *Time* magazine's 2006 list of Top 100 People Who Shape Our World as a "champion of internet egalitarianism," believes that the expert is born rather than bred and that talent can be found in the most unexpected places. It is a metaphysical conceit that can be traced back to his libertarian roots. To Wales, neither our reputations nor our qualifications have any intrinsic value. In his ideal world, everyone should be given equal voice, irrespective of their title, knowledge, or intellectual or scholarly achievements.

Jimmy Wales and Larry Sanger launched Wikipedia in January 2001. "Humor me," Larry Sanger wrote to all his friends. "Go there and add a little article. It will take all of five or ten minutes." Well, millions of amateur Wikipedians have humored Sanger and Wales more than they could ever have imagined. But in the cult of the amateur, those who know most can be persecuted by those who know the least.

Dr. William Connolley, a climate modeler at the British Antarctic Survey in Cambridge and an expert on global warming with many professional publications to his credit, recently went head-to-head with a particularly aggressive Wikipedia editor over the site's global warming entry, when, after trying to correct inaccuracies he noticed in the entry, he was accused of "strongly pushing his POV [point of view] with systematic removal of any POV which does not match his own."

Connolley, who was pushing no POV other than that of factual accuracy, was put on editorial parole by Wikipedia, and was limited to making one entry a day. When he challenged the case, the Wikipedia arbitration committee gave no weight to his expertise, treating Connelley, an international expert on global warming, with the same deference and level of credibility as his anonymous foe—who, for all anyone knew, could have been a penguin in the pay of ExxonMobil.

The consequences of this dismissal of traditional, credentialed experts on sites like Wikipedia are both chilling and absurd. Can a social worker in Des Moines really be considered credible in arguing with a trained physicist over string theory? Can a car mechanic have as knowledgeable a "POV" as that of a trained geneticist on the nature of hereditary diseases? Can we trust a religious fundamentalist to know more about the origins of mankind than a Ph.D. in evolutionary biology?

Unfortunately, the Web 2.0 revolution helps to foster such absurdities. By empowering the amateur, we are undermining the authority of the experts who contribute to a traditional resource like the *Encyclopaedia Britannica*—experts who, over the years, have included the likes of Albert Einstein, Marie Curie, and George Bernard Shaw. Indeed, what defines "the very best minds" available, whether they are cultural critics or scientific experts, is their ability to go beyond the "wisdom" of the crowd and mainstream public opinion and bestow on us the benefits of their hard-earned knowledge.

In undermining the expert, the ubiquity of free, user-generated content threatens the very core of our professional institutions. Jimmy Wales' Wikipedia, with its millions of amateur editors and unreliable content, is the seventeenth most-trafficked site on the Internet; Britannica.com, with its 100 Nobel Prize winners and 4,000 expert contributors, is ranked 5,128.

Fighting against free is hard, if not impossible. The current Britannica company, for example, employs over a hundred professional editors and fact-checkers, and pays its 4,000 contributors. Wikipedia, in contrast, pays for none of its content and employs only a handful of paid employees. The 232-year-old Britannica went through a series of painful layoffs in 2001 and 2002, cutting its 300-person staff in the United States almost by half; with the advent of Wikipedia, no doubt more layoffs are to come.[5]

So what do we get in exchange for free amateur content? We get, of course, what we pay for. We get what the great thinker and writer Lewis Mumford called "a state of intellectual enervation and depletion hardly to be distinguished from massive ignorance." Today's editors, technicians, and cultural gatekeepers—the experts across an array of fields—are necessary to help us to sift through what's important and what's not, what is credible from what is unreliable, what is worth spending our time on as opposed to the white noise that can be safely ignored. So while the professionals—the editors, the scholars, the publishers—are certainly the victims of an Internet that diminishes their value and takes away their jobs, the greater victims of all this are *us*, the readers of Wikipedia and of the blogs and all the "free" content that is insistently reaching out for our attention. And when misinformation is spread, it is we the people who suffer the consequences. For the sad fact is that while Dr. William Connolley may be able to discern the misinformed ravings of moonbats (a term Eric Raymond, a respected open-source pioneer, used to describe the

Wikipedia community) from the wisdom of experts, the average Internet user cannot. Most of us assume that the information we take in can be trusted.

But when the information is created by amateurs, it rarely can be. And the irony in all this is that democratized media will eventually force all of us to become amateur critics and editors ourselves. With more and more of the information online unedited, unverified, and unsubstantiated, we will have no choice but to read everything with a skeptical eye. (That is why, in February 2007, the Middlebury College history department banned students from citing Wikipedia as a source for research papers.) The free information really isn't free; we all end up paying for it one way or another with the most valuable resource of all—our time.

Citizen Journalists

Wikipedia is far from alone in its celebration of the amateur. The "citizen journalists," too—the amateur pundits, reporters, writers, commentators, and critics on the blogosphere—carry the banner of the noble amateur on Web 2.0. In fact, citizen journalism is a euphemism for what you or I might call "journalism by nonjournalists," or as Nicholas Lemann, Dean of the Columbia University Graduate School of Journalism,[6] described them in *The New Yorker:* people who are not employed by a news organization but perform a similar function. Professional journalists acquire their craft through education and through the firsthand experience of reporting and editing the news under the careful eye of other professionals. In contrast, citizen journalists have no formal training or expertise, yet they routinely offer up opinion as fact, rumor as reportage, and innuendo as information. On the blogosphere, publishing one's own "journalism" is free, effortless, and unencumbered by pesky ethical restraints or bothersome editorial boards.

The simple ownership of a computer and an Internet connection doesn't transform one into a serious journalist any more than having access to a kitchen makes one into a serious cook. But millions of amateur journalists think that it does. According to a June 2006 study by the Pew Internet and American Life Project, 34 percent of the 12 million bloggers in America consider their online "work" to be a form of journalism.[7] That adds up to millions of unskilled, untrained, unpaid, unknown "journalists"—a thousandfold growth between 1996 and 2006—spewing their (mis)information out in the cyberworld.

Most amateur journalists are wannabe Matt Drudges— a pajama army of mostly anonymous, self-referential writers who exist not to report news but to spread gossip, sensationalize political scandal, display embarrassing photos of public figures, and link to stories on imaginative topics such as UFO sightings or 9/11 conspiracy theories. Drudge, who once wrote that "the Net gives as much voice to a thirteen-year-old computer geek like me as to a CEO or speaker of the House. We all become equal,"[8] is the poster boy of the citizen journalist movement, flashing his badge of amateurism as a medieval crusader would wield a sword.

These four million wannabe Drudges revel in their amateurism with all the moral self-righteousness of religious warriors. They flaunt their lack of training and formal qualifications as evidence of their calling, their passion, and their selfless pursuit of the truth, claiming that their amateur status allows them to give us a less-biased, less-filtered picture of the world than we get from traditional news. In reality this is not so.

In 2005, in the aftermath of Hurricane Katrina, for example, many of the initial reports of the damage came from citizen journalists, people on the scene blogging about the chaos and taking photos of the devastation with their camera phones. But, as it turned out, these initial reports helped to spread unfounded rumors—inflated body counts and erroneous reports of rapes and gang violence in the Superdome—that were later debunked by the traditional news media. The most accurate and objective reports instead came from professional news reporters who brought us high-quality photographs of the disaster and information from key figures like the New Orleans police, rescue workers, the U.S. Army Corps of Engineers, as well as first-hand accounts from the citizens and victims themselves.

Citizen journalists simply don't have the resources to bring us reliable news. They lack not only expertise and training, but connections and access to information. After all, a CEO or political figure can stonewall the average citizen but would be a fool to refuse a call from a reporter or editor at the *Wall Street Journal* seeking a comment on a breaking story.

One leading champion of citizen journalism, Dan Gillmor, author of the crusading *We the Media: Grassroots Journalism by the People, for the People,* argues that the news should be a *conversation* among ordinary citizens rather than a lecture that we are expected to blindly accept as truth. But the responsibility of a journalist is to inform us, not to converse with us.

If you simply want to converse with a journalist, invite them to your local bar for a few drinks. That's exactly what I did in the fall of 2006 when I spent an evening with Al Saracevic, deputy business editor of the *San Francisco Chronicle.*

Halfway through the evening, we got onto the subject of amateur journalism. "So what do you think distinguishes bloggers from professional journalists?" I asked him.

I'd expected Saracevic to focus on the quality of the end product. I expected him to tell me that amateur reporting on recent events like the 7/6 London bombings or New Orleans after Katrina wasn't up to real journalistic standards because it wasn't vetted by knowledgeable editors or wasn't corroborated by multiple sources. But I was wrong. While Saracevic might have agreed with the above, he had something else on his mind.

"In America, bloggers don't go to jail for their work," he told me. "That's the difference between professionals and amateurs."[9]

Saracevic was referring to Lance Williams and Mark

Fainaru-Wada, his colleagues on the *Chronicle,* a two-person team of baseball reporters who had just been sentenced to eighteen months in prison for refusing to testify about the identity of the person who leaked them secret grand jury testimony from Barry Bonds.

In Saracevic's view, the blogosphere is a sideshow, all eyeballs and no real relevance, a poker game played with fake chips. Bloggers are very rarely sued or prosecuted because the government and corporations don't seem to really care what they write. As a result, they aren't held accountable for their work in the way that real reporters are.

In contrast, professional journalism matters. Companies sue newspapers, and reporters get sent to jail. Professional journalism is hardball. It counts—for the journalists, for corporations, for the government, and, most important, for all of us. This is because it is still only mainstream journalists and newspapers who have the organization, financial muscle, and credibility to gain access to sources and report the truth. As Saracevic later e-mailed me:

> It's as if libel law has taken a brief vacation so that citizen journalists can get their feet wet, while trashing the mainstream media for "not speaking truth to power," as Craig Newmark puts it. Well, speaking truth to power takes money. Money to pay lawyers. Lots and lots of lawyers. Say what you will about the mainstream media, it takes big companies with a

commitment to real investigative journalism to take
on big institutions with any hope of surviving.

Contrast this with another conversation I'd had, a few
months earlier, with Dan Gillmor, the champion of citizen journalism I introduced earlier. I'd asked Gillmor
what citizen journalism could provide that we can't get
from mainstream media.

Gillmor's answer reflected the self-absorption of the
typical amateur journalist. He told me that the real
value of citizen journalism was its ability to address
niche markets otherwise ignored by mainstream media.

When I asked him for an example, he replied, hybrid
cars. To him, proof of the value of citizen journalism
was in news blogs about the Toyota Prius. Leave wars to
the real reporters, he implied. The responsibility of
amateurs was to report the latest feedback about the
Prius. But is reporting about your favorite car really journalism? I asked him. According to Gillmor, it is.

> Is this journalism? I would say yes; it's a conversation, absolutely, but it's a collective bringing
> together of what people know, and when someone
> posts something that's not true, other people jump
> in and say well this is wrong.[10]

In other words, professional journalists can go to jail
for telling the truth; amateurs talk to each other about
their cars.

Unfortunately, the Internet is bloated with the hot air of these amateur journalists. Despite the size of their readership, even the A-List bloggers have no formal journalistic training. And, in fact, much of the real news their blogs contain has been lifted from (or aggregated from) the very news organizations they aim to replace.

It is not surprising then that these prominent bloggers have no professional training in the collection of news. After all, who needs a degree in journalism to post a hyperlink on a Web site? Markos Moulitsas Zuniga, for example, the founder of Daily Kos, a left-leaning site, came to political blogging via the technology industry and the military. Glenn Reynolds, who leans to the right, was a law professor and an amateur music producer before jumping on his digital soapbox. Drudge was a mediocre student who came to the media business via a job managing the CBS studio gift shop. Such amateurs treat blogging as a moral calling rather than a profession tempered by accepted standards; proud of their lack of training, standards, and ethical codes, they define themselves as the slayers of the media giants, as irreverent Davids overcoming the news-gathering industry Goliaths.

In the first Internet revolution, a Web site's value was determined by the number of eyeballs; in the Web 2.0 epoch, value is determined by its accumulation of amateur voices. In August 2006, I talked with digital media impresario Arianna Huffington (whose Huffington Post is one of the most highly trafficked blogs on the Internet), who boasted to me about ways in which her blog was planning to incorporate voices not traditionally heard in mainstream media. While papers like the *Los Angeles Times* or the *Washington Post* strive to maintain a singular, authoritative voice through the expert journalism they offer, Huffington claimed that her site was more truthful than traditional media because of its richer tapestry of amateur viewpoints. The problem is, these voices often distort the news, turning the music into noise (although as this book is going to press, Huffington is planning to add original reporting to her blog).

The New Yorker's Lemann points out that "societies create structures of authority for producing and distributing knowledge, information, and opinion."[11] Why? So that we know we can trust what we read. When an article runs under the banner of a respected newspaper, we know that it has been weighed by a team of seasoned editors with years of training, assigned to a qualified reporter, researched, fact-checked, edited, proofread, and backed by a trusted news organization vouching for its truthfulness and accuracy. Take those filters away, and we, the general public, are faced with the impossible task of sifting through and evaluating an endless sea of the muddled musings of amateurs.

Blogs on both the left and right have perfected the art of political extremism. Unlike professionally edited newspapers or magazines where the political slant of the paper is restricted to the op-ed page, the majority of blogs make radical, sweeping statements without evidence or substantiation. The most popular blogs are those that offer the seductive conspiracy theories and sensationalist antiestablishment platitudes that readers crave. As Lemann notes, even "the more ambitious blogs, taken together, function as a form of fast-moving, densely cross-referential pamphleteering—an open forum for every conceivable opinion that can't make its way into the big media, or . . . simply an individual's take on life."[12]

The downside of all this "democracy," which the *Washington Post*'s Robert Samuelson described as the "greatest outburst of mass exhibitionism in human history,"[13] is the integrity of our political discourse. Amateur journalism trivializes and corrupts serious debate. It is the greatest nightmare of political theorists through the ages, from Plato and Aristotle to Edmund Burke and Hannah Arendt—the degeneration of democracy into the rule of the mob and the rumor mill.

In 1961, Pulitzer Prize–winning playwright Arthur Miller wrote that "a good newspaper is a nation talking to itself." Fifty years later, in a nation where professional newspapers are losing readership to a seemingly endless stream of blogs and opinon-based sites, this conversation has taken a disturbing turn. Instead of starting our conversations about politics, economics, and foreign affairs from a common informed perspective, the amateur bloggers wax on trivial subjects like their favorite brand of breakfast cereal, or make of car, or reality television personality.

What Miller would see today in the Web 2.0 world is

a nation so digitally fragmented that it's no longer capable of informed debate. Instead, we use the Web to confirm our own partisan views and link to others with the same ideologies. Bloggers today are forming aggregated communities of like-minded amateur journalists—at Web sites like Townhall.com, HotSoup.com, and Pajamasmedia.com—where they congregate in self-congratulatory clusters. They are the digital equivalent of online gated communities where all the people have identical views and the whole conversation is mirrored in a way that is reassuringly familiar. It's a dangerous form of digital narcissism; the only conversations we want to hear are those with ourselves and those like us.

Recently, Jürgen Habermas, one of Europe's most influential social thinkers, spoke about the threat Web 2.0 poses to intellectual life in the West.

> The price we pay for the growth in egalitarianism offered by the Internet is the decentralized access to unedited stories. In this medium, contributions by intellectuals lose their power to create a focus.[14]

In this egalitarian environment, any intellectual—be it George Bernard Shaw, Ralph Waldo Emerson, or Habermas himself—is just another strident voice in the cacophony.

Not only can we now publish our own journalism, however substandard, we can self-publish our own literary works as well (I use the word "literary" loosely). Today's digital print-on-demand services are turning amateur novelists into modern-day Gutenbergs, enabling anyone to publish anything, regardless of quality, for a fee. Blurb.com, for example, sells a self-publishing technology that enables unpublished writers, photographers, and bloggers to transform their online blogs into physical books. With Lulu, another publish-on-demand service, all you have to do is upload your files, choose a binding and a cover, and a published book magically appears.

Blurb and Lulu are really just cheaper, more accessible versions of vanity presses, where the untalented go to purchase the veneer of publication. As of this date, Lulu has had little impact on professional book publishers. But whom are such sites benefiting? With 40,000 new books published each year by major houses—a number that most publishers would admit is far too many—do we really need to weed through the embarrassing efforts of hundreds of thousands of unpublished or self-published novelists, historians, and memoirists? According to John Sutherland, chairman of the 2005 Man Booker Prize committee, "It would take approximately 163 lifetimes to read all the fiction available, at the click of the mouse, from Amazon.com."[15] And these are just the professionally selected, edited, and published novels. Do we really need to wade through the tidal wave of amateurish work of authors who have never been professionally selected for publication?

The Liquid Library

Silicon Valley utopian Kevin Kelly wants to kill off the book entirely—as well as the intellectual property rights of writers and publishers. In fact, he wants to rewrite the very definition of the book, digitalizing all books into a single universal and open-source free hypertext—like a huge literary Wikipedia. In a May 2006 *New York Times Magazine* "manifesto," Kelly describes this as the "Liquid Version" of the book, a universal library in which "each book is cross-linked, clustered, cited, extracted, indexed, analyzed, annotated, remixed, reassembled, and woven deeper into the culture than ever before."[16] And Kelly couldn't care less whether the contributor to this hyper-textual utopia is Dostoyevsky or one of the seven dwarfs.

"Once digitized," Kelly says, "books can be unraveled into single pages or be reduced further, into snippets of a page. These snippets will be remixed into reordered books and virtual bookshelves." It is the digital equivalent of tearing out the pages of all the books in the world, shredding them line by line, and pasting them back together in infinite combinations. In his view, this results in "a web of names and a community of ideas."[17] In mine, it foretells the death of culture.

To anyone with the most elemental appreciation for the sanctity of the book and respect for the toils of the author, the implications of what Kelly suggests are, well, obscene. Is *Crime and Punishment* still *Crime and Punishment* if you remove the scene where Raskolnikov

murders the pawnbroker? Should I be allowed to annotate and remix *Moby-Dick* so that Ahab spots the whale
in the beginning of the journey? Is Plato's *Republic* still
the same book if it contains a chapter from Locke and a
paragraph from Kant? A finished book is not a box of
Legos, to be recombined and reconstructed at whim.

Kelly's 2.0 vision may be the ultimate endpoint of the
noble amateur. In his version of the future, individual
writing will be freely distributed online. Writers will
no longer receive royalties from their creative work, but
will have to rely on speeches and selling add-ons to make
a living.

The result: amateur writers and amateur content—all
Drudge and no Dostoyevsky. Without a viable publishing
business model, Kelly's universal library would degenerate into a universal vanity press—a hypertextual confusion of unedited, unreadable rubbish. Bookstores and
publishing houses will disappear. All we will have left to
read are our versions of our own stories.

In the music business, rock stars like Beck are singing
the same tune as Kevin Kelly. Like Kelly and Jimmy
Wales and the other Web 2.0 utopians, Beck is sold on
the seductive nobility of the amateur. Beck's grand idea
is to allow his fans to create personalized versions of his
music—allowing them to design their own cover art,
write their own lyrics, create their own electronic mixes.
Beck would readily replace his own professional cover
artists, lyricists, and recording engineers with the amateur enthusiast. As he told *Wired* magazine:

I'd love to put out an album that you could edit and mix and layer directly in iTunes. We did a remix project on a Web site a few years back where we put up the tracks on a song and let people make their own versions. There was something really inspiring about the variety and quality of the music that people gave back. In an ideal world, I'd find a way to let people truly interact with the records I put out—not just remix the songs, but maybe play them like a videogame.[18]

Similarly, the popular Toronto band Barenaked Ladies recently launched a "remix" contest, allowing fans to download songs from their latest album and re-mix and re-edit them into new versions, the best of which will eventually be released on CD. It's rather like an expert chef who, instead of cooking a fine meal, provides the raw ingredients for the diner. Or the surgeon who, instead of performing the surgery, leaves the amateur in the operating chamber with some surgical instruments and a brief pep talk.

As a profoundly unmusical music fan myself, I can scarcely conceive of Johann Bach releasing a raw version of his Brandenburg Concertos to be remixed or mashed up by his public. Or Mozart letting his listeners rewrite his operas and concertos. Can you imagine Bob Dylan releasing an interactive *Blood on the Tracks* that could be rearranged to sound like you? And once all of these amateur remixes and mash-ups end up on YouTube, as

the noble amateur

most ultimately do, it is us who are faced with the task of sitting through the millions of efforts to find the rare few that are worthwhile.

What the Web 2.0 gives us is an infinitely fragmented culture in which we are hopelessly lost as to how to focus our attention and spend our limited time. And this culture of the amateur goes far beyond books and music. Today, hundreds of thousands of amateur radio broadcasters or podcasters—would-be Howard Sterns and Rush Limbaughs—are using their computers to produce and distribute podcast shows. The latest fad—the new new thing—is video blogs, transforming anyone with a webcam and a microphone into instant stars on amateur video networks like YouTube and Bebo. What's next? Some believe we'll soon see the advent of "wiki-television," in which amateurs can submit content to be embedded in the story lines of their favorite television programs.

Broadcasting technology is becoming so pervasive that everything we do and say can, in a couple of clicks, be disseminated throughout the Internet. But is any of it worth watching?

A Burrito in Every Hand

The cult of the amateur even threatens the world of design, fashion, and advertising. In the October 2006 issue of *Fast Company* magazine, design maven Joe Duffy, founder of Duffy Designs, argued, in a debate with me about the democratization of the art of design, that anyone can and should be a designer. Joe Duffy argues that "the broader the participation in design, the more enthusiasm and demand for great design."[19] But to maintain their value, high-end clothing and cars and electronic equipment require not only great design and great engineering, but mystery and scarcity. What Duffy optimistically calls "participation in design," I argue, lessens the value of real innovation. Are great designs truly that easy to create? Today, the devil might wear Prada. But tomorrow, if Duffy gets his way, we may all be wearing self-designed Prada knockoffs.

Nevertheless, companies like Wal-Mart have begun to calculatingly play to our false assumptions about the "realness" of the amateur, getting free advertising in the process. In July 2006, untrained high school students were invited on Wal-Mart's "Hub" social network to create personalized video advertisements for the Arkansas retail giant. Cosponsored by Sony, the best of these "School My Way" amateur advertisements will be used in a Wal-Mart cable television commercial. It is yet another way in which the cult of the amateur is celebrated, even if it's only a marketing ploy. Companies have come to realize that not only is the amateur ad cheaper, but consumers have come to see it as rawer, less polished, and somehow more "real" or true than an ad prepared by a professional agency.

Nor is Wal-Mart alone. Nike, MasterCard, Toyota, and L'Oréal have run similar user-generated marketing contests, as have Cingular, Nestlé, and American Express. At the 2007 Super Bowl—one of the advertising industry's most important venues, which, with its audience of close to 100 million people, is known to be a showcase for the most creative and biggest-budget commercials,[20] Frito-Lay, Chevrolet, Diamond Foods, and the National Football League ran thirty-second commercials created by amateurs. The economics of these user-generated Super Bowl advertisements are particularly troubling. Take, for example, the competition that Frito-Lay ran to "discover" an amateur commercial for their Doritos corn chips. According to the American Association of Advertising Agencies, the average professionally produced thirty-second spot costs $381,000. Yet Frito-Lay paid a mere $10,000 to each of the five finalists in the competition, leaving $331,000 on the table. That's $331,000 that wasn't paid to professional filmmakers, scriptwriters, actors, and marketing companies—$331,000 sucked out of the economy.

A whole user-created "advertising platform" is even being pioneered by an Atlanta-based company called ViTrue, enabling consumers to create, produce, and upload their own video advertisements. One of ViTrue's early customers is the fast-growing restaurant franchise Moe's Southwest Grill, whose latest campaign to put a "Moe's Burrito in Every Hand" is being produced by amateur videographers (the creators of the best ad will receive Moe's burritos for life).

These campaigns manipulate our sensibility while undercutting the work of traditional advertising agencies and the talented people they employ. Unwittingly, we are giving away our time and our creative output to corporations like Wal-Mart or MasterCard in return for free burritos.

Becoming a doctor, a lawyer, a musician, a journalist, or an engineer requires a significant investment of one's life in education and training, countless auditions or entrance and certifying exams, and commitment to a career of hard work and long hours. A professional writer spends years mastering or refining his or her craft in an effort to be recognized by a seasoned universe of editors, agents, critics, and consumers, as someone worth reading and paying attention to. Those in the movie industry submit to long hours, harried schedules, and insane pressure to create a product that will generate profit in a business in which expenses are high and hits are unpredictable. Can the cult of the noble amateur really expect to bypass all this and do a better job?

Glenn Reynolds, the author of the Instapundit blog, claims that we are on the brink of the amateur century. Technology, Reynolds asserts, will give each individual the power only available traditionally to "nation-states, superheroes, or gods." We will, he argues, acquire the "intelligence of the gods" on everything from amateur journalism and music production to medicine, nanotechnology, and space travel.[21]

As we will see in the next chapter, this celebration of the amateur is having a corroding effect on the truth, accuracy, and reliability of the information we get. Think that's an exaggeration? Read on.

3

truth and lies

Not a day goes by without some new revelation that calls into question the reliability, accuracy, and truth of the information we get from the Internet. Sometimes it's a story about ads made to look like a personal page on social networks like MySpace or Facebook. Or a popular YouTube video that turns out to have been produced by a corporation with a vested interest in shaping consumers' opinions. Every week a new scandal further erodes our trust in the information we get from the Web.

In the digital world's never-ending stream of unfiltered, user-generated content, things are indeed often not what they seem. Without editors, fact-checkers, administrators, or regulators to monitor what is being posted, we have no one to vouch for the reliability or credibility of the content we read and see on sites like Xanga, Six Apart, Veoh, Yelp, Odeo, and countless others. There are no gatekeepers to filter truth from fiction, genuine content from advertising, legitimate information from errors or outright deceit. Who is to point out the lies on the blogosphere that attempt to rewrite our history and spread rumor as fact? When we are all authors, and some of us are writing fiction, whom can we trust?

Can You Believe It?

The September 2006 news clip on the German version of YouTube certainly looked genuine. It showed a professionally attired male news anchor seated at a wooden desk, with a map of Europe hanging behind him. It seemed to be a clip from *Tagesschau*—the most trusted news show in Germany. According to the anchor, the neo-Nazi NPD party had done well in the recent local elections:

> The NPD has received 7.3% of the votes in the German state of Mecklenbeurg-Western Pomerania—more than enough to enter the regional parliament.

Many German viewers were alarmed. Only those with the keenest of eyes could see that this YouTube video was not from the real *Tagesschau*—instead of the Das Erste studio logo, the top right-hand corner of the screen displayed the logo of a multi-spoked black sun

that can be easily rearranged into three swastikas—
the symbol that has been adopted by the German neo-
Nazis.

Yes, the newscast, luckily, was a fraud. Made to look
like a broadcast from the trusted Das Erste, this show
was actually produced by the extremist neo-Nazi NPD as
a trial run for a weekly Internet "news" show they were
planning to launch as a vehicle for party propaganda and
a tool for member recruitment.

Welcome to the truth, Web 2.0 style.

Things aren't much better on the American version
of YouTube. During the November 2006 congressional
elections, one of the most watched videos on YouTube
was a campaign advertisement for Vernon Robinson, the
Republican candidate for North Carolina's Thirteenth
Congressional District.

The video was a distasteful attack on Brad Miller,
Robinson's Democratic opponent. "Instead of spending
money on cancer research, Brad Miller has spent your
money to study the masturbation habits of old men," the
commercial announced. "Brad Miller even spent your
tax dollars to pay teenage girls to watch pornographic
movies with probes connected to their genitalia!"

When criticized for mud-slinging, Vernon Robinson
claimed that this video had never been approved for distribution. "We never put that out as an ad," he told Fox
pundit Sean Hannity. "Someone put it on YouTube."

Is this a valid excuse for defamatory campaign tactics
and blatant distortion of truth? In the Web 2.0 era, the

"Somebody put it on YouTube" excuse has become the equivalent of "the dog ate my homework."

Or what about Conrad Burns, the ex-senator from Montana, who lost the 2006 election against Democrat Jon Tester in part because of political propaganda spread on YouTube. In one popular video, Burns was shown falling asleep during a congressional hearing; in another he was captured on camera making a joke about the "nice little Guatemalan man" who did the gardening at his Virginia residence. And a third caught him warning his constituents about those who "drive taxicabs in the daytime and kill at night."

Given that Burns really did commit these gaffes, the videos weren't technically lies. But they weren't exactly truth either. Arrowhead77, the anonymous videographer who authored and posted the videos, was the pseudonym for a couple of Jon Tester's staffers. Between April and October 2006, a Tester aide, camcorder in hand, had gone on video safari, putting 16,000 miles on his car and following the Montanan senator on the campaign trail with his camera, ready to pounce at any slip of the tongue.

The problem is that the viral, editor-free nature of YouTube allows anyone—from neo-Nazis, to propagandists, to campaign staffers—to anonymously post deceptive, misleading, manipulative, or out-of-context videos. Conrad Burns was far from the only victim of this type of slander. In the 2006 Virginia senatorial race, the Democrats famously milked George Allen's *macaca* media moment to death. There are, no doubt, all sorts of wannabe Arrowhead77s out there, camcorders at the ready, preparing to big-game hunt Hillary Clinton, Rudy Giuliani, John McCain, and Barack Obama in the 2008 presidential campaign.

This is the future of politics in a Web 2.0 world. The supposed democratization medium of user-generated content is creating a tabloid-style gotcha culture—where one thoughtless throwaway remark overshadows an entire platform, and lifelong political careers are destroyed by an off-the-cuff joke at the end of a long campaign day.

And when information on politics and policy is so easily skewed or distorted, it's us, the electorate, who lose. When we, the citizens, don't know whom to believe or whom to trust, we may end up making the wrong decisions, or, worse yet, just switch off—from the candidates, from politics, from voting at all.

The YouTubification of politics is a threat to civic culture. It infantilizes the political process, silencing public discourse and leaving the future of the government up to thirty-second video clips shot by camcorder-wielding amateurs with political agendas.

The Truth About 9/11

In 2005, three young would-be filmmakers from the small town of Oneonta in upstate New York used two thousand dollars saved up from shifts at a Friendly's ice cream store to create an eighty-minute movie called *Loose Change*, a "documentary" (originally conceived as a fictional story) that claimed the 9/11 terrorist attacks were organized and carried out by the Bush administration. In a collage of out-of-context quotes and since-discredited news clips, the film painted a grossly distorted version of events. In this version, one of the Flight 11 hijackers was found alive after the crash, a few blocks from the Trade Center, and United Flight 93 didn't crash in a Pennsylvania field, but instead was redirected to Cleveland's Hopkins Airport. And the towers didn't collapse as a result of the impact from planes flown by Islamist suicide hijackers, but rather from the detonation of previously planted explosives. Originally posted on the Internet in the spring of 2005, *Loose Change* rose to the number-one spot on Google Video's "Top 100" by May 2006, generating ten million viewings in its first year alone.[1] That's ten million people being fundamentally misled about one of the most cataclysmic events in American history.

The "claims" made in *Loose Change* were completely discredited in the final report of the 9/11 Commission, a report that took two years to compile, cost $15 million, and was written by two governors, four congressmen, three former White House officials, and two special counsels. So whom do you trust? Three twenty-something amateurs with no college education or a team of experts that included America's brightest and most experienced elected officials and investigators? The Oneonta revisionists used the self-authoring technology of Web 2.0 to trash history about an event that cost thousands of

American lives, provoked a global backlash against Islam, and instigated two wars.

Yes, you could argue, to some people it was obvious the movie was a hoax. But how many other "hoaxes" are less obvious? How much of what we read or see on the Internet is equally deceptive? Is the person who posts an online ad or sends us a witty e-mail genuine, or is he or she a con artist, sexual predator, or hustler of one kind or another?

Scammers and Spammers

We've all received the e-mails from the Nigerian entrepreneur who promises us a million-dollar return on a "small" investment in his oil company, or the e-mails from an unknown address claiming to be from your credit card company asking you to verify your card number. Most of us know these are cons. But unfortunately, in an age the *New York Times* dubs Spam 2.0, digital scams are becoming harder and harder to spot.

One of the most persistent contemporary scams is called the "pump and dump," in which the perpetrators buy up penny stocks and then sell them, via spam, at artificially inflated prices. When the stock's price spikes a few days later, the spammers sell off their shares, receiving a 5 to 6 percent return and causing the values of the hoodwinked investors' shares to plummet.

Take, for example, a penny stock called the Diamant Art Corporation. At the end of the day on Friday,

December 15, 2006, this share was valued at 11 cents. Over that weekend, a botnet began "spewing out millions of spam messages" about the value of the shares. By Monday, many unsuspecting spam victims bought up shares, driving the price up to 19 cents, and finally peaking at 25 cents. Then, of course, the spammer sold off his shares at a huge profit. By Wednesday, December 20, the price was down to 12 cents.[2]

Or, in another popular con, spammers seize control of innocent computer networks, turning them into "botnets" by programming them to automatically send out spam that will then appear to be from a trustworthy source. Secure Computing, a leading Silicon Valley anti-spam company, has reported that 250,000 computers each day are transformed into botnets without their owner's knowledge.

Sex, Lies, and the Internet

In early September 2006, a Seattle-based techie named Jason Fortuny posted an ad under an invented female identity in the "casual encounters" section of Craigslist—the virtual marketplace for one-night stands and anonymous sex partners. Fortuny received 178 responses and proceeded to post them on his Web site—including the men's names, photos of them naked, even the identities of their wives. With the click of Fortuny's mouse, reputations were destroyed, careers ruined, marriages and families shattered, all for a petty prank. Yes, some of the victims were going behind their wives' backs, and perhaps they deserved what they got. But others were simply lonely people looking to make a connection.

This case underscores the dangers inherent in an editorless medium where the only rules are that there are no rules. With a few simple keystrokes, Fortuny was able to create a false identity and publish the fruits of his deceit to the world. Like too much of what is on the Web today, his prank was both dishonest and harmful. The irony of the case, of course, is that the very people who seek anonymity in the Web 2.0 were done in by it. The Web's cherished anonymity can be a weapon as well as a shield.

The fact is that rumors and lies disseminated online can tarnish reputations and ruin careers. In the summer of 2005, a woman named Julie posted a horrific tale on the Web site dontdatehimgirl.com, a message board that invites scorned women to vent about egregious behavior of ex-boyfriends. According to Julie's posting, a man named Guido had gotten her drunk earlier that summer, raped and sodomized her, infected her with a sexually transmitted disease, and left her so humiliated and depressed that she attempted suicide. This tragic story, accompanied by a photograph of the alleged offender, was viewed over 1,000 times, prompting one visitor to write, "This son of a bitch deserves to be in jail. We need to circulate his picture everywhere and let everyone know what he did."

Had the story been true, most of us would be inclined

to agree. The problem is, not a word of it was. "Guido" was actually Erik, a friend of "Julie" (shockingly, not her real name). She eventually admitted she had posted the sordid tale "as a joke."[3]

Where content is unvetted, no proof or evidence is required to back up one's claims (on dontdatehimgirl. com, users only have to check a box declaring the information to be truthful), and anonymous postings are allowed, wild exaggerations and fabrications are not uncommon. As "Julie" told the *Miami New Times,* "There is nothing to stop [someone] from slandering a guy with impunity. . . . I would guess the vast majority of the 'stories' posted are completely full of shit."

In traditional media, antidefamation and libel laws protect people from these kinds of vicious character assassinations. But due in part to the anonymity and casualness of most Web postings, these laws have been hard to enforce in the digital world. A Pennsylvania lawyer named Todd Hollis found messages on dontdatehimgirl. com accusing him of having herpes, being gay, and having knowingly spread a sexually transmitted disease. Hollis promptly sued the owner of the site, as well as the women who made the defamatory statements, for being "a secondary distributor of false information." But his effort to clear his name had some negative consequences. As a result of the publicity surrounding the suit, five more unflattering profiles of him were posted on the site; they have collectively been viewed over 50,000 times.[4]

Then there is Rafe Banks, an attorney who sued a former client for attacking him on his blog. The former client had a vendetta against Banks after Banks failed to refund a $3,000 fee, so he falsely accused Banks of bribing judges to dismiss charges against drug dealer clients, then threatened more accusations if Banks didn't pay up. Banks eventually won a settlement, but not before irreparable damage had been done to his professional reputation.[5]

The owners of traditional newspapers and news networks are held legally accountable for the statements of their reporters, anchors, and columnists, encouraging them to uphold a certain standard of truth in the content they allow in their paper or on their air. Web site owners, on the other hand, are not liable for what is posted by a third party. Some say that this is a protection of free speech. But at what cost? As long as the owners of Web sites and blogs are not held accountable, they have little encouragement or incentive to question or evaluate the information they post.

On the Web, rumors or misinformation from even a single source can spread with frightening speed. Take the experience of Amy Tan, the bestselling author of *The Joy Luck Club*. In an essay entitled "Personal Errata,"[6] she describes how erroneous facts about her career, background, and personal life, likely originating from a single posting, have multiplied in cyberspace to the point where they have become part of her official biography. According to online accounts, Tan attended eight different colleges, lived in a mansion in Silicon Valley, raised two children, has been married several times, and has won both a Pulitzer Prize and the Nobel Prize for literature. The real Amy Tan has, in fact, been married once, has no kids, lives in a San Francisco apartment, and has won neither prize (yet). With no one to step in and question the veracity of information in the digital world, mistakes, lies, and rumors multiply like germs.

Before the Web 2.0, our collective intellectual history has been one driven by the careful aggregation of truth—through professionally edited books and reference materials, newspapers, and radio and television. But as all information becomes digitalized and democratized, and is made universally and permanently available, the media of record becomes an Internet on which misinformation never goes away. As a result, our bank of collected information becomes infected by mistakes and fraud. Blogs are connected through a single link, or series of links, to countless other blogs, and MySpace pages are connected to countless other My Space pages, which link to countless YouTube videos, Wikipedia entries, and Web sites with various origins and purposes. It's impossible to stop the spread of misinformation, let alone identify its source. Future readers often inherit and repeat this misinformation, compounding the problem, creating a collective memory that is deeply flawed.

Lonely Girls and Sock Puppets

It's not just the information itself that we can no longer trust; with the anonymity that Web 2.0 technology affords, the sources of information are of unknown origin, and as we've seen, they often can't be trusted. The Internet is flooded with fake identities—fake bloggers, fake MySpace profiles, fake YouTube starlets, fake e-mail addresses, fake reviews on sites like Amazon (some of which clearly are the result of a personal vendetta). Fake identities on the Internet have, in fact, become so widely adopted, they've been given their own term: "sock puppet," meaning the alter ego through which one speaks on an online community or posts on a blog.

Two of the more well-known examples are a couple of puppets called Mikekoshi and sprezzatura. Mikekoshi—whose real name is Michael Hiltzik—is a Pulitzer Prize–winning journalist who, ironically enough, won his 1999 award for his reporting on corruption in the entertainment industry. Hiltzik, who up until April 2006 wrote the *Los Angeles Times'* "Golden State" blog, is a "strident liberal" frequently embroiled in polemical fireworks with conservative bloggers. But Hiltzik—whose tagline on his blog was "Michael Hiltzik on business, economics, and more with a California edge"—cheated. He invented an online identity called Mikekoshi, and then, under this moniker, aggressively defended his own work on his opponents' Web sites.

Lee Siegel, a senior editor at the *New Republic* magazine and the winner of the 2002 National Magazine Award for Reviews and Criticism, invented an online identity called "sprezzatura" (an Italian word meaning nonchalance), under which he harshly attacked the liberal media. Siegel went so far as to post explosive remarks by sprezzatura on his *own* blog. When accused of being sprezzatura, Siegel took his deception to the next level by categorically denying it.[7]

Hiltzik and Siegel were temporarily suspended from their respective publications for violating journalistic ethics by misrepresenting themselves online (the *Los Angeles Times* ethics guideline states that editors and reporters must identify themselves when dealing with the public) in a way that would never have been possible before the advent of 2.0 technologies. In traditional news media, there is no such thing as anonymity. Articles and op-eds run with bylines, holding reporters and contributors responsible for the content they create. This not only holds them to ethical standards, but also provides a level of assurance for the public; the writer is accountable for his or her reporting or opinions. If an op-ed writer works for a political party or a partisan think tank, for example, the reader is made aware of his or her affiliation and potential conflict of interest. If a reporter misrepresents himself, or misrepresents the facts, the infraction will be caught and he or she will be taken to task and possibly fired, as was the case with Jayson Blair of the *New York Times*. But in the anonymous world of the blogosphere, there are no such assurances, creating a crisis of trust and confidence.

Sock puppetry (both literal and figurative) is rampant on YouTube as well. In fact, the lies on YouTube are so well told that they have become detective stories in their own right. Take, for example, the famous story of YouTube's lonelygirl15, a sixteen-year-old who starred in a popular series of self-made YouTube videos chronicling the life of an angst-ridden and lonely teenage girl. Some viewers, over time, noticed that in places, the amateur lonelygirl15 videos appeared to have a professional hand behind them, raising questions about the girl's true identity. Soon the blogs were peppered with speculation. Some thought that YouTube itself might be producing the video to boost viewership. Other sleuths suspected the hand of the Beverly Hills–based talent agency Creative Artists Agency. Jon Fine of *BusinessWeek* wondered if it could have been something "dreamed up" by Scientologists, occultists, or some other obscure millenarian Christian sect.[8]

The question of the authenticity of the video became the story itself. Meanwhile, the audience grew and grew, and lonelygirl15 became YouTube's second-most-subscribed channel. None of her hundreds of thousands of viewers seemed to care whether they were watching sophisticated advertising or the musings of an angst-ridden teenager. Eventually, lonelygirl15's creators, a screenwriter and filmmaker from California, confessed: "Bree," the girl in the video, was, in fact, a twenty-something Australian actress named Jessica. The videos had been an experiment in what the creators called "a new art form"—scripted clips that they hoped to eventually turn into a movie.

But if we can't trust the authenticity of Bree's confessions—if her teenage angst is all a sham—then we've simply been hoodwinked. And it makes me wonder what else on YouTube, or in the blogosphere, is fiction or advertisement.

Howard Kurtz of the *Washington Post* summarized the farce of lonelygirl15 this way:

> The great thing about the Internet is that anyone, even a lonely 16-year-old girl, can record her thoughts and draw a big following. The maddening thing about the Internet is that she might not be lonely or 16.[9]

All this points to a fundamental flaw with our user-driven content. We're never sure if what we read or see is what it seems. The user-run Internet not only allows, but encourages, the invention of false identity. Yet no one questions why so many of us are determined to hide who we are or what our affiliation is. The problem for those of us who wish to know more about who we're communicating with is that, as Jack Shafer, media critic at Slate.com, says, "There are just too many places to hide now."

The Blogosphere and the Bazaar

Some argue that the Web 2.0, and the blogosphere in particular, represents a return to the vibrant democratic intellectual culture of the eighteenth-century London coffeehouse. But Samuel Johnson, Edmund Burke, and

James Boswell didn't hide behind aliases while debating one another. The fact is that too many of us aren't innately honest creatures, either on- or off-line. When a medium like the Web is unchecked by regulation or professional editors or filters, and when we're left to our own amateur devices, we don't always behave well.

Trust is the very foundation of any community. Every social contract theorist—from Hobbes and Locke to Jean-Jacques Rousseau—recognizes that there can be no peaceful political arrangement without a common pact. And, as anthropologist Ernest Gellner argues in his classic *Nations and Nationalism*, the core modern social contract is rooted in our common culture, in our language, and in our shared assumptions about the world. Modern man is socialized by what the anthropologist calls a common "high culture." Our community and cultural identity, Geller says, come from newspapers and magazines, television, books, and movies. Mainstream media provides us with common frames of reference, a common conversation, and common values.

Benedict Anderson, in *Imagined Communities*, explains that modern communities are established through the telling of common stories, the formation of communal myths, the shared sense of participating in the same daily narrative of life. If our national conversation is carried out by anonymous, self-obsessed people unwilling to reveal their real identities, then Anderson's imagined community degenerates into anarchy.

The Web 2.0 is exacerbating the disconnect between

truth and politics, too, if indeed there can ever be any absolute truth in politics.

The Web site Insight, for example, a remnant of a defunct print magazine owned by the Unification Church, caused a stir in January 2007 by publishing an erroneous story that the *New York Times* called the first anonymous smear of the 2008 presidential race. Insight posted a story—by an anonymous reporter citing anonymous sources—claiming that Senator Hillary Clinton's campaign was hatching a smear campaign against her rival for the Democratic nomination, Barack Obama. According to the Insight story, which was promptly discredited, the Clinton campaign was planning to accuse Obama of having been enrolled in an Islamic religious school in Indonesia as a child, and of having covered it up. Even though the report was denounced by both campaigns, uncorroborated by other news organizations, and unconfirmed by sources (because there were no identifiable sources), it was picked up by Fox News and was discussed extensively on the morning news programs and on conservative talk radio.

It is deeply disturbing that in our filter-free Web 2.0 world, rumors and lies concocted by anonymous (and no doubt amateur) reporters are lent legitimacy and propagated by mainstream media channels. As Ralph Whitehead Jr., a professor of journalism at the University of Massachusetts, told the *New York Times,* "If you want to talk about a business model that is designed to manufacture mischief in large volume, that would be it."

When Charles Johnson, a rabidly pro-Israeli blogger at Little Green Footballs, discovered a doctored photo of a war scene in Beirut from a Reuters photographer named Adnan Hajj, tens of thousands concluded that the whole mainstream media was pro-Hezbollah, pro-Syria, and pro-terrorist. What the Reuters reporter did—staging and manipulating a photograph in order to create a more dramatic image—was a travesty; it utterly violated our expectations of truth and objectivity in journalism. And as a representative of a trusted, 155-year-old news organization, Hajj was duly excoriated for it. Following Reuters' immediate investigation of the matter, both Hajj and his editor were fired, and all 920 photos Hajj had taken in his career at Reuters were removed from the Web site. Reuters even went one step further to prevent such breaches in the future, by requiring all staff and freelance photographers to sign an enhanced code of ethical conduct.[10]

In contrast, on YouTube, one can watch thousands of short videos of grieving Lebanese men and women in the ruins of Beirut, holding dead babies in their arms. On a Web site with no filters, no ethical codes, no accountability or disciplinary consequences, one has no way of knowing how many of these films were doctored. As the *Washington Post* concluded, YouTube is a "video Dumpster" for a "disorganized bazaar of images."[11] For every Adnan Hajj in the mainstream media, there are hundreds of amateur polemicists peddling their propaganda and distortions on the Web.

In fact, the Web 2.0 media has put the horse before the cart—the new information disseminated on it is endless and mind-numbing. What is in short supply is reasoned, informed analysis. All the raw sensationalized information in the YouTube Dumpster—whether or not it is genuine—has no real value without expert interpretation and commentary. A photograph of a dead Lebanese or Israeli baby is not a helpful guide to understanding the complex situation of the Middle Eastern conflict.

In the golden age of media, revered journalists like Edward R. Murrow and Walter Cronkite were cultural heroes—universally admired, trusted, and respected. But in today's world, they would be C-list celebrities, as fewer and fewer of us pay any attention to the traditional news media. Instead, many of us—especially younger Americans—get our own, personalized version of the news at sites like Instapundit.com or at the Daily Kos, where we can be sure that the prevailing sentiment matches our own. Wittingly or not, we seek out the information that mirrors back our own biases and opinions and conforms with our distorted versions of reality. We lose that common conversation or informed debate over our mutually agreed-upon facts. Rather, we perpetuate one anothers' biases. The common community is increasingly shattering into three hundred million narrow, personalized points of view. Many of us have strong opinions, yet most of us are profoundly uninformed.

Library of Babel

In 1939, Jorge Luis Borges, a half-blind Argentine from Buenos Aires with a genius for dark literary fantasy, wrote a short essay called "The Total Library," predicting the horrors of the infinite library, one that has no center, no logic. Instead, it is a chaos of information, "composed of an indefinite and perhaps infinite number of hexagonal galleries."

Borges' "The Total Library" is today's Internet— anonymous, incorrect, chaotic, and overpowering. It is a place where there is no concrete reality, no right and wrong, no governing moral code. It is a place where truth is selective and constantly subject to change. The experience of surfing the Internet is akin to wandering around the hexagonal galleries of Borges' Library of Babel. Truth is elusive, always one click or Web site away.

Even conventional blogs aren't always what they seem to be. They can be faked, hidden, or hacked. They can become the tools of corporations, political propagandists, or identity thieves. The newest phenomenon on the Web are "splogs"—a combination of spam and blogs. Generated from software that allows users to create thousands of blogs per hour, splogs are fake blogs designed to mirror the real blogs in a sneaky ploy to trick advertisers and search engines and drive traffic and thus pay-per-click revenue. According to a researcher at the University of Maryland, splogs make up 56 percent of active blogs, clogging up the blogosphere with some 900,000 posts a day. Dave Sifry, the CEO of Technorati, the dominant search engine that indexes blogs, believes that splogs make up 90 percent of new blogs. As the September 2006 issue of *Wired* magazine noted, these sploggers "build entire online ecosystems of sleaze, twaddle, and gobbledygook," designed to waste the time of Internet users and steal revenue from innocent advertisers.[12]

A first cousin of splogs are flogs. Floggers are bloggers who claim to be independent but are actually in the pay of a sponsor, like the three Edelman PR staffers who, in 2006, attacked Wal-Mart critics while posing as grass-roots "Working Families for Wal-Mart" bloggers. Wal-Mart's commercial relationship with Edelman PR was not something, of course, that these floggers wrote about on their flogs.

PayPerPost.com, a Web 2.0 start-up backed by respected Silicon Valley venture capital firm Draper Fisher Jurvetson, acts as middleman between advertisers and floggers, paying floggers anything from $5 to $10 per post. PayPerPost.com calls itself a "marketplace for Consumer Generated Advertising." More accurately, it's a dark alleyway on the Internet where bloggers sell their souls to the highest bidder.

It may surprise you to know that advertisers, too, are victims. As much as we may focus on the way in which they deceive us, they, too, it turns out, are being deceived. In 2006, the professional monitoring service Click Forensic proved that at least 14 percent of the advertisements sold by search engines are bogus clicks, generating a payment for the search company without creating any real advertising value in return.[13]

In fact, a whole underground network of "domain parking" sites consisting solely of links and recycled banner ads has risen up, existing strictly to generate more clicks for which advertisers can be billed. And click-fraud scams are growing in both scope and number. In some, "paid to read" rings, often with hundreds or thousands of members scattered all over the world, are paid to sit at their computers and click over and over on a link. In others, automated programs called "clickbots" generate high volumes of anonymous, bogus clicks that are harder to track down than manual clicks. The result is that businesses, which pay per click on their ads, dole out huge, inflated sums to advertising companies for clicks that generate no returns in sales, customers, or genuine "stickiness."

The Atlanta-based company MostChoice.com was one such victim. In 2006, the company's founder, Martin Fleishman, noticed a growing number of clicks from places like South Korea and Syria—particularly puzzling since MostChoice serves mostly U.S.-based customers. After hiring a programmer to design a system that could analyze the length and origin of every click on a company ad, he discovered that most questionable clickers had left the site in a matter of seconds, and that none of those clicks had resulted in any new clients or business. Indeed, he had fallen prey to an elaborate click-fraud scheme—one that had cost his company over $100,000 in fruitless advertising fees. And this case is far from an anomaly. Click fraud, which, according to *The Economist* magazine, made up somewhere between 10 percent and 50 percent of all online advertising in 2006—adding up to between $3 billion and $13 billion—is perhaps the single biggest threat to the viability of the advertising-centric Web 2.0 economy. It makes Enron look like a rounding error.[14]

From splogs and flogs to botnets and clickbots, the Web 2.0 world has been invaded by liars, cheats, and fraudsters.

TiVo and Tea Parties

Before the Web 2.0, independent media content and paid advertising existed separately, in parallel, and were easily distinguishable from each other. On television and on the radio, commercials ran in thirty- or sixty-second slots, spaced predictably between every fifteen or so minutes of traditional programming. In newspapers and magazines, certain pages and columns were reserved for ads, and others were reserved for news and editorial content. Even in the first Internet revolution of the Nineties, content was separate from banner ads or interstitial paid advertisements. On the Web 2.0, that is no longer true. According to a Pew Internet and American Life Project study, while most people can distinguish between regular programming and infomercials on television, and between regular content and advertisements in print publications, 62 percent of Web browsers could not distinguish between paid and unpaid sites among search results.[15]

One reason for this is that new Web 2.0 technologies enable advertisers to transform what appears to be traditional content into commercials. Take a controversial new technology called "in-text" advertising, which allows companies like Microsoft and Target to sponsor keywords in traditional editorial articles so that when a reader moves their cursor over an underlined word, a pop-up ad appears. From the user's perspective, it's often not even clear what the association is between the underlined word and the advertisement. But from the advertiser's perspective, as long as they view the ad, it hardly matters.

This blurring of lines between advertising and content is partly due to our growing distrust in marketers and advertising. In January 2006, Edelman PR's "Trust Barometer" revealed a dramatic societal shift in whom we trust, from traditional media to trust in ourselves and our peers. In 2003, only 22 percent of American respondents reported trusting "a person like yourself or your peer." In January 2006, just three years into the Web 2.0 revolution, this had more than tripled, to 68 percent.[16]

As consumers, we have become increasingly suspicious of commercial messages, as well as increasingly intolerant of them. A 2005 report from the market research firm Yankelovich found that 69 percent of American consumers "were interested in ways to block, skip, or opt out of being exposed to advertising." As the editor of *PR Week* explained:

The past few years have seen something of a crisis in traditional TV and advertising, due in large part to two words that have only come into existence in the past half-decade or so: TiVo and blogs. These two phenomena have been the cornerstone of the shift in formula of most marketing programs away from the 30-second TV ad centerpiece toward a more fluid interaction with a highly knowledgeable audience.

The advertising industry certainly has gotten the message about "fluid" interactivity. In a much-quoted 2004 speech, James Stengel, Procter & Gamble's head of advertising, acknowledged that because today's consumers are "less responsive to messaging on traditional media," Web 2.0 consumers "are embracing new technologies that empower them with more control over how and when they are marketed to."

Given our mistrust of traditional commercials, the challenge for marketers in the Web 2.0 democratized media is to advertise without appearing to do so—by creating and placing commercial messages that appear to be genuine content. The challenge, and the opportunity, is to do this while building "authenticity"—authentic content, authentic brands, authentic commercial messages. But, of course, such authenticity is utterly contrived.

An executive at the Weber Shandwick PR agency described such strategies in *PR Week* as "seeding" the market with guerrilla publicity, product placement, and public relations stunts. The anonymous, editor-free Web 2.0 media provides an ideal environment for this, because if we don't know who produced an advertisement, we can be convinced that it was created by people "like us." Amateurism sells. The more unofficial the message, the more likely the consumer will take ownership of it.

Case in point? A short video called "Tea Partay" was posted on YouTube at the beginning of August 2006. Directed by Julien Christian Lutz, a music video veteran known as "Little X," "Tea Partay," a short rap video set on Cape Cod, which parodies the lifestyle of New England preppies, was viewed half a million times in the first couple of weeks of its YouTube release. But "Tea Partay" was not posted purely for our entertainment. In fact, it was paid for by Smirnoff to advertise a new malt drink called Raw Tea. Produced by the global advertising agency of Bartle Bogle Hegarty at a production cost of $200,000, it has proved to be one of the first big hits of viral advertising. And few consumers realized the extent to which they'd had the wool pulled over their eyes.

The beverage industry is not the only one to embrace guerrilla advertising. Nike ran a similarly successful video featuring the happy feet of Brazilian soccer star Ronaldinho as a promotion for its range of sports footwear. Other successful YouTube videos include Sony's "Colour Like No Other" spots, advertising its range of Bravia flat-screen TVs, and Volkswagen's "Unpimp Your Ride" features for their new GTI model. What is so disconcerting is that, to the uncritical eye, all these commercials appear to be entertainment. YouTube is a long commercial break dressed up as democratized media. It's the ultimate fantasy for the marketing and advertising industries.

As Chad Hurley, the founder of YouTube, told *Adweek:*

> We think there are better ways for people to engage with brands than forcing them to watch a commercial before seeing content. . . . We wanted to create a model where our users can engage with content and create a two-way communication between advertisers and users.

What Hurley is really suggesting is that on YouTube advertising and content can be successfully collapsed; that advertising is entertainment and entertainment is advertising. This "two-way communication" model has made YouTube into a grab bag of video commercials; everyone is using YouTube to peddle their brand.

What makes this deceptive to consumers is that YouTube's paid-for advertising appears no different from the rest of its content. In August 2006, the site began selling what it called "participatory video ads" (PVA), paid user-initiated spots that run on its front page. The first PVA was for a techno-dystopian movie called *Pulse,* and the ad was viewed 900,000 times over four days in August 2006.[17] The difference between the PVA and the standard YouTube content is virtually undetectable. And so is the distinction between participatory content and advertising on YouTube's "Brand Channels," which have been established solely to enable advertisers to sell products online. The first, paid for by Warner Brothers and dedicated to Paris Hilton's debut album *Paris,* was launched in the summer of 2006. With its Brand Channels, YouTube is turning itself into a democratized Shopping Network that does not distinguish between independent content and advertising.

But there *is* a fundamental difference between advertising and user-generated content—one is a paid message carefully calibrated to entice people to buy a product, while the other is an expression of information, creativity, or art. What happens to truth when politicians begin buying channels on YouTube to trash their opponents? And what becomes of artistic integrity when media companies use YouTube to broadcast "reviews" of their own products?

The irony of a "democratized" media is that some content producers have more power than others. In a media without gatekeepers, where one's real identity is often hidden or disguised, the truly empowered are the big companies with the huge advertising budgets. In theory, Web 2.0 gives amateurs a voice. But in reality it's often those with the loudest, most convincing message, and the most money to spread it, who are being heard.

The Wisdom of Crowds

In the Web 2.0 world, the crowd has become the authority on what is true and what is not. Search engines like

Google, which run on algorithms that rank results according to the number of previous searches, answer our search queries not with what is most true or most reliable, but merely what is most popular. As a result, our knowledge—about everything from politics, to current affairs, to literature, to science—is being shaped by nothing but the aggregation of responses. The search engine is a quantitative historical record of previous requests. So all the search engine offers is a ranking system that feeds back to us the wisdom of the crowd. In terms of links clicked on and sites visited, Google is an electronic mirror of ourselves.

But the problem is that the Web 2.0 generation is taking search-engine results as gospel. Imagine your child is doing a paper about the American presidency. He or she enters the words "White House" to learn more about the executive office, and decides to visit the links for the top three responses. Well, the third link in the Google search takes your kid to WhiteHouse.org—a spoof Web site that is dedicated to fake news, gossip, and offensive headlines.

And what's more, the Google search engine can be easily manipulated or corrupted. "Google bombing," which involves simply linking a large number of sites to a certain page, can raise the ranking of any given site in Google's search results. So anyone with a bit of tech savvy can rig the supposedly democratic Internet by repeatedly hyperlinking or cross-linking certain pages that they want to show up first in Google searches. These bombers are attempting to corrupt the collective "wisdom" stored in the Google algorithm.

Rather than user-generated content, what Google bombing represents is another kind of UGC—user-generated corruption. Google bombing has become a popular strategy for trying to sway popular opinion. In the 2006 congressional elections, for example, Google bombers at a liberal group blog called MyDD.com tried to discredit Republican senatorial candidate Jon Kyle by manipulating the algorithm so that when users searched for his name, a highly critical article published in the *Phoenix New Times* was among the first links to show up. And in a more humorous but no less agenda-pushing example of Google bombing, try entering the term "miserable failure" into Google and see what comes up.

"Social news" or "social bookmarking" sites like Digg, Reddit, Delicious, and the relaunched Netscape.com, which rely on the collective behavior of other users to prioritize the articles they display, also limit our access to fair and balanced information. These sites track the reading habits of their users and make recommendations based on aggregated preferences of the entire community. But such a method cannot be relied upon to keep us informed. When our individual intentions are left to the wisdom of the crowd, our access to information becomes narrowed, and as a result, our view of the world and our perception of truth becomes dangerously distorted.

For all their claims to be more democratic and honest, these supposedly editor-free social news sites are actually creating a more oligarchic and corrupt media. Social news sites such as Digg and Reddit are being manipulated by so-called "influencers"—people who artificially drive up the rankings of certain stories on these recommendation engines. According to the *Wall Street Journal*'s analysis of over 25,000 recommendations on six social sites, a tiny coterie of thirty users at Digg, a community of 900,000 users, were responsible for one-third of all front-page postings. And on Netscape.com, one user—with the screen name "Stoner"—was responsible for 217 (13%) of all the stories on the site's most popular list over a fourteen-day period. The *Wall Street Journal*'s research reveals that these sites reflect the preferences of the few rather than the "wisdom" of the masses.

The most disturbing thing of all about social news sites is that many influencers are gaming the engines to promote their own agendas. According to the *Wall Street Journal* report, some marketing companies are now selling "front-page exposure" on Digg. Others openly pay influencers to push stories. In October 2006, for example, User/Submitter.com began paying Digg users 10 cents for each story recommendation. And one seventeen-year-old Illinois high school senior, once ranked the number-two user on Digg, is now paid a monthly stipend of $1,000 by Netscape just to post his recommendations on the Netscape site.[18] Clearly, the wisdom of the crowd is an illusion—the anonymous influencers on Digg or Reddit are no more to be trusted than the anonymous amateur editors at Wikipedia or the anonymous amateur filmmakers on YouTube.

But even if there was such a thing as the wisdom of

the crowd, should we trust it? The answer, of course, is no. History has proven that the crowd is not often very wise. After all, many unwise ideas—slavery, infanticide, George W. Bush's war in Iraq, Britney Spears—have been extremely popular with the crowd. This is why the arbiters of truth should be the experts—those who speak from a place of knowledge and authority—not the winners of a popularity contest.

In 1841, a Scottish journalist called Charles Mackay wrote a classic critique of the irrational crowd called *Extraordinary Popular Delusions.*[19] Mackay used the Dutch Tulipmania fiasco and the South Sea Bubble to show that "whole communities suddenly fix their minds upon one object and go mad in its pursuit." If Mackay were around today, he would add Web 2.0 to the list of extraordinary popular delusions that have gripped the crowd. There is a twist, however, to today's grand digital delusion. With Web 2.0, the madness is about the crowd falling in love with itself.

Is that really the wisdom of the crowd?

4

the day the music died
[side a]

LARGEST RECORD STORE IN THE KNOWN WORLD—OPEN NINE TO MIDNIGHT, 365 DAYS A YEAR, read the sign outside the store on the corner of Bay and Columbus in San Francisco.

Originally opened in April 1968, the store might not have been as physically overwhelming as the Tower Records that spanned three blocks in New York's Greenwich Village, where the major music labels regularly debuted new releases, or as rich in star sightings as the Tower Records on Los Angeles' Sunset Strip, but to me it was the *biggest* record store in the world. It was where, in the early Nineties, as a music writer and reviewer, I would hang out in the richly stocked classical music annex, learning about new releases from knowledgeable

Tower staff, meeting with other writers, and attending the annual in-store appearances of opera stars like Luciano Pavarotti or Renée Fleming. Bin after bin of records, and later CDs, filled the aisles, while die-cut easel-backed posters of the new albums and beloved artists filled the empty spaces.

Rock-and-Roll Hall of Famer David Sholin, the man "with the golden ears" who changed the face of music programming on the radio, has similar memories of the San Francisco store:

> On Friday nights, the place was like an event. Just going in and seeing everybody in the place, the aisles jammed, all the new releases—it would be hard to describe to someone who wasn't there.[1]

But today, when I got to the corner of Columbus and Bay, the old beloved Tower—the Tower of Pavarotti and Fleming, U2 and the Rolling Stones, Madonna and Aretha—was dead. The windows of the old store were plastered with cheerless purple, red, and yellow signs bellowing the same out-of-tune song:

SALE ON EVERYTHING.
NOTHING HELD BACK
EVERYTHING MUST GO
GOING OUT OF BUSINESS

One week earlier, the fat lady had sung.

The price on the table was now $134.3 million. Cash.

The robust bidding had been going on for thirty hours. The once pristine law firm boardroom was littered with the debris of the marathon auction: ties and jackets of disheveled bidders sprawled on the backs of chairs, half-eaten pizza in soggy cardboard boxes, stacks of empty soda cans. But the end was finally in sight. After an auction lasting a full day and a half, all but two bidders had dropped out.

They called it a bankruptcy auction, but, in truth, it was the last picture show, the day when another piece of the music died. At 8:00 A.M. on Thursday, October 3, 2006, Tower Records, where we've been buying our music and our dreams for almost half a century, went under the hammer for the final time. Seventeen bidders had shown up at the offices of Delaware's largest law firm in downtown Wilmington to bid on the remains. And by 4:00 P.M. on Friday, October 4, only one liquidator and one low-end retailer were left standing.

It was the final stop on Tower's journey from a record department in a Sacramento drugstore, to America's best-known music retailer, to the latest victim of the digital revolution. Had there been any justice, the auction would have taken place on eBay, bringing an appropriately digital conclusion to the sad Tower story. The end had finally come for the store that had become synonymous with broad, deep choices in every musical genre—from jazz, country, classical, and opera to R&B, rap, and heavy metal.

The retailer had been in decline since the mid-Nineties, ever since the birth of the Internet. Big-box, low-cost retailers like Wal-Mart hadn't helped Tower's business. But the bigger culprit behind Tower's demise was the digital revolution. As a specialty retailer, it hadn't been able to compete against digital piracy or the low prices of Internet retailers like Amazon.com and iTunes.

Between 2003 and 2006, 800 independent music stores closed their doors for good. The independent record store is becoming an endangered species, especially in California, where a quarter of all music stores closed between 2003 and 2006. In the first five months of 2006 alone, 378 record stores closed nationally, against 106 closures in 2005. Ironically, the one record store that seems to be thriving today is the three-dimensional Sony BMG store on SecondLife.com, where virtual citizens seek to re-create the vitality of a real-life record store.

"We don't see the kids anymore," Thom Spennato, the owner of Sound Track, an independent record store in Brooklyn told the *New York Times* in July 2006.

That's because the kids are sitting at home in front of their computers, file-sharing digital music with one another—legally or illegally—or downloading 99-cent songs from iTunes.

The CD market plummeted 25 percent between 1995 and 2005. Between 1999 and 2005, music sales dropped by $2.3 billion from $14.6 billion to $12.3 billion. Global sales of music fell by another 4 percent in the first half of 2006, with revenues from physical formats such as compact discs down 10 percent.[2]

By the Friday afternoon of the Tower auction, the bidding for the chain was going up in $500,000 increments. The price on the table had risen to barely $130 million. It was a grim sum, given that Forbes had valued the company at $325 million in 1990. But sales, which had been in the $1-billion-a-year range during the Nineties, had dropped more than half since the digital revolution—bottoming out at $430 million in 2005.

The two parties left in the auction were the Great American Group, a California liquidator, and Trans World Entertainment, a New York low-end retailer, which had already rolled up the previously bankrupted Sam Goody and Wherehouse Music. They were bidding on everything: the entire inventory of CDs, DVDs, and books in the remaining eighty-nine stores in twenty states, as well as the Tower name.

Everything, that is, except Tower's 3,000 employees (including eighty-one-year-old founder Russ Soloman), the most valuable part of the company. None of the 3,000 flesh-and-blood people had any value to the liquidators at the Delaware auction.

At around 4:00 P.M. on Friday afternoon, Trans World Entertainment folded. Tower had been sold for $134.3 million. The Great American Group immediately announced their intention to liquidate. Tower Records was dead.

After a company barbecue in Sacramento, described

by participants as a funeral, Soloman wrote an emotional final e-mail to all his staff:

> The fat lady has sung. . . . She was way off key. Thank You. Thank You. Thank You.

At the Sunset Boulevard store, a marquee read, "It's the end of the world as we know it. Thanks for your loyalty." On the sidewalk, a mock gravestone was erected. It read, simply, "Tower." And at the flagship location in New York, Tower's row of blackened-out windows spanned the length of a city block that once thronged day and night with customers.

Inside the Bay and Columbus Street store, consumers were picking through the Tower carcass—the DVDs and CDs at 15 percent off, the books and magazines discounted by 30 percent. It was a miserable scene. I stood beside a shelf stacked with a reminder of music's glory days—compact discs of Pink Floyd's *Dark Side of the Moon* and the Beatles' *Abbey Road*. As people wandered past, I conducted my own on-the-spot research into Tower's demise.

"What will you miss?" I asked several shoppers.

"Choice," they replied. "Their deep, broad catalog. . . . Salespeople who love music. . . . Awesome selection. . . . Friday evenings and rainy Saturday afternoons browsing. . . . The serendipity of discovery of a new album or group. . . ."

The disappearance of Tower's unparalleled musical selection will certainly be mourned by all music lovers. As one Tower executive put it, "If you wanted the Amazon tree frog noises, we had it."

The expertise of the Tower staff will sorely be missed, too—the clerk who could have stepped out of Nick Hornsby's bestselling novel and film *High Fidelity*, the guy with the earring who has heard everything before anyone else, and who passes on that inside knowledge to the rest of the world. The people responsible for what Dave Marsh, the great rock critic, called "the transmission of music" from one generation to the next. This is no small thing. *Los Angeles Times* pop music critic Ann Powers confesses that a Seattle Tower clerk who turned her on to Elvis Costello and the Clash "changed my life."

Tower's remarkably diverse selection cannot be replicated. Perhaps no one summarizes the value of Tower's deep catalog better than Powers, who once worked as a clerk at the Tower on Bay and Columbus herself:

Deep catalog was the commitment Tower made to the regular shopper: the jazzbo looking for that weird fusion project on the American Clavé label, the dreadlocked hippie browsing the Jamaican imports, the hard-core punk looking for anything with speedy guitars and a shouted chorus. By allowing its product buyers—a motley crew of aspiring musicians, bohemian lifers and undergrads willing to accept retail wages just to be near all that music—to stock the shelves with virtually every pop derivative imaginable, Tower created a physical space where the music's variety came alive, where the snobbish geek and the casual listener were equally served.[3]

Ironically, Powers' "deep catalog" community sounds like a Silicon Valley vision of the digital future. Indeed, Chris Anderson's long tail of infinite musical choice could be a snapshot of the now defunct Tower store on Bay and Columbus.

But Tower's demise actually represents the end rather than the beginning of a long tail. By some estimates, Tower represented around 40 to 50 percent of the niche-genre labels' entire market. With Tower now closed, the niche labels have, in one fell swoop, lost half of their business. How these labels—in classical, jazz, opera, hip-hop, world, and the rest—are now going to reach the music-buying public is unknown. The sad truth is that with the demise of the physical record store, we may have less musical choice, fewer labels, and the emergence of an oligarchic digital retail economy dominated by Amazon.com, iTunes, and MySpace.

Chris Anderson, ever optimistic, would tell us that all the small labels can now sell directly, thereby no longer sacrificing their margins to middlemen. But doing so requires marketing skills and investment in Web site infrastructure and direct sales—specialized expertise that the majority of niche labels don't possess. A more likely consequence of Tower's closure is the increasing consolidation of the major labels—a development reflected by German media group Bertelsmann's choice to sell the publishing rights to the music owned by its BMG Music Publishing Group to Vivendi's Universal Music for $2.1 billion to raise cash for a buyout of one of their European partners.

Chris Anderson's *The Long Tail* claims that the future of music lies with the infinite selection of online stores like Amazon.com or iTunes. That may be true. But what these online stores don't have is the deeply knowledgeable Tower clerk to act as cultural tastemaker. Instead, our buying choices depend upon the anonymous Amazon.com reviewer—a very poor substitute for the bodily encounters that Tower once offered.

The Toy at the Bottom of the Cornflakes Box

One Saturday morning I found myself sitting opposite self-proclaimed music futurist Gerd Leonhard in San Francisco's Café Trieste. Leonhard is the author of *The Future of Music*,[4] a manifesto that imagines a world where music has become a public utility like water or electricity.

We couldn't have found a more appropriate spot to talk about the future of the recorded-music business. Located in the heart of the city's North Beach, a few blocks south of the now defunct Tower store on Bay and Columbus, this San Francisco landmark is a venerable

Italian café, lined floor to ceiling with black-and-white photographs of old opera divas. The Trieste is famous for its regular Saturday-afternoon concerts where local opera singers put on free shows for the café audience.

"Music will be a utility like water, like electricity, because essentially right now only two out of ten people are buying the music that they are listening to," the futurist shouted at me above the din. "But nine and a half out of ten are interested in music; together with sex and with games, it's the biggest thing on the Internet."

Leonhard's estimate of the number of people buying music was, in fact, far too optimistic. According to a joint 2006 report by European (IFPI) and American (RIAA) researchers, *forty songs* are actually downloaded for every legal music download. That adds up to 20 billion songs illegally downloaded in 2005, compared to a legal digital market of 500 million tracks, resulting in a paltry $1.1 billion in revenue.

Imagine the impact on the Café Trieste's bottom line if only one in forty coffee drinkers paid for their cappuccinos. But this is the reality of the digital economy. It's why the recorded-music industry doesn't have much of a financial future.

At the iTunes price of 99 cents a song, the 20 billion digital songs stolen in a single year adds up to an annual bill of $19.99 billion, one and a half times more than the entire $12.27 billion revenue of the U.S. sound recording industry in 2005. That's $19.99 billion stolen annually from artists, labels, distributors, and record stores. Year by year, the entire music industry, which has brought us classic recordings of everyone from the Beatles, Pink Floyd, and The Clash to Luciano Pavarotti and Maria Callas, is being strangled by one of the most brazen mass larcenies in history.

"Just look around you," Gerd Leonhard told me, sweeping his hand across the crowded, noisy café. "Music has never been so popular."

The audience in Café Trieste indeed seemed captivated by the performance of the café's divas. The problem is, nobody was actually paying for it. The only money changing hands was in the sale of cappuccinos, pastries, and soda. It was not so dissimilar to what was happening on a far more vast scale on the Internet—art and culture being reduced to vehicles for the sale of other products.

Is this the future of music? As a free "come-on" to sell other stuff? Rather than a utility like electricity or water, music in the Web 2.0 revolution may become equivalent to the plastic toy found at the bottom of the cornflakes box.

Digital piracy and illegal file-sharing from services like BitTorrent, eDonkey, DirectConnect, Gnutella, LimeWire, and SoulSeek have become the central economic reality in the record business. It is why there are now 25 percent fewer music stores in America than there were in 2003. It is why the International Federation of the Phonographic Industry filed 8,000 new lawsuits against illegal downloaders in October 2006 alone. It is why, in the first half of 2006, shipments of CDs and other physical music formats in America were down 15.7 percent from the first half of 2005.⁵ It is why there is no longer a "cultural hub" on the corner of San Francisco's Bay and Columbus Streets.

"If you can't beat 'em, join 'em" seems to have become the mantra of the increasingly desperate record industry. The situation has become so dire that labels are now planting decoys or fake files that contain messages from advertisers on peer-to-peer sites. For example, the rapper Jay-Z formed a 2006 alliance with Coca-Cola in which the Universal Music Group artist agreed to allow distribution of a clip from a live Radio City Music Hall performance on peer-to-peer sites. This clip came with a promotion for Coca-Cola and, thus, became a way for the soft-drink company to market their message to music thieves. Many other popular contemporary bands, including Audioslave, Ice Cube, and Yellowcard, are also selling advertising off the back of piracy.

"The concept here is making the peer-to-peer networks work for us," Jay-Z's attorney explained of this surreal strategy. "While peer-to-peer users are stealing the intellectual property, they are also the active music audience."

Given that only one in forty digital songs are being paid for, digital music is, like it or not, essentially free. For 98 percent of today's "consumers," music *is* now freer than electricity or water. And the recorded-music business is being forced to confront this *de facto* economic catastrophe head-on. Universal Music, the largest of the major labels, with millions of songs from artists as diverse as Eminem and Hank Williams, announced in September 2006 that it intended to freely distribute its catalogue on the Internet through a Web 2.0 service named SpiralFrog. A month earlier, EMI, another of the big four labels, announced a similar deal with a Web 2.0 company called QTrax. Both services give out the music for free on the Internet in exchange for exposing the listener to advertising.

To gain access to *Abbey Road* or *Dark Side of the Moon* on QTrax, will I have to first listen to a pitch for Q-Tips? Will future generations of opera fans who want to hear Mozart's opera *Così Fan Tutte* on SpiralFrog be interrupted at key moments by interstitials from the Italian airline Alitalia enticing them to visit Italy?

As Gerry Kearby, the founder and CEO of Liquid Audio, Silicon Valley's original digital music company, stated recently, "Perhaps the music is free, but inside the music is a condom or whatever the hell they are trying to sell you."

Services like QTrax and SpiralFrog threaten to reduce the experience of listening to music into a cat-and-mouse game between consumer and advertiser. And while Universal and EMI bring in money from Johnson & Johnson or Alitalia, the artists might get nothing in royalties.

Does the recorded-music industry have any alternative to partnering with services like SpiralFrog and QTrax? According to Web 2.0 idealists like Chris Anderson, the Internet offers musicians their own sales and marketing platform. But this doesn't translate into revenue. MySpace is now offering itself as a digital storefront by selling the music of three million unsigned bands. But as David Card, an analyst at Jupiter Research, said, "I've yet to see an entertainment company that can be successful by creating a business only out of the long tail."[6]

The problem is that even strong Internet visibility and popularity don't necessarily generate money. Take, for example, the band The Scene Aesthetic, a rock acoustic duo started by vocalist Eric Bowley and Andrew de Torres, a couple of twenty-year-old kids from Everett, Washington. Possessing the boyish good looks and gentle, self-conscious lyricism of a young Paul Simon and Art Garfunkel, The Scene Aesthetic have become huge stars on MySpace, YouTube, and PureVolume.com.

As of September 2006, the band, which posted its first song "Beauty on the Breakdown" on MySpace in January 2005, had built up nine million total plays on the social network, 2.3 million visitors had visited The Scene Aesthetic page on MySpace, and the duo had amassed more than 140,000 friends. On PureVolume.com, a free music site, its most popular album, *Building Homes from What We've Known*, had been downloaded 1.3 million times. On YouTube, the band's video of "Beauty in the Breakdown" had been watched half a million times.

And the total dollar revenue derived in digital music sales from its nine million plays on MySpace, the 1.3 million downloads on PureVolume.com, and the half million screenings on YouTube? Yes, you've guessed it. Zero.

In spite of their phenomenal online popularity, The Scene Aesthetic has yet to sign a record deal with a label. True, Eric Bowley was able to cobble together enough cash to quit his job selling televisions at Everett's Best Buy store and go on "national" tour in the summer of 2006. But the only gigs the band's amateur booking agent could leverage from their MySpace popularity were at such venues as the Wilton Teen Center in Connecticut, Todino's Pizza in Bloomington, Illinois, and Blue Ridge High School in Pinetop, Arizona. These venues, which seat about 200 fans and charge just $5 or $10 a head, barely cover the bands' hotel and travel costs. On good days, if the band manages to sell enough T-shirts and tickets, they can even buy dinner. On bad nights, Bowley and de Torres ended up sleeping on the basement floors of fans' homes.

This is no way for a band to become the next supergroup. Gerd Leonhard is right. Music is as popular now as it's ever been. But Internet fame doesn't equal dollars. The sheer volume of music online, and the ease with which it can be downloaded—for free—is snuffing out the careers of budding artists like The Scene Aesthetic. With so many songs available for free, or for 99 cents from iTunes and the like, why would anyone pay $15 to $20 for a CD? As a consumer, why buy an album when you can cherry-pick the one or two songs you really want? With fewer and fewer people buying the physical albums, where is the money for the record industry and the recording stars?

The Sound Aesthetic might still join the ranks of Arctic Monkeys and the handful of other bands who have managed to leverage their Internet popularity into commercial success. But their struggle to translate their massive virtual following into either significant record sales or a major label contract is an ominous augury for the other three million bands on MySpace trying to make a living selling their music.

The contrast between The Scene Aesthetic and Simon and Garfunkel is revealing. By the time Paul Simon and Art Garfunkel were Bowley's and de Torres' age, they already had a minor hit, "Hey Schoolgirl," which they recorded as the teenage duo Tom & Jerry and was released by Big Records in 1957. And by the time Simon and Garfunkel were twenty-three years old, they had their first album, *Wednesday Morning, 3 AM,* which was released on Columbia Records in October 1964 and contained their first hit song, "The Sound of Silence." That Bowley and de Torres will achieve comparable success in three years' time is unlikely.

In late October 2006, I had a conversation with Paul Simon about how the music business was being changed by the Web 2.0 revolution. Like Gerd Leonhard, Paul Simon confirmed that music today was as popular as it's ever been. But, unlike Leonhard, Simon wasn't optimistic about the future of high-quality recorded music.

To make a top-quality recording today, what he called an "exquisitely slow and detailed" album, Simon explained, ideally would take a full year and, given the price of top contemporary musicians, could cost a million dollars. But this kind of investment, he said, can't be earned back in a market where people are buying fewer and fewer compact discs. So recording artists necessarily compromise their music because it is not economically viable to hire the best musicians and take enough time making the recording.

"I'm personally against Web 2.0 in the same way as I'm personally against my own death," he said, in a line that might have been borrowed from one of his own songs.

But for all his antipathy, Simon is resigned to the Web 2.0 revolution, an event he compared to an uncontrollable forest fire. "Maybe," he said, "a fire is what's needed for a vigorous new growth, but that's the long view. In the short term, all that's apparent is the devastation." Citing what he called the "destruction" of the twentieth-century record business, he recalled the last verse from "Look at That," a song from his 2000 album *You're the One*. "You might learn something," Simon claims, one never knows. "But anyway, you've got to go."

But Simon wasn't finished. "We're going to 2.0," he concluded. "Like it or not, that is what is going to happen."

Perhaps Paul Simon is right. We're going to 2.0.

Like it or not.

5

the day the music died
[side b]

By the time Charles Dickens came to North America on a reading tour in 1842, hundreds of thousands of copies of his books—including *Sketches by Boz, Nicholas Nickleby, The Pickwick Papers,* and *Oliver Twist*—had been published in the United States. But Dickens "never derive(d) sixpence,"[1] because at the time, there was no copyright protection for works created in Britain and sold in the United States (and vice versa); U.S. publishers could copy British books without paying a dime in royalties.

Dickens and other authors with followings on opposite sides of the Atlantic—Henry Wadsworth Longfellow, Sir Walter Scott, and Harriet Beecher Stowe—were the early victims of intellectual piracy. By the 1840s, though a household name, Dickens was facing debtor's prison. Sir Walter Scott nearly went bankrupt in the middle of his career, and is said to have died at age sixty-one, "broken in body and mind by years of financial difficulties." And Harriet Beecher Stowe, an American, was estimated to have lost $200,000 (millions in today's currency) rightfully due her for European sales of *Uncle Tom's Cabin.*[2]

But, of course, had Dickens' rich character portraits or Longfellow's evocative poems never reached the opposite shores, the greater victims of piracy would have been readers. In any profession, when there is no monetary incentive or reward, creative work stalls. As Dickens, one of the first to actively lobby Congress for copyright protection, aptly noted, American literature could only flourish if American publishers were compelled by law to pay writers their due; allowing publishers to print the works of foreign authors for free would only discourage literary production.

Yet on the Web 2.0 such indiscriminate piracy is becoming the norm. "Booksellers, defend your lonely forts!" John Updike roused the book-loving audience at Book Expo America in late May 2006. Seventy-four-year-old Updike was in a feisty mood that day, shouting with the force and vigor of a man half his age. The object of his rage was Kevin Kelly, the "senior maverick" at *Wired* magazine who, earlier that month, had published his manifesto in the *New York Times Magazine* in support of the "universal book."

Kevin Kelly claims that the technology to digitize and

infinitely copy texts will inevitably overthrow hundreds of years of copyright protection. According to Kelly, we can no longer protect intellectual property from piracy, so all texts should be available for free. It is a bit like saying that because our car *might* get stolen, we should leave it unlocked with the keys in the ignition and the driver's-side door open, to usher would-be thieves on their way.

In Kelly's view (who, it doesn't hurt to note, has published several books for which he has received substantial advances), the value of the book lies not in the professional author's achievement in creating something true out of empty air and a blank page, but in the myriad ways the cult of the amateur can recall, annotate, tag, link, "personalize, edit, authenticate, display, mark, transfer and engage a work." According to Kelly, "The real magic will come . . . as each page in each book is cross-linked, clustered, cited, extracted, indexed, analyzed, annotated, remixed, reassembled, and woven deeper into the culture than ever before." In other words, a finished masterpiece like F. Scott Fitzgerald's *The Great Gatsby* is not important—what is important in today's digital world are the ways we annotate, link, and change to adapt the original texts. Fitzgerald's masterpiece is just a jumping-off point for what truly matters: the ways each of us annotate and remix, tag, and make it our own work. Fitzgerald was merely a skilled workman. To Kelly the real value of a work like *The Great Gatsby* is in what we—the amateur—bring to it.

Kelly argues that in the future, instead of making money on the sale of books, authors can "sell performances, access to the creator, personalization, add-on information, sponsorship, periodic subscriptions—in short, all the many values that cannot be copied." It's the old razor blade business model. The book is but a giveaway, and the writer will supposedly make money from consulting gigs, book signings, and public lectures.

But books aren't razors, and reading has nothing in common with shaving. As Updike shouted from the podium, "For some of us, books are intrinsic to our human identity." When writers, and composers and music makers for that matter, can no longer hope to make a living from their work, how many works will never be written or created? When there are no books to base talks on, no performances to sell merchandise at, no creators to greet and meet, and no music to sell ads with, culture and the industries that have arisen around it will wither and die.

Even Kelly admits that the protection of the physical copy has "enabled millions of people to earn a living directly from the sale of their art to the audience" and that it has "produced the greatest flowering of human achievement the world has ever seen." Isn't this a model worth preserving?

Hollywood in Crisis

But the economic consequences of the Web 2.0 revolution go far beyond just books and music. Thanks to pirated products, free news on the blogs, free radio from podcasters, and free digital classifieds on Craigslist, our media industries and content providers of all sorts—radio, television, newspaper, the movie businesses—are in decline. As *Atlantic Monthly* writer Marshall Poe told me, companies simply can't make money by providing high-quality content—be it music, movies, or news—for free. "The Internet is a huge moral hazard for people in general," he said, "and it is a huge economic hazard for the serious providers of content."

In the movie business, digital piracy, the explosion of free movie downloads, and the growing popularity of amateur video sites like YouTube and Veoh video are already causing a decline in box-office revenue and DVD sales.

Peter Jackson, the movie maestro who brought us the *Lord of the Rings* trilogy and the remake of *King Kong*, summed up the crisis succinctly: "Piracy has the very real potential of tipping movies into becoming an unprofitable industry, especially big-event films," he told the *International Herald Tribune* in August 2005.

Jackson's tipping point may have already arrived. In May 2006, LEK Consulting authored a report for the Motion Picture Association of America (MPAA), showing that the American movie industry lost $6.1 billion in global wholesale revenue to all forms of digital piracy in 2005; for the global movie industry, the figure was $18.2 billion. The LEK report, which was conducted over eighteen months and surveyed 20,600 movie consumers in twenty-two countries, showed that $2.3 billion of the losses stemmed from Internet piracy, $2.4 billion from street sales of bootlegged copies of DVDs and video cassettes, and the remaining $1.4 billion from the illegal copying of films in movie theaters. The MPAA's last official global revenue figures were of $44.8 billion in 2004.[3] In other words, piracy shaves around 12 to 13 percent off America's total movie industry revenue.

Another research group, the Texas-based Institute for Policy Innovation, argues that motion picture piracy results in a "total lost output" from all U.S. industries of $20.5 billion annually. Yes, that's right—$20.5 billion, including lost annual earnings to U.S. workers, lost tax revenue, and the loss of jobs across the economy.

According to MPAA's most recent statistics, the American movie business is in big trouble. In 2005, box office revenue was down 5.7% to $8.99 billion, and admission in movie theaters dropped 8.7 percent. In fact, admissions have dropped to their lowest levels since 1997. Most worrying of all, DVD sales, which had driven Hollywood studios' strong growth over the last decade, have now reached a plateau. This is due to the growing popularity of movie-downloading services (Wal-Mart, once one of the nation's leading DVD retailers, recently announced plans to offer one such service on its Web site). Pali Research analyst Richard Greenfield has forecast that 2007 will be the first year that DVD sales will decline in the United States.[4]

Nor has the Internet been the marketing solution to its economic crisis that the movie industry briefly hoped. New Line Cinema's 2006 horror movie S*nakes on a*

Plane was enormously hyped on the Internet and was expected, as a result, to be a big hit. New Line included ideas from bloggers in the script. They developed a Web site that allowed Internet users to receive telephone calls from the movie's star, Samuel L. Jackson. And they allowed anyone who purchased movie tickets online to participate in exit polls by sending text messages to the studio. But none of this buzz made any difference to the movie's bottom line. As the president of theatrical for New Line conceded to the *New York Times*, "There were a lot of inflated expectations on this picture. But it basically performed like a normal horror movie."[5]

Fewer people are paying to watch fewer movies in fewer theaters, and Hollywood is clearly feeling the pain. At the Walt Disney Company, domestic ticket sales plummeted from $1.5 billion to $962 million between 2003 and 2005, and studio entertainment revenues dropped 13 percent in 2005, largely due to lagging DVD sales. Recently, Disney was forced to eliminate 650 jobs and substantially cut the number of films it produces each year.[6] Disney isn't the only one downsizing. Paramount Studios also cut hundreds of jobs in their movie and DVD units, and Warner Bros. axed 400 jobs globally in December 2005, including its heads of comedy, casting, and scheduling.

But the worst is still to come. As the bandwidth revolution makes it increasingly easy to download movies from the Internet, Hollywood is about to become engulfed in the same storm that has wrecked the music industry. Today, according to research firm Park Associates, only 660,000 people regularly download movies from the Internet. Park expects this number to grow to 50 million by 2010.[7] Given the metrics on music thieves, 49 million of those downloaders are likely to be stealing.

The Internet is beginning to undermine the viability of the movie theater. ClickStar, an Intel-funded start-up founded by actor Morgan Freeman and launched in December 2006, is debuting some independent films on the Internet the same day they are released in the theaters. Such practices, which go against long-held Hollywood strategy, will compound the crisis facing movie theaters. When a movie is available on the Internet as soon as it has been released, why go to the extra inconvenience and cost of seeing it in a local theater? For many technophiles accustomed to watching all media on their computers already, the big screen viewing experience of the multiplex will hardly be missed.

It's not just movie theaters that are being undermined by the digital revolution. Local video stores are also under attack, thanks not only to piracy but also to the wildly successful Web-based operation Netflix. Video chains like Blockbuster are already hedging their bets by planning downloading services of their own in the future. But for local places, like Berkeley's Reel Video, an independent rental store stocking several thousand DVDs and videocassettes, the future is bleak.

"We'll always have a place," the *San Francisco Chronicle* quoted a clerk at Reel Video in October 2006. "We

have a lot of obscure movies that you can't find anywhere else."

Sure. Just as the Tower at Bay and Columbus had a lot
of obscure music. Or the recently closed Cody's bookstore
on Berkeley's Telegraph Avenue had a vast array of books.

Sadly, Cody's isn't alone. There's Duttons in Beverly
Hills, A Clean Well-Lighted Place for Books in San Francisco, Coliseum Books, Enticott Books, and Murder Ink in
Manhattan, and thousands of other beloved bookstores
across America that have been forced to close their doors
because of cut-priced e-competition from the Internet.
According to numbers put together by the *New York
Times,*[8] 2,500 independent bookstores have gone out of
business since 1990. Meanwhile, Amazon.com, the online
megastore and chief slayer of the independent bookstore,
announced a 21 percent increase in "media sales" (which
includes books) over the final quarter in 2005.

So what does Chris Anderson, the supposed champion
of the little guy at the end of the Long Tail, think about
all these closures? "The clear lesson of the Long Tail is
that more choice is better," Anderson told the *Los Angeles Times* in February 2007. "Since bookstores can't compete on choice, many once-cherished stores are going to
be road kill."[9]

But does the closure of independent stores result in
more choice for consumers? Instead of 2,500 independent bookstores, with their knowledgeable, book-loving
staffers, specialty sections, and relationships with local
writers, we now have an oligarchy of online megastores

employing soulless algorithms that use our previous purchases and the purchases of others to tell us what we want to buy. Like the death of Tower Records, the demise of the independent American bookstore means even less choice for the consumer—especially the book buyer who relies on their local bookstore for suggestions about interesting books.

Television stations, too, are navigating rough waters. More people are using DVR or TiVo, downloading shows through software like Azureus and Torrent, or getting their news online. As a result, fewer people are watching the commercials on both national and local stations that underwrite television, and advertisers are shifting more of their dollars online.

In historical terms, local television stations have represented what the *Wall Street Journal* called the "backbone" of the broadcast-TV business. But according to the Television Bureau of Advertising, total local broadcast revenue fell 9 percent in 2005 to $16.8 billion. The reason? Key sponsors like Daimler-Chrysler and Ford are cutting advertising budgets—13 percent and 15 percent, respectively—or moving online. With local stations failing to generate enough profits, corporate owners like Viacom, News Corp., and NBC Universal are selling them off. Some companies, like the Tribune Company, are even considering spinning off entire TV-station groups.

There was a time, not so long ago, when, if we wanted to watch television, we'd turn on our television sets. Now, we turn on our computers, flip open our cell phones, switch on our TiVos, or plug into our video iPods. The consequence of all this is perhaps best evidenced by the story that ran on the front page of several major papers on October 19, 2006: NBC Universal was slashing costs in news and prime-time programming. After three years of declining revenue, NBC Universal announced aggressive plans to save $750 million in operating costs and return the station to double-digit growth. The initiative, disturbingly dubbed "NBCU 2.0," included plans to eliminate 700 jobs, 5 percent of the company's total workforce. The first major TV company to acknowledge the limited growth potential of the television news business, NBC announced that most of its initial layoffs would be in the company's eleven news divisions; the company planned to cut spending on news programming and consolidate a number of local news stations. Former NBC correspondent David Hazinski predicted, "This trend will mean more processing, more in-studio things, probably more star celebrities to get people to watch based on the personalities, and less real news." According to a 2006 Pew Research study, 71 percent of adults in the key eighteen to twenty-nine age demographic already get most of their news online, where, as we have seen, information is often unreliable or biased. As television stations cut their news programming, this number will only increase.

When media companies flounder, employees and executives lose their jobs and shareholders lose their investments. But all the rest of us lose out, too, as the quality of programming is compromised. Case in point? NBC Universal also announced that its 8 to 9 P.M. time slot would no longer run high-cost, scripted dramas. Instead, this prime-time hour—one that has, over the years, featured favorites like *Friends* and *Seinfeld,* will now air cheaper-to-produce programming like the game show *Deal or No Deal* or more dime-a-dozen reality programs. According to Jeff Zucker, chief executive of NBC Universal's television group, "Advertiser interest just wasn't high enough to justify spending on scripted shows."

As they announced a $750 million cut in news programming and scripted dramas, NBC Universal also stated plans to invest $150 million in new digital projects and Internet offerings such as specialized broadband sites, actors' blogs, and Internet-only "webisodes," which are cheaper to produce and use unknown actors rather than the actual stars (like in the online version of *The Office,* in which Steve Carell is noticeably absent). As NBC Universal chairman Bob Wright told the *Wall Street Journal,* "As we reprioritize ourselves towards digital, we've got to be as efficient in our current businesses as possible. We can't have new digital expenses and the same analog expenses."

So, instead of the newest drama from Dick Wolfe or Aaron Sorkin, all we'll soon have to watch will be the Paris Hilton Channel, cheap knockoffs of existing sitcoms, reality television, or clips from Sam Waterston's video blog.

Radio is in the midst of its own identity crisis. Teenagers, historically radio's biggest and most devoted audience, simply aren't listening to radio anymore. Over the last ten years, the listening hours of eighteen to twenty-four-year-olds have dropped 21 percent. Since 2006, the stocks of the five largest publicly traded radio companies dropped between 30 percent and 60 percent. In the first six months of 2006 alone, the operating income of CBS' radio business declined 17 percent, forcing CBS to sell off some of its local radio channels. In the summer of 2006, The Walt Disney Company got out of the radio business entirely. And, in November 2006, Clear Channel, the largest radio operation in America, announced that it would be seeking offers for 448 of its 1,200 stations.[10]

When the Ink Bleeds Red

Traditional newspapers and magazines, too, are getting hammered by the free content and advertising on the Internet. Newspapers are getting smaller—in circulation, in ad revenue, and in relevance. They are even shrinking in physical size. The *Wall Street Journal* trimmed its width three inches in January 2007, reducing the space devoted to news by 10 percent and eliminating an entire column on the front page. The *New York Times* plans to trim its width by 1.5 inches,[11] as was done at the *Los Angeles Times*, where editors have also begun to push reporters for shorter stories, to cater to the attention span of the average online reader.

Circulation at America's newspapers is plunging. In the six months between March and September 2006, daily circulation for 770 newspapers in America was down 2.8 percent from the same period in the previous year—one of the worst declines on record.[12] The circulation of the *San Francisco Chronicle*, which lost $40 million just in 2004, fell over 16 percent between 2005 and 2006. The *Los Angeles Times'* circulation dropped 8 percent between 2004 and 2006; it has plummeted from its peak of 1.2 million in 1990 to its current circulation of 908,000—less than it was in 1968. The circulation of the Sunday edition of the *Boston Globe* dropped 25 percent between 2003 and 2006. The *Dallas Morning News'* circulation was down 13 percent in the first six months of 2006.[13] Even at the *New York Times*, where circulation remains relatively stable, predictions for the future are not optimistic; its share price has fallen 50 percent in the past 5 years.[14]

As circulations continue to drop, advertisers are shifting their dollars to online media, where they can reach a larger and more targeted audience. According to Merrill Lynch, in 2006 advertising sales at newspapers were flat and are predicted to drop in 2007—the first time in history that newspaper advertising revenue will have declined in a nonrecessionary year. The story is depressingly similar at almost every metropolitan and national newspaper. Advertising revenue at the *Boston Globe* was 12.4 percent less in the second quarter of 2006 than it was in the equivalent 2005 quarter. The *Wall Street Jour-*

nal's advertising revenue in September 2006 fell 5.9 percent compared to September 2005. The Belo Corporation, which publishes the *Dallas Morning News* and the *Providence Journal*, reported a 19 percent drop in general advertising revenue in the third quarter of 2006.[15] The migration of classified ads from print papers to free Web sites like Craigslist is draining even more revenue from newspapers. According to a report by the Pew Internet and American Life Project, the number of people who use online classified advertising through these services increased 80 percent in 2005, with almost nine million of those visitors using the free service on Craigslist.[16]

The first response to sagging revenue, of course, is layoffs. Predictably, the number of people employed in the industry, according to the Newspaper Association of America, fell by 18 percent between 1990 and 2004, largely due to downsizing and layoffs.[17]

More recently, The New York Times Company laid off 200 people in May 2005, including 130 at the *New York Times* itself and the rest at the *Boston Globe* and the *Worcester Telegram & Gazette*. Later that same year, another 500 jobs, or about 4 percent of the company's total workforce, were eliminated. The year 2006 was the annus horribilis for American journalists, with job losses surging 88 percent (from 9,453 job cuts in 2005 to 17,809 in 2006), according to the tracking firm Challenger, Gray, and Christmas.[18] In March 2006, the *Washington Post* announced plans to cut about eighty jobs from its newsroom over the next year. October 2006 was a particularly bloody month, with redundancy announcements from the *Plain Dealer* in Cleveland (sixty-five layoffs), the *San Jose Mercury News* (101 layoffs), the *Philadelphia Inquirer,* and the *Philadelphia Daily News.*

And in the fall of 2006, in a dramatic showdown that played out for months, Jeffrey M. Johnson and Dean Baquet, the publisher and editor of the *Los Angeles Times,* were very publicly ousted for refusing to carry out the budget cuts and firings ordered by the *Times'* parent company, the *Chicago Tribune.* Loyal employees of the company for a combined total of over twenty-five years, Johnson and Baquet had already complied with orders to cut 200 positions, or 20 percent of the news-room employees, since the *Tribune* bought the paper in 2000. But when more cuts were ordered, they said enough was enough. Newspaper editors, Baquet declared in a fiery speech in New Orleans that precipitated his fir-ing, must push back against cutbacks ordered by corpo-rate owners in order to maintain the journalistic integrity and credibility of their papers.[19] Ironically, one important reason for the *Los Angeles Times'* financial crisis has been what the *Financial Times* called the "dra-matic pullback" in Hollywood's spending on advertising (down 17 percent in 2006). It's the reverse of the new media ideal of synergy. Bad economic news in one sector of traditional media causes more bad news in another sector.

Things have not been much better in the magazine world. Time Inc. cut over 100 jobs in December 2005; in January 2007, they cut 300 more at popular magazines such as *People, Sports Illustrated,* and their flagship, *Time,* shutting down bureaus in Los Angeles, Chicago, Atlanta, Miami, and Austin. In August 2004, Gruner & Jahr USA, the publisher of major magazines such as *Fast Company, Fitness,* and *Family Circle,* announced plans to cut costs by $25 million and reduce staff by as much as 15 percent, before finally selling off the magazines entirely and taking a huge write-off.[20]

Those are a lot of lost jobs. Some will argue that seismic economic change always results in downsizing in one sector but the creation of jobs in another. The problem is, the Web 2.0 economy is not creating jobs to replace those it destroys. Take Craigslist, for example, which has done more to undermine classified newspaper advertising than any other single institution. In spite of being the seventh-most-popular Web site in the world, Craigslist operates out of a rickety Victorian building in a residential San Francisco district close to the Pacific Ocean and has an employee roster of twenty-two full-timers—the number of players on the field in a soccer game. But while these listings on Craigslist, a site founded in 1995 by a counterculturist named Craig Newmark whom *New York* magazine described as a "shlumpy IBM refugee,"[21] are ostensibly free, in reality they aren't. Every supposedly "free" new car or house or job advertisement takes money straight from a local newspaper. Bob Cauthorn, former VP of digital media at the *San Francisco Chronicle,* has estimated that Craigslist siphons off an annual $50 million from Bay Area newspapers alone. In other words, the people at the *Chronicle* and at the *San Jose Mercury News* who lost their jobs in 2006 can thank shlumpy Craig and his twenty-two employees and their "free" advertising.

Wikipedia, which is almost single-handedly killing the traditional information business, has only a small handful of full-timers, in addition to Jimmy Wales. It brings to mind Sir Thomas More's much-quoted remark from his 1515 satire *Utopia*, where, in reaction to the Enclosure Laws that banned the peasantry from the fields of the great estates, he wrote that "sheep are devouring men." Five hundred years later, in the Web 2.0 world, computers are consuming journalists with the same results: Many people are losing their livelihood, and a few lucky souls—landowning aristocrats in More's day and executives at companies like MySpace, YouTube, and Google in our own—are getting very very rich.

The YouTube guys are getting particularly rich. On Wednesday, October 11, 2006—just five days after eighty-nine Tower Record stores were sold for $134.3 million in a Delaware law office—Chad Hurley and Steven Chen, the founders of YouTube, had lunch with Google co-founder Larry Page and CEO Eric Schmidt in a booth at a Denny's near YouTube's small office in Silicon Valley. At the end of the meal, the four men agreed that the unprofitable YouTube, with its staff of sixty engineers, would be acquired by Google for $1.65 billion—a lot of money for a company at which amateurs create all the content for free. Since YouTube doesn't need journalists, editors, producers, publicists, customer-service staff, or a back-office support staff, this $1.65 billion is virtually all upside.

Of course, the demise of newspapers cannot all be blamed on the Internet. The rise of cable news, too, has contributed to newspapers' waning profit margins. And many newspapers are cannibalizing themselves by migrating to the Web, where there is typically free, unfettered access to the content. The print version of the *New York Times* has only 2.7 million paid subscribers (1.1 million to the daily papers and 1.7 to the Sunday edition), while the free online version receives 40 million users a month. The problem is that while the print version generates annual revenues of $1.5 to $1.7 billion a year, the online version pulls in just $200 million.[22] If people continue to migrate to the online version, the *Times* may be forced to rein in its editorial department and compromise its renowned editorial content. It may need to lure a wider audience made up of younger, less-educated readers with fluff pieces on entertainment and lifestyle topics in place of hard-hitting reporting on international affairs and politics.

This is already happening at some major papers. At the *Los Angeles Times,* which won fifteen Pulitzer Prizes between 2000 and 2005, managers have responded to declining circulation and advertising (daily circulation in 2005 was down 18 percent, and full-run advertising was down 26 percent) by pressuring editors to increase coverage of Hollywood and celebrity gossip. In October

2006, the paper launched an initiative christened The Manhattan Project (in an apparent reference to the gravity of its mission) to generate fresh ideas for stories expected to re-energize the paper and attract a wider readership. Most of these changes will likely involve linking the content of the print paper more closely to the online edition, which covers less hard news and more local events and entertainment.[23]

But what happens if even these tactics fail, and print papers are unable to retain the readership they need to stay economically viable? *The Economist* predicts that over the next few decades, half the newspapers in the developed world may fold.[24] The business model of the *New York Times* is instrumental to understanding the grave challenges that digital media pose to established newspapers. According to New York media maven Michael Wolff, for the *Times* to replicate its newsprint revenue would require it to either increase its online audience to around 400 or 500 million readers or to compromise its editorial content by catering to the interests of its advertisers. As Wolff put it:

The *Times* as we know it, as a pastiche of its paper self, can't succeed online (the whole idea that an old-time business can morph seamlessly into a huge, speculative entrepreneurial enterprise is a kind of quackery). At best, it might become a specialized Internet player, having to drastically cut its current $300 million news budget. What it might providentially become, however, is About.com, a low-end, high-volume information producer, warehousing vast amounts of advertiser-targeted data, harnessing the amateurs and hobbyists and fetishists willing to produce for a pittance any amount of schlock to feed the page-view numbers—and already supplying 30 million of the *Times*'s 40 million unique users.[25]

Should mainstream newspapers and television fold, where will online news sites get their content? Where will the Matt Drudges and the instapundits get their information? How can they comment on the war in Iraq, or the 2008 election, if there is no organization with clout and sufficient resources to report on it? In the absence of traditional news, will the online sites be forced to abandon the effort to search out the truth altogether and simply make the facts up? Who will have the resources to investigate and report on the next Watergate scandal or to pay the wages of the 2.0 versions of Carl Bernstein and Bob Woodward? Or will this kind of quality reportage simply cease to exist? As a 2006 report from the Carnegie Corporation of New York put it, "As newspapers begin to fade, are the institutions that replace them "up to the task of sustaining the informed citizenry on which democracy depends?"[26]

Wolff claims that the idea of the end of the *New York Times* is a "God Is Dead" sort of statement for an old guard Manhattan intellectual like himself. It's "too big, too existential" an idea to contemplate, he says. But the *New York Times* is only one small part of the story. Our entire cultural economy is in dire straits. I fear we will live to see the bulk of our music coming from amateur garage bands, our movies and television from glorified YouTubes, and our news made up of hyperactive celebrity gossip, served up as mere dressing for advertising. Will investigative reporting go the way of the peasantry in Thomas More's sixteenth-century England? In our coming digital future, God may not be dead—but commerce and culture may well be.

Where Is the Money?

Throughout history, art and culture have helped to bridge generations, establish a rich heritage, and generate wealth. Today, the primary value of Web 2.0 companies is in advertising dollars, not in establishing a rich cultural legacy. Take Google, for example, the economic paragon of a truly successful Web 2.0 media company. With a market cap of approximately $150 billion, the Silicon Valley company took in $6.139 billion in revenue and $1.465 billion in profits in 2005. What is telling is the fact that unlike companies such as Time Warner or Disney, which create and produce movies, music, magazines, and television, Google is a parasite; it creates no content of its own. Its sole accomplishment is having figured out an algorithm that links preexisting content to other preexisting content on the Internet, and charging advertisers each time one of these links is clicked. In terms of value creation, there's nothing there apart from its links.

The core of Google's business, 99 percent of its revenue, lies in its sale of advertising. In fact, of the $16 billion spent on online advertising industrywide in 2006, $4 billion, a whopping 25 percent, is estimated to have gone to Google.[27] Indeed, Larry Page and Sergei Brin, the multi-billionaire founders of Google, are the true Web 2.0 plutocrats—they have figured out how to magically transform other people's free content into a multi-billion-dollar advertising machine.

Indeed, one can argue that the entire Web 2.0 economy is a magnified version of Google. Over $500 million in venture capital was invested in 2006 in Web 2.0 me-too social media businesses like Bebo, Zimbra, Facebook, Six Apart, and Xanga, which offer nothing but the distribution of free user-generated content. The new, new thing in Silicon Valley is the "Bring-your-own-content" business model, in which sites that provide their users with nothing more than the platform to express themselves, network, and link with one another, are worth millions or billions of dollars. This idea is being exploited in every market from travel (RealTravel), to virtual communities (Second Life), to events planning (Zvents, Eventful, and Upcoming), to blogs (Technorati), to classifieds (Edgieo), to audio content (Podshow), to pornography (Voyeurweb). Even, absurdity of absurdities, to e-mails (FWDitOn).

In the first Internet boom, "eyeballs" (the number of views per page) was the criterion for determining the value of a Web company. Now, the value is determined by the number of pages of user-generated content potentially available for advertising. With money being pumped into online advertising increasing at an astronomical rate (total spending on Internet ads increased 30 percent in 2005 and another 28 percent in 2006), YouTube, MySpace, and Facebook are potential gold mines. That is why, despite having negligible revenues today, YouTube was acquired for $1.65 billion, MySpace went to News Corp. for $580 million (cheap at today's price), and Facebook is rumored to be worth upward of $1 billion. While MySpace may not be making money yet (according to *Fortune* magazine, it lost money in 2005), RBC Capital's Jordan Rohan predicts it will be worth $15 billion within three years.

Think about it. Fifteen billion dollars for a site containing nothing but user-created profiles. If each added page on MySpace increases the company's value, what's next? How about a social-networking business that offers amateurs cash each time they post a comment or upload a photo?

Don't laugh. This is not a long way off from Panjea. com's commitment to share 50 percent of its advertising profits with users who contribute their music or photography. YouTube is also flirting with the same crazy idea of a revenue-share to reward user "creativity." In January 2007, at the World Economic Forum in Davos, Switzerland, YouTube founder Chad Hurley told the BBC that his company was working on a technology that would give users a share in the company's ad revenue.[28]

So while our record stores, newspaper companies, and

radio stations are struggling just to survive, we're pumping all our money instead into businesses that offer nothing more than infinite advertising space in exchange for user-generated nonsense that couldn't be published or distributed through any professional source.

God Is Dead

My own "God Is Dead" moment came in late 2005. I was talking with Alan Parsons, the legendary record producer best known for engineering the Beatles 1969 album *Abbey Road* and Pink Floyd's 1973 album *Dark Side of the Moon*.

Both albums are huge economic successes. As of 2004, sales of *Dark Side of the Moon* were at over forty million units, making it the twentieth-bestselling album in history. And *Abbey Road,* with its iconic cover photograph of the Beatles crossing a North London street, is the forty-sixth-bestselling album of all time, and has gone platinum fifteen times.

Abbey Road and *Dark Side of the Moon* represent the apotheosis of the mass media economy that shaped the twentieth century. These albums made mass cultural, political, and social statements that may never again be repeated. And they made money, too. In 2002, *Dark Side of the Moon* was still selling 400,000 copies, making it the 200th-bestselling album of the year, almost thirty years after its initial release.

I had first met Parsons at a Silicon Valley conference

called "Media Business Five" (MB5), which I produced in the fall of 2000. I invited a hundred leading media visionaries to imagine the future of the information and entertainment industries.

"Where is the money?" was the question I asked everyone at MB5.

In addition to Parsons, MB5 alumni included Jonathan Taplin, the Hollywood insider who produced Martin Scorsese's *Mean Streets;* Frank Casanova, head of Streaming Media at Apple; Chuck D of Public Enemy and the first serious rap artist; Chris Schroeder, then-CEO of the online *Washington Post;* Michael Robertson, founder of MP3.com; and many other leading figures in Silicon Valley and Hollywood.

When I spoke to Parsons in 2006, he announced the end of the record business as we know it. My original question at MB5—Where is the money?—still couldn't be answered. By 2005, Parsons had concluded it would *never* be answered. The record business was dying. The party had come to an end.

"Are you sad?" I asked him.

"It's very sad, yes," he said. "But I'm glad I've lived through the—what's the word—the glorious years."

There might be money to be made by linking music to advertisements, or other content to the sale of condoms or cappuccino. But the glory days of selling epoch-making albums like *Abbey Road* are over.

Today, the lyrics from a song like "Money" on *Dark Side of the Moon* reverberate with a strange irony. In a way they describe Parsons' "glorious years"——the dying gasps of mass media when an album sold forty million units in record stores like Tower, and thievery was limited to small-scale, in-store shoplifting rather than an industry-destroying, paradigm-shifting dismantling of 200 years of intellectual property law. As the biggest record store in the world closes its illustrious doors on the corner of Bay and Columbus, we say good-bye to one of the most venerated culture industries of modern times.

6

moral disorder

When Yours Is Mine

Thou Shalt Not Steal.

n the summer of 2003, twelve-year-old Brianna LaHara discovered the addictive pleasure of downloading online music. Instead of spending vacation days riding bikes with friends or lounging at the community pool, this New York City middle schooler sat at her computer and illegally downloaded over 1,000 songs before copying and distributing them among friends using file-sharing applications. She thought nothing of it until that September, when the Recording Industry Association of America knocked on her door, informing her that she was being named as a defendant in one of 261 lawsuits being filed in a crusade to crack down on "exclusively egregious file swappers." (The case was eventually settled out of court.)

Was LaHara running an international ring of digital thieves, or had she simply committed the naive mistake of an unwitting youth? Of course, she was no hardened felon—in fact, she had had no idea she was doing anything wrong. "I thought it was OK to download music because my mom paid a service fee for it," she told the *New York Post*. Technically, her paid subscription did not entitle her to download, copy, and share songs. But in an era where file sharing, music downloading, and cutting and pasting—especially among the younger set—is the norm, is what she did really that surprising? But as innocent as LaHara's intentions were, the fact remains that theft of intellectual property on today's Web 2.0 is as pervasive—and potentially as destructive—as a new strain of avian flu.

The Judeo-Christian ethic of respecting others' property that has been central to our society since the country's founding is being tossed into the delete file of our desktop computers. The pasting, remixing, mashing, borrowing, copying—the *stealing*—of intellectual property has become the single most pervasive activity on the Internet. And it is reshaping and distorting our values and our very culture. The breadth of today's mass kleptocracy is mind-boggling. I'm not referring only to the $20 billion pilfered and pickpocketed, day by day, from the music industry or the $2.3 billion and growing from the movie industry. Sadly, the illegal downloading of music and movies has become so commonplace, so ordinary, that even the most law-abiding among us, like Brianna LaHara, now do it without thinking. "How are we supposed to know it's illegal?" asks a bookkeeper in Redwood City, California, as he copied a playlist of songs to give out to his friends as a party favor.

The problem is not just pirated movies and music. It's become a broader quandary over who-owns-what in an age when anyone, with the click of a mouse, can cut and paste content and make it their own. Web 2.0 technology is confusing the very concept of ownership, creating a generation of plagiarists and copyright thieves with little respect for intellectual property. In addition to stealing music or movies, they are stealing articles, photographs, letters, research, videos, jingles, characters, and just about anything else that can be digitized and copied electronically. Our kids are downloading and using this stolen property to cheat their way through school and university, passing off the words and work of others as their own in papers, projects, and theses.

A June 2005 study by the Center for Academic Integrity (CAI) of 50,000 undergraduates revealed that 70 percent of college students admitted to engaging in some form of cheating; worse still, 77 percent of college students didn't think that Internet plagiarism was a "serious" issue. This disturbing finding gets at a grave problem in terms of Internet and culture: The digital revolution is creating a generation of cut-and-paste burglars who view all content on the Internet as common property.

This warped definition of intellectual property and ownership isn't confined to students and digerati alone.

These days, even the clergy are turning into plagiarists. With sites like sermoncentral.com, sermonspice.com, and desperatepreacher.com offering easily downloadable transcripts of sermons, more and more pastors, according to the *Wall Street Journal,* are delivering recycled sermons, almost verbatim, without crediting their original author. "There's no sense reinventing the wheel," says Florida pastor Brian Moon, who admits to delivering a sermon that he bought for $10 on another pastor's Web site. "If you got something that's a good product, why go out and beat your head against the wall and try to come up with it yourself?"[1] In our Web 2.0 world, it's just so easy to use other people's creative efforts; even our priests, whom we expect to be paragons of virtue, are doing it.

Stanford University law professor Lawrence Lessig argues that "legal sharing" and "reuse" of intellectual property is a social benefit. In fact, as I discussed in Chapter 1, Lessig wants to replace what he calls our "Read-Only" Internet with a "Read-Write" Internet, where we can "remix" and "mashup" all content indiscriminately. Lessig, misguided as he is, suggests that digital content—whether it be a song, a video, a short story, or a photograph—should be commonly owned for the benefit of everyone. What Lessig fails to acknowledge is that most of the content being shared—no matter how many times it has been linked, cross-linked, annotated, and copied—was composed or written by someone from the sweat of their creative brow and the disciplined use of their talent.

Of course, one can't blame digital technology alone for this explosion of plagiarism and illegal downloading. The Web 2.0 culture grew up celebrating file sharing; and now it has provided, on a mass scale, the tools that make cheating and stealing so much easier and so much more tempting. Addictive, almost. With the digital world at each of our fingertips, why not, and besides, who's to know? After all, as any shoplifter will tell you, it's a lot easier to steal if you don't have to look the shopkeeper in the eye.

The fact is that co-opting other people's creative work—from music file sharing, to downloading movies and videos, to passing off others' writing as one's own— is not only illegal, in most cases, but immoral. Yet the widespread acceptance of such behavior threatens to undermine a society that has been built upon hard work, innovation, and the intellectual achievement of our writers, scientists, artists, composers, musicians, journalists, pundits, and moviemakers.

Stanford University professor Denise Pope tries to explain away cheating as a consequence of the excessive academic pressures on kids. "On the part of students, there's an eerie logic to justify cheating. It's three o'clock in the morning, you're exhausted, you've worked hard. . . . Rather than getting a zero, you'd take your chances with plagiarism."[2]

But students who cheat aren't genuinely learning anything. And by depriving artists and writers of the royalties due them, they aren't just hurting those from whom they steal—in the end, they are hurting us all.

Betting the House

The nineteen-year-old bank robber held a handwritten note in his sweaty palms. The rush he experienced was like the feeling he had when he played poker online. The same mix of euphoria and nausea. The same rapid heartbeat, the same parched mouth, the sense that his face was on fire. The same feeling of powerlessness, as if he weren't the author of his own actions.

Then he slid the note across the counter toward the bank teller. It was as if somebody else had scrawled the message. As if somebody else were robbing the bank.

I WANT $10,000 IN CASH. I HAVE A GUN! BE QUIET AND QUICK, OR I WILL SHOOT. NO BAIT!

In his mind, everything went silent. It was the same silence that followed the final raise in an online poker game. In the sleepy little Pennsylvania bank, time stood still. Everything froze.

It was the teller's move. Would she fold and hand him the cash? Or would she call his bluff on the gun?

The Wachovia Bank teller, a local Allentown woman named Hiyam Chatih, stared at the baby-faced teenager standing in front of her. Dressed in a green fleece jacket and a red baseball cap, he resembled an altar boy gone off the rails. His glazed stare and disheveled state suggested drug addiction or demonic possession.

Chatih folded; emptying her till, she handed him

$2,871 in used banknotes. He stuffed them into his back-pack and ran out into the snowy afternoon. There, beside the shoveled walkway, the getaway car, a black Ford Explorer, waited for him. He jumped in, and the car roared off into the late-gathering gloom.

Later that evening, the robber was apprehended by armed police on the nearby campus of Lehigh University, when the young desperado, who also happened to be the second cellist in the Lehigh Philharmonic, showed up for nightly orchestra practice.

His name was Greg Hogan. In addition to being a member of the university's philharmonic orchestra, Hogan was the President of Lehigh's Class of 2008 and the assistant to the university chaplain.

"Mom, I'm in bad shape," the Lehigh sophomore confessed into a cell phone, after he'd been booked by the cops for bank robbery. "I've done something really stupid."[3]

Why did the President of the Class of 2008 wreck his life for $2,871? The reason was simple. Greg Hogan had become addicted to Internet gambling.

In the twelve months leading up to his bank heist, the Lehigh sophomore was down $7,500. He had forty-five bank overdrafts. He owed money to his parents, siblings, and Sigma Phi Epsilon fraternity brothers. He had emptied his own family's safe of $1,200 in bonds saved for him since his birth. What started as a $75 bet on pok-erstars.com became a single-minded obsession. Hogan was soon skipping classes, missing meals, and going on sleepless binges that lasted fourteen hours at a time.

Soon, online poker had taken over his life. So it was fitting that the heist resembled the final hand in a game of high-stakes hold 'em. The last big raise, in this case, would result in ten years behind bars.

The son of an Ohio Baptist minister, Hogan was a musical prodigy who, by the age of thirteen, had twice given piano recitals at Carnegie Hall. He was home-schooled by his mother until the age of fourteen, when he won a scholarship to Ohio's exclusive University School. There, he excelled musically and academically, playing both cello and piano in the school orchestra and working as a Young Republican volunteer for leading Ohio politicians and judges. On graduation, Hogan selected a quote by Winston Churchill for his senior yearbook page: "History will be kind to me, for I intend to write it." At Lehigh, the gregarious Hogan did indeed write his own history, but not quite as he might have expected.

Hogan isn't alone in his secret addiction. Thanks to sites like PartyGaming, SportingBet, 888.com, BetonSports, and Bodog.com, Internet gambling has quickly become a national disease. In 2005, the year Hogan robbed the Allentown Wachovia Bank, $60 billion was bet on online poker alone. That year, according to Annenberg Public Policy Center research, an estimated 1.6 million college students and 1.2 million kids under twenty-two were gambling regularly online, and the number of male college students gambling online on a weekly basis quadrupled. Some college students are so addicted to online gambling that they are spending all their waking hours glued to their laptop screens, never leaving their broadband-enabled dorm rooms, sometimes even falling asleep in the middle of a hand.

Research scientists tell us that online gambling is as addictive as cocaine, alcohol, and other substance abuse. A 2006 study by Dr. Nancy Petry, an expert on online gambling at the University of Connecticut Health Center, says that over 65 percent of Internet gamblers are pathologically addicted, and that Internet gamblers are far more likely to be addicted to gambling behavior than those who frequent the real-world casinos. Why? Because unlike real casinos, which require you to travel to where they are located, these sites can be accessed from anywhere, twenty-four hours a day. According to Petry, "The availability of Internet gambling may draw individuals who seek out isolated and anonymous contexts for their gambling behaviors. Accessibility and use of Internet gambling opportunities are likely to increase with the explosive growth of the Internet."[4]

Internet poker is fast becoming the opium of the college crowd. With campuses so fully wired with broadband connections, addicts can place wagers from their dorm rooms, study lounges, even while sitting in class. As a result, cases like Hogan's are far from rare. "It fried my brain," confessed a kid from Florida who lost a quarter of a million dollars on online poker. "I would roll out of bed, go to my computer, and stay there for twenty hours. One night after I went to sleep, my dad called. I woke up instantly, picked up the phone, and said, 'I raise.'"

In a June 2006 *New York Times Magazine* exposé on online gambling, Mattathias Schwartz blames the colleges for this national pandemic: "Administrators who would never consider letting Budweiser install taps in dorm rooms have made high-speed Internet access a standard amenity, putting every student with a credit card minutes away from twenty-four-hour, high-stakes gambling."

The growth of the online gambling sector recalls what happened when the European powers exported opium to China in the eighteenth century. It resulted in the same nightmarish consequences—powerless addicts, a pandemic of opium dens, a demoralized, destabilized population. By the end of the nineteenth century, over half of China's population were opium addicts, and Chinese society had become unraveled. Could this happen to us today, online? Could a growing segment of our population, like Greg Hogan, lose control of their lives?

One can see how seductively easy online gambling is. Just switch on your computer, type in a URL, and you're in virtual Las Vegas. Broadband delivers a twenty-four-hour, nonstop, personalized city of sin to every dorm room and every off-campus apartment in every college in America. It's the equivalent of Vegas on steroids.

In *Amusing Ourselves to Death*, his 1985 polemic against the trivialization of American life, Neil Postman argues that Las Vegas had become a "metaphor of our national character and aspiration, its symbol a thirty-foot-high cardboard picture of a slot machine and a chorus girl." Today, in the Web 2.0 epoch, Postman sounds as dated as Gibbons describing the decline of the Roman Empire. That poster of a slot machine has been digitalized and virtualized and is now ubiquitous and available at all times. Nobody needs to travel to Las Vegas—Las Vegas now comes to us. As Schwartz wrote about college students and Internet gambling:

> Freshmen arrive already schooled by ESPN in the legend of Chris Moneymaker, the dough-faced 27-year-old accountant who deposited $40 into his Pokerstars.com account and parlayed it into a $2.5 million win at the World Series of Poker in Las Vegas. Throughout the dorms and computer labs and the back rows of 100-level lecture halls, you can hear the crisp wsshhp, wsshhp, wsshhp of electronic hands being dealt as more than $2 billion in untaxed revenue is sucked into overseas accounts each year.

For a year, Greg Hogan had carried his Las Vegas around with him wherever he went. *Wsshhp, wsshhp, wsshhp.* He would sometimes play Texas Hold 'em for four days straight in his dorm room. In the computer lounges of the Lehigh library, he pulled all-nighters playing 60 to 100 hands an hour. He even brought his own casino to his clergyman father's basement office in Ohio during the winter vacation, where, with the music of Green Day, Incubus, and 311 blaring in the background, he celebrated Christmas by playing nonstop digital poker with other anonymous addicts around the world.

Like theft, gambling has existed long before the Internet, probably as far back as the beginnings of human civilization. But the proliferation of casinos and online gambling has dramatically heightened our addiction to gambling by reducing much of the social stigma and allowing us to gamble, surreptitiously or not, anywhere at any time: from our homes, our offices, on our commute to work, or even on the sidelines of our kids' soccer games.

Online gambling is prohibited in the United States under the 1961 Federal Wire Act. Yet, until the summer of 2006, not a single site had ever been indicted and the industry thrived, generating around $6 billion of revenue in America in 2005.[5] Businesses like BetonSports, 888.com, SportingBet, and PartyGaming grew up overnight, basing their computer servers offshore in tax-free Costa Rica, Gibraltar, Antigua, and the Channel Islands, where they were largely ignored by American law enforcement. Only now, as we shall see in Chapter 8, is the danger of online gambling being confronted.

A significant portion of society feels that adults are responsible for their own actions, that they should be free to gamble their lives away if they wish. But the social costs of the online gambling culture extend far beyond the destruction of individual lives. Families become unglued. Desperate addicts go to desperate and sometimes criminal lengths to get their hands on more cash. Any way you look at it, online gambling is dangerous and illegal, and by doing nothing to clamp down on it, the government undermines our faith in the rule of law.

Moreover, Internet gambling sends a terrible message to our kids about the value of money. The easy-come, easy-go attitude that online gambling instills is an insidious ethic to pass on to our kids. Online gambling feeds a kid's fantasy of getting something for nothing.

Greg Hogan was seduced by the promise of easy-money poker when he saw the $160,000 in winnings of another student gambler. To the naive eighteen-year-old, that kind of money could have been his if he played his cards right, if you'll excuse the pun. The irony is that if he had simply worked and studied hard throughout college, he could have ended up with a high-flying career on Wall Street or Main Street that would have ultimately been far more lucrative.

Most Silicon Valley pundits would, of course, snigger at the old-fashioned celebration of hard work, self-discipline, frugality, and self-sacrifice. Maybe that's because the Web 2.0's YouTube economy, with its irrational valuations and instant millionaires, where a couple of twenty-something kids can cash in $1.65 billion and over $300 million apiece in stocks for an unprofitable eighteen-month-old Internet site, has infiltrated and infected the rest of America with

irrational attitudes and beliefs. Gambling—with its illu-
sionary shortcut to instant wealth—has become a way of
life not only in Silicon Valley but in society at large.

Perhaps we can't overcome online gambling any more
than we can outlaw other addictive Internet obsessions,
like pornography and file sharing. But don't we have a
responsibility in society to try to control these behaviors so
that they don't become the opium of the twenty-first century? As James Madison, one of America's wise founders,
once remarked, we aren't angels. We don't always do the
right thing. That is why we have enacted laws that help us
regulate our darker impulses and behaviors.

Of course, this is first and foremost a moral issue, and
the Web 2.0 world is uncomfortable with ethical debate.
It raises questions about the kind of society we want and
the kinds of kids that we seek to raise.

One thing is for sure—we don't want to raise a generation of Greg Hogans. So perhaps, just as alcohol needs
to be restricted to licensed establishments that can check
IDs and be held accountable if their patrons drink too
much and attempt to drive, legal gambling needs to be
confined to licensed casinos—rather than allowed inside
dorm rooms and university libraries.

Sex Is Everywhere

The ways in which the Web 2.0 is compromising our
morals and our values is most evident in the realm
of pornography. Between 1998 and 2003, the *Internet*

Filter Review reported, the amount of Internet pornography mushroomed 1,800 percent from 14 million to 260 million pages.[6] The number of pornographic sites has multiplied, too—seventeenfold, in fact, from 88,000 porn sites in 2000 to 1.6 million in 2004.

Not surprisingly, addiction to online pornography has risen dramatically, as well. The National Council on Sex Addiction and Compulsivity believes somewhere between 3 percent and 8 percent of Americans are "sex addicts" in some shape or form, and the San Jose Marital and Sexuality Center estimates that between 6 percent and 13 percent of online pornography users are "compulsive," spending at least eleven hours a week on porn sites. As a consequence, twelve-step programs for pornography addiction are springing up all over America.

The Web 2.0 twist to this explosion of addictive smut is the rise in user-generated pornography. Amateur porn sites that subsist on user-generated content like Voyeurweb, or Pornotube, a rip-off of YouTube that posts thousands of new amateur pornographic videos weekly, are among the most highly trafficked sites on the Web. In fact, according to traffic-ranking authority Alexa.com, Pornotube—founded in February 2006—has, in just one year, become one of the top two hundred most-popular Web sites, with significantly more daily visitors than "professionally" created porn sites like playboy.com.

More sobering, the National Center for Missing and Exploited Children (NMEC) estimates that the number of images of child porn on the Internet has increased by

1,500 percent. One would have to be in the pay of the ACLU not to see that this poses real concerns for both the future of an open Internet and for the moral tenor of our society. Yes, most civilized societies have their red-light districts and peep shows, and pornographic DVDs have been a high-growth industry for years. But it wasn't until the advent of the Internet, and the rise of amateur content on the Web 2.0, that porn has become so ubiquitous, so available, so diverse and perverse in its offerings that it is virtually inescapable.

This is no exaggeration. In a telephone survey of 1,500 Internet users between the ages of ten and seventeen, the Crimes against Children Research Center at the University of New Hampshire found that of the 42 percent of kids who were exposed to online pornography, 66 percent reported that this exposure was "unwanted." This report, released in January 2007, suggests that a shocking two-thirds of our kids who see online pornography are doing so against their will.[7] As Dr. Michael Wasserman, a pediatrician with the Ochsner Clinic in Metairie, Louisiana, put it, "It's beyond the Wild West out there."

To many parents of teenage and pre-teenage kids, including myself, hard-core online pornography is a moral scourge. Do you want your kids trawling around voyeur.com (where they could catch the amateur porn show of a neighbor or teacher)? What kind of lessons are they learning online about real love and the role of sex in a mature relationship? How can they *not* come away with a twisted notion of what sex is about? Is it okay that our kids are being exposed to this twisted content with every spam e-mail solicitation and pop-up advertisement?

Web 2.0's social-networking sites are certainly not helping to prevent pornography addiction among minors. On MySpace, fourteen-year-old girls, with screen names like "nastygirl," post photos in which they pose provocatively in their underwear, bathing suits the size of postage stamps, skin-tight leather clothing, or cleavage-revealing tops. This is the "culture" that the online cult of the amateur promotes and perpetuates. How far have things gone? In February 2006, *Playboy* magazine issued a casting call for a "Girls of MySpace" nude magazine spread.

And this is the tamer fare. Solicitations of sex among young teens and preteens on sites like MySpace are becoming commonplace. Message boards on MySpace have become confessionals on which thirteen- and fourteen-year-olds one-up each other with boasts about their sexual exploits and experimentations. While no one over the age of eighteen can access a fourteen- or fifteen-year-old's profile without knowing their full name or e-mail address (unless, of course, they lie about their age, which people routinely do), fourteen- and fifteen-year-olds can view any profile they wish. Inevitably, they begin to mimic the offensive and lewd material posted by older members.

What's more, social-networking sites are reaching kids at younger and younger ages. The *Wall Street Journal* recently reported that in December 2006, 22 percent of all visitors to MySpace were under the age of eighteen.

And sites targeted at eight- to twelve-year-olds—such as clubpenguin.com, imbee.com, and tweenland.com—are springing up like mushrooms after a spring rain to mimic the popularity of MySpace. Some of these sites receive as many as two million visitors a month. While theoretically there are parental controls in place, they are easy to circumvent. Kids often use code words and acronyms to trick the content filters and use their parents' password to bypass controls and sign themselves in.

I would argue that the ubiquitous sex on the Internet and the hypersexual content of online social-networking sites is accelerating kids' sexual and social development in very dangerous ways. Need proof? The online sex magazine *Nerve* recently published an interview with a thirteen-year-old eighth-grade girl named "Z" about Internet pornography:[8]

NERVE: *Have you ever seen any pornography on the internet?*

Z: Obviously.

NERVE: *How old were you would you estimate when you first saw porn?*

Z: I guess ten, but that was because there were pop-ups, like advertisements, shit like that.

NERVE: *So do you know anyone who's really into internet porn?*

Z: Basically all of my friends are.

NERVE: *Are you?*

Z: Yeah. I'm not like ashamed to say that. Most of the time the way my friends look at it it's not like, "Oh my God, that's so hot." It's like, "Yeah, that's all right." I sort of like gothic porn.

Thirteen-year-olds should be playing soccer or riding bikes, not sitting in locked bedrooms looking at hard-core pornography. The Internet is transforming future generations into a nation of kids so inundated by and desensitized to hard-core smut that they've even developed genre favorites. And what the heck is *gothic porn*?

But, of course, this is hardly the darkest, scariest part of online sex. The fact is, social-networking sites have become magnets for real-life sexual predators. Thanks to the vast amount of detailed personal information kids post on their profiles—including hometown, school location, favorite hangouts, and, of course, photos—pedophiles have never had an easier time acquiring sexual images of underage kids or of tracking down their potential victims in the real world.

The dangers of a social-networking site like MySpace are horribly real. In January 2007, the families of four girls ages fourteen and fifteen sued MySpace for failing to provide safety measures for protecting their daughters from sexual predators, after the girls had been sexually abused by men whom they met on the MySpace Web site.[9] We all have a responsibility to protect our kids from a similarly premature end to their age of innocence.

Online Addiction

Forty-seven-year-old Carla Toebe couldn't control her Internet dating habit.

The first thing this mother of four would do in the morning, before getting out of bed, was boot up her laptop and begin chatting and instant messaging on online dating sites. Often, she would spend as many as fifteen hours on these sites, rarely leaving her bed and ignoring her daily tasks, leaving her Richland, Washington, home at times with stacks of unwashed dishes and dirty laundry. "I am self-employed and need the Internet for my work, but I am failing to accomplish my work, to take care of my home, to give attention to my children who have been complaining for months," she wrote.[10] She had become a slave to the digital universe, preferring her online existence to the day-to-day realities of life itself.

Internet addiction is not new. But in a Web 2.0 world in which so much of our lives—from social networking, to exchanging ideas, to watching videos, to self-broadcasting—is conducted online, Internet addiction is inevitably on the rise. According to a recent Stanford University study, Internet users are now averaging 3.5 hours a day online, and in the first scientifically rigorous research project, conducted by the Stanford University School of Medicine, on the addictive properties of the Internet, it was found that out of 2,513 adults, more than one in eight manifested some symptom of Internet addiction.

the cult of the amateur

Beyond the disturbing individual stories of women like Carla Toebe, there are many other symptoms of this incipient social disease. As we have seen, addiction to online theft, gambling, and pornography has become a social curse afflicting everyone from twelve-year-old digital-music downloaders, to college-age poker players, and pornography-obsessed teenagers. Indeed, in the age of always-on media, Internet addiction is corrupting our values and culture.

Our Second Lives

The popularity of online multiplayer games like Second Life, where users create online personas and engage in any and every form of real-life activity—from starting a business, to getting married, to buying and decorating a home—is resulting in dangerous confusion between virtual reality and life. Virtual worlds like Second Life, which has grown from 100,000 users at the end of 2005 to 1.5 million by the end of 2006, are becoming highly addictive alternatives to the pressures and frustrations of the real world. The addiction here is to a consequence-free existence, where absolutely anything—including being able to fly, becoming a different gender, even killing someone without real-world repercussions—is possible. And, for many, that is irresistibly seductive.

Second Life has a thriving virtual economy based on Linden dollars, which users can purchase with real money. On Second Life, real developers sell virtual land, real advertising executives sell virtual billboard space, real clothing retailers sell virtual clothing, real hotel chains sell virtual rooms, and real therapists sell virtual counseling sessions to real couples. In January 2005 alone, players spent over $5 million in transactions for virtual items.[11] While this makes the site a potentially lucrative source of income for entrepreneurial types, it can have dangerous financial consequences for addicts who prioritize their second lives over their real lives and drain their bank accounts buying goods and services to consume in their second lives.

And because, in true Web 2.0 fashion, Second Life is virtually unregulated and unsupervised, it has become a channel for all kinds of social and ethical vices. Though there are (largely unenforced) rules against inappropriate behavior in public (virtual) spaces, users can act out all of their most base or prurient instincts in virtual private. For 220 Linden dollars, one can even act out virtual rape fantasies; options include "rape victim," "get raped," or "hold victim."[12]

"But it's just a game," some users protest. Sure. A game so all-consuming that many of its users spend up to twelve hours a day online running their virtual businesses, spending time with their virtual families, and tending to their virtual homes, ceasing to be functioning, productive members of society.

"The Internet problem is still in its infancy," Dr. Elias Aboujaoude, the principal author of the October 2006 Stanford study on online addiction, admitted.

So what will the world look like in 2020 if nothing is done to rein in addictions of an online culture?

Baroness Susan Greenfield, a member of the British House of Lords and a professor of Neuroscience at Oxford University, argues that the consequences for the future generation are grave. Her research indicates that the ubiquity of digital technology is altering the shape and chemistry of our brains, and that violent video games and intense online interactivity can generate mental disorders such as autism, attention deficit disorder, and hyperactivity. Thus children of the Web 2.0 generation, she suggests, will be more prone to real-world violence, less able to compromise or negotiate, apt to be poor learners, and lacking in empathy.

A scary vision of the future, indeed.

From hypersexed teenagers, to identity thieves, to compulsive gamblers and addicts of all stripes, the moral fabric of our society is being unraveled by Web 2.0. It seduces us into acting on our most deviant instincts and allows us to succumb to our most destructive vices. And it is corroding and corrupting the values we share as a nation.

7

1984
(version 2.0)

Everybody Knows

t began as a moral dilemma. *Should you plan sex before meeting a cyber lover?* she asked the search engine on April 17, 2006.

The problem was that she was *married but in love with another man,* as she confessed to the search engine on April 20.

A week later, she had made up her mind to meet her Internet lover. *What do men think is sexy?* she inquired ten days later as she finalized her plans—the plane tickets, the hotel and restaurant reservations—to fly from her home in Houston to meet him in San Antonio.

She spent the night of May 4 with him in San Antonio's Omni Hotel. It was a disaster. *i met my cyber lover and the sex was not good,* she confessed on May 8. *Online friend is horrible in person.*

Does God punish adultery? she asked on May 13.

How do I know all these intimate details about a stranger?

I know it because I've read her entries on her AOL search engine. I've scanned every entry she made between March 1, 2006, and May 31, 2006.

She had opened her heart to this technology, transforming her search-engine queries into a window to her soul. She's as real as lonelygirl15, the fictionalized actress on YouTube, is fake. The thoughts and feelings that she poured into AOL's search engine reveal a woman struggling to maintain her sanity in the face of despair.

From March through the end of May, she fed 2,393 questions into the search engine—questions that she would have been too shy to ask even her closest friends; questions about her body, male sexuality, Internet addiction, and God's justice. She was a digital *Madame Bovary,* with just one caveat—her entries in the AOL search engine weren't intended to be published. There was no Flaubert behind her confessions. They weren't supposed to be read by anyone. She trusted her search engine absolutely. Amid her snoring spouse, her invisible children, her heartbreaking adultery, her struggle to make sense of God's word, it was her sole confidante, the one certainty that could never let her down.

How wrong she was. Her utter frankness with the

search engine represented her most serious misjudgment, one even more misguided than her decision to spend the night with her Internet lover. For soon the Internet turned her into a global media celebrity. Her search engine entries between March and May—all 2,393 of them— would be released on the Internet for public consumption. Her confessions would be read and "interpreted" by thousands of voyeuristic bloggers. Little did AOL user #711391 know that she would become one of the first casualties of a digital surveillance culture in which our deepest fears and most intimate emotions can be broadcast, *without our knowledge or permission,* to the world.

Everybody knows her now, including, no doubt, some Houston neighbors who could tell us her name, her address, and the ages of her kids. We now know this Texan woman as intimately as we know our own spouse—her bedroom attire (*purple lingerie*), her body flaws (*can spider veins swell up and turn red?*), the color of her pubic hair (*blond*), and her post-adultery wisdom (*don't ever have sex with your best friend*).

The online magazine *Slate* described the release of her entries as a flagrant invasion of fundamental individual rights. It was, the magazine claimed, "Orwellian."

As so it is. Welcome to 1984, version 2.0.

Our new Orwellian age got its public screening on the evening of Sunday, August 6, 2006, when AOL leaked the search data of 658,000 people (including AOL user #711391). Critics immediately dubbed this information leak "Data Valdez," after the 1989 *Exxon Valdez* oil tanker spill. Twenty-three million of the AOL users' most private thoughts—on everything from abortions and killing one's spouse to bestiality and pedophilia—were spilled on the Internet to the world without their knowledge or permission.

All this data became the intellectual plaything of AOL researchers—not surprising in an industry where search companies like Google and Yahoo treat the billions of queries in their search engines as their own property, to store, analyze, and profit from.

But the legal ownership of search-engine queries remains murky. Marc Rotenberg, the executive director of the Electronic Privacy Information Center, described it as a "ticking privacy time bomb." That bomb exploded on August 6, when AOL researchers accidentally posted the database of queries online. Hackers promptly downloaded this data and "democratically" distributed it across the Web. Now anyone—workmates, friends, and family, of course, as well as blackmailers and other cybercriminals—could pore through this enormous database of private intentions.

It was the equivalent of the Catholic Church mailing out 658,000 confessions to its worldwide parishioners. Or the KGB, the Soviet secret police, throwing open their surveillance files and broadcasting them on national television.

The information in these AOL files is a twenty-first-century version of *Notes from Underground*—replete with information that reveals us at our most vulnerable, our most private, our most shameful, our most human. They include every imaginable query, from *"how to kill your wife"* and *"I want revenge for my wife"* to *"losing your virginity,"* *"can you still be pregnant even though your period came?"* and *"can you not get pregnant by having sex without a condom?"*

"My goodness, it's my whole personal life," a sixty-two-year-old widow from Georgia told the *New York Times*, horrified, when she learned that her personal life had been splayed across the Internet. "I had no idea somebody was looking over my shoulder."

Of course, this was far from being the only major privacy debacle of the digital age. In February 2005, scam artists broke into the databases at ChoicePoint, an Atlanta-based data broker, which, MSNBC reports, maintains background information on almost every U.S. citizen. This breach, in which identity thieves obtained data through the fake accounts they had set up by posing as legitimate clients, exposed over 163,000 financial records and resulted in close to 800 cases of identity theft. "We believe that several individuals, posing as legitimate business customers, recently committed fraud by claiming to have a lawful purpose for accessing information about individuals," ChoicePoint told its shocked victims. "You should continue to check your credit reports frequently for the next year."

In May 2006, a couple of teenagers stole a laptop from the Department of Veterans Affairs, leaking the financial histories of 25 million veterans. And then there were the hackers who, in September 2006, broke into the Second Life database and stole the real-life records—including names, addresses, contact information, and financial information—of its 600,000 virtual inhabitants.

Worse still, the data from 40 million MasterCard and Visa accounts was stolen in July 2005. Just think about that the next time you enter your credit card number on an online shopping site.

And with doctors and hospitals increasingly storing their records online (on sites like WebMD.com), medical records, too—which can include anything from prescription-drug information, to surgical histories, to treatments for sexually transmitted disease—can easily fall into the wrong hands. In one recent case, records of 260,000 patients in Indiana were compromised when an outside contractor downloaded the records onto CDs and placed them in a computer bag, which he later returned to the store with the CDs still inside.[1] In cases like these, consequences go beyond mere embarrassment or invasion of privacy. According to the *San Diego Business Journal*, there are over 200,000 medical identity-theft cases each year, and that number is on the rise.[2] With just a fraudulent Social Security number or a stolen insurance card (easily obtained by even an amateur hacker), thieves can amass thousands of dollars in medical bills, create legal liabilities by submitting fraudulent insurance claims, or tamper with existing records in such a way that jeopardizes future insurance coverage.

The consequences of a stolen identity on the Web can perhaps best be seen in the following story of a man who had his life turned upside down for two years.

There are two kinds of guys in the world: those who own their own tuxedo and those who rent.

Paul Fairchild falls firmly into the latter category. A thirty-four-year-old Web developer from the bedroom community of Edmond, Oklahoma, with a wife and two small kids, Fairchild is the quintessential renter. He rents his small ranch-style home in the little suburb of Oklahoma City. And he also rents his tuxedos when he needs to, which, given his modest lifestyle, is rarely.

In the summer of 2003, Paul Fairchild had good reason to rent a tux. His sister was getting married in Portland, Oregon. Having cobbled together the money to fly his family out to the wedding, Fairchild went to a local tuxedo rental store to outfit himself for the ceremony.

Do you take American Express?

Sure.

The assistant took Fairchild's credit card to process the rental, but reappeared a few minutes later, looking slightly flustered.

Excuse me, sir, but your card has been declined.

Paul Fairchild didn't understand it. He rarely used his American Express card. Money was tight in the Fairchild household—so tight, indeed, that his family could barely afford the $12 shoes from Payless that he and his wife bought for their son to wear at the wedding.

He called customer service. Your account is delinquent, a woman told him.

That's impossible, he said.

Are you the sole proprietor?

Huh?

The sole proprietor, she repeated. Of the Ebony Passion Escort Service in Brooklyn, New York. That's you, right?

I'm afraid there must be some mistake.

There had been a mistake. A huge one.

Paul Fairchild's identity, including a false ID displaying his genuine photograph, had, so to speak, been digitally rented. It had been borrowed without his permission or knowledge by the proprietor of the Ebony Passion Escort Service, a prostitution service that operated out of Brooklyn, New York.

There was another Paul Fairchild. A fake East Coast version, the kind of guy who buys rather than rents tuxedos using other people's credit cards. He was an identity thief, a flesh-shop operator who had run up over $500,000 in debts on credit cards, cell-phone and car-rental bills, as well as a store account with a New York jewelry wholesaler. On this Fairchild credit card, instead of a $12 charge for shoes from Payless, there was a $750 charge for Manolo Blahnik footwear, as well as charges for furs and diamonds, and a $500 charge for high-end tobacco. Most egregiously, this Paul Fairchild had committed to a mortgage of $315,000 for an apartment building in downtown Brooklyn—an operational center, no doubt, for his escort service.

For the real Fairchild, the consequences of the theft were, to quote the *New York Times*, "two years of hell." He spent forty hours a week for the first four months after the revelation of the identity theft just dealing with police reports and filing notarized affidavits to each defrauded company. Extracting himself from the mortgage proved particularly time-consuming and expensive. Wells Fargo Bank, one of the owners of the debt, ended up suing Fairchild, who was forced to hire a lawyer to defend himself. Even two years after the identity theft was exposed, he was still getting billed by telephone companies for charges racked up by the fraudster.[5]

Meanwhile, the fake Fairchild, the owner of Ebony Passion Escort Service, remains on the loose. And there's little chance of catching him. Of the estimated ten million identity thefts each year, it is estimated that only one in 700 are ever apprehended.

The only good news is that Paul Fairchild is now the one and only Paul Fairchild. And he's still that modest guy from Oklahoma who rents, rather than owns, a tuxedo. Even more so now. You see, since the identity theft, his credit rating has been hit hard and his credit limits have been severely cut. So it might be a stretch to afford the rental on a tux next time somebody in his family gets married.

What is in many ways more shocking than the amount of stolen information on the Web is the amount of private information traded *legally* on the Internet each day.

In July 2006, Google performed 2.7 billion and Yahoo performed 1.8 billion unique searches. In the Web 2.0 world, where each and every one of these searches is readily available to corporations or government agencies, the right to privacy is becoming an antiquated notion. In the physical world, we can tear up bank statements and phone bills, discard private notes or letters, shred embarrassing photos, or keep our medical records under lock and key. But once immortalized by AOL or Google, our online records are here to stay.

Google, Yahoo, and AOL, who have no legal responsibility to purge old data, keep records of what subjects we search, what products we buy, what sites we surf. These search engines want to know us intimately, they want to be our closest confidante. You see, the more information they possess about us—our hobbies, our tastes, and our desires—the more information they can sell advertisers and marketers, allowing them to better personalize their products, pitches, and approaches. But our information is not distributed to advertisers alone. Everyone from hackers to cyberthieves to state and federal officials can potentially find out anything from the last movie ticket we bought, to the prescription medications we're taking, to the balance of our savings account.

So how do Google and AOL acquire such detailed information? Through the innocently named "cookies"—tiny parcels of data embedded in our Internet browser that establish a unique ID number on our hard disk and enable Web sites to collect precise records of everything we do online. These data parcels represent a Faustian pact made with the Internet devil. Each time we land on a Web page, a cookie is activated, telling that site who is visiting it. Cookies transform our habits into data. They are gold mines for marketers and advertisers. They record our site preferences, they remember our credit card information, they store what we put into our electronic shopping carts, and they note which banner advertisements we click on.

And they are everywhere.

How long do these cookies last? The life span of each company's cookie differs. Google's cookie, for example, doesn't expire until 2036. (In March 2007, they changed that policy for new searches.) It is possible to disable the use of cookies on your computer; but as the so-called "Yahoo Privacy Center" warns all users:

> If you reject all cookies, you will not be able to use Yahoo! Products or services that require you to "sign in" and you may not be able to take full advantage of all offerings.

No cookies, no Yahoo! Mail, no personalized My Yahoo! Homepage, none of the digital goodies that our friends at Yahoo give us for free. From my own My Yahoo! page, the company knows that I live in Berkeley, go to the movies a lot, read the *New York Times*, and follow an English soccer club called Tottenham Hotspur. Meanwhile, my g-mail account, which is scanning all my e-mails for key words that it uses to generate customized advertisements, knows that I'm planning a trip to New York City on JetBlue, pre-ordered a copy of *The Long Tail* on Amazon, and subscribe to BMG's classical music club. Everything I do and everywhere I go on the Internet is recorded by somebody for some commercial end.

This compilation of personal information is not just limited to the Internet search engines. On August 10, 2006, four days after AOL's release of its search queries, the Internet retail giant Amazon.com lodged a request with the United States Patent and Trademark Office to patent "a system to gather and keep massive amounts of intimate information about its millions of shoppers." This "system" is designed to compile the most intimate economic, ethnic, sexual, and religious information about Amazon shoppers. Amazon not only wants to own our online shopping experience, they want to own the online shopper—turning each of us into another data point within an infinite database of e-commerce intentions.

Sir Francis Bacon, the Elizabethan father of inductive science, wrote optimistically that "knowledge is power." But in our contemporary digital age, it is information, rather than knowledge, that lends power. And the more personal the information, the more power it promises to those who hold it.

The age of surveillance is not just being imposed from above by the aggregators of data. It's also being driven from below by our own self-broadcasting obsession. The

Web 2.0's infatuation with user-generated content is a data miner's dream. The more we reveal about ourselves on our MySpace page, in our YouTube videos, on our blog, or on the blogs of others, the more vulnerable we become to snoops, blackmailers, voyeurs, and gossips. The confessional nature of user-generated culture is resulting in a cultural explosion of personal, sexual, and political self-revelation.

Privacy is no longer cool. Just look at the high traffic on sites such as DailyConfession.com, NotProud.com, and PostSecret.com, which are made up of anonymous confessions of everything from greed to slothfulness to insatiable lust. It is a haven for voyeurs—a place where people can go to poke their noses into other people's business. And while ostensibly anonymous, these sites, of course, all use cookies to identify both readers and writers. How long will it be before somebody hacks into one of these sites and leaks the names and addresses of all the confessors?

Not surprisingly, the Central Intelligence Agency—that government-funded organization of official nose-pokers—is now investing in Web 2.0 technology. The CIA has embraced something it calls "spy-blogging," which involves the spooks sharing one another's research, aerial photographs, and secret videos.

To justify spy-blogging, one defense expert at the Naval Postgraduate School, parodying Orwellian doublespeak, told the *New York Times,* "To fight a network like al Qaeda, you have to behave like a network."[4] Next thing, they'll be telling us that to beat the terrorists, they have to fly planes into tall buildings.

According to the *New York Times,* the wisdom-of-the-crowd premise of the CIA's spy-blogging initiative is that "a million connected amateurs will always be smarter than a few experts collected in an elite star chamber."

That's a very large crowd of democratically organized secret policemen. I just hope that they aren't sharing information about my private life with a million of their closest colleagues.

This democratized, user-generated media, where everyone gets to spy on everyone else, represents the collective implosion of our privacy rights. In this digital panopticon, teachers watch the kids, college administrators watch the students, and peers watch peers. Orwell's *Nineteen Eighty-Four* painted a picture of a top-down surveillance society where Big Brother sees everything, knows all, watches our movements, listens to our conversations, and reads our minds. Well, the Web 2.0 is the democratization of that Orwellian nightmare; instead of a single all-seeing, all-knowing Orwellian leader, now anyone can be Big Brother. All you need is an Internet connection.

And maybe a digital camera. At HollaBackNYC.com, for example, users are invited to "holla back at street harassers" by taking their photo and then posting them online. HollabackNYC now has popular sister sites in many American cities, as well as in Canada and Europe, where users post photos of people supposedly ogling them in the street. So the next time you flash someone on the street a friendly smile, be prepared for them to snap your photo and make you an involuntary member of the HollaBack community. It's an ideal way to publicly humiliate innocent people trying to mind their own business and live their lives.

It's not just sites like HollaBack that are transforming citizens into snoops. In December 2006, Reuters and Yahoo introduced an online initiative to feature amateur videos and photographs on both their Web sites. Reuters also plans on distributing these images to the many thousands of broadcast, online, and print media subscribers to their news service.

"What if everybody in the world were my stringers?" the president of Reuters media group told the *New York Times* in December 2006 without, it seems, any hint of irony.

What if, indeed. This Reuters and Yahoo partnership encourages anyone to take photographs of anybody else in the vague guise of news.

"There is an ongoing demand for interesting and iconic images," the Reuters president explained, justifying this initiative of transforming anyone with a camera into paparazzi.

But who gives who permission to take *interesting* and *iconic* photos? When does this sort of citizen journalism become intrusive? And who is to distinguish between a tasteless prying into other people's lives and the genuine pursuit of news?

From our entries on search engines, to the content of our e-mails, to our blog postings, to the insalubrious details we post about ourselves on social-networking sites, the Web 2.0 revolution is blurring the lines between public and private.

What happens when all our queries and postings and casual comments become open to public consumption, and the Web becomes a permanent repository of the details of our lives? Our rights to free expression are jeopardized.

Do you think for a moment that what is posted by or about you doesn't matter? Think again. Reed College denied admission to a student in 2006 because he had posted rude comments about the college on his LiveJournal blog. Twenty students at a middle school in Costa Mesa, California, were suspended for making anti-Semitic remarks in a MySpace group. Athletes at Louisiana State and the University of Colorado were suspended for rude remarks on Facebook about their coach. And a graduating senior at Vermont Technical College had a job offer rescinded after the employer saw references to partying and alcohol on the student's Facebook page.

In the fall of 2006, Aleksey Vayner, a senior at Yale, applied for a job at the Swiss investment bank UBS; he also submitted a detailed résumé, an eleven-page cover letter, and a self-made video entitled "Impossible is nothing," which showed off his bench-pressing and tennis-playing prowess. Somebody at UBS put Vayner's application materials online and his video on YouTube;

within days, he was getting hundreds of derisive and even threatening e-mails. The digital lynch mob ended Vayner's career in banking before he'd set foot in Zurich. Now the Yale senior is considering a job in real estate.

The public humiliation of Aleksey Vayner or the AOL users can't, however, compare to the experience of thirty-seven-year-old Chinese dissident journalist Shi Tao. In April 2005, Tao, who reported for *Contemporary Business News* in Hunan Province, was sentenced to ten years in prison by a Chinese court for "illegally providing state secrets to foreign entities." His crime? He'd e-mailed some Western correspondents information about the Chinese government's media coverage of the fifteenth anniversary of the Tiananmen Square massacre. Shi Tao was caught when Yahoo provided the Chinese government with information that traced the dissident through his e-mail account and personal computer.

The Ultimate Search Engine

Big Brother is very much alive and well in the Silicon Valley town of Mountain View, California. It is here that Google, the world's most powerful Web 2.0 company, has its global HQ. And it is out of their offices that the dawn of digital surveillance is being built, algorithm by algorithm, by an army of the world's leading engineers, mathematicians, and software architects.

According to Nigel Gilbert, a professor at Surrey University and head of a 2006 Royal Academy study into surveillance, Google is within five years of having sufficient information to be able to track the exact movements and intentions of every individual, via Google Earth (which can already be used by foreign governments to pinpoint exact locations of secret U.S. army bases), Google Calendar, or the new Web site currently under development, Google Health.[5]

Gilbert's concerns are shared by the UK's Information Commissioner, Richard Thomas, who wrote, "I fear that we are waking up to a surveillance society that is already all around us." It is an apprehension that has also been echoed by a number of leading American critics, including Adam Greenfield, the author of *Everyware: The Dawning Age of Ubiquitous Computing.*

In the short-term future, Greenfield predicts, small computers will become embedded in everything from clothes to beer mats. The consequence of his "Everyware" scenario will be a world in which we, as citizens, will be interfacing with computers in everything we do, from meeting chip-wearing strangers on the street to drinking an intelligent pint of beer. Each of our daily interfaces with smart buildings, smart furniture, smart clothing, or even smart bathtubs will produce data, and all this information will end up in a Google-like database—the database to end all databases.

Everyware represents the real dawn of the age of surveillance. Once computers exist in clothing, on walls and streets, in living rooms and bathrooms, then absolutely everything is knowable. All this information can be collected, networked, and distributed. As Professor Gilbert says, we will be able to type into Google, "What was a particular individual doing at 2:30 yesterday? and would get an answer."

It is a world without privacy, a world in which individuals are turned inside out.

According to the *New York Times*, the next Web boom (3.0, if you will) is likely to be driven by "intelligent" software that can use information from the Web to intuit our future decisions and intentions. A University of Washington project called KnowItAll, for example (funded by none other than Google), has rolled out a test software that can mine databases of online hotel reviews and link them to past customer preferences, then use cognitive deduction to find the best hotel for each individual user. This may seem unthreatening at first glance. After all, who wouldn't want a computer to pick out the hotel with the most convenient location, the best swimming pool, and a room-service menu serving our favorite dish? But do we really want to open the door to technology that takes the place of human reasoning and individual decision-making? Do we really want Google to know enough about us that they can anticipate our actions and predict our ways of thinking?

Google, with its Ministry of Truth credo of *Do No Evil*, is leading the charge into this brave new world of ubiquitous information. Speaking at the appropriately named "Zeitgeist '06" conference for Google's European partners, Google cofounder Larry Page imagined the "ultimate" search engine.[6]

"The ultimate search engine would understand everything in the world. It would understand everything that you asked it and give you back the exact right thing instantly."

Page's "ultimate search engine" is Google's holy grail. It's the modern-day version of the ancient Greek oracle. It's the Judeo-Christian idea of an omnipotent, omnipresent God.

So what happens to the human beings of the future who must coexist with Google's ultimate database? What becomes of us in an age of total digital surveillance?

Everybody knows.

8

solutions

So what is to be done?

How can we channel the Web 2.0 revolution constructively, so that it enriches rather than undermines our economy, culture, and values? What can we do to ensure that our most valuable traditions—celebrating knowledge and expertise, fostering creative achievement, sustaining and supporting a reliable and prosperous information economy—aren't swept away by the tsunami of the cult of the amateur?

I'm neither antitechnology nor antiprogress. Digital technology is a miraculous thing, giving us the means to globally connect and share knowledge in unprecedented ways. This book certainly couldn't have been completed without e-mail or the Internet, and I'm the last person to romanticize a past in which we wrote letters by candle-light and had them delivered by Pony Express.

Digital technology has become an inescapable part of twenty-first-century life. Kevin Kelly told Silicon Valley's TED Conference in February 2005, "You can delay technology, but you can't stop it." And that is true. For better or for worse, Web 2.0 participatory media is reshaping our intellectual, political, and commercial landscape. We can't outlaw Wikipedia, or resurrect Tower Records, or change the realities that have made sites like MySpace and YouTube enormously popular and increasingly profitable. Our challenge, instead, is to protect the legacy of our mainstream media and two hundred years of copyright protections within the context of twenty-first-century digital technology. Our goal should be to preserve our culture and our values, while enjoying the benefits of today's Internet capabilities. We need to find a way to balance the best of the digital future without destroying the institutions of the past.

Citizendium

In January 2000, thirty-year-old doctoral student Larry Sanger came to Internet entrepreneur Jimmy Wales with the idea of building a cultural blog. As I've described in Chapter 2, Wales hired Sanger, and the two men first created a peer-reviewed encyclopedia called Nupedia, then, in January 2001, founded Wikipedia.

But unlike Sergei Brin and Larry Page at Google, or Steve Chen and Chad Hurley at YouTube, the Wales-Sanger partnership didn't have a happy ending.

Why? Because Larry Sanger came to his senses about Wikipedia. He recognized the appallingly destructive consequences of the Wikipedia experiment. Sanger ran Wikipedia's day-to-day operations. He was responsible for policing the lunatic-fringe amateurs who posted and reposted thousands of entries a day. After two years, he had had enough of anonymous anarchists like "the Cunctator" and their ceaseless debates and bickering over Wikipedia controls and quality.

The lesson Sanger drew from his experience at Wikipedia is that the democratization of information can quickly degenerate into an intellectually corrosive radical egalitarianism. The knowledge of the expert, in fact, *does* trump the collective "wisdom" of amateurs. He learned that an open-source encyclopedia like Wikipedia could only function effectively if it reserved some authority to screen and edit its anonymous contributions. He learned that fully democratic open-source networks inevitably get corrupted by loonies.

Wikipedia's problem, Sanger realized, was with its implementation, not its technology. So he went away and rethought how to incorporate the voice and authority of experts with the user-generated content. And he returned with a solution that incorporates the best of old and new media.

He called it Citizendium. Launched in September

2006, Sanger describes it as "an experimental new wiki project that combines public participation with gentle expert guidance." In other words, it is an attempt to fuse the strengths of a trusted resource like the *Encyclopaedia Britannica* with the participatory energy of Wikipedia. On Citizendium, experts in specific subjects have the power to review, approve, and settle disputes about articles within their intellectual specialty. A select group of "constables" maintain order on the site by censoring rule-breakers and troublemakers.

What is so refreshing about Citizendium is that it acknowledges the fact that some people know more about certain things than others—that the Harvard English professor does, in fact, know more about literature and its evolution than a high school kid. If even a Web 2.0 pioneer like Larry Sanger can come to recognize this, maybe there is hope after all for the user-generated Web 2.0.

Larry Sanger is not the only Web 2.0 pioneer who has come to his senses about the inferiority of amateur content. Niklas Zennstrom and Janus Friis, the founders of the original file-sharing service Kazaa as well as the online telephony company Skype (which they sold to eBay for $2.5 billion in September 2005), have launched Joost, a new digital media initiative for a world in which the Internet and television are rapidly converging. Joost is a service that promises to provide professional creators of video with a peer-to-peer platform for distributing and selling their content over the Internet. The platform will enable professional content producers to combine the traditional one-to-many broadcasting functionality of network television with the many-to-many interactivity of online content. A second television platform that offers the similar promise is Brightcove, a Boston-based start-up founded by former Macromedia chief technology officer Jeremy Allaire, which, by January 2007, had raised $60 million in venture capital.

"TV is 507 channels and nothing on and we want to change that!" Friis—borrowing a Springsteen verse—wrote.

But the alternative to 507 channels doesn't have to be 507 million channels. Unlike user-generated content services such as YouTube, platforms like Joost and Brightcove maintain the all-important division between content creators and content consumers. They are designed to enable professional creators of video content to deliver high-quality, interactive content to both the personal computer and the television (thus Viacom's decision, in February 2007, to license some of its MTV, Comedy Central, and BET programming to Joost). These next-generation platforms will offer the best of both the old and new media worlds—enabling us to simultaneously video chat and instant message with one another while watching our favorite shows. In 1990, technology visionary George Gilder published *Life After Television*. With exciting new technology companies like Joost and Brightcove, the world after TV can really begin to take shape.

This gives me hope that the Web 2.0 technology can be used to empower, rather than overshadow, the authority of the expert, that the digital revolution might usher in an age in which the authority of the expert is strengthened. Take, for example, a site called iAmplify—a publishing platform that allows professionals to sell audio or video downloads that offer instruction and expertise (in everything from weight-loss to finance to parenting) directly to the site's subscribers. iAmplify shows how Web 2.0 technology can provide professionals with more direct channels to reach their market.

So is the future iAmplify or MySpace? Is it YouTube or Joost? Wikipedia or Citizendium? The question is ideological rather than technological—and the answer is largely up to us. We can—and must—resist the siren song of the noble amateur and use Web 2.0 to put trust in our experts again.

Many traditional newspapers and magazines, too, are responding to the challenges they face by marrying new media and traditional content without compromising editorial standards or quality.

One such institution is the left-of-center British newspaper the *Guardian*, which has managed to shift a portion of its business online while still maintaining its high-quality news gathering and reporting. Its online version, *Guardian Unlimited*, has done such a brilliant job of integrating the authoritative traditions of the newspaper with the interactive democracy of the Web 2.0 world that it now boasts more online readers in the United States than such top domestic newspapers as the *Los Angeles Times*. Sure, the *Guardian Unlimited* has anonymous message boards littered with uninformed, unregulated, reader-generated opinions. But unlike many online editions, where readers' blogs and paid advertisements are indistinguishable from actual articles, on the *Guardian Unlimited*, the division between professional reportage and amateur opinion is clearly delineated.

And though the *Guardian Unlimited* is free, it has managed to achieve some measure of economic success by effectively balancing its costs with its online advertising sales. The good news is that other print newspapers are now following the *Guardian*'s embrace of the online medium. In January 2007, for example, the new editor of the *Los Angeles Times*, James E. O'Shea, launched a high-profile initiative to invest significantly more resources in digital technology and online reporting, particularly in the coverage of "hyper local" news. O'Shea's goal was to more cost-effectively deliver the news to his readers—what he described as the "daily bread of democracy."[1]

Recently, the *Wall Street Journal* decided to move some of its analysis and opinion online as well, reducing the size and cost of the paper edition but without compromising its news-gathering ability or journalistic integrity. Such success gives one hope that newspapers can simultaneously embrace the online medium, maintain their professional standards, enlarge readership, and increase revenues.

The Internet is also maturing as a medium for professionally produced news sites. The January 2007 launch of *Politico*, a Washington, D.C., based online news publication, proves that professional journalism is suited to the more flexible and informal medium of the Internet. Founded by John Harris, former political editor of the *Washington Post, Politico* is staffed by well-trained journalists from publications such as the *Washington Post, Time* magazine, National Public Radio, and *Bloomberg News.* These A-list journalists will bring to the Web start-up not only credibility and name recognition, but also the ethical standards, inside-the-Beltway network, and institutional knowledge lent by their successful careers in traditional media.

And in November 2006, Arianna Huffington, the charismatic Southern Californian impresario behind the eponymous HuffingtonPost.com, announced that she would be hiring professional journalists from publications like the *New York Times* and *Newsweek* to report on Congress and the 2008 presidential elections for her blog, adding news-reporting capability to the mix of opinion and commentary. As a result, the Huffington Post will enjoy the best of both worlds—the immediacy and energy of a blog site with original, quality reportage. Still, a handful of reporters covering politics and the elections hardly replaces a full-scale newspaper in the breadth and scope of its reporting. At the end of the day, perhaps the long-term viability of our media depends upon the actions and behaviors of each of us. If we agree with the notion of a free press and strong news-gathering media, we need to support it by continuing to subscribe to and read the papers. Nothing is more important in a democracy such as ours than an informed citizenship. In the meantime, the news organizations, too, are trying to adapt and change.

As advertising dollars migrate to the Web, more newspapers are attempting to boost ad revenue through strategic partnerships with online businesses. In November 2006, Yahoo formed a partnership with 176 daily newspapers by which the papers' classified ads could be accessed through the Yahoo site. That month, Google announced a similar deal, agreeing to share content, advertising, and technology with a group of fifty major newspapers, including the *Washington Post,* the *Chicago Tribune,* and the *New York Times.* Monster.com, the online career site, has agreed to post job listings from forty national newspapers, including the *Philadelphia Enquirer* and the *Philadelphia Daily News.* The question is whether such partnerships help newspapers generate enough ad dollars to make up for plunging circulations.

And what of the music industry? Can music companies rethink their business models to stay competitive despite the surge in digital downloading and piracy? According to the *New York Times,* cost-analysis data on a successful hip-hop record recently released by Warner Records revealed that only 74 percent of the total revenue from the release came from actual CD sales—the rest was from the sale of ring tones, related cell-phone games, and cell-phone wallpaper and screen backgrounds. Clearly, there is money to be made in digital products tied to album releases. In other parts of the world, the sale of digital add-ons is even more profitable. Can the music industry find ways to make enough money off such products to make up for the lost revenue from piracy?

It continues to astound me each time I walk into Amoeba, one of the few local record stores left in Berkeley, that a newly released CD, on average, still costs $16. When consumers can get an album on iTunes for $10, or cherry-pick individual songs for a dollar, why does the music industry cling to its archaic pricing structure? The industry should find ways of streamlining the costs of packaging, storing, and distributing physical albums so that CD prices can become more competitive with digital albums. Sure, that is not the end-all and be-all with regard to piracy, but such a gesture could be a first step in the fight to win back its customers.

It is also astounding that the big labels cling to their faith in the power of digital rights management software (DRM) to somehow magically stem the tide of digital piracy. DRM is the copy-protection software that comes with the downloaded music sold by the big labels, blocking us from easily transferring our legally purchased digital music from our Apple iPod player to other players, and from our iTunes jukebox to our Napster or Real Networks libraries. But what the recent history of the music business clearly demonstrates is that thieves steal music online no matter what intricate digital electronic lock is supposed to be protecting it. This may be why even Apple CEO Steve Jobs—whose brilliantly designed iPod player and iTunes store have pioneered the growth of digital music into a $2 billion global market in 2006[2]—has come out against DRM. Given that the Apple iTunes store sold around 85 percent of the legal 525 million digital music downloads bought in the United States in 2006,[3] Jobs' controversial position is certainly something that the record industry should contemplate carefully. In a February 2007 essay, the Apple CEO wrote that the vast majority of today's digital piracy stems from illegally traded music copied from compact discs (which are DRM-free) rather than from digital downloads. What does Jobs conclude are the benefits of DRM? "There appear to be none," he says.[4]

Once again, it is we, the consumers of music, who play a role in this ongoing saga. We have to understand that the illegal downloading and sharing of music is killing off an industry that has treated us to recordings by everyone from Paul Simon and the Beatles to Beyoncé and Carrie Underwood. A viable future of the music business lies somewhere between that $16 compact disc and the free, stolen digital file. One potential version of this future lies with eMusic, the new big player in the digital music business (second only to Apple). eMusic sells DRM-free music files in the MP3 format, which means its subscribers can download songs into any digital player or jukebox. Although the four big labels have so far resisted including their catalogs on the eMusic service, the site nonetheless boasts 250,000 subscribers who pay $9.99 per month to download thirty songs selected from the 11,000 independent labels who sell their catalogs on the site.[5] And in the third quarter of 2006, it recorded a 10 percent share of the entire digital music market—the same as the total share of Napster, MSN Music and Yahoo Music combined. The success of eMusic's business model shows that consumers are willing to pay for music when it is competitively priced and easy to buy. And eMusic's successful aggregation of catalogs from 11,000 independent labels suggests that the labels and artists *can* still make money by selling their music at significantly less than 99 cents a track. eMusic paints a hopeful picture that a vibrant recorded music industry and satisfied music consumers *can* coexist in the digital future. In February 2007, one of the big four labels—EMI—was rumored to be wrestling with the idea of releasing their catalog in the MP3 format.[6] So perhaps by the time you read this, one or more of the big labels will have taken that all-important first plunge into a DRM-free digital world.

The way to keep the recorded-music industry vibrant is to be willing to support new bands and music, and new services like eMusic, with our dollars—to stop stealing the sweat of other people's creative labor.

Crime and Punishment

In March 2006, I became embroiled in an online debate with Instapundit blogger Glenn Reynolds about morality. In reviewing his book, *Army of Davids* for the *Weekly Standard*, I argued that Reynolds, in the romantic tradition of Marx, had invested an unreasonable level of trust in mankind's ability to use technology responsibly.

But this is the key question in the debate between pragmatists like myself (or so I like to think) and digital utopians like Reynolds. Can we really trust society to behave properly in the Wild West culture of the Web 2.0 revolution?

I would argue that we are easily seduced, corrupted, and led astray. In other words, we need rules and regulations to help control our behavior online, just as we need traffic laws to regulate how we drive in order to protect everyone from accidents. Sometimes it takes government regulation to protect us from our worst instincts and most self-destructive behavior. The fact is, modest regulation of the Internet works. Let me give you an example.

On Sunday, July 15, 2006, David Carruthers, a smartly attired British executive in his late forties with wire-rimmed glasses and a balding pate, and his wife, Carol, were changing planes at the Dallas–Fort Worth International Airport on their way from London to San José, Costa Rica. But as it happened, he never made it to Costa Rica. Before he could board American Airlines flight 2167, he was arrested and detained by federal authorities under charges of racketeering, conspiracy, and fraud.

Carruthers was the CEO of BetonSports, an online gambling company publicly traded on the London Stock Exchange, which, in 2005, earned $20.1 million in profits on $1.77 billion revenue. Although online gambling is prohibited in the United States under the 1961 Federal Wire Act, which forbids the use of wire communication (including the Internet) for the transmission of bets or wagers, casino businesses like BetonSports, 888.com, SportingBet, and PartyGaming have nevertheless sprung up, generating about $6 billion in revenue from Americans betting on everything from football to poker to roulette. Until now, these companies got around the American justice system by locating their computer servers offshore in tax-free Costa Rica, Gibraltar, Antigua, or the Channel Islands, where they managed to operate largely off the radar of the American authorities.

The arrest of David Carruthers at DFW Airport, and the subsequent arrest of another online gambling kingpin, Peter Dicks, the chairman of SportingBet, a few months later, dealt a swift blow to the illegal online betting business. With its CEO sitting in a Dallas courtroom in his prison-issued orange jumpsuit and facing a twenty-two-count criminal indictment, BetonSports stopped accepting bets from users with American IP addresses, and SportingBet has sold off its entire U.S. operation.

More recent congressional legislation has helped curb illegal gambling operations further. On September 30, 2006, Congress passed the Unlawful Internet Gambling Enforcement Act, which created new criminal penalties for banks and credit card companies that process payments to online gambling companies. And in January 2007, indictments were handed down to four major investment firms for underwriting the initial public offerings of online gambling operations.

Strong legislation and effective law enforcement *can* be

effective. The number of online casinos has been reduced. And according to *The Economist* magazine, the 2006 legislation "proved enough to cripple an industry already reeling from the earlier arrests," prompting PartyGaming to immediately halt its U.S. business. But the government still needs to continue to legislate against online gambling and go after and shut down offshore gambling businesses.

Gambling is not the only Internet activity that would benefit from more regulation. I feel we need the same uncompromising crackdown on online fraud, identity theft, and the unbridled stealing of intellectual property.

In February 2006, Massachusetts congressman Ed Markey introduced a bill requiring search-engine companies to delete any information about visitors that is not required for legitimate business purposes. It is a step in the right direction. Only by putting legal limitations on the type of data that can be stored and collected about us, as well as the amount of time it can be held, can we protect ourselves against the kinds of data leaks that result, at best, in public humiliation, and at worst, in devastating identity theft.

Unfortunately, past legislation has done little to curb illegal file-sharing of music and movies on the Internet. However, the media companies are starting to finally take legal action. In November 2006, Universal Music Group filed a copyright-infringement suit against MySpace for allowing users to post and swap pirated versions of its musicians' videos and music. Universal is seeking damages of $150,000 per infraction—no small potatoes considering that a significant percentage of the site's 140 million users are probably in violation. Meanwhile, in January 2007, News Corp.'s Twentieth-Century Fox television studio subpoenaed YouTube to reveal the user who illegally uploaded digital copies of *The Simpsons* and *24*.[7] And, in February 2007, media conglomerate Viacom—which owns MTV, Nickelodeon, Black Entertainment Television (BET), and the Comedy Channel—formally requested that YouTube take down 100,000 clips, which, Viacom copyright lawyers assert, have been illegally posted on the video site. And in March 2007, Viacom pursued legal actions, suing the Google-owned company.

This sends a powerful message about the high price of intellectual property theft. And in October 2005, a coalition of publishers—Simon & Schuster, McGraw-Hill, John Wiley & Sons, and Penguin Group (USA)—sued Google for its plans to scan and digitize millions of copyrighted books. The more that companies follow this example in protecting the rights of their authors and artists, the more effective they will be in deterring digital piracy and reversing the cut-and-paste culture of the Web.

I would argue that regulation is most urgently needed in protecting our children against sexual predators and pornography on social-networking sites like MySpace. Bills have been proposed in several states that would require the e-mail addresses and instant messaging screen names of convicted sex offenders be registered so that they can be cross-referenced with social-networking sites' user databases. Such a protection from registered sex offenders *nationwide* would be even more effective. And MySpace, too, as the leading social-networking site, is creating a database with names and physical descriptions of sex offenders and developing technologies that could find and expel users with matching descriptions or profiles. But this only addresses part of the problem. What concerns me are all the offenders out there who are undetected because they have never been convicted, or those who join MySpace under false identities.

This is why government intervention can only go so far. The responsibility to protect young users really falls upon MySpace and similar sites to monitor content more vigilantly, and better police their sites to shield minors from indecent material or inappropriate sexual advances. Parents, too, can play a key role, using word filters to prevent minors from sending or receiving explicit messages. I would suggest that all photos sent to and by minors be screened for sexual content. Sites like MySpace should prohibit minors from including information in their profile that would identify them—such as a cell phone number or home address—and parents (and schools) should strongly discourage their children and teens from posting other potentially revealing information as well. The sites should implement more-secure background checks to ensure that when users set up their profiles, they can't lie about their age. And of course, when offenders are caught, they should be immediately and permanently banned from the site and, if appropriate, prosecuted.

And as a parent, I feel we need to enforce the laws designed to protect our kids from morally corrosive Internet content. I would urge enforcement of the 1998 Child Online Protection Act (COPA), the bipartisan legislation designed to protect children from online material deemed "indecent" as determined by "contemporary community standards." The law requires that operators of pornographic Web sites demand proof of age from their users before allowing them to access their content. COPA punishes Web-site operators with a $50,000 fine and a six-month prison term if they fail to comply with the law. Yet, despite its noble intention of criminalizing online pornographers who allow children to access their obscene material, COPA remains widely unenforced, as ACLU lawyers have taken advantage of the vague wording and successfully argued that it is impossible to define indecency "by an objective contemporary community standard." If the law does prove unenforceable in the courts, I would urge legislators to revise the law in such a way that the courts will accept it.

In May 2006, Congress passed the Deleting Online Predators Act, requiring that elementary and secondary schools ban access to social-networking sites on all school and library computers. The average schoolday is about seven hours long, and with computers now in every classroom, and student-to-teacher ratios often as high as 30 to 1, educators simply can't monitor what the kids are looking at all the time. By blocking access to social-networking sites, as well as to chat rooms and any other sites where minors may have access to sexual material or be "subject to" sexual advances in the schools, this bill, if signed, would go a long way to ensuring that our children are protected from harmful content, at least while on school grounds.

Is this censorship? If so, tell that to the parents of the ten-year-old girl who stumbled onto a hard-core anime porn Web site while doing research for her science project in the school library. Or to the parents of the curious twelve-year-old boy who accessed a site about bestiality and incest in the computer lab and showed it to his classmates.

Bringing It All Home

Which brings me to my final point: Parents must man the front lines in the battle to protect children from the evils lurking on the Web 2.0. In today's Web 2.0 world, one thing is clear—kids are spending more and more time online. And while this may be unavoidable, if you're a parent, when, where, and how your kid spends his or her time online is largely up to you. Move their computer to a family room, rather than allowing them to go online in the privacy of their bedrooms. This will help you to monitor the amount of time spent at MySpace and other sites that can monopolize their time at the expense of homework, exercise, or interacting with friends in the real world.

We can control when our kids are allowed online, where we keep the family computer, and especially now, with all the various Internet safety products available, what sites they visit and what content they see. With products like Net Nanny, Cybersitter, and SmartAlex, for example, parents can program their child's Internet browser to block specific sites or images, restrict chat and instant messaging to a "safe list" of friends, limit time online, control downloads, and block private information like phone numbers and addresses from leaving the computer. And by downloading the free parental notification software that MySpace unveiled in January 2007, parents can track the name, age, and location their children use to identify themselves on their MySpace page.

"But I don't want to spy on my kids," some parents might object. Well, neither do I. But I also don't let them watch the Playboy Channel, get in a car with strange men, or hop on a plane to Las Vegas for the weekend.

Parents have a responsibility to educate their kids about the dangers on the Internet. Just as we teach our kids to look both ways before they cross the street and not to take candy from strangers, so we must teach them safe online behaviors. And more important, we must be unwavering in our efforts to instill in them good judgment so that, if put in a compromising situation online, they will make the right—and safe—decision.

The Last Word

At the 2005 TED Conference, Kevin Kelly told the Silicon Valley crowd that we have a moral obligation to develop technology. "Imagine Mozart before the technology of the piano," he said. "Imagine Van Gogh before the technology of affordable oil paints. Imagine Hitchcock before the technology of film."

But technology doesn't create human genius. It merely provides new tools for self-expression. And if the democratized chaos of user-generated Web 2.0 content ends up replacing mainstream media, then there may not be a way for the Mozarts, Van Goghs, and Hitchcocks of the future to effectively distribute or sell their creative work.

Instead of developing technology, I believe that our real moral responsibility is to protect mainstream media against the cult of the amateur. We need to reform rather than revolutionize an information and entertainment economy that, over the last two hundred years, has reinforced American values and made our culture the envy of the world. Once dismantled, I fear that this professional media—with its rich ecosystem of writers, editors, agents, talent scouts, journalists, publishers, musicians, reporters, and actors—can never again be put back together. We destroy it at our peril.

So let's not go down in history as that infamous generation who, intoxicated by the ideal of democratization, killed professional mainstream media. Let's not be remembered for replacing movies, music, and books with YOU! Instead, let's use technology in a way that encourages innovation, open communication, and progress, while simultaneously preserving professional standards of truth, decency, and creativity. That's our moral obligation. It's our debt to both the past and the future.

9

web 2.0 and politics

Is User-Generated Media Killing American Democracy?

had just given a speech about the dangers of user-generated media at the Warsaw offices of *Polityka*, Poland's most respected political weekly. So it didn't surprise me that the toughest question of the night was about the political consequences of the Web 2.0 revolution.

"You say that user-generated media is assaulting the American economy, its culture and values," I was asked by a Polish journalist, "but what about politics—how is the Web 2.0 revolution going to affect the 2008 American election?"

It was the same question that I had been repeatedly asked since *The Cult of the Amateur* hit the bookstores last year. Everywhere I traveled in the world—Germany, England, Denmark, France, Holland, Greece, even Brazil (where I'd been invited to address a United Nations conference about the Internet)—everyone wanted to know how Web 2.0 was going to change the face of American politics.

Yet it was also the one question that I couldn't answer with any confidence. "Next year *could* be the year in which the blogosphere elects the next president. In 2008, it's *possible* that the cult of the amateur will infiltrate the White House," I responded, sounding, no doubt, like a typically prevaricating political pundit. "But before the primaries start in early 2008, it's all speculation."

Well, it's 2008 now, the American primary season has begun and there's no longer any excuse for vagaries or evasion. So let me return to the Polish journalist's question. Are blogs, MySpace, and YouTube killing American democracy? Is our politics—like our economy, our culture, and our values—being destroyed by user-generated media? Are Huxley's monkeys swinging their way up Pennsylvania Avenue into the White House?

Huxley's monkeys, you will remember, are that crowd of self-publishing amateurs saturating the Internet with their homemade, (generally) worthless, user-generated content. But when it comes to the impact of Web 2.0 on democracy in America, it is hedgehogs rather than Huxley's monkeys who threaten the health of American democracy.

Let me explain. The English philosopher Isaiah

Berlin once argued that there are two kinds of political thinkers—hedgehogs and foxes. "The fox knows many things," Berlin quoted the Classical Greek poet Archilochus, "but the hedgehog knows one thing." Berlin's hedgehog, then, sees all history in terms of a single fixed idea, while his fox regards it from a number of angles, and in a variety of ways. American democracy was built by foxes, like James Madison, who recognized that our representative political system, with its division of powers, should reflect both the imperfectability and complexity of the human condition. In contrast, today's techno utopians, who see the world—and our place in it—solely in terms of how technology can be used to "improve" every aspect of society, are hedgehogs.

In May of last year, I found myself in New York City, a lone fox in a mob of hedgehogs. I had been invited to an event called the Personal Democracy Forum to debate Craig Newmark, the multimillionaire founder and self-appointed "customer service representative" of Craigslist, about digital democracy. *Technology is changing politics*, the conference organizers triumphantly announced. Personal Democracy Forum was FOO Camp for politicos and, like Tim O'Reilly's open-source retreat for radical elites, I found its mood to be inappropriately self-congratulatory.

The one fixed idea at Personal Democracy Forum was this: that technology could *perfect* democracy. It was hedgehog heaven. Idealist after idealist—including Google CEO Eric Schmidt and Stanford Law professor

Lawrence Lessig—spoke on behalf of the American people about the benefits of digital democracy. They said that the current political system didn't work and, like bad software, it needed to be upgraded. Democratizing technologies such as blogs, wikis, and social networks, they promised, would radically empower the electorate. User-generated media would strip the traditional political elites of their authority, "disintermediate" and democratize bureaucracy, allow occasional voters to become full-time citizens, and, most ominously of all, transform professional politicians—Craig Newmark–style—into customer service representatives of the American people.

Over lunch, one hedgehog—a veteran of the 2004 Howard Dean campaign—personally tutored me in the radical impact of technology on politics. Dressed, Steve Jobs–style, in black Levi's and a cashmere turtleneck, he was trying to sell me the idea that digital technology is the best antidote to the tyranny of government.

He looked me straight in the eye. "You have to understand that this is the real American Revolution," he explained. "Politics 2.0 is going to be the most revolutionary development in democracy since—"

"Politics 1.0?" I interjected foxily.

Like most hedgehogs, he lacked humor. "Politics 2.0 isn't a joke," he said testily. "The blogs, YouTube, and the social networks are changing everything. In 2008, the next president of the United States will be user-generated."

But 2008 has arrived and the joke is now on him. True, the year is still young as I write this; it's only the middle of January, a handful of days after the Iowa caucuses and New Hampshire primaries. So far, however, Web 2.0 has far from revolutionized the political process; it hasn't been a YouTube election; the blogosphere hasn't overtaken mainstream media as the primary source of information or vehicle for discussion; and (Ron Paul being case in point) the size of the candidates' social networks haven't determined the number of votes they've received. And so far, thank goodness, a user-generated American president remains the most absurd of hedgehog fantasies.

If I had a dollar for every time a political pundit (myself included, I confess) predicted that 2008 would be the "YouTube election," I'd have the cash to fund my own open-source video Web site. But the only political impact YouTube had in 2007 were the two CNN/YouTube presidential debates—and even in this the role of the amateurs was extremely limited. True, the questions posed to candidates from both parties were delivered by ordinary citizens via user-generated videos. Yet the debate was strictly monitored by consummate professional and long-time CNN anchor Anderson Cooper, who limited responses to a mere 30 seconds and even dictated which candidate would respond to which question. Moreover, it was Cooper and his team of CNN gatekeepers who carefully selected which videos to run from among the thousands submitted. So while the debate was lauded as being the first in which candidates would have to answer directly to their constituents, in reality they were answering only to those constituents whose questions the CNN producers cherry-picked as being worthy of putting on the air.

What's more, the pundits have been (so far) mistaken about the likelihood that YouTube would destroy a front-running candidate or derail a successful campaign. They incorrectly envisaged the 2008 election as a film festival of "Macaca moments" in which political career after career would be destroyed, witch trial–style, by incriminating YouTube moments. Fortunately, this has not come to be. The closest we got to a Macaca moment in 2007 was when John McCain got filmed remixing the old Beach Boys hit "Barbara Ann" with the words "bomb bomb bomb, bomb Iran." But when an anti-McCain activist posted this video on YouTube, Americans reacted indifferently. Our electorate was smart enough to recognize the Vietnam veteran's silly ditty as a joke; one in bad taste, but nonetheless just a joke, and the incident barely made the news. So, far from suffering George Allen's fate as I write this, less than a week after his victory in the New Hampshire primary, the four-term Arizona senator is leading the race for the Republican nomination.

It can't be denied that the blogosphere is abuzz with political discourse, and that the leading candidates have huge followings on MySpace and Facebook. And it can't be denied that Web 2.0 has improved voter turnout, and even driven grassroots fundraising—on all ends of the political spectrum. But were the results of the Iowa caucus or the New Hampshire primary determined by user-generated media? Did Obama and Huckabee win Iowa because the candidates had 400,000 "friends" on Facebook, or a well-staffed virtual political operation on Second Life? Did libertarian candidate Ron Paul win more than a laughable percentage of votes—despite the $20 million he raised on the Internet in the fourth quarter of 2007 alone? Did blogging bullies like Glenn Reynolds or Markos Moulitsas actually change the minds of any voters, or force the candidates to change their stance on any key issues?

No. Instead, what we saw in Iowa and New Hampshire were fair, reasoned, issue-based races whose results were determined for reasons almost entirely independent of user-generated media. The message from the voters of Iowa and New Hampshire is that Politics 1.0 works in America. The electorate wanted political change, of course—but not changes to the rules of the political game. Obama and Huckabee won Iowa for the same reason candidates have been winning races for over two centuries: because of their superior political organization and fundraising, because of their political charisma and strong speaking skills, and because their positions on the issues were best aligned with those of the voters—not because of their Web sites, e-mail marketing campaigns, or real-time online chat sessions. Similarly, John McCain won New Hampshire because he was endorsed by the local media and because he participated in over a hundred local town meetings during the campaign, not because he was a favorite among bloggers or had the most friends on MySpace.

And what about Hillary Clinton? How did she overcome Obama's post-Iowa momentum to win the 2008 New Hampshire Democratic primary? Simple. Like hundreds of politicians before her, she finally emotionally connected with the American public. But that teary moment in a Portsmouth, New Hampshire, coffee shop on the morning of Monday, January 8, wasn't a Macaca moment, filmed on a $200 camcorder by a voyeuristic amateur and then slapped up on YouTube. No, Hillary Clinton's newfound intimacy with the American people was captured by mainstream media and was conventionally broadcast on CNN, ABC, and every other major network. It was as much a historic moment as Nixon's sweaty television debate with JFK in 1960 or Edmund Muskie's tears on a snowy Manchester, New Hampshire, street in 1972.

So I have an answer now to the question from that Polish journalist. And it's good news for a change. Despite what the hedgehogs would have us believe, Web 2.0 media isn't about to revolutionize American democracy. That's because most American voters are foxes, rather than hedgehogs, and care about more than just one thing. Today's voters care more about the complicated political issues confronting America—Iraq, Iran, the economy, the environment, health care, immigration—than about discussing these issues in the most technologically complicated way. Sure, blogs, Facebook, YouTube, and Wikipedia will be relevant to the way voters learn about the candidates; that is simply a result of our new media landscape. But television, newspapers, radio, books, and other traditional media will remain the primary vehicles of information—and for this we can be grateful. The next president of the United States is *not* going to be user-generated. Politics 1.0 remains the standard platform for American democracy, and I, for one, see no need for an upgrade.

notes

introduction

1. For more about Huxley's theory, see Jorge Luis Borges' 1939 essay "The Total Library."

2. Evan Hessel, "Shillipedia," *Forbes*, June 19, 2006.

3. http://mashable.com/2006/07/22/youtube-is-worlds-fastest-growing-website/

4. Scott Wooley, "Video Fixation," *Forbes*, October 16, 2006.

5. Audit Bureau of Circulations, September 2005, reports. BBC News, January 23, 2006. (http://news.bbc.co.uk/2/hi/entertainment/4639066.stm.)

6. Jeff Howe, "No Suit Required," *Wired*, September 2006.

7. Frank Ahrens, "Disney to Reorganize Its Lagging Movie Studios," *Washington Post*, July 20, 2006.

8. The term "cult of the amateur" was first coined by Nicholas Carr in his essay "The Amorality of Web 2.0," roughtype.com, October 3, 2005.

1 the great seduction

1. "Liquid Truth: Advice from the Spinmeisters," *PR Watch*, Fourth Quarter 2000, Volume 7, No. 4.

2. Antonio Regalado and Dionne Searcey, "Where Did That Video Spoofing Al Gore's Film Come From?" *Wall Street Journal*, August 3, 2006.

3. Michael Barbaro, "Wal-Mart enlists bloggers in PR campaign," *New York Times*, March 7, 2006.

4. "Ken Lay's Death Prompts Confusion on Wikipedia," *USA Today*, via Reuters, July 5, 2006.

5. Marshall Poe, "The Hive," *The Atlantic*, September 2006.

6. Kevin Kelly, "Scan This Book!" *New York Times Magazine*, May 14, 2006.

7. www.AMillionPenguins.com.

8. Reuters, "Publisher launches its first 'wiki' novel," February 1, 2007.

9. Chris Anderson, *The Long Tail*, Hyperion, 2006.

10. Trevor Butterworth, "Time for the Last Post," *Financial Times*, February 17, 2006.

11. http://blog.guykawasaki.com/2007/01/a_review_of_my_.html.

12. Brookes Barnes, "Big TV's Broadband Blitz," *Wall Street Journal*, August 1, 2006.

2 the noble amateur

1. Interview with author, August 24, 2006.

2. Stacy Schiff, "Know It All: Can Wikipedia Conquer Expertise?" *The New Yorker*, July 31, 2006.

3. Ibid.

4. Marshall Poe, "The Hive," *The Atlantic*, September 2006.

5. CNET News, March 13, 2001, and January 2, 2002.

6. Nicholas Lemann, "Amateur Hour: Journalism Without Journalists," *The New Yorker*, August 7 & 14, 2006.

7. Ibid.

8. Matt Drudge to National Press Club, June 2, 1998.

9. Interview with author.

10. Interview with author, March 17, 2006.

11. Nicholas Lemann, "Amateur Hour: Journalism Without Journalists," *The New Yorker*, August 7 & 14, 2006.

12. Ibid.

13. Robert J. Samuelson, "A Web of Exhibitionists," *Washington Post*, September 20, 2006.

14. Jürgen Habermas, Acceptance speech for the Bruno Kreisky Prize for the Advancement of Human Rights, March 9, 2006.

15. William Grimes, "You're a Slow Reader? Congratulations," *New York Times*, September 22, 2006.

16. Kevin Kelly, "Scan This Book!" *New York Times Magazine*, May 14, 2006.

17. Ibid.

18. Eric Stuer, "The Infinite Album," *Wired*, September 14, 2006.

19. Open Debate, "Can Anyone Be a Designer?" *Fast Company*, October 2006.

20. Louise Story, "Super Bowl Glory for Amateurs with Video Cameras," *New York Times*, September 27, 2006.

21. Glenn Reynolds, *Army of Davids*, Nelson, 2006.

3 truth and lies

1. Nancy Jo Sales, "Click Here for Conspiracy," *Vanity Fair*, September 2006.

2. John Markoff, "Attack of the Zombie Computers Is Growing Threat," *New York Times*, January 7, 2007.

3. Joanne Green, "Blind Date," *Miami New Times*, September 14, 2006.

4. Laura Parker, "Courts Are Asked to Crack Down on Bloggers, Web Sites," *USA Today*, October 2, 2006.

5. Ibid.

6. Amy Tan, "Personal Errata," from *The Opposite of Fate*, Penguin Putnam, 2003.

7. "Sock Puppet Bites Man," *New York Times* editorial, September 13, 2006.

8. Jon Fine, "The Strange Case of LonelyGirl15," *BusinessWeek*, September 11, 2006.

9. Howard Kurtz, "Loneliness, Lies, and Videotape," *Washington Post,* September 18, 2006.

10. Tom Glocer, transcript of speech given at the Globes Media Conference in Tel Aviv on Monday, December 11, 2006. http://tomglocer.com/blogs/sample_weblog/archive/2006/12/12/142.aspx

11. Sara Kehaulani Goo, "Videos on Web Widen Lens on Conflict," *Washington Post,* July 25, 2006.

12. Charles C. Mann, "Blogs+Spam=trouble," *Wired,* September 2006.

13. Brian Grow and Ben Elgin, with Moira Herbst, "Click Fraud," *BusinessWeek,* October 2, 2006.

14. Ibid.

15. Tom Zeller Jr., "Gaming the Search Engine, in a Political Season," *New York Times,* November 6, 2006.

16. Edelman PR Press Release, January 23, 2006.

17. Caroline McCarthy, "Paris Hilton Showcases YouTube's New Ad Concept," cnet.com (News), August 22, 2006.

18. Jamin Warren and John Jurgenson, "The Wizards of Buzz," *Wall Street Journal,* February 10, 2007.

19. Charles Mackay, *Extraordinary Popular Delusions*, Harriman House Classics, 2003.

4 the day the music died [side a]

1. Joel Selvin, "For S.F. rockers, Tower Records was where it was all happening—now the party's over," *San Francisco Chronicle,* October 19, 2006.

2. *The Financial Times,* October 12, 2006, based on research by International Federation of the Phonographic Industry (IFPI).

3. "Ann Powers Remembers Tower Records," *Los Angeles Times,* October 11, 2006.

4. Dave Kusek and Gerd Leonhard, *The Future of Music: Manifesto for the Digital Music Revolution,* Berklee Press, 2005.

5. Recording Industry Association of America.

6. Richard Waters, "MySpace seeks to become a force in online music sales," *The Financial Times,* September 1, 2006.

5 the day the music died [side b]

1. www.victorianweb.org/authors/dickens/pva/pva75.html

2. www.victorianweb.org/authors/dickens/pva/pva76.html

3. Jay Epstein, "The World According to Edward," *Slate*, October 31, 2005.

4. *Hollywood Reporter*, December 21, 2006.

5. Sharon Waxman, "After Hype Online, 'Snakes on a Plane' Is Letdown at Box Office," *New York Times*, August 21, 2006.

6. Frank Ahrens, "Disney to Reorganize Its Lagging Movie Studios," *Washington Post*, July 20, 2006.

7. Yuanzhe Cai and Kurt Scherf, "Internet Video: Direct to Consumer Services," Park Associates Report, November 2006.

8. Mark Porter, "Competition Is Killing Independent U.S. Bookstores," Reuters, December 26, 2006.

9. David Streitfeld, "Bookshops' latest and sad plot twist," *Los Angeles Times*, February 7, 2006.

10. *San Antonio Business Journal*, November 24, 2006.

11. Katharine Q. Seelye, "In Tough Times, a Redesigned Journal," the *New York Times*, December 4, 2006.

12. Katharine Q. Seelye, "Newspaper Circulation Falls Sharply," *New York Times*, October 31, 2006.

13. Ibid.

14. Michael Wolff, "Panic on 43rd Street," *Vanity Fair*, September 2006.

15. "Ad woes worsen at Big Newspapers," *Wall Street Journal*, October 20, 2006.

16. Maria Aspan, "Great for Craigslist But Not for Newspapers," *New York Times*, November 28, 2005.

17. "Who Killed the Newspaper?" *The Economist*, August 24, 2006.

18. Katharine Q. Seelye, "Times Company Announces 500 Job Cuts," *New York Times*, September 21, 2005.

19. Katharine Q. Seelye, "Los Angeles Times Publisher Is Ousted," *New York Times*, October 6, 2006. Katharine Q. Seelye, "Los Angeles Paper Ousts Top Editor," *New York Times*, November 8, 2006.

20. David Carr, "Gruner and Jahr Chief Intends to Cut Costs by $25 Million," *New York Times*, August 7, 2004.

21. Philip Weiss, "A Guy Named Craig," *New York* magazine, January 16, 2006.

22. Michael Wolff, "Panic on 43rd Street," *Vanity Fair,* September 2006.

23. Katharine Q. Seelye, "A Newspaper Investigates Its Future," *New York Times,* October 12, 2006.

24. Who Killed the Newspaper?" *The Economist,* August 24, 2006.

25. Michael Wolff, "Panic on 43rd Street," *Vanity Fair,* September 2006.

26. "Who Killed the Newspaper?" *The Economist,* August 24, 2006.

27. eMarketer Report, October 17, 2006.

28. Tim Weber, "YouTubers To Get Ad Money Share," BBC News, January 27, 2007.

6 moral disorder

1. Suzanne Sataline, "That Sermon You Heard on Sunday May Be from the Web," *Wall Street Journal,* November 13, 2006.

2. Karoun Demirjian, "Denise Pope Comments on Student Plagiarism," *Christian Science Monitor,* May 11, 2006.

3. Matt Assad, "How Online Gambling Toppled Greg Hogan's World," *Morning Call,* August 17, 2006.

4. George T. Ladd and Nancy M. Petry, "Disordered Gambling Among University-Based Medical and Dental Patients: A Focus on Internet Gambling," *Psychology of Addictive Behaviors,* March 2002, Vol. 16, No. 1, 76–79.

5. Mattathias Schwartz, "The Hold-'Em Hold Up," *New York Times Magazine,* June 11, 2006.

6. Robyn Greenspan, "Porn Pages Reach 260 Million," Internetnews.com, September 5, 2003.

7. *Pediatrics: the Official Journal of the American Academy of Pediatrics,* Vol. 19, No. 2, February 2007, pp. 247–57.

8. Nerve.com, "The Prurient Interest: An Eighth Grader Weighs In," October 10, 2006.

9. Joe Garofoli, "Families of sexually abused girls sue MySpace, alleging negligence," *The San Francisco Chronicle,* January 19, 2007.

10. January W. Payne, "Caught in the Web," *Washington Post,* November 14, 2006.

11. "My Virtual Life," *BusinessWeek,* May 1, 2006.

12. Laura Conaway, "Rape Still Haunting Cyberspace," *Village Voice* online, December 15, 2006.

7 1984 (version 2.0)

1. Daniel Lee, "Lost and Found: Info on 260,000 Patients," *Indiana Star,* October 25, 2006.

2. Katie Weeks, "Fast-Growing Medical Identity Theft Has Lethal Consequences," *San Diego Business Journal,* October 16, 2006.

3. Tom Zeller Jr., "For Victims, Repairing ID Theft Can Be Grueling," *New York Times,* October 1, 2005.

4. Clive Thompson, "Open-Source Spying," *New York Times Magazine,* December 3, 2006.

5. Alexi Mostrous and Rob Evans, "Google Will Be Able to Keep Tabs on All of Us," *The Guardian,* November 3, 2006.

6. Richard Wray, "Google Users Promise Artificial Intelligence," *The Guardian,* May 23, 2006.

8 solutions

1. James Rainey, "Editor James O'Shea unveils Web initiative at Times," *Los Angeles Times,* January 24, 2007.

2. IFPI, Digital Music Report 2007.

3. Nielsen SoundScan report, December 14, 2006.

4. Steve Jobs, "Thoughts on music," www.apple.com, February 7, 2007.

5. Devin Leonard, "Rockin' Along in the Shadow of iTunes," *Fortune,* February 19, 2007.

6. Joshua Chaffin, "EMI Goes Radical on Digital Rights," Andrew Edgecliffe-Johnson and Richard Waters, *Financial Times,* February 12, 2007.

7. Nicole Urbanowicz, "Fox Subpoenas YouTube over Pirated TV Shows," *Wall Street Journal,* January 26, 2007.

acknowledgments

began with a confession, so let me end with one, too.

I confess that, as a writer, I remain a bit of an amateur. This is my first book, and I'm still learning the craft of this complex business. It has been my great fortune, however, to have received a first-rate literary education from a remarkable group of professional agents, editors, publishers, and marketers.

This education began in New York City one morning in late 2005. I was walking down Broadway toward Times Square. Tucked under my arm were the first 100 pages of a "book" that I'd been working on since FOO Camp 2004. Part anti-Web 2.0 polemic, part Silicon Valley dystopia, part paean to Alfred Hitchcock's movie *Vertigo*, part autobiography, this muddled first draft was classic amateur self-indulgence—100 percent unreadable and 100 percent unpublishable.

I found myself in Steve Hanselman's garret of an office on Forty-second Street, just off Broadway. Steve and his partner, Cathy Hemming—both ex–HarperCollins senior executives—had just opened a literary agency called LevelFive Media. With over twenty-five years of experience in the publishing business, Steve instinctively knew what I wanted to say better than I did.

"An anti-Web 2.0 polemic," Steve said. "That's what you are really trying to write."

Exactly. So, with Cathy's and Steve's expert guidance, and under the editorial tutelage of LevelFive's Julia Serebrinsky, I deleted those original 100 pages and started again. Cathy introduced me to Jonathan Last, the online editor of the *Weekly Standard* magazine. Jonathan graciously agreed to look at an article comparing Web 2.0 ideology to Marxism. That article, expertly edited by Jonathan, got published in February 2006 and became an instant hit, getting syndicated on CBS News and transforming me into the *bête noire* of the digital utopian crowd.

I remained an amateur. But now, at least, I was a controversial one.

When, in the spring of 2006, Steve sold my book to Roger Scholl's Currency imprint at Doubleday, I assumed that I'd made it into the exalted ranks of professional authors. How wrong I was. This is when my serious learning began.

acknowledgments

"Any advice on how to write a first book?" I asked Roger when we first met.

"Just have fun," he replied.

I've had fun. But it's been the Puritan version—the sweaty fun of learning a craft, the Sisyphean fun of turning myself into a professional writer. Working with Roger and ever-responsive assistant editor Talia Krohn has been an intensely educative six months. They taught me the importance of focus, economy, organization, sticking to the preexisting plan—above all, writing *one* book at a time. The most lucid bits of *The Cult of the Amateur* were squeezed out of me and then polished up by Roger and Talia. Please blame me for any amateurish digressions that even their eagle editorial eyes missed.

There would be no *Cult of the Amateur* without Steve, Roger, Talia, Cathy, Jonathan, or Julia. As agents, publishers, and editors, each represents a paragon of the mainstream media ecosystem. I'm just the symbolic tip of a very large iceberg—what in Silicon Valley we call the "front end" of a business enterprise.

Nor would there be a book without the noble efforts of the marketing and sales team at Doubleday. The only bigger fallacy than anyone being able to write a book is that anyone can market and sell one. Web 2.0 book publishing start-ups like Lulu and iUniverse seduce amateur writers with the false promise of instant mass distribution. But, as even Chris Anderson reminds us, the vast majority of books sell fewer than 100 copies. What dis-

acknowledgments

tinguishes a mainstream publisher like Doubleday are the incredibly rich sales and marketing resources that they offer their writers. I've been particularly lucky to work with Doubleday's deputy publisher, Michael Palgon, as well as David Drake and Liz Hazelton in publicity, and Meredith McGinnis in marketing, Rebecca Gardener in foreign rights, and Louis Quayle in domestic rights. I would also like to thank my own small but highly professional marketing, research, and technology team of Catrin Betts, Sabine Elser, and Peter Rowland, who have contributed significantly to this project, from before the beginning till after the end. Finally, I would like to thank Nicholas Carr, whose richly insightful "The Amorality of Web 2.0" essay (2005) about the cult of the amateur helped define and refine my own arguments in this book.

Thanks to all of you for an unforgettable education. I only hope that this little book does some justice to your splendid job of finding, polishing, and selling talent.

—Berkeley, December 27, 2006

index

index

Andrew Keen is a leading contemporary critic of today's Internet whose writings on culture, media, and technology have appeared in the *Los Angeles Times*, the *Wall Street Journal*, the *Guardian*, the *San Francisco Chronicle*, *Forbes*, the *Weekly Standard*, *Fast Company*, and *Entertainment Weekly*. He has been featured and quoted in many publications including *Time* magazine, the *New York Times*, *U.S. News and World Report*, *BusinessWeek*, *Wired*, the *Financial Times*, the *Wall Street Journal*, the *Sunday Times*, the *Independent*, MSNBC.com, and he has appeared on *The Today Show*, *Fox News*, CNN International, NPR's *Weekend Edition*, the *McNeil-Lehrer NewsHour*, BBC's *Newsnight*, and *The Colbert Report*. His controversial blog, www.cultofthe amateur.com, incurs the ire of techno-utopians worldwide. He lives in Berkeley, California.

MOMENTS WITH GOD

Whispers
of Hope

CHRISTIAN ART
PUBLISHERS

January

New Year's Resolutions

There is a time for everything, and a
season for every activity under heaven.

– Ecclesiastes 3:1 NIV –

Once again, New Year's resolutions are being made every-where. Well, I also have a couple of resolutions for the year that lies ahead ... like making more time for silence in my life. God doesn't compete with all the noise in and around me. I realize that I have to hear Him on His terms, not mine in the New Year. That's why I actively plan to be still and quiet more often in the New Year in God's presence. I absolutely need to get to know the Lord better.

Another resolution – I don't want to send or answer any nasty e-mails or text messages this year. It's an unnecessary waste of energy to argue with those who believe that they know better, or with those who are always the only correct ones. This year I also don't want to fret about road users furiously chasing their tales just to win two minutes of saved time, but also two hours of higher blood pressure as their only "reward."

Finally, I want to live this new year in front of me at "today-speed" – one day at a time for a full 365 days. I reckon that's just about fast enough.

A High Price

Bless – that's your job, to bless. You'll
be a blessing and also get a blessing.

– 1 Peter 3:9 THE MESSAGE –

Maybe you've heard of Maximilian Kolbe. He was a Franciscan priest who ended up in Auschwitz, the notorious German concentration camp, during World War Two. One day a fellow prisoner from his block escaped. Now when someone escaped from Auschwitz it was standard protocol that 10 prisoners be chosen at random to be gruesomely killed. In short, you knew that if you escaped ten others would die in your place.

When Kolbe heard that one of the men who was randomly chosen to die had a wife and children, he immediately offered to take the man's place. Following two brutal weeks of torture, Kolbe finally died after being injected with a deadly acid. Kolbe's sacrifice always reminds me of Jesus' words that there's no greater love than when someone sacrifices his own life for his friends!

What do we ever sacrifice for each other? Which of the people around us have fuller and richer lives because of us? Who knows, maybe our faith is way too safe and boring. Maybe we are too much of a burden instead of a 24/7 blessing to others.

A Life of Their Own

May the words of my mouth and the meditation
of my heart be pleasing in Your sight, O LORD.

– Psalm 19:14 NIV –

Our words are alive. Just consider how powerful a run-of-the-mill phrase like "thank you" can be. Or a short sentence, like "I love you!" In the same way, sharp words can be very hurtful. Hard, loveless words are like gunshots. They wound people.

That's why the Bible instructs us to count our words before we let them loose on the world. By the way, this isn't merely good advice. God created us to be able to form second opinions. Our emotions are our first opinion formers. Researchers are of the opinion that our emotions are as much as a million times faster than our thoughts, which are our second opinion formers. When we literally count to three, we allow our thoughts to kick in. They can then eliminate the words that our emotions want to let loose prematurely.

We must think about our words before they leave our lips in the direction of other people's ears. Words that have already been spoken have a life of their own. The damage they inflict cannot be easily undone. Ask the Lord to dip your words in gold before they escape your mouth. Ask Him to turn your words into good medicine. Speak words of life and see what happens!

Put it Down

Carry each other's burdens, and in this
way you will fulfill the law of Christ.

– Galatians 6:2 NIV –

I once read a tale of two monks who went on a journey. At a river they encountered a woman who couldn't cross the fast-flowing water without help. The first monk refused to help her, since it was against their order's rules to touch a woman. The other monk immediately offered to help by carrying her on his shoulders across the river. Afterward, the rule-abiding monk went on for hours about his "shocking" breach of conduct. "I don't understand your unhappiness," the helpful monk eventually answered. "I put that woman down hours ago, but you're still carrying her around." How true! We don't get other people off our shoulders easily, especially not those who breach our own religious rules.

Stop your prejudiced opinions about others. You can't make your unasked-for religious views applicable to them. Only when you have the courage to establish an authentic relationship with them do you earn the right to talk to them about the Lord. Maybe today is the right time to put down your opinions about other people. Even better, place it on the shoulders of One stronger, Christ! Then you'll be able to carry the burdens of others much more easily.

Too Much Weight

Blessed are those who trust in the
LORD, and have made the LORD their hope and confidence.

– Jeremiah 17:7 NLT –

"People say …" Isn't it remarkable how often you hear this? The opinions of "others" far too often determine what "we" or "I" think. Far too many churches and businesses are managed because of the opinions of others. Comments like "what would the church members say?" or "the opinions of our customers count the most!" are well-known expressions in these circles. People have to be kept happy at all costs otherwise they might withdraw their loyalty from us. But wait … do you really want to be a lifelong victim of other people's opinions? Do "they" have to keep you hostage? Is that really what the Lord expects of you? Should you work hard to win the favor of others, like some Christians think, or should you trust God to confirm your integrity in front of others in His own way?

If you constantly live for the approval of others, you're a victim. There's a better alternative. Strive only for God's approval. Put His kingdom first. Ensure that His approval motivates you. Try to receive the best compliment ever from the Lord one day: "Well done, good and faithful servant." Then you'll be free of "their opinions."

Disconnected from Christ

Train a child in the way he should go, and
when he is old he will not turn from it.

– Proverbs 22:6 NIV –

We're all accustomed to the stereotypes some people use when talking about the younger generation. I'm referring to expressions like, "the youth of today has completely lost their way." Older people far too easily accept that today's younger generation is a "lost generation." That's why a young guy recently caught me off-guard. After a youth service where I spoke, he told me that he's deeply concerned about older people.

I couldn't believe my ears. Normally these statements work the other way round. "What is it about older people that concerns you?" I asked. "I think their religion doesn't really bring peace to their hearts. They're disgruntled with their lives and blame it on others," he replied. "Be careful not to generalize," I said. "I know many elderly people whose lives are flooded with wisdom." In any case, it's wonderful that young people are also concerned about the older generation. Young and old people alike are branded as "difficult" far too easily, but it's not automatically true. Age is not the problem ... discontented and disconnected people are. Every day we must choose to be a blessing to others. Otherwise we're living one day at a time in discontent. That's really not how God wants us to go through life.

The Speed of Sound

Teach us to number our days aright, that
we may gain a heart of wisdom.

– Psalm 90:12 NIV –

Time is money. There's no time for lounging around and doing nothing. No wonder we have phrases like "time management" or "effective use of time." Nowadays we even need to learn how to save time to be effective! There you have it: We're time addicts! We constantly run around at the speed of light to every new demand, in the hope that we'll save two or three minutes somewhere. If we do, we immediately forget about the "saved time" when we arrive anxiously and tired at our destination.

No, we don't really save time. We just chase up our heart rate and heap loads of stress on our shoulders through our hectic daily pace of life. This is because we're chasing after wind and dust storms. The Lord doesn't intend for us to live like this. It's not part of His plan that we live at the speed of light every day. We were made for relationships. And we need time for these – time to stand still, time to take hands.

Well, do you ever have time for that? Do you have the courage to reduce your speed-of-light lifestyle to walking pace? Then you'll start experiencing God and others again.

Sensitivity

So be careful how you live. Don't live like fools, but like those who are wise. Make the most of every opportunity.

– Ephesians 5:15-16 NLT –

Sometimes I'm left dumbfounded at people's utter lack of sensitivity. Not long ago, a woman told me about a colleague whose brother had died at a young age. Then, someone too-holy-for-words sent him a text message to "comfort" him with the words of Proverbs 10:27 that says "the years of the wicked are cut short." Proverbs does indeed say that, but it's not directly applicable, one for one, to each and every person who dies prematurely. Similarly, not every person who attains a ripe old age is enjoying God's favor (as some readers of the Ten Commandments might deduce!). We don't have any right to summarily condemn people who die young.

Indeed, the book of Proverbs was written to teach people how to discern between wisdom and folly. Proverbs definitely wasn't intended to be used by spiritual bullies intent on increasing other people's pain and suffering further through thoughtless text messages and other forms of Bible bashing. It is also not for people who say they need an instant answer for every possible crisis or heartache. Let's learn to handle God's Word with respect and care. Let's serve one another rather than injuring others with our knowledge of the Bible.

Ambassadors for Christ

"Let your good deeds shine out for all to see, so that
everyone will praise your heavenly Father."

– Matthew 5:16 NLT –

A church leader recalls how he and his wife once showed up
at a restaurant late one evening, a couple of minutes before
closing time. The owner didn't want to serve them because
the kitchen was about to close. The church leader caused a
big ruckus and expressed his unhappiness with the poor service. The next morning his phone rang. It was the restaurant
owner's wife. "Were you maybe at our restaurant last night?"
she inquired. Then she added, "My husband, who doesn't attend church at all, keenly watches your messages on television. He says it looked like you at the restaurant last night, but
he couldn't believe that you'd be so rude. I'm phoning just to
make sure."

The church leader had to admit that it was indeed he who
visited the restaurant. He apologized, but the restaurant owner said that he was now finished with Christianity for good.
This story caused me to reflect deeply on my own behavior. I
know I'm often an embarrassment to the Lord and to others
rather than an effective ambassador. Sometimes I speak without thinking, and other times I'm abrupt, even unfriendly.

How about you? Are you a dependable ambassador?

Chasing Fear Away

"Have I not commanded you? Be strong and courageous.
Do not be terrified; do not be discouraged, for the
LORD your God will be with you wherever you go."

– Joshua 1:9 NIV –

Elie Wiesel, a Romanian-born Jewish American, Holocaust survivor, author of fifty-seven books and Nobel Peace Prize winner, tells the story of his visit to a Jewish community during the reign of the old communistic regime in Moscow. During a religious feast, some of them openly danced in the streets. When asked why they were dancing, a woman answered: "All year I live in fear. But once a year, on this day, I refuse to be afraid. Then I'm a Jew and I dance in the streets!"

We should also learn how to dance. We live in times where fear is one of the dominant emotions for many of us. Tragic, or what!

Did you know that we're born with only two basic fears? The fear of loud noises and the fear of falling. Still, many adults now have hundreds of fears. That's why we need to learn anew how to celebrate, not just once a year, but every day. Our identity is anchored in the Lord, who is infinitely bigger than the biggest of our fears. Jesus is our Lord. Thus, we can dance and sing, even with tears on our cheeks ... we can be glad and call the bluff of every old or new fear that threatens us.

Promotion

> "Do not store up for yourselves treasures
> on earth, where moth and rust destroy,
> and where thieves break in and steal. But
> store up for yourselves treasures in heaven."
>
> – Matthew 6:19-20 NIV –

For many people promotion means only one thing – *more stuff*! *more* money, *more* tangible benefits, *more* houses, *more* cars, *more* vacations, *more* status ... For followers of Jesus, the word "promotion" should mean something completely different. It can't equate to more tangible things. Promotion should rather mean to grab every opportunity that the Lord offers you, sacrificing your valuable time and energy in His service.

The right type of promotion in God's service is to cast aside all the construction plans for your own little earthly kingdom, and to exchange them for the privilege being a daily blessing to other people. True promotion is to be part of the lifelong adventure of building God's kingdom. This yields dividends that have eternal value. Promotion in God's kingdom becomes visible when you spend *more* time at the Lord's feet; when you make *more* time for the poor and the lonely; when you do *more* kind things for others; and also when you worry *less* about yourself and your own temporary needs.

The Difference

The LORD your God will bless you in all
your harvest and in all the work of your
hands, and your joy will be complete.

– Deuteronomy 16:15 NIV –

There's a big difference between dreamers and doers. Doers live out their dreams, while dreamers constantly talk about how they will one day change the world. But it never gets beyond idle talk. The problem with most dreamers is their desire for control, predictability and security. The Roman philosopher Tacitus said the desire for safety always stands in the way of the good intentions of those who merely dream of changing the world.

Doers are very different from dreamers. Doers never sleep through their dreams. They constantly search for the fastest and most effective routes between the vision that God placed in their hearts, and their hands and feet. Doers give body to their dreams. Their calling is to take God's people forward and closer to the manifestation of His vision. Therefore, doers are brave individuals who don't allow believers to fall into spiritual comfort zones. They're not interested in winning any spiritual popularity contests, or in being the center of attention.

No, they fulfill their calling by empowering others to give wings to the vision that God placed in their hearts through His Spirit. So then, are you a dreamer or a doer?

Built for Relationships

Do nothing out of selfish ambition or vain conceit,
but in humility consider others better than yourselves.

– Philippians 2:3 NIV –

Genesis 2 tells us that there was trouble in the Garden of Eden, of all places. The reason: Adam was home alone and relationship hungry! He couldn't find a soul mate. God said this was not good, since man was not made to be alone.

All these "Rambo" figures that take on the world alone might be Hollywood's idea of success, but it's false. No human is an island. We're built for relationships. We long for God and other people. We want to cherish and love. Our hearts remain restless until we find rest in the arms of God, but also in the closeness of others.

From His side, God also yearns for a living relationship with everyone bearing His signature. We are His artwork, His personal property. We are the highlight of His beautiful creation. That's why He sent His Son to look for us when we were lost in the dark. When we wandered the farthest from Him, Jesus came, caught up with us, and accompanied us back to the Garden. By the way, there's still some space left in Paradise Street. Move back there immediately, back into the relationship where you belong!

Sharing

John answered them all, "I baptize you with water.
But one more powerful than I will come, the thongs
of whose sandals I am not worthy to untie. He
will baptize you with the Holy Spirit and with fire."

– Luke 3:16 NIV –

John the Baptist's words to the soldiers, tax collectors and poor – who asked him what they should do to live in the right relationship with God – touches my heart immensely (Luke 3). No, he doesn't offer them some quick escape route to heaven. Neither does he offer them a safe bomb-shelter to protect them from life's assaults. On the contrary, John brought heaven down to earth by saying that he who has two sets of clothing should give one set away to those who have less. Soldiers needed to learn to be happy with their pay, and tax collectors needed to stop making unfair profits.

John doesn't teach people who suffer to passively wait for help from elsewhere else. Even the poorest of the poor have something to share. This is an important biblical principle that we often overlook. The poor widow who gives her last couple of cents to God in Luke 21 is a good example of this. At that very moment when she gave everything she had she became the latest spiritual millionaire. Our faith shines the brightest through the money and stuff we give away. Even the poorest among us can share something of ourselves with others.

In Remembrance

"I tell you the truth, wherever the gospel is
preached throughout the world, what she has
done will also be told, in memory of her."

– Mark 14:9 NIV –

This is how Jesus responded to the remarkable woman who poured a bottle of very expensive perfume over His head at a dinner in Bethany. It was more than a year's income for the average person in Palestine that she "wasted" on Jesus. But it was exactly the right kind of wasting! It was the right thing to do since Jesus was the recipient.

To pour out your life before the Lord, by giving your money, talents, time and energy to Him in an overly generous way, might seem like a useless waste in the eyes of those around you. However, that's not the case when the Lord is the Recipient.

Learn from this woman that the wasting of earthly things is in order sometimes. Learn from the Lord's contemporary heroes who are doing such wasting in the proper way. Go and practice the art of over-the-top wastefulness in such a way that heaven and earth will start noticing. It's not too late.

Living Generously

You should remember the words of the Lord
Jesus: "It is more blessed to give than to receive."
– Acts 20:35 NLT –

Paul's farewell speech to the church in Ephesus in Acts 20 on the island of Milete touches my heart over and over again. It should be one of the more well-known and popular texts in the church than is the case today. Especially precious are the apostle's words that he worked hard to always have something to give to the poor. This verse belongs in the same category as John 3:16, the Lord's Prayer and Psalm 23. Why not? It's the heart of God, pure and simply expressed.

In these deep words of Paul we encounter the true heart of the gospel in a nutshell, namely that we must always live generously. That's what the gospel is all about – giving, not receiving. And not storing up things just for ourselves. We don't work only for our own retirement package or the next luxury item on our never-ending shopping list. No, we also work hard to be able to care for those who are suffering. Our biggest investment in God's kingdom is to reach out every time we encounter someone who is less privileged than ourselves. So, how about a fresh re-appreciation of Acts 20:35 today, here and now?

Spiritual Finesse

Start with GOD – the first step in learning
is bowing down to GOD; only fools thumb
their noses at such wisdom and learning.

– Proverbs 1:7 THE MESSAGE –

Some have it ... others don't. I'm speaking about spiritual finesse. In the book of Proverbs it's called wisdom. Wisdom, the type that starts with reverence for God according to Proverbs 1:7, touches your daily life dramatically. This kind of wisdom is to know when to say your say, and when to keep your mouth closed. It's to never storm blindly into any situation with an artificial quick fix. Wisdom makes you dare to do God's will, but also mindful of the traps of folly.

Spiritual finesse is to know the difference between wisdom and folly and to apply that knowledge wisely. Where do you find this type of finesse? Listen afresh to Proverbs where it's taught that it all starts with a life of dedication to God. Wisdom is equal to full-time, day in and night out respect for the Lord. This type of wisdom is the reason why you can't help but treat other people with respect. Respect for God continually flows over into respect for other people.

Such a life filled to the brim with spiritual finesse causes you to read the "handle with care!" sticker on others every time ... and to respect it!

Danger

"My grace is enough; it's all you need."
– 2 Corinthians 12:9 THE MESSAGE –

Experts say that one of the biggest dangers staring modern society in the face is our endless consumer mentality. Too many people are like bottomless pits who need to satisfy one desire after the other ... here and now. Tomorrow is way too late, because tomorrow there's already a new CD, cell phone, car or set of clothes that must be acquired. How true was this in the festive season just passed? It was barely over and people descended on every possible sale like vultures. Our closets are taking strain. Our houses are stacked, and still the end is not in sight!

How tragic that the abundance of possessions has become the yardstick for measuring success in our day. But the question still remains: When is enough finally enough? One can walk around in only one set of clothes at a time, and drive around in only one car at a time. Are the lives of consumers truly filled with peace when they have all the right things to their name? No, because I suspect they are still drinking at the wrong well. Living water is found elsewhere – at Jesus' well of life. Only His water gives life eternally.

Junk In, Junk Out!

Guard your heart above all else, for
it determines the course of your life.

– Proverbs 4:23 NLT –

You are what you watch! Watching television isn't always just an innocent time-killer. It forms your thoughts. It shapes your humanity without you even realizing it. No wonder television addiction is highlighted by social researchers as one of the biggest inhibitors of our psychological health and relational adaptability. It changes far too many good people into lazy couch potatoes and robs them of their creative thoughts and active participation in the rest of life. TV time is often wasted time.

Choose carefully what you watch. Watch with discernment. No, you don't have to be against everything and everyone on the tube. It definitely won't help to throw out the baby with the bathwater. There are still valuable lessons to be learned from movies, stories, and other programs. Let your faith in Jesus Christ be the filter through which you watch television. Let your core values of respect, caring and integrity take new lessons from everything you watch. Share this with others. Use the lessons you learn as conversation points to teach people to watch differently, to think differently, to live differently. Let television work for you rather than the other way around.

Being Thankful

> Since we are receiving a kingdom that is
> unshakable, let us be thankful and please God
> by worshiping Him with holy fear and awe.
>
> – Hebrews 12:28 NLT –

You're not a victim of your emotions. You can be thankful every day. You can have an "attitude of gratitude" lifestyle. How? Here are a few pointers:

Choose to live every day proactively in the Lord's name, never merely reactively. Refuse to react to everyone and everything. You don't have to have an opinion about everything under the sun.

Don't get attached to strangers in a dysfunctional manner. Don't allow bad drivers or criminals to fill you with anger. Detach yourself emotionally from negative people. Don't allow them to pull you down. Don't seek revenge. God has freed you from "an eye for an eye" and "a tooth for a tooth" games long ago. Don't play along.

Show thankfulness in little ways to every person you encounter today. Be quick to thank them. Give suitable compliments often. Pray with someone regularly.

Count the blessings in your life today and thank God willfully for these. Live today's portion of life in a rhythm of thankfulness, not a "shuffle of critique."

From Chaos to Calm

God is our refuge and strength,
an ever-present help in trouble.

– Psalm 46:1 NIV –

In one moment even the stormiest seas can become calm. In the blink of an eye huge storms can abate. The same can also happen in your life. Chaos can instantaneously make room for peace. Noise can be replaced by soft silence in an instant. Unrest can be chased away by heavenly peace. How? Just realize afresh that the Lord is God. He alone! Believe the Word that the Lord is with you right there in the storm. Believe the Word that He is the only hiding place in time of danger.

Subside. Calm down. Come to rest. Let your heart become still and calm. Let your turbulent mood find a hiding place at the Lord's feet. Look up. Notice the Lord, high over nations and far above the dead gods of this world. See Him in faith. Bow gently before Him in the name of Jesus. Kneel in worship.

Know that the Lord is the Almighty. He has all power in His hands. He alone is Lord, only He. He is your only Hope, your only Savior. Notice Him, and come to rest in His presence. Look up to Him and experience His heavenly peace.

God's Dreams

"Before I formed you in the womb I knew you."

– Jeremiah 1:5 NIV –

God dreams, and He dreams big. He dreams about a new world, one where His will prevails. He dreams about a society where hate comes second, and injustice loses. He dreams about the poor having enough food to eat and about lonely people being cared for. He dreams about people who live together safely and who love one another. He dreams about His kingdom spreading across the earth like a runaway bushfire, and billions of people bowing before Jesus. He dreams of people who discover His treasure in the field, as Jesus tells us in Matthew 13, and then surrender everything to get hold of it.

God dreams new dreams. Here's the good news – you have a pertinent place in God's dreams. He noticed you when He dreamed big about people and His creation. He wants to use you to make His dreams a reality. You should report for duty at once. He'll take care of the rest. The Lord will cause streams of living water to flow through you. He'll use you to touch the lives of those around you. He will give His dreams wings in and through your life. So, what are you waiting for?

Unconditional Love

What marvelous love the Father has extended to
us! Just look at it – we're called children of God!

– 1 John 3:1 THE MESSAGE –

I'm sold out on Philip Yancey's definition of grace. In his book
What's So Amazing about Grace? he says there is nothing we
can do to make God love us less, and there is nothing we can
do to make God love us more. He loves us regardless. God
loves us on Christ's behalf. He loves us despite ourselves, not
because of who and what we are. God's amazing love is not
performance driven; it is always relationship based. Listen
again … He doesn't look at who does the most for Him and
then loves those people more. He doesn't love us more when
we are obedient and less when we fail.

God is our Father. That's why His love for us is a constant
reality. It comes without a performance clause that's flourish-
ing everywhere in the business world. Grace is nothing more
different than God's free caring for us. Grace is a godly verb.
It says that Jesus is on our heels with a handful of fresh goodness. That's why grace is also a rest-word for you and me.
Now then, stop running. Go and rest in God's arms. He'll do
the rest. He loves you.

A New Identity

You are all one in Christ Jesus.

– Galatians 3:28 NLT –

Someone I know bought a new house a couple of years ago. While he was working in his new garden, a neighbor came over with some tea. She asked, "Is the master of the house here?" He naughtily replied that the master would only be home that evening. She inquired at the front door again that evening. When he opened the door, she said, "Oh, I see you are the butler, too!" After he corrected her in a friendly way they became really good neighbors.

Unfortunately, such misunderstandings and faulty perceptions are daily realities. Luckily, Paul teaches in Ephesians 2 that Christ permanently demolished the wall of separation between Jew and non-Jew. There is now a new generation of people who follow Jesus and who are blind to man-defined differences such as nationality, ethnicity, gender or social status. The apostle reiterates this point in Galatians 3:28. As followers of Jesus, we don't need to erect "safety barriers" around us to protect our identity. Our identity is seated in Christ.

Our lives are now all about Him in whom we find our safety and peace – only about Him! That's why the differences between ourselves and others need not threaten us at all.

Life in Abundance

Don't copy the behavior and customs of this world, but
let God transform you into a new person by changing
the way you think. Then you will learn to know God's
will for you, which is good and pleasing and perfect.

– Romans 12:2 NLT –

Live abundantly! Live generously. For a change, live on "abundance hill" instead of in "shortage valley." How? Give away, that's how! Give generously, give excessively, and give constantly. What should you give away? No, the question is not what, but who. Give yourself. As a rule, don't primarily give away your money ... or your valuable time. Give of yourself. The Lord asks your whole life. He asks all your commitment, time, and energy. Give yourself generously and profusely to Him. Let your life be God's full-time temple! Don't hold back.

Also give yourself to others. Be present with your whole heart to everyone in whose presence you find yourself each day ... but not only with your head. Also not with a few crumbles of left-over time that you found somewhere deep in your diary. Give your heart to every person that the Lord wants you to serve today. Then you're living abundantly. Then your heart is truly free. Then you realize how the treasure chambers of heaven open up.

Opinions

Your words are my joy and my heart's delight.

– Jeremiah 15:16 NLT –

"Everyone is entitled to an opinion," someone says. "And to their own idea of the truth," he adds. "Yes, surely, but does that mean that all opinions are equal?" I wanted to know. Danger lights start flashing when every thinkable opinion is considered to be valid. Of course we can look at life in many different ways, but there is also right and wrong. This applies from traffic rules to the most basic questions about God and life.

My compass for truth is the Bible. It is the life book for everyone who wants to live in tune with God's will. No, the Bible is not a book to hurt others with. Nor is it a verse book from which a few favorite texts can be drawn arbitrarily and the rest forgotten. It is also not a scientific handbook by which today's scientists need to be proven right or wrong.

When the Bible is read correctly, it becomes medicine. The Bible is a compass pointing directly to Christ. But then I need to read it book by book and understand the context within which it was written correctly. Then the Bible shapes my conscience correctly and in the right direction.

Honesty

An honest witness tells the truth.

– Proverbs 12:17 NLT –

I wonder if people also crack jokes in the company of dietitians, like, "Now we must be careful what we eat, because there's a dietitian present ..."? Strangely, some people feel that they need to make funny remarks in the presence of spiritual leaders, such as, "We should watch what we say now, because the pastor is here." Masters of ceremony at weddings often fall into this trap.

Once at a wedding the MC even came and apologized to me after he let loose some rough jokes on the crowd. "You are at the wrong address," I answered him. "I think you need the Lord's forgiveness more than mine right now."

That's all I could think of saying at that moment. Tactful? Maybe not quite. However, for a while now I don't sing in that choir of religious folks who are burdened by other people's behavior in secret, but don't do anything about it in public. I don't want to be as tactful as some people who don't do anything about what's wrong except to be worried about it. That's why I opt for honesty, even though it sometimes can be costly.

A Grandfather in Heaven

I am convinced that neither death nor life, neither angels
nor demons, neither the present nor the future, nor any
powers, neither height nor depth, nor anything else in all
creation, will be able to separate us from the love of God.

– Romans 8:38-39 NIV –

In his phenomenal book *The Problem of Pain,* the well-known theologian and Christian thinker, C. S. Lewis, asks if the world really wants a father in heaven. He thinks many people rather want a heavenly grandfather. They want a forgetful figure who lost track with reality and whose only desire is for everyone to have a good time here on earth. These words of Lewis give expression to many people's naïve idea of a universal deity that plays heavenly nanny and constantly needs to fulfill our requirements and all our desires. For the rest, it is better that He stays out of humanity's way. Obviously, this is not a reliable, biblical view of God.

God is not the one who needs to ensure that my life is a constant ball. Sometimes, pain and suffering is exactly the megaphone the Lord uses to reach a deaf world, as C. S. Lewis puts it. God's presence is definitely not equal to the absence of hurt and hardship. That's humanity's big mistake about God. Even clergy fall into this trap. That's why rediscovering the words of Romans 8 is so important today – God is always near, in prosperity and in pain.

While We Are Sleeping

I will lie down and sleep in peace, for You
alone, O LORD, make me dwell in safety.

– Psalm 4:8 NIV –

Your faith does not only happen when you're awake. Put differently, your trust in God ought to have a direct influence on how you sleep every night. The psalmist tells us in Psalm 3 that he lies down in peace and falls asleep instantly, even when a thousand people are storming toward him. He knows his life is permanently in God's hands, even when he closes his eyes at night. He knows God does not sleep, as Psalm 121 tells us. God is never off duty – never! He is awake 24/7 and 365 days of the year.

When you and I are in dreamland, God is wide awake. That's why we can trust Him with our lives and those of our loved ones when we close our tired eyes at night. Even our dreams should bring us closer to God, says the well-known Christian song.

We are always in the hands of the living Lord. Therefore, we can lie down in peace, even though the land is on fire. We can even trust God, in the words of Psalm 127:3, to give us what we need while we are sleeping every single night!

God Is in Control

We know that God causes everything to work
together for the good of those who love God and
are called according to His purpose for them.

– Romans 8:28 NLT –

A few years ago, Lloyd's Bank of London tried to determine what happens to all the paperclips in their bank. Of the approximate 100,000 in use then, close to 25,000 ended up in vacuum cleaners or were thrown away; 14,163 were broken from excessive bending during telephone conversations; 4,434 were used for scratching ears or cleaning teeth; and only 20,286 were used as paperclips. In short, even the simplest of items – like paperclips invented by Samuel B. Fay in 1867 – are used in ways other than intended.

It seems to me that if we can't even control the use of paperclips, we will far less likely be able to control each other or the flow of life. Maybe it was never our calling to do so. The secret of life is simply to love God and each other. And to find daily joy in simplicity, as Ecclesiastes teaches us. That's why God's invitation to us is to eat our food with pleasure and create joy before God with daily portions of simplicity. When we stop trying to control everyone and start trusting God to provide for us in His way, we make joy a welcome expectation in our lives.

Never Give Up

You yourself must be an example to them by doing
good works of every kind. Let everything you do
reflect the integrity and seriousness of your teaching.

– Titus 2:7 NLT –

In his excellent book *The Orthodox Heretic*, the amazing church leader and author Peter Rollins tells the tale of a lady named Sophia who had a dream to translate the Bible into her local language. After more than 15 years of begging in her poor community, she had enough money for the big project. Then tragedy struck a neighboring town. Immediately Sophia gave all the money she had so arduously collected to the victims, and started collecting money again from scratch.

Nine years later Sophia had enough money to again start the Bible translation. But then another big tragedy struck nearby. On the spot she gave all the money away once again to help those in need. Hereafter, as an old lady, Sophia started gathering money for her Bible translation project for a third time. This time she was successful, and after a few years the Bible was translated into the local language. Shortly after this translation was completed Sophia died.

At her funeral it was said that she translated the Bible three times during her lifetime, of which the first two were the most successful. What a woman. Follow in her footsteps!

February

Grace and Forgiveness

Make a clean break with all cutting, backbiting,
profane talk. Be gentle with one another,
sensitive. Forgive one another as quickly and
thoroughly as God in Christ forgave you.

– Ephesians 4:31-32 THE MESSAGE –

The guilty party in an illegal money-making scheme was caught and thrown into jail. Everyone in the local community, where this fraudster was also a well-respected leading figure, was deeply shocked. Many of them lost their life savings by investing in this man's money-making scheme. Shortly afterward, the local priest preached a sermon where he praised God that justice was done and that this man was behind bars. He seriously prayed that the church members would be repaid their losses.

When a congregation member who also lost everything suggested that they all visit the fraudster in jail and pray for him, everyone was shocked. "We are not ready for such action yet. Our people got hurt too badly," was the official reply. The man decided to go alone. In jail, he knelt next to the fraudster who had robbed him. Together they prayed for grace and forgiveness. That day the Lord's grace was visible in the jail. Christ showed up there as Savior. Thereafter, these two started a wonderful prison ministry. And the religious townspeople? Well, they remained bitter.

February 2

Machine Versus Organism

You must grow in the grace and knowledge
of our Lord and Savior Jesus Christ. All
glory to Him, both now and forever! Amen.

– 2 Peter 3:18 NLT –

There's a very important difference between a machine and a living organism. Machines are impressive, but machines can't grow. Machines become more powerful, but never more alive. Machines are clones of one another. They work exactly the same. Unfortunately, some people think and live like machines, even in the church. You soon realize when someone has a machine-like approach ... they stack everyone in the same boring boxes. They expect everyone to talk, think and act the same.

We need to rediscover a sense of the beautiful and unique ways in which God deals with each of us. We are not living machines. Each of us is precious, growing and constantly changing. The Lord is busy, at his own tempo and with endless heavenly wisdom, shaping everyone who believes in Christ into His image. Let's refuse to go through life in a clinical way, without emotion – like machines. Let's take up our places in the Lord's large earthly vineyard where a unique grace-spot is reserved for each of us. With Him there's more than enough space, grace, food and water for everyone. He offers exactly the right type of growth-power for every one of us.

Jesus – The New Hobby?

Humility and the fear of the LORD
bring wealth and honor and life.

– Proverbs 22:4 NIV –

Jesus has become a hobby for far too many people. Whenever they show up at His "place" on Sundays He must entertain them with good sermons and fine worship music. Sadly, Jesus must make people feel good all the time. That is His job description according to many. Apparently He is there to serve the selfish needs of people. Well, Jesus is not for sale, like a toy on the shelf of any store. You do not play around with Him and decide at your own leisure when and how you will allow Him into your life. He is the Son of God. He is the Messiah, not little Jesus, the meek and mild toy for those bored, selfish, egotistic, me-myself-and-I "Christian" types.

Read the stern warnings in Jesus' own words before you decide to walk with Him: death, rejection, disappointment, a cross, far more questions than answers, suffering, joy, a strange happiness, true service ... these experiences will become your companions on the road with Jesus. He will lead you on new routes. He will also let you discover old and new treasures in his Father's house that will fill you with a strange new joy, but then on His terms alone.

Giving

But when He, the Spirit of truth, comes,
He will guide you into all truth.

– John 16:13 NIV –

"I give to my church." Have you ever said these words to beggars or those people who collect money on the street for welfare organizations? May I ask an uncomfortable question? Is your responsibility suddenly dealt with because you make a monthly contribution at your congregation? Is the reach of your calling inside God's kingdom only as far as the boundaries of your local church? Does your monthly contribution set you free from the responsibility to help people that appear unexpectedly on your radar?

Have you ever considered that the first and last line of relief is not only your local church, but also you yourself? Did you forget that helping the poor is like making a loan to God, as the book of Proverbs teaches? You are a full-time, daily representative of Christ. That's why it is not right to say you only make contributions at your local church. Open yourself to be where God asks you to be. Be His full-time 911 relief number. No, you can't help everyone. But be sensitive to the guidance of the Spirit. Give extravagantly when He calls on you! Give as a sacrifice!

Dissatisfaction

May the words of my mouth and the meditation
of my heart be pleasing in Your sight, O LORD.

– Psalm 19:14 NIV –

People's nerves are at breaking point nowadays. At least, so it seems to me. Recently, when cash registers at a certain shop were not functioning, and that on the first Saturday of the month, there were many unhappy faces. The poor personnel got much attention from some sharp tongues. When my wife remarked to the lady behind the cash register that it can't be nice to constantly be spoken to in such a harsh way, she was in tears on the spot.

I know I am the last one to speak, but we seriously need to stop finding fault with everything, and constantly complain about bad service. We criticize way too much and too easily. Our faith needs to be felt in the way that we drive our cars, treat our housekeepers, or speak to cashiers.

Our smallest deeds tell way more about ourselves than we will ever realize. And also about our relationship with God! Coincidentally, it is in these simple matters that we write most of our faith exams. What does it help that we are faithful in all the big things, but are found wanting in the smaller matters?

Unremarkable

This is the day the LORD has made;
let us rejoice and be glad in it.

– Psalm 118:24 NIV –

"My life is completely unremarkable," someone told me recently. "Bleak days, bleak clothes, bleak happenings – that's more or less the story of my life," she concluded. Ouch! I felt so sorry for her. She sounded so discouraged and helpless. How many bleak days are slipping lifelessly through the fingers of thousands of people every single day? Maybe that is why Shirley Valentine says in the great movie of the same name: "I got lost in unused time." Don't let this happen to you.

Do what Paul suggests to the Ephesians: Buy out the time! Take the best out of every day. Let every day count. After all, you only have one day to live at a time.

Declare today a feast and invite a friend to celebrate it with you. Serve a feast to someone less privileged. Carry the burden of someone who's struggling for an extra mile. Memorize your favorite chapter of the Bible, and go and tell it cheerfully to someone else. Don't get caught up in the unremarkable. Not today. It's going to steal your soul. It's going to break you down. It's your choice!

Bigger and Better

Cast your cares on the LORD and He will sustain you.

– Psalm 55:22 NIV –

In *Prince Caspian*, the fourth book in the popular Narnia series of the larger-than-life Christian author, C. S. Lewis, there is an encounter between Aslan the Lion (who resembles Christ) and one of the little girls. After seeing him again, she tells him that he is bigger. To this Aslan replies, "That is because you are older, little one." "But aren't you bigger?" she asks him. Then he replies, "I am not. But every year you grow, you will find me bigger."

That is precisely what happens on the Lord's journey. He grows bigger and bigger in our eyes as we begin to grow in our faith. Of course He is the Almighty God, the One who transcends time and eternity. He *is* big. He *is* the Lord, whether people grasp that or not. God is not dependent on our recognition, knowledge or acceptance.

Still, the more we learn to walk close to Christ, the more we see the Lord's glory. Then our problems and worries shrink. Do you know something of this reversed growth journey? The bigger the Lord grows in your life, the more all your cares dissipate.

Integrity

"When you pray, go into your room, close the door and
pray to your Father, who is unseen. Then your Father,
who sees what is done in secret, will reward you."

– Matthew 6:6 NIV –

Integrity is a verb ... it happens. Integrity is not automatically
the same as religious deeds. In Matthew 6:1-18, Jesus says
that religion can easily be practiced without integrity. Deeds
like prayer, fasting, and helping the poor can be misused to
earn respect in the eyes of others. Therefore, followers of Jesus
should deliberately choose not to do things merely to be seen
by others. God's approval matters most to them. They choose
to live outside of the spotlight, not on the *stage* of life.

Integrity happens, even if no one else knows about it. You
don't have to give big testimonies, or enjoy favor in the eyes
of everyone before you start having integrity. Integrity is first
and foremost about your deep, enduring love for the Lord.
Integrity shows in your genuineness and character in the eyes
of the living God. Integrity also happens in all those critical
choices that you make daily that no one knows about. Choices like whether you will look at filth on the Internet, whether
you will help a poor person without making a scene about it,
whether you will pack away your prejudices about others that
irritate you ... again and again. The choices you make in such
instances reveal whether you have integrity or not.

Prayer

Be joyful always, pray continually, give
thanks in all circumstances; for this
is God's will for you in Christ Jesus.

– 1 Thessalonians 5:16-18 NIV –

Father of all grace and goodness,
In the name of Christ I rest at Your feet
In still reverence I look up at You
Your greatness is far too big for me to comprehend
Your goodness is too overwhelming to understand
But the little that I do grasp of You makes me joyful
It causes me to leave myself and my loved ones
in Your care today
Holy God, Your approval really counts the most of all
Your love is all that matters
That's why Your praise is all that's on my lips today
And why my life wants to sing Your praise
Teach me to serve You well
Lord please be merciful; Lord be close
Let Your light shine everywhere
Let Your wisdom be our wisdom
In Jesus' name,
Amen.

Life in CAPITAL LETTERS

Live a life filled with love, following the example
of Christ. He loved us and offered Himself
as a sacrifice for us, a pleasing aroma to God.

– Ephesians 5:2 NLT –

Martin Luther King, Jr. once said that even if you have a lowly job you should do it with the same commitment and enthusiasm that Michelangelo relied on when he was sculpting his great works, or that Mozart used in composing his genial music. That's also what Paul meant when he wrote in Colossians 3 that everything we do and say should glorify God. Put another way, the Lord's name should preside in CAPITAL LETTERS over every word we speak and everything we do. Like a flashing advertising board, our lives should reflect God's splendor and importance.

How do you live your life in the right CAPITAL LETTERS? Well, you invite God humbly to be the Guest of Honor in your life every day. Ensure that He's the Guest of Honor in every conversation you have. Then all your words will be carefully chosen, tasteful and uplifting. Ensure that the Lord is the Witness to everything you do. Then your work will be done for His glory alone and not primarily for your boss or company. Then you'll do your work with pride, thoroughness, and commitment. Your light will shine for Christ in new ways.

Trust God

Trust in the LORD with all your heart; do not depend
on your own understanding. Seek His will in all
you do, and He will show you which path to take.

– Proverbs 3:5-6 NLT –

It's not uncommon for us to be overly protective of those who
are close to us. As parents we want to protect our kids from
the rough edges of life. We also like to go the extra mile for
our close family and friends. However, we can't always be
physically there for each other. And it's surely not always the
wisest thing on earth to try and keep our loved ones away
from the adventures of life, even though life is full of dangers,
challenges, and surprises. Sadly, life doesn't happen on some
cloud, but right here in the real world fraught with danger.
This side of the grave, life isn't perfect.

Maybe our calling is rather to pray for those we love while
they are living in the danger zones of life, rather than to keep
them hidden. We should rather keep their names in front of
our heavenly Father.

We should trust God with their lives, and pray that He
keeps them safe and on the right path. We need to trust God
to guide us and our loved ones in life *and* death.

Depreciating with Age

Therefore we do not lose heart. Though
outwardly we are wasting away, yet
inwardly we are being renewed day by day.

– 2 Corinthians 4:16 NIV –

Depreciation is a problem that affects most items in our homes. At some time or another, the value of all earthly possessions decreases, sometimes so much that they become completely worthless. Take something like a new car. The moment you drive out of the dealer's showroom its value plummets by thousands of dollars! Equally sad is that people are also the victims of depreciation. The older we get, the less consumer value we have to society around us.

The same does not apply to God. The Bible teaches us that the exact opposite happens in His presence. Paul says in 2 Corinthians that even as our bodies are wasting away, inwardly we are being renewed day by day. Followers of Jesus are on an upward-sloping growth curve. Because God is busy with an appreciation exercise in us, our value and quality increases continually. Day by day we grow substantially in wisdom and spiritual knowledge. Above all, we move closer to our wonderful final destination. Therefore, we can and must live with joy. Even when we feel lonely or rejected we are valuable in the hands of God. Our worth increases before Him. Appreciation is our new password.

Living with Purpose

I have fought the good fight, I have finished
the race, and I have remained faithful.

– 2 Timothy 4:7 NLT –

Many years ago, good friends of mine involved their elderly friend Ernie in the youth ministry of their church. Ernie stayed involved until his death in his nineties. Ernie's work at the youth ministry was to pack the dishwasher every Wednesday evening after they served a great feast to the youngsters.

One day Ernie told my friends that he asked the Lord the previous night to take him home. At this stage he was deaf in both ears and could no longer bear the deep longing for his late wife. But then he thought of all the young people that he served and wondered who would pack and unpack the dishwasher after they spent time together each week. Right there Ernie chose to carry on living with a new vigor. He did exactly that until the end of his life. Ernie knew that once the race was over, Jesus would be waiting for him with the crown of righteousness in His hand (vv. 7-8). That's why he couldn't stop living or stop running before the race was over. Just like Ernie, we are called by God to live with purpose, no matter how old or young we are.

The Hairs on Your Head

"Even the very hairs of your head are all numbered."
– Matthew 10:30 NIV –

Those guys who shave their heads, and those of us whose hair is getting less and less by the day, are making things easy for God. There's far less hair left on our heads to count! On a more serious note, Jesus says in Matthew that God is so close to us that He even numbers the hairs on our heads. He knows how many of those hairs fall out every day. If I can remember correctly, I read somewhere that a normal person loses on average about 125 per day. None of them escapes heaven's attention.

Why do we receive such special attention? The answer's simple: As followers of Jesus, we are God's most precious earthly assets. We are His handiwork. We are His permanent property. That's why the Lord carries us around in His hand every day, as Jesus tells us in John 10:28-30. Absolutely nothing that happens in our lives ever escapes His attention. He hears every prayer that passes from our lips in the name of His Son. He knows of every step that we take. He is in attendance at every conversation that we have. The Lord is involved in the detail of all that we do. He that numbers the hairs on our heads is in our vicinity again today.

Memory Loss

The LORD is compassionate and merciful,
slow to get angry and filled with unfailing love.

– Psalm 103:8 NLT –

Do you ever close that little black book in which you carefully record other people's mistakes and shortcomings? Do you go to bed angry night after night? Well, here's a newsflash if you struggle with amnesia regarding other people's misdemeanors: God suffers from memory loss. He gladly forgets people's sins, shortcomings, failures, wrong deeds, defects and factory faults. He doesn't worry about everything people do wrong against Him, as we learn in Psalm 103. Even better, He forgets every time, over and over again. For whom does He do this? Well, for everyone that knocks on His door in the name of Jesus.

God is forgetful when it comes to those things that people bring to Him in remorse. The reason? There's not enough storage space in God's heavenly home for all our written-off faults and paid-off accounts. The cross of Calvary is the permanent heavenly eraser in His hand. Grace says in five life-changing letters that God is on our side. It says that He fully loves us no matter how deep and far we have fallen. Grace says that God starts over time and again in our lives. He forgives and forgets. He closes old books forever.

A Spectator Sport

"I have come that they may
have life, and have it to the full."

– John 10:10 NIV –

Pavilions are wonderful places. From there, you can shout anything from praise to criticism. You can encourage the players on the field, or you can write them off. But best of all – after the match you can go home untouched. All that your loyalty costs is a tired voice and a glad or not-so-glad heart, depending on the outcome.

Spectators are normally friendly ... as long as their team is winning. But, when their team is losing, they become critical. Therefore, the only guys making a real difference are the players on the field. For them, the match is far more than a time-killer for a few hours every week. They make huge sacrifices. They give their hearts and bodies for their sport.

We must decide once and for all whether we're players or spectators on the playing-field of faith. God doesn't want us not to consider our faith as a spectator sport. The Lord asks that we turn our playing-field into His territory. We don't know whether we'll get another playing opportunity tomorrow. But, at least we've received today as a gift from heaven. Therefore, we can't dare being spectators on some church pavilion. Let's play with full commitment on the Lord's playing-field, according to His instructions.

No Safe Bid

God called you to do good, even if it means
suffering, just as Christ suffered for you. He is
your example, and you must follow in His steps.

– 1 Peter 2:21 NLT –

Just listen to those wishes we express at the beginning of the new year or on someone's birthday. Such wishes are normally "safe." They teem with words like happiness, health, and prosperity. It's fine to express a wish that good things will happen to another person on their journey, but are these the only good things in life? Is it only in prosperity that your faith grows? Is life only about green pastures and still waters? Or isn't the deep, dark valley of Psalm 23 maybe one of God's favorite places of growth?

What about a daring challenge today? One like provocateur and author Erwin McManus signs in his books: "Risk everything!" Isn't that exactly what we need sometimes in our faith? Even more, is faith as such not a constant challenge? Isn't it the chance of a lifetime to walk with the living God? Faith asks for courage in the midst of disbelief, selfishness and opposition. As Paul tells us in Romans 8, faith asks that we must carry on hoping despite all hopelessness. It asks for boldness to walk on God's heels when you'd rather be going off in your own direction.

Unfashionable

We are being transformed into His
likeness with ever-increasing glory, which
comes from the Lord, who is the Spirit.

– 2 Corinthians 3:18 NIV –

"You have to take me just as I am," a difficult church member told me once. "Why?" I asked. "Well, that's just how it is since I'm not the one that's going to change," he replied. "No, you're wrong," I said. Second Corinthians 3:18 teaches us that God's Spirit transforms us into the likeness of Christ with ever-increasing glory. We are definitely not lifelong victims of ourselves, our education or circumstances. We don't have the luxury of staying as we are for the rest of our lives. Christ gives us the grace *and* the privilege to change and grow.

Too many people around us are victims of this member's "I can't change" syndrome. That's why negative issues such as our deep-rooted prejudices toward each other still run strong, despite our "deep religiosity." Does this happen because we believe we have the right to think like we always did? Does it happen because in church we often only speak about faith or moral sins while dodging questions about how we need to treat each other across cultural and racial divides? Or maybe because we ourselves are such bad examples of true transformation in this area? Listen, we can change. No. God can change us ... and He will!

Danger Zone

"I have told you these things, so that in Me you
may have peace. In this world you will have trouble.
But take heart! I have overcome the world."

– John 16:33 NIV –

Some believers are caught up between the church and the
world. They prefer to spend more time in what they consider
God's exclusive terrain, the world of the church. There they
feel safe. There God's Word resounds and there He is praised.
The "real world" outside the church is dangerous and unpredictable for those who prefer the safety and predictability of
religious bomb shelters. No wonder they keenly use texts
such as 2 Corinthians 6:14-7:1 as their motivation to stay clear
of the "sinful world."

Does Paul mean that we should build the walls of our
religious shelters thicker and wider when bad things happen
around us? Should we see the world as a place of enmity
where "we" take a stand against "them"? Should we withdraw
ourselves from the world and only be busy with "spiritual"
things? Should others first become exactly like us before we
make space for them in our midst? I don't think so. Paul didn't
mean that we as followers of Jesus should flee or withdraw to
religious bomb shelters. What he meant in 2 Corinthians 6 is
that our lifestyle should be radically different.

The Harbor or the Storm?

I know the LORD is always with me. I will
not be shaken, for He is right beside me.

– Psalm 16:8 NLT –

Think with me about the following question: Where do you discern God's will the clearest – in the harbor, or in the storm? Let me explain – with the harbor I mean the well-known religious terrain among fellow believers in church or Bible studies. The storm represents the everyday world with its unpredictability, dangers, unbelievers, and challenges. Listen to that question again: Where do you discern God's will the clearest – in the harbor or in the storm?

Let me make it easier. Think about Jesus' behavior on earth. Now, where did He spend most of His time – in religious harbors, or in dangerous storms? Was Jesus more often among the religious, or more often among the doubters, sinners, outcast, strangers, losers ... ? I think you know the answer – obviously Jesus spent more time amongst the non-religious! Why? Because He came specifically for those people, as He says in Mark 1.

If it's true that Jesus spent more time in the storms than in the "safe harbors," where should we then spend most of our time? In the storm, of course. Now why are we always trying to discern God's will in spiritual harbors? Let's all get back to stormy waters.

Hindering God's Work

Be strong and do not give up,
for your work will be rewarded.

– 2 Chronicles 15:7 NIV –

I often think of a pastor who once told me that God works when we get out of the way. That's why he spends his time practicing how to get out of God's way. Wise words! I know that I sometimes stand squarely in the way of the Lord's work. I often speak without being asked for my opinion. At other times, there are no brakes to my eagerness to work. Mistake!

It seems like the best way to get out of the way is to discover God's heavenly rhythms. Sometimes He's in a hurry. Then we don't have the luxury of sitting still and waiting, like when Lot and his family had to flee to escape the destruction of Sodom.

At other times, God seems to have years of patience. Just ask Abraham. At the age of 75, God asked him to move. But God only fulfilled His promise of a child 25 years later (Gen. 12-17). The required method for Lot and Abraham, and their families, was to know at what speed they were journeying with God. Sadly, they failed. Lot's wife looked back and paid a dear price. Sarah and Abraham twice laughed at the Lord. Learn from them and set your pace to God's!

Teaching Stones to Talk

This hope will not lead to disappointment. For we
know how dearly God loves us, because He has given
us the Holy Spirit to fill our hearts with His love.

– Romans 5:5 NLT –

Can stones talk? Yes. When? When humanity starts silencing
God. That's what Jesus says when the religious leaders try to
silence those who are welcoming Him to Jerusalem. Maybe
we should start listening to the stones around us.

Humanity is trying to kill God's voice by silencing it, shouting louder, and looking straight past it. No wonder that we
are currently experiencing what a friend of mine once called
"a God-eclipse"! With our technologically advanced fire-ex-
tinguishers, we think we can extinguish God's burning bush.
With our clever theories about the Bible we think we have
the power and authority to do a so-called "postmortem" on
the Scriptures. And then we wonder why the world is in such
chaos and why we feel so alone.

Luckily, God's not the prisoner of our radical unbelief, anger, bitterness and arrogance. He doesn't stop being Himself
when we stop being respectful, faithful and humane. Even
then He stands unchanged. Then He still allows Himself to
be found by every seeker of grace. Then He removes every
God-eclipse as His grace flows over and eradicates our darkness. That's why today is framed with hope.

Dangerous or Tame?

You have one God and Father, who rules over
all, works through all, and is present in all.

– Ephesians 4:6 THE MESSAGE –

My favorite quote is that of Ernst Käsemann, a well-known German theologian of the previous century. He writes the following about Jesus: "People and institutions do not like to be kept continually on the alert, and they have constantly devised screens to protect themselves from too much heat. In fact, they have even managed to reduce Jesus' red-hot message, which promised to kindle a fire throughout the world, to room temperature."

What comes to mind as you read these words? Does it stop you in your tracks? I hope so. Isn't it true that we have radically "reduced the heat" of Jesus and His message? Why? In order to have Him fit neatly into our small, predictable little worlds. We have tried to change Jesus into our image instead of allowing Him to change us into His. We have tried to bring Him under control instead of Him bringing us under control and shaping us as He thinks fit. The result is that many of us are stuck with a safe and uninspiring Jesus who we encounter in church around a few moral lessons that aren't exactly life changing. Outside of that, we just carry on with our lives as usual. Let's stop this cooling-down process here and now.

Charging into the Storm

Whether you turn to the right or to the
left, your ears will hear a voice behind
you, saying, "This is the way; walk in it."

– Isaiah 30:21 NIV –

Some people are wandering around aimlessly in the wind and the weather. We should be there for them. We should serve and love them in the name of Jesus, without writing them off. Why do we then spend more time sitting in religious harbors than serving and helping out there on the open sea? Is God's will not clearly audible, visible, and tangible when we are among the poor, the lonely and the lost? Who knows, maybe that's the reason why so many believers never find God's one and only will for their lives ... they're not at the right place often enough – out there in the storm where Jesus is busy saving people who drown in their own sins and shame!

How do you get into God's rhythm of navigating the storms of life? Well, there are no quick recipes or shortcuts. It's a lifelong journey of humility, obedience, reflection on God's will, and carefully listening for the voice of His Spirit. He'll teach you how to survive and thrive in the storm. He'll help you over and over again how to be the hands and feet of Christ and how to touch the lives of those in serious need of grace.

Whatever

"Though your sins are like scarlet, they
shall be as white as snow; though they
are red as crimson, they shall be like wool."

– Isaiah 1:18 NIV –

Is the word "whatever" part of the vocabulary of Jesus? Perhaps. Often He looked at the religious people of His day who were so busy obeying their strict religious laws they didn't have any time left to serve their neighbors.

Jesus observed how the religious professionals harshly judged others that didn't obey their laws to the very last letter. Then He shook His head in dismay and said, "Whatever!" Jesus saw how the religious people rigorously obeyed harsh Sabbath laws without caring a hoot for the sick or the poor. Then He shook His head in amazement and said, "Whatever!"

Religiosity doesn't bring people a single inch closer to God. It turns many of them into self-appointed saints. It creates that us (the saints) versus them (the sinners) distinction. No wonder that religious people still don't mix with non-religious types. "If only they could change and become nice, religious people like us, we would gladly accept them into our midst." Well, Jesus just weeps at this. No, He does more than this. He invites people like you and me to join Him in His undiluted love for sinners.

The Guest of Honor

Blessed are those who are generous,
because they feed the poor.

– Proverbs 22:9 NLT –

Food is a concrete part of our faith. That's why most feasts in the Bible had to do with food and eating. Whenever the Israelites celebrated a feast in the presence of God, they ate. The "get-togethers" of the early Christians were also characterized by simple meals. Our communion is a faint representation of the early Church's festive meals. Food, joy and faith go hand-in-hand. The first Christians recognized this as important. That's why they enjoyed eating together, despite the persecution and opposition they encountered. They invited the risen Lord as a Guest of Honor to every meal.

It's sad that we're still struggling to find the proper connection between our faith and food. Yes, I know that we are in a festive setting between Christmas and New Year. But, for the rest of the year, we seem to lose our festive mood. Could that be because food just isn't "spiritual" enough for most of us? Go and learn from the first Christians and from other believers, like the writer of Ecclesiastes who found joy in the simplicity of bread and wine. Eat your bread with joy every day. Declare every meal spontaneously a feast.

False Perceptions

Wisdom will multiply your days and add years to your life.
– Proverbs 9:11 NLT –

Did you know that more people die annually across the globe as a result of falling coconuts than of shark attacks? Really! The shark researcher George Burgess found that around 150 people die annually as a result of falling coconuts. That's fifteen times more than all the people who die annually due to shark attacks. People get anxiety attacks when watching movies like *Jaws*, and sit frozen in front of National Geographic's shark programs, but no one would take a movie like *The Killer Coconut Tree* seriously.

It's funny how faulty perceptions can be formed and how easily we drink them in like lemonade on a hot day. That's why we should be careful not to be taken in by the media, text messages, e-mails, and even some religious folk.

Proverbs teaches us to continuously think about life, and to be cautious. We're not allowed to storm blindly into any situation, or believe every new rumor that's doing the rounds. Don't believe every carrier of bad news. Don't lend your ears to people who say, "Have you heard what this or that church leader has done this time?" or similar stories. Protect your ears from false stories. Stop spreading rumors.

Duty!

Whatever you do, work at it with all
your heart, as working for the Lord.

– Colossians 3:23 NIV –

Traditional English culture was built on the principle of duty. Everyone in society had certain duties that they had to fulfill – an army officer towards his troops, a husband towards his wife, citizens toward governments, members toward their churches, etc. This duty thing found its way into our society. Many things were done purely out of a sense of duty … not necessarily from an inner conviction. People fulfilled their religious duty by attending church on Sundays, by making a small monthly contribution to the church, and so forth.

Then came the new digital era that brought an abrupt end to many of these duties. All of a sudden, everyone wondered where order and discipline evaporated to. Much of what people saw as order earlier was, however, just the consequences of an outward sense of duty that everyone formally adhered to. True transformation always happens *inside* people. When you do the things you do for the Lord and others out of love instead of duty, you're doing them correctly. Duty is only fulfilled when people are driven by authoritarian figures or feelings of guilt – conversely, love always comes from the heart.

Be motivated by the words of Colossians 3.

The Salt of the Earth

"You are the salt of the earth. But what good is salt if it has
lost its flavor? Can you make it salty again? It will be thrown
out and trampled underfoot as worthless."

– Matthew 5:13 NLT –

In some places today, salt is used to repair and improve roads.
Namibia is such an example: unsaturated salt from salt pans
north of Swakopmund was used to improve the condition of
the roads along the coast. Salt is also used in cooler climates
like Canada and the U.S. to de-ice roads in winter. So it was
in Jesus' day – roads were covered with salt. It appeared to be
genuine salt, but had lost its saltiness.

In today's Scripture verse, Jesus says that we are the salt
of the earth. Elsewhere, He instructs believers to be the "salt
and light" in society. Salt is used to season and preserve food,
and in the past people even used it to flavor their tea. Salt was
highly esteemed by the Romans and at one time its army was
even paid in salt.

What the world desperately needs today is Christians who
are willing to be the salt and light in their families, schools,
churches, and communities. Our mandate is to make a difference in a dark and dying world.

On this earth, we are Jesus' hands and feet. Where do we
start? By showing His love and light one smile, one thought,
one gesture, and one act of kindness at a time.

march

Protecting Others

If you need wisdom, ask our generous God, and He
will give it to you. He will not rebuke you for asking.

– James 1:5 NLT –

Always protect the integrity of other people. It's your full-time calling as a follower of Christ to first believe the very best of other people, like 1 Corinthians 13 teaches. Read it and make this valuable spiritual lesson your own. The Lord expects you to honor, serve and respect fellow believers and all other people. Don't summarily believe unproven stories or general perceptions about them. What does faith help if you play along with the rest of the world's game of gossip, suspicion spreading and backstabbing others? Don't live with a critical heart – it'll make you spiritually sick. Rather become a thinking, careful believer that lives with God's wisdom.

Ask the Lord to give you some of His wisdom today. Read James 1 where the author says that the Lord gives wisdom to anyone who asks for it. But then we should accept and embrace it without doubting God's readiness to give. Also read portions from the book of Proverbs this week and learn a few new wisdom principles. Thank God for His flooding grace.

Pray for the heavenly wisdom that will help you discover the difference between duty and love. Pray for a society that's love driven instead of duty driven.

Invisible

Always give yourselves fully to the work of the Lord,
because you know that your labor in the Lord is not in vain.

– 1 Corinthians 15:58 NIV –

I once read an interview with the well-known South African boxing referee, Stanley Christodoulou. When asked about the greatest compliment he received as a referee, he referred to a world title fight that he handled somewhere in the USA. After the fight, he relaxed at the hotel's restaurant. Someone with whom he struck up a conversation asked whether he watched the fight earlier that evening. For Stanley it was the best compliment imaginable that he as referee was so "invisible" in the ring that the spectator didn't even recognize him.

I think as followers of Christ we must become just as invisible. We sometimes stand in the way of others seeing the Lord. Our church infighting, theological debates that's front page news daily, and our inability to love each other, are blocking our sight. Let's get out of the way. Won't it be a wonderful spiritual practice to just get out of the way and allow God to do what only He can do through His Holy Spirit? How?

Well, by a) Expecting no recognition for what we do for the Lord, b) Expecting no "thank you" when we do good for someone, c) Staying out of religious and other arguments, and d) Loving God quietly, but intimately, every day.

Happiness

There is nothing better than to be happy
and enjoy ourselves as long as we can.

– Ecclesiastes 3:12 NLT –

Followers of Jesus aren't automatically the happiest people in the world. The same applies to those of other religions. The happiest people on earth are apparently those of Costa Rica, followed closely by Denmark (*World Database of Happiness*, 2000-2009). According to the research among 149 of the world's nations, the unhappiest people are those in Togo, followed by the citizens of Tanzania.

Happiness has to do with quality of life for most people. The problem with this understanding of happiness is that it will disappear like an early-morning mist as soon as external circumstances change. Just observe what happened in many first-world countries after the economic collapse that started in 2008. Many people's happiness was blown away in an instant.

Happiness that doesn't come from the heart is temporary. It's paper thin. Find your happiness in your relationship with God. His presence is neither dependent on your circumstances nor on that of your country. Listen again. *The Lord's grace is not measured by your circumstances!* The Bible is filled with wisdom that teaches how God allows Himself to be found in special ways during hard times.

Your Last Move

Real wisdom, God's wisdom, begins with a holy life and
is characterized by getting along with others. It is gentle
and reasonable, overflowing with mercy and blessings,
not hot one day and cold the next, not two-faced.

– James 3:17 THE MESSAGE –

You're only as good as your last move on the chess board of
life. Football players are assessed on Mondays based on their
game the previous Saturday. Preachers are evaluated based on
their last sermon. A writer's most-recent book determines his
success. Ditto for an actor's performance in his latest movie.
This is not the way things should be. We should give each
other more chances than just the last thing we did, or for that
matter didn't do. The latest controversy should never overshadow all the good things that a person has done, especially
not between friends.

We can't live with short-term memories when the integrity of others is at stake. We shouldn't dare write each other
off based on something that didn't impress us. The Lord's love
causes us to always start over and afresh with each other. We
should believe and expect the best of each other as 1 Corinthians 13 teaches. Our last move is never the only move in
the eyes of our friends and fellow believers. It's about a whole
lifetime of integrity before God and others.

Caring for Creation

The earth is the LORD's, and everything in it.
– Psalm 24:1 NIV –

A 2007 study by British television Channel 4, about what the average Briton's "life footprint" looks like, pointed out that the average person in his or her lifetime uses 3.5 washing machines, drives eight cars, goes through 15 computers, receives 628 Christmas presents, uses 36,000 gallons of fuel, knows 1,700 people, produces 750 tons of CO_2, reads 532 books, reads 2,455 papers (equivalent to 24 trees), and cries 61 liters of tears!

What does your life footprint look like? What are you spending most of your time and energy on? What role do possessions play in your life? Do your footprints during the week leave a trail leading to those who are in need? Are the friends of Jesus – the poor, the outcast, and the lost – your friends too? Does your faith cause your footprint to look any different than what it previously did?

Talking about footprints – what does your carbon footprint look like? We can't allow God's creation to be destroyed right under our noses. Drive less. Use less electricity. Every kilowatt-hour of electricity you save is equal to one kilogram less CO_2 in our air. The creation is God's gift to us. We should take better care of it in His name.

Living Humbly

It is a good thing to receive wealth from God and
the good health to enjoy it. To enjoy your work and
accept your lot in life – this is indeed a gift from God.

– Ecclesiastes 5:19 NLT –

King Hezekiah got a second chance. When the prophet Isaiah
gave him the bad news that he would soon die (Isa. 38), he
fell down and begged God for mercy. God heard his cry for
help. Right there, the king got a handful of extra life – a full
15 years. Instead of allowing God's mercy to make him humble, he later openly bragged about his wealth and power to a
foreign delegation. He even took them on a sight-seeing tour,
showing off his weapons and his palace to make them understand just how large and glorious his kingdom was.

Hezekiah's arrogant behavior upset the Lord to the ex-
tent that He announced that his rule would come to an end,
and that his sons would not rule in his place. Then followed
Hezekiah's shocking reaction, "As long as it doesn't happen in
my lifetime." Talk about selfishness! Let others suffer as long
as I'm excluded! Don't be like Hezekiah. Make room for others, for the generation that follows. Don't keep the best part
for yourself. Don't live arrogantly. Everything you have is a
gift of grace from the hand of the living God.

Not Like "Everyone"

For we are God's workmanship, created in Christ Jesus.
– Ephesians 2:10 NIV –

"You made my day," the shop attendant told me. A wide smile spread across his face. I was stunned. "What did I do?" I asked, surprised. "You called me sir!" he answered. Then he told me that people often treated him with disrespect. He wanted to know why I called him "sir." All I could think of was that God's Word teaches me to treat other people with respect, and this is how I try to live.

After driving away from the shop, I realized anew how easy it really is to do small things in the name of the Lord ... like treating others with respect. How sad that we don't succeed in constantly walking the extra mile for everyone who crosses our path. Just as I shared this story with another person, someone told me that I don't live in the *real world* where *everyone* is bad.

Well, I don't have the luxury of generalizing. I don't know "everyone." I also don't know what the aim of everyone is. But Jesus teaches me in Matthew 5-7 that I don't have the luxury to live and think like everyone. I know that each person is not everyone, but a unique creation of God.

A Prayerful Life

Are any of you suffering hardships? You should pray. Are any of you happy? You should sing praises.

– James 5:13 NLT –

"We just need to pray more. Then God will bless our country," someone said. Everyone agreed. "How do you know that?" another person asked. While everyone just sat there, one answered, "The Bible says so." "Yes," the rest agreed. "Where in the Bible do you read that prayer's primary function is to ensure safer circumstances for everyone?" this person continued. Again there was silence. Someone said, "It's written somewhere that you should 'pray and you shall receive.'"

"Yes, but does that mean that everything will suddenly be better if we send larger volumes of prayer heavenwards?" the questioner wanted to know. "Do you really think that there's a prayer meter that measures how long each of us prays and how many people pray for a particular matter and then these matters get a higher priority from God?"

He carried on, "Prayer is not a quick fix. It is primarily about God and His glory. If there is someone who needs to be changed by prayer, then it is primarily the one who prays himself." Then everyone started talking at the same time. Some agreed, some not. I walked away with some new perspectives on prayer.

The Fate of Millions

"My Father! If it is possible, let this cup of suffering be taken away from Me. Yet I want Your will to be done, not Mine."

– Matthew 26:39 NLT –

That Thursday evening in Gethsemane was a time of blood-sweat for Jesus. One last time, He stood there before the choice of moving forward or backward. It was forward to the cross, or back to heavenly security. Jesus could now leave the life-threatening playing field and return to his Father's home.

In between the olive trees and a few sleeping disciples, Jesus' options were suddenly very limited. But He made exactly the right choice. In those dark moments God's will was His only route indicator. That's why Jesus spoke some of His best-known words during His greatest anxiety: "Father, let this bitter cup pass Me by, but if not, let Your will be done!" Gethsemane finally sealed the course of Jesus. To turn away here, short of the goal line, was never even an option. There was always only one choice for Jesus. He knew very well that He would have left us exposed to our own mercy for eternity if He deviated from His calling.

The fate of millions carried the path of Jesus past Gethsemane to Calvary. We are the reason He braved that course through darkness. But it's precisely this choice on that dark night in Gethsemane that swung the door to God's mercy wide open for us.

The Sun Stands Still

The Sun of Righteousness will
rise with healing in His wings.

– Malachi 4:2 NLT –

Our sun is slowly but surely burning out while it provides light and life to all here on the planet. What a strange live-and-let-die rhythm! This fireball will be burned out completely in another few million years. Something similar also happened with the Sun/Son of Righteousness on the cross of Calvary. On that day, Jesus hung on Jerusalem's most dangerous and deadly piece of wood. There He was, the dying Light to a pitch-dark world.

While Jesus' own life-light was being extinguished, a new heavenly light was switched on in a dark world. Death in exchange for life – this is the new life-rhythm of Calvary. There on the cross Jesus stood in God's way on behalf of all, in order for us to be able to walk away freely. Unearned and absolutely free ... that's the fresh language of Calvary. The cross speaks prominently about the eternal Sun/Son being switched off for three days. It tells about the death of One who's equal to life for all who embrace His sacrifice in faith. Calvary tells that God switched off the "Sun of Righteousness" for a short while so that His light and life can shine through us forever. That's why we can't but stand in awe in front of the Man of the cross.

The Hardest Heart

"I will give you a new heart and put a new spirit in you; I will remove from you your heart of stone and give you a heart of flesh."

– Ezekiel 36:26 NIV –

Sometimes even the strongest among us discover grace in unexpected places. The Roman officer on duty at the cross when Jesus hung there on dark Good Friday had his life brought to an abrupt standstill when the sun went out. When Jesus breathed His last breath on that Friday afternoon, this officer said out loud that Jesus truly is the Son of God. A hardened soldier, whose work it was to ensure that convicted criminals died the cruelest death possible, encountered the One who can move heaven and earth.

Even in the tragic dying moments of Jesus, His true identity could not be hidden. This Roman officer never in his wildest dreams imagined he would encounter God's Child in real life, even less likely on a wooden cross, in Jerusalem of all places. But that's exactly how God works. On a certain day, at a place where you don't expect it, He makes Himself known to you. Like a treasure in a field that someone discovers (Matt. 13), you discover God in the most unexpected places. Then the hardest heart crumbles as new words are confessed about God's Son.

The Empty Tomb

"Be sure of this: I am with you
always, even to the end of the age."

– Matthew 28:20 NLT –

The deceased leader of Christendom didn't lie somewhere in wake in Jerusalem while mourners walked hopelessly past. His grave is empty. Jesus is no longer to be found there. Death could not hold on to its most important victim. On the third day after His crucifixion, Jesus rose from the dead. The difference between hope and despair is the empty grave of Jesus. That's what the New Testament tells us over and over again. The resurrection of Jesus is the big difference between life and death. The empty grave is the answer to all the pain and insanity of this life. It shouts out loudly and visibly that another kind of life is possible, one filled with hope and meaning.

Now Jesus' place in heaven is filled again. He is the One before whom everyone in heaven and on earth will bow. The words of the angels at His empty grave on Good Sunday, after Jesus threw off the ties of death for good, echoes over all the earth: "He is not here. He has risen!" The last words of Jesus here on earth were that He would be with us always, until the last day (v. 20)! We are not religious orphans. He is here with us.

A New Song

Sing to the LORD a new song; sing to the LORD, all the earth.

– Psalm 96:1 NIV –

Paul and Silas held a celebration in a jail in Philippi (Acts 16) one night. Do you remember how the two of them were cruelly assaulted and beaten to a pulp earlier that same day? Afterwards they were thrown into the maximum security cell of Philippi's stinking jail. At midnight, Paul decided to sing. It was not hate songs against their enemies. They did not ask for those who assaulted them to be punished by God. Nothing of the sort. All that was on the lips of Paul and Silas was praise for God.

With bloodied bodies and false voices – how can you sing properly when your body is in shock? – they sent the purest sounds imaginable to God. Paul and Silas wouldn't have won an *Idols* competition that night, but their sincerity to bring God praise under the worst imaginable circumstances touched God's Father heart. That's why the earth suddenly started shaking.

It is about time that we as followers of Jesus started singing different songs. All too easily we join the choirs of the discouraged. We constantly listen to hit parades where hate songs and inflammatory lyrics have the upper hand. Let's learn from Paul that true hit music is praise to God.

Look Who's Walking

He has showed you, O man, what is good. And
what does the LORD require of you? To act justly
and to love mercy and to walk humbly with your God.

– Micah 6:8 NIV –

Cleopas was upset after hearing that the grave of Jesus was empty on that Sunday after the crucifixion (Luke 24:1-35). Angry and disappointed, he and his wife walked the 8 miles back to their little town Emmaus in the hot desert sun. Then Jesus joined them – but they didn't recognize Him. Actually, Jesus should have been celebrating with His angels on that day. He should have been with His disciples to celebrate the victory feast. But He chose to spend the greatest Sunday in world history with two doubters, walking back to their insignificant little town. He chose to eat a simple meal with them that evening. Then their eyes were opened. After a full day in the presence of Jesus, Cleopas and his wife recognized Him when He shared a meal with them!

Jesus celebrates His victories very differently from how we do. He does it by lovingly walking with people who are angry at Him. He does it by breaking a piece of bread with those of little faith – and then allows God to open their eyes. Jesus is always on the cul-de-sac routes of life, where He is busy catching up with the bitter, lonely and lost ones. The feast of a lifetime is awaiting them!

Mile Three

"If someone forces you to go
one mile, go with him two miles."

– Matthew 5:41 NIV –

In his amazing book *The Orthodox Heretic,* Peter Rollins tells the story of a man who listened to Jesus' Sermon on the Mount (Matt. 5-7). He was captivated when Jesus said that we need to walk a second mile for our enemies. Later, this man encountered a Roman soldier and offered to carry his weapons for two miles instead of the one mile that Roman law required. Some time later he met Jesus again, and told Him that he practically applied his "two-mile law." Immediately Jesus told the man that he had misunderstood and that it was actually three miles!

What is the point of this story? Jesus didn't simply come to bring a new set of rules. For Him, it is all about new relationships that are driven by love. No, the Ten Commandments did not expire (vv. 17-20). Jesus just clarifies that the original meaning of these was to live in fresh new relationships with God and others. The law is not a bunch of dos and don'ts.

The question is if we are successful at walking extra miles at all? Do we truly understand what Jesus means when He tells us to add a mile or two on every route with our enemies?

Fire on Your Tongue

Watch your words and hold your tongue;
you'll save yourself a lot of grief.

– Proverbs 21:23 THE MESSAGE –

Language is alive. The book of Proverbs says that our words are like knife stabs. Or like fine silver. Just consider how powerfully a phrase like "I appreciate you" can influence the life of another. Or a sentence, like "you are special!" On the other hand, sharp words can deeply hurt others. Hard words are dangerous. That's why the Bible says that we must carefully weigh our words and calculate their weight before they finally leave our mouths. We need to ruminate on our words twice before they leave our mouths.

Once spoken, words take on a life of their own. Therefore, ask the Lord to dip your words in pure gold before they escape from your mouth. Ask Him to change your words into medicine instead of life-threatening weapons that bruise others. Ask Him to touch your tongue like He did Isaiah's. Do you remember that when Isaiah told God that his lips were unclean, there was a coal taken from the heavenly altar to touch his tongue? His mouth was immediately purified with heavenly fire. After that, Isaiah could speak God-honoring language and share words of hope and life with others.

Starting Over

If anyone is in Christ, he is a new creation;
the old has gone, the new has come!

– 2 Corinthians 5:17 NIV –

Imagine you had the chance to start over – what would you do differently? Well, according to researchers most people would want to be someone else if they could start over. How sad that the story of our lives, of which we are the main authors, often degenerates into chaos. Well, you do have a chance to start over on God's terms. You have at least the rest of today available to do just this.

Today is full of unused hours, minutes and seconds. You have the choice between seizing them to make the best of them to the glory of God, or just being your old self for the rest of today. Don't do that! Choose today to start over in the name of the Lord. Let His light shine. "How?" you ask. Well, I somewhere saw the ad of an American motor oil producer that might be applicable here. It said: "We don't want to change the world. We just want to change your oil!" You don't have to change the whole world. You just need to be a living blessing to one other person who crosses your path somewhere during the day. That's the right kind of starting over.

Light Versus Darkness

You are my lamp, O LORD;
the LORD turns my darkness into light.

– 2 Samuel 22:29 NIV –

Who wins when light and darkness meet? Well, the Pharisees believed that darkness wins. When holy and unholy was on the same terrain, they were of the opinion that the unclean walked away with the victory. That's why religious folk had to avoid sinners. Even today many churchgoers believe this. That's why they make so little impact for God. They're continually hiding in religious shelters and moaning about evil being on the increase.

Jesus differs radically from this hide-and-criticize mentality. He was not scared to be among the "unclean ones." Lepers and sinners could even touch Him. This upset the overly religious ones, but Jesus was not scared that sinners were "contagious." Too many believers are scared of people who do not believe like they do. Learn from Jesus that light is always stronger than darkness. Holiness is more contagious than unholiness. Those who are hiding in the dark are the ones who need to watch out. They might just bump into God's grace when they deal with God's children. The sad part is that many Christians don't believe this.

Forgiveness

Be kind and compassionate to
one another, forgiving each other.

– Ephesians 4:32 NIV –

In one of his books, the well-known writer Ernest Hemingway tells the story of Paco who flees from his father after a disagreement and goes to live in Madrid. Later his father is so saddened by this that he posts an advertisement in the daily *El Liberal*: "Paco, all is forgiven. Meet me at Hotel Montana, noon Tuesday." That Tuesday, 800 boys named Paco showed up at the hotel.

It is easy to speak about forgiving ... until you have someone to forgive, as C. S. Lewis says. It is easy to speak about forgiveness from pulpits. It is something completely different when you or your loved ones are the victims of injustice. Or when you are exploited by someone close to you. Well, here's a newsflash: you cannot forgive. You will never manage this yourself. But you know Someone who specializes in forgiveness. He's the best in the universe with this. His name? Christ! Only He can, through His Spirit, help you to close those books and find new joy in life. Here's the route: take your darkest feelings to Him today. Put your hurt and unforgiveness on His shoulders. Also, leave it right there. Repeat this exercise every time that bitterness starts welling up in you.

Be the Difference

Keep your eyes open, hold tight to
your convictions, give it all you've got,
be resolute, and love without stopping.

– 1 Corinthians 16:13-14 THE MESSAGE –

Is it only my imagination or is selfishness presently the order of the day? Not to mention hate, suspicion, and fear. Have the headlines of the world now become the headlines of Christians as well? Are we following the example of the Pharisees only to do good to those who will return the favor, and to hate our enemies? Do we follow Jesus just as long as it is comfortable? Let's break this vicious circle. Let's follow the advice of Romans 12 by showing kindness to our opponents. Let's make those that stand against us red with shame by repaying their anger with goodness. Let's pray that the Lord will teach us what it means to follow Him. Let's remember that God's route is not only the road to church on Sundays. Let's allow the Holy Spirit to free us from hate and suspicion.

We can bring joy to at least one other person today through a text message, a call, or a quick visit. Then our own life-cup will be filled automatically. We can allow Jesus to let His love flow through us like a stream of living water (John 7:38). We can break this stronghold of selfishness in the name of Jesus.

Victory Tomorrow

"I have told you these things, so that in Me you
may have peace. In this world you will have
trouble. But take heart! I have overcome the world."

– John 16:33 NIV –

If tomorrow looks dark, today is cast in shadows. If the future feels uncertain, the present is a bad place to be. Unfortunately, many believers also feel like this about tomorrow. That's why they look just as despondent. They stare themselves blind against that future that the media, the economy, and politicians hold up in front of them, not to mention that never-ending choir of hopeless individuals who constantly share the latest round of bad news with everyone in range.

How about a piece of truly good news? Well, here it is: God has sorted out the future already. It is not classified information that the future belongs exclusively to the Lord. Just read what the final scoreboard says in Revelation 20-22: THE LORD WINS! Nothing and nobody can prevent Him from reaching His goal. God is full speed underway to let His new heaven and new earth dawn. *Know* every day afresh that the Lord will win.

Never forget that Christ awaits you at the end of your own journey with a heavenly crown of righteousness in His hand (2 Tim. 4:7-8).

Wisdom Wins

Joyful is the person who finds wisdom,
the one who gains understanding.

– Proverbs 3:13-15 NLT –

The well-known composer Joseph Haydn's orchestral members were very tired. The duke for whom they worked promised them a vacation, but time and again he postponed it. Haydn then came forth with a clever plan. His solution was to write his well-known *Farewell* Symphony in 1792. As this piece of music unfolds, one instrument after another becomes quiet. Haydn arranged beforehand that every musician had a candle in front of him, which he would extinguish after he finished his part in the symphony. As the symphony progressed the stage became darker ... until finally it was pitch black. The duke got the message and allowed them to take their long-overdue vacation.

Haydn's behavior sounds like the wisdom found in the book of Proverbs. Proverbs teaches that there are sometimes better ways of getting things done than using words. Sometimes keeping quiet is better. At other times, a symbolic gesture or an unexpected soft answer is just the thing to defuse a difficult situation. Ask the Lord to flood you with His kind of wisdom – then you will know how to act appropriately in every situation.

Living Wisely in a Hurried World

Wisdom is sweet to your soul. If you find it, you will have
a bright future, and your hopes will not be cut short.

– Proverbs 24:14 NLT –

We live in a super-fast, information-overloaded world. Already in 1990 Octo Barnett found that if a medical professional read two new medical research papers every day for one year, he or she would be about 800 years behind at the end of that year. That's the telling tempo at which new information appears on the medical terrain.

It is not only science that grows at the speed of light. The digital realm is also exploding. For instance, during February of 2010 Facebook grew from 373 to 394 million active monthly users. Meanwhile, Twitter grew by 1,382% between February 2009 and February 2010.

Information overload is paralyzing us. It causes difficulty in making decisions because we never feel we have enough information. Well, here's a newsflash: You will never have enough information at your disposal. Live with the light that you have. Trust the Lord and make your decisions bravely. Trust your intuition, and not the constant flow of new data. This time tomorrow, today's information is old news. Only the grace and wisdom of God is timeless. It endures forever.

Ask and Receive

If you need wisdom, ask our generous God, and He will give
it to you. He will not rebuke you for asking.

– James 1:5 NLT –

How do you receive wisdom from God? It's simple, actually.
James writes in chapter 1 that you just go ahead and ask for it.
That's all. There's no secret. Just ask. Also believe that you will
receive it. If you don't believe that you will receive the wisdom
you prayed for you are like an ocean wave being thrown back
and forth at will. Then there's no solidity in your faith. That's
why you need to believe that you will receive what you've
asked for – in this case divine wisdom. You don't have to feel
it. Wisdom is not a simple feeling – it is a way of living before
God and others.

Follow the advice of James today. Pray for the necessary
wisdom to live a godly life. Also receive it in faith, because
James warns that we shouldn't pray as if God were absent. He
gives His wisdom abundantly to those who don't doubt Him.
He lavishly hands out His goodness to those who are not
flung around like the waves on the ocean of doubt. Humbly
ask for wisdom. Ask God to teach you to live a wise, humble
and considerate life.

The Purpose of Life

Not even the wisest people discover
everything, no matter what they claim

– Ecclesiastes 8:17 NLT –

"When I finally discovered the purpose of life ... someone else changed it," an author once wrote. It seems like we are all searching for purpose in life. We are searching for that one big answer that would make all our questions disappear.

The wise author of Ecclesiastes says that no one can discover everything God is doing under the sun. Not even the wisest people discover everything. He comments, "In my search for wisdom and in my observation of people's burdens here on earth, I discovered that there is ceaseless activity, day and night. I realized that no one can discover everything God is doing under the sun. Not even the wisest people discover everything, no matter what they claim." There you have it! You can only start understanding God and His works when you admit your inability to understand life around you.

Christ Is the Way

Jesus said, "I am the Road, also the Truth, also
the Life. No one gets to the Father apart from Me."

– John 14:6 THE MESSAGE –

The author of the book of Ecclesiastes refuses to offer simple answers to the puzzles, questions and problems of life. Our inability to understand this hard life of ours, where crime, disease, unemployment and broken families are the order of the day, does not mean that God cannot be understood, or that He is absent. To the contrary, God is near and knowable.

Jesus is the open door to His heart. He is the way! To bump into Jesus is, in the same breath, to run into the arms of God. To find Jesus is the answer to life's big riddle. To rest in Him is to find that peace which surpasses understanding.

To find Christ does not mean that all your answers about life's riddles will disappear at once, as if by magic. But it does mean that you will get to know the ONE who is larger than life. It means that you know Him who will let you live for eternity on this and the other side of death. It means that you will find purpose and meaning in your life as you learn to follow in the footsteps of Christ day after day.

The NBS Game

Choose a good reputation over great riches; being
held in high esteem is better than silver or gold.

– Proverbs 22:1 NLT –

Have you been the victim of "friendly fire"? This happens
when someone says something negative about another person behind his or her back ... then everyone believes it and
spreads the story further, free of charge. How tragic that even
those on the right side of the friendship-fence and the faith-
fence continually gossip about each other. I have noticed that
there are three basic elements present in most back-stabbing
stories. I refer to this as the "NBS game"; that is, "Naming,
Blaming and Shaming." Those who play this dangerous game
like to give others a bad name behind their back. With their
sharp tongues (against which the book of Proverbs warns us),
they say things like, "I wonder if so-and-so is a Christian."
Then, the blame part kicks in when they accuse this person
of all kinds of bad things. And then the shaming part follows.
"We need to avoid contact with her. She is dangerous."

This NBS game happens without the accused knowing
about it. Do you know this game? Are you aware of people
who are playing it at present? Intervene immediately. Stand up
for the integrity of the accused when you find yourself amongst
NBS players. Exhort the guilty ones in the name of Jesus.

Fail Forwards!

If we confess our sins, He is faithful and just and will forgive us our sins and purify us from all unrighteousness.

– 1 John 1:9 NIV –

The best countermeasure against sin is simply to avoid committing it! See to it that you are never in the presence of sin. Take shelter with the Lord and you will be safe. But if you should stumble and fall, then at least do it forwards. Yes, *fail forwards*! That is, go forward and take your sins directly to the Lord. Of course God hates sin, but He nevertheless invites all wrong-doers to lay their sins at His feet immediately so that He can deal with it effectively.

Take your broken heart to the Holy Trinity without fail. He forgives and forgets. He does not keep a record of sinful deeds that have been confessed in the name of Jesus. God removes all the information from His heavenly records immediately. He wipes the slate clean of everyone who sincerely asks for His forgiveness.

If your life seems to be chaotic and out of control at present, take it to the right place at this very moment. Lay your messed-up life at His feet, receive His redemption and begin over again with a grateful heart. Yes, renounce all sin and live in obedience to God!

Controlling Your Thoughts

Humble yourselves, therefore, under God's
mighty hand, that He may lift you up in due time.

– 1 Peter 5:6 NIV –

"Does one's brain sweat if you think hard?" someone asked the other day on Twitter. Well, to think always takes up energy. Our brains have relatively little energy available ... about 40 watts' worth. That's why our mind is the original energy saver! When it can take shortcuts without thinking, it does exactly that! Your mind has many "routes," "scenarios" and "maps" stored in your subconscious about all those experiences from your past. You don't even remember these, but your mind uses exact maps to determine your behavior here and now ... unless you deliberately intervene!

If we don't *continually* establish new God-honoring thought patterns in our minds, we will be the victims of our own stereotype, or even of destructive thoughts. Fortunately we are not slaves of our present thought patterns. We can and need to intervene. How? Well, by choosing to arrest those negative thoughts that rush through our heads in the name of Christ, and to refocus our thoughts on Him. If not, our old thoughts will continually program us in the wrong direction. Actively arrest destructive and negative thoughts. Focus on Christ. It will set your mind free to think God-honoring thoughts.

Focusing on Christ

Whatever is true, whatever is noble, whatever is right, whatever is pure, whatever is lovely, whatever is admirable – if anything is excellent or praiseworthy – think about such things.

– Philippians 4:8 NIV –

Your brain is the original energy saver. It constantly uses all those experiences, emotions, and thought patterns from the past to dictate your behavior, emotions and feelings here and now. Your old thoughts can keep you captive for the rest of your life if you don't deliberately choose daily *what* and *how* you want to think every day. Therefore, Paul tells us in Ephesians 4 not to get stuck with weak minds that think sinful thoughts all the time. He knows all too well that our thought patterns can degenerate into useless, addictive routines.

In the same breath, the apostle Paul writes in 2 Corinthians 10 that we need to take our thoughts captive. Every one of them needs to be arrested in the powerful name of Christ. Those thoughts that fuel anger, suspicion, bitterness and immorality need to be unmasked time and again and handed over to God. Such thoughts need to be identified, unmasked, and refused free access to our minds. Otherwise we can become prisoners of addictive thoughts and accompanying behavioral patterns. Renewed minds offer the key to a new understanding of Christ. Let's focus our thoughts on Christ and be free!

Accountability

"I tell you that men will have to give account on the
day of judgment for every careless word they have spoken."

– Matthew 12:36 NIV –

When we think we can live all on our own for God, like a brave
spiritual "Rambo," we are missing the point. In 1 Corinthians
12:13, Paul says that the one Spirit made us into one body,
the living body of Christ. That is why we are now accountable
to others. Subsequently, many Christians today have mentors
that keep them accountable regarding how they live.

Recently, I encountered a more handy term than "accountability," namely "editability." Derived from "edit," it refers to
the work of book editors. They ensure that their writers succeed. The publishers of world-renowned authors guide their
authors behind the scenes and enable them to write their
best-sellers!

A Christian mentor is someone who guides me to enable
me to reach my goal in God's kingdom. An effective mentor
needs to guide me to proactively serve the Lord and other
people on the road ahead. Leonard Sweet writes, "Accountability is designed to prevent you from doing bad. Editability
is designed to help you do good. The real question is not 'are
you accountable?' but rather 'are you editable?'"

April

Editing Life

Friends come and friends go, but a
true friend sticks by you like family.

– Proverbs 18:24 The Message –

Each of us needs to be in a healthy growth-oriented relationship with someone else who "edits" us to make the right
impact for God. We aren't islands! We need each other's constant advice, shaping, intercessory prayer, exhortation, and
encouragement. If you don't have someone like this in your
life, it's about time! Pray that God will send the right person
to assist you in your spiritual growth. Be specific: Ask the Lord
to make you transparent so that the right mentor will easily
find you.

By the way, how many people are you also mentoring at
present? In whose lives are you investing some of God's good
gifts on a daily or a weekly basis? Listen, you really need to be
a mentor for someone else. You need to constantly share what
you've received from God. Become a "publisher" for at least
one other person who is busy writing a good story to honor
God with his/her life. Pray today that God will show you exactly who it is that you need to "edit" to serve God and others
more effectively. As a follower of Christ you must actively influence and encourage people around you to live godly lives.

A Safe Haven

The heartfelt counsel of a friend is
as sweet as perfume and incense.

– Proverbs 27:9 NLT –

It seems to me that safe people are as scarce as safe places. Who or what is a safe person? It is someone in whose presence you can open your heart. It is someone with whom you can just be yourself without fearing that he or she will use it against you. A safe person will always protect your integrity in front of others – and always enjoys speaking to God about you.

Shedding tears is a gift from God to wash our insides clean of hurt and pain. But our tears are not safe with everyone. Some see it as a sign of weakness, or an inability to stare life bravely in the eyes. How great that the Lord made some people so free that they are safe havens for those around them. With these folks you can be fragile and broken. And even sensitive. In their presence you find healing for your tired soul.

Do you know safe people? Cherish them! Thank God over and over for them. Are you someone like this? Not? Then get to know Romans 12 – learn how to mourn with those who are mourning and to rejoice with those who are rejoicing. There you will also learn how to associate with the humble and to dry the tears of others.

Unique

Thank You for making me so wonderfully complex!
Your workmanship is marvelous – how well I know it.

– Psalm 139:14 NLT –

No two people on earth share the same fingerprints. But did you know that our "eye prints" are equally unique? The developer of the Iris ID, John Daugman of Cambridge University in England, already compared the "eye prints" of 30 million people. No one of them is the same. Each of us also has 23 pairs of chromosomes that can combine in 8,388,608 different ways. Every one of us is unique.

However, not only our fingerprints and our eyes tell us that we are unique, valuable and special. God confirms it over and again in the Bible. Just take Psalm 139:14 where David writes how the Lord put us together in a wonderful way. We are the climax – the magnum opus – of all God's works here on earth. Maybe that is why Vincent van Gogh once said that Christ is the greatest artist ever. However, according to van Gogh He works with living pieces of art instead of dead statues.

Why do we talk so destructively about ourselves if we are so uniquely sewn together? Why do we so eagerly focus on our shortcomings? Notice that there's only one you in the whole universe. Let your one and only life produce continuous heavenly music for God. Make good sounds with those opportunities you have at your disposal.

Light Years

The prayer of a righteous man is powerful and effective.

– James 5:16 NIV –

A snippet of good news especially for you – the distance between heaven and earth is shorter than you've ever thought. On the day that the feet of Jesus touched the earth, this distance shrunk dramatically. On that day the chasm between heaven and earth was bridged for ever. No longer do we have to rely on our own attempts to reach God. Such attempts will come to nothing in any case. Jesus Christ really is the only connecting road between God and us.

The best way to keep to Christ's road is through prayer. The minute you start praying you are present in the throne room of the Almighty. By way of a simple prayer in the name of Jesus you are transported to the presence of God in a divine instant. A prayer spans the distance between heaven and earth faster than any text message.

The speed of prayer easily beats any high-speed Internet connection. For a prayer to overtake the speed of light is plain sailing. Banish any distance between heaven and earth today in your prayers. Connect to God in the name of Christ.

The Right Name

"My Father's will is that everyone who looks to
the Son and believes in Him shall have eternal life."

– John 6:40 NIV –

Here is a vitally important rule for you to remember until that
very moment when you take the first step on the other side,
the side of death. Also remember it for the rest of eternity:
When you stand face-to-face before God and He wants to
know why you are there, you must appeal immediately to the
only Savior in the entire universe.

Declare that you know the name of the One on whom
you have built all your hope: Jesus Christ. He alone is your
Lord! This simple confession will unlock the doors of eternity
for you. Jesus will be there to welcome you to an everlasting
feast!

What a privilege to know the most important Person in
the universe by name. What an honor to have the most exclusive name of all on one's lips, to speak it with respect and love
and to give it a place of honor in one's heart. You should never
become used to this privilege. You should let the Spirit guide
you to stand before our great God with a sense of wonder
time after time. Respectfully give praise to His name in your
every prayer.

The Right Connections

If you confess with your mouth, "Jesus is
Lord," and believe in your heart that God
raised Him from the dead, you will be saved.

– Romans 10:9 NIV –

Remember that the only "legitimate" way you can have a conversation with God is by knowing a second name of equal importance, that of Jesus! No one can reach God except through Him (John 14:6; Acts 4:11-12). If the words that you speak profess the name of Jesus, and if you believe in Him with all your heart (Rom. 10:9-10), then you have the only key to unlock the door to true life forever. Only the saving grace of His name can give you this unbelievable guarantee.

The warrantees that large international companies provide on their products are valid for a few years at the most, but not for ever. But Jesus guarantees His work of redemption in your life for ever! Jesus has promised in black and white that everyone who submits to Him will receive everlasting life in His heavenly home (John 5-6). Not even death can bring this new life to an end. In fact, this is the start of true life! This is the first time that you are really going Home.

Today and every day, use the correct Heavenly Connection if you want to live in God's home!

God Goes about Quietly

I know the LORD is always with me. I will
not be shaken, for He is right beside me.

– Psalm 16:8 NLT –

Simply by speaking, God can quiet a violent storm in an instant! Just ask the seafarers in Psalm 107. One day they saw the calm sea around them suddenly turn into violent waves; their boat rolled to and fro uncontrollably. They realized that they were in serious trouble. There and then they started to pray. All at once, God performed a miracle. He calmed the waters; something He likes to do! God addressed the giant waves to calm down when His people started to pray.

Still today, the Lord walks quietly on stormy waters. The most powerful winds cannot blow Him off course, especially not when His children flounder helplessly in dangerous storms.

Even when the winds are at their strongest, the Lord calmly reaches out to His people. He knows when they feel trapped and helpless. He knows their feelings of fear and despair when giant waves wash over their lifeboats. When they anxiously call for help He hears every word. He will constrain the winds that blow all round them at once. In no time He will clear the dark clouds that have gathered above them. He will also do it today. All you have to do is ask!

The Shadow of His Wings

Those who live in the shelter of the Most
High will find rest in the shadow of the Almighty.

– Psalm 91:1 NIV –

God always knows where you are. He watches your movements closely, 24/7. He can trace you in no time at all, wherever you might be wandering. Each earthly address where you spend your time is recorded in the heavenly books. You will never be able to change your address on the quiet without God discovering it in a divine instant. That is why He knows full well when you land in real storms. You can be sure that He will be there in the blink of an eye.

Always know that when you feel caught up among giant waves, the Lord is very close to you. You are too precious for Him to allow gales to blow you away from Him. You are one of God's very special possessions, and He will speak out to calm the storms round you. He will protect you. Ask Him to do it!

Remember to bow to Him in thankfulness afterwards. Honor Him for being with you in your dark hour of need. Worship the only Lord who can change even the most intense darkness, surrounding you with the brightest light, turning your night into day!

A New Creation

Imitate God, therefore, in everything
you do, because you are His dear children.

– Ephesians 5:1 NLT –

The name God uses to address everyone that bows before Jesus is "child." "How great is the love the Father has lavished on us, that we should be called children of God! And that is what we are!" (1 John 3:1). "He who did not spare His own Son, but gave Him up for us all – how will He not also, along with Him, graciously give us all things?" (Rom. 8:32). God calls us His children. Through the blood of His Son He has made us part of His heavenly family. Thus, God is our Father and we are the special children of His kingdom! He loves us all equally and for the same length of time (= forever).

To God we aren't mere numbers in an ID document. No, God calls us His *beloved children*. We share in all the privileges that go along with this name of honor, such as a permanent place to sit at His feet, as well as a brand-new life.

Wow, we should rejoice that God has chosen this incredible new name for each of us. Naturally our lives should reflect that we are part of the family of the kingdom of God; indeed, that our Father is the King of all creation.

Beyond the NOW

God has said, "Never will I leave
you; never will I forsake you."

– Hebrews 13:5 NIV –

One can so easily become blind to everything but one's own circumstances. Then it's easy to fall back on that old ever-green complaint:"The Lord has forsaken me."Listen, it is definitely not true. Your own feelings and circumstances should never be the yardstick against which you measure how far (or near) God is from you. Don't think that God is far away simply because you feel that it is the case. Don't let your troubles make you decide that He has forgotten you, because God will never forsake you in difficult times.

We allow our feelings to lead us by the nose far too easily. Whenever it feels as if the road to heaven is closed, we decide that God has given us up as a bad job. Yet the Bible tells us that not even dire circumstances can ever separate us from Him (Rom. 8:31-39).

God proved that we are extremely valuable when He sent His only Son to make us His permanent property. We are so important that God sent His Spirit to transform us into permanent dwellings for the Almighty.

In Step with God

I will teach you wisdom's ways and lead you
in straight paths. When you walk, you won't be
held back; when you run, you won't stumble.

– Proverbs 4:11-12 NLT –

Keep pace with the rhythm of the Lord. How? Well:

Make time for the Word (Psalm 1): Make time in your daily program to read God's Word. The Bible must be your daily guide. You must replenish yourself regularly with the right kind of good news.

Make time for prayer: To really hear God's voice, you have to switch off the noise around you: the TV, the radio, the telephone, as well as your busy schedule. You have to put aside quiet time for sitting alone at the feet of the Lord (Matt. 6:5-6). Choose a quiet garden or a room, where noise won't disturb you, and where you are also able to silence the noise within you.

Make the right kind of friends: Instead of keeping company with people who are frivolous or devoid of any hope, you should rather spend time with people who uplift you as a person. Make a point of befriending people who can teach you to walk close to the Lord. Your role models and mentors should be people who walk the Lord's road of grace every day.

In God's Hands

"I know you well and you are special to Me."
– Exodus 33:12 The Message –

Asaph, one of the believers in the Bible who always went against the tide, wrote in Psalm 73:13 that he had been near to losing his faith after he had seen the prosperity of wicked people compared to his own suffering. Fortunately the Lord opened his eyes to see what it was all about (v. 17). Asaph came to realize that God deals with sinners in His own way (vv. 18-20). He also learnt that the Lord never forsakes His children. God is the Rock where people who are afraid can hide (v. 23). Listen to Asaph's words, "My flesh and my heart may fail, but God is the strength of my heart and my portion forever" (v. 26).

The Lord will never forsake us, not even when we are in revolt against Him. That is why Asaph confesses, "When my heart was grieved and my spirit embittered, I was senseless and ignorant; I was a brute beast before You. Yet I am always with You; You hold me by my right hand" (vv. 21-23).

Well, there you have it – the true facts! Do you believe it? Or do you listen to all the noise in your head?

The Joy of Life

"Come to Me, all you who are weary
and burdened, and I will give you rest."

– Matthew 11:28 NIV –

One of the reasons for our rushed lives could be our desire for more earthly possessions. We exhaust ourselves in order to afford a new car, a house, a holiday, furniture, the children's education ... We worry today about the problems and expenses of tomorrow.

But listen to this: God measures out grace only "one day at a time" (Matt. 6:11). He provides in all our needs – one day at a time. But when we appoint ourselves as the architects and owner-builders of our plans, that is when our faith diminishes while the speed at which we live increases by the day, so much so that we begin to devise plans to get even more unnecessary food on the table.

The solution is to hand over full control of the building plans of our lives to God. He should be the only architect of our life's house. Then we will move forward in the right direction, one day at a time. We will no longer have unnecessary manmade building plans in our lives that sap our energy and swallow our faith. Peace and simplicity will become the most precious possessions we have – gifts bestowed upon us by the Lord!

Cease-Fire

He Himself is our peace, who has
made the two one and has destroyed
the barrier, the dividing wall of hostility.

– Ephesians 2:14 NIV –

The peace of Christ proclaims that there is no more *enmity* between heaven and earth. His death and resurrection constitute the cease-fire that connects God and us. There is no other road to God. Only Jesus brings true peace and can guarantee that it will last. The peace of Christ gives the receiver permanent access to God. If we follow Jesus' road of peace, we are assured of a place at the throne of God.

Read what Paul says in Romans 5:1-2: "Therefore, since we have been justified through faith, we have peace with God through our Lord Jesus Christ, through whom we have gained access by faith into this grace in which we now stand. And we rejoice in the hope of the glory of God."

There is no more punishment from God. Peace = good news. This means that there is no condemnation for those who are in Christ Jesus (Rom. 8:1). The peace of Jesus brings about peace between people on earth who fight with one another.

Company

"For where two or three gather together as
My followers, I am there among them."
– Matthew 18:20 NLT –

God loves the wrong kind of people. He loves sinners, enemies, rebels, good-for-nothings. For that reason He devised a master plan to free all His enemies that He loves so dearly from the death-traps of sin. He needed only one Man to carry out this master plan. Not hordes of angels, not super beings with laser guns; nor an army with mega bombs. No, He needed only one person who didn't carry dangerous weapons or wear shiny clothes. I am talking about Jesus, of course!

One day Jesus took a decisive step that had an everlasting effect on world history. He decided to exchange His heavenly honor for a humble life here on earth. No red carpets were rolled out in His honor during His wearisome journeys on earth. Stripped of all glory, Jesus braved our dusty dirt roads to tell sinners and outcasts about the kingdom of God.

Jesus wants to be present in the company of everybody, and that includes you. Kneel before Him. Give yourself to Him unreservedly. In exchange, everlasting new life will be your gift.

Set Your Sails

> Don't you realize that your body is the temple
> of the Holy Spirit, who lives in you and was given
> to you by God? You do not belong to yourself.
>
> – 1 Corinthians 6:19 NLT –

Do you want the power of the Holy Spirit to swell your life's sails? Well, be assured of the following:

Know that the Spirit lives in you (1 Cor. 3:16; 6:19): The Holy Spirit was given to the church of Christ (Rom. 8:9). He transforms you and other believers into temples of the Almighty. He changes your life into a temple of the living God.

Know that the Spirit is the Guarantee that you will reach the finish line (Eph. 1:13-14): The Spirit guarantees that a heavenly feast awaits you. He guarantees that you will reach the finish line safely because you believe in Christ. He also guarantees that He will be with you wherever you are on the road. He will make sure that you reach the eternal home of the Lord safely.

Let the Spirit fill your life every day (Eph. 5:18): Your life should be like an empty vessel that is filled with the Spirit each day. Be the clay in His hands for Him to model. Ask Him to fill the vessel of your life to the brim with life-giving water, enough to spill over to others.

The Heavenly Gardener

"Remain in Me and I will remain in you. Those who remain in Me and I in them, will produce much fruit."

– John 15:4-5 NLT –

God lets Jesus, His heavenly Gardener, till the garden of your life so that you may bear more fruit to His glory. He plants a nameplate next to your life that reads, "Under the special care of the heavenly Gardener!" Therefore, as far as He is concerned, you have to prepare for a blessed year. He is going to shape and mould you so that His Word takes even deeper root in your heart. You will have new insights into the words of the Bible.

What is more, you will find it much easier to carry the burdens of others on your shoulders from now on. In short, this time is going to be God's season of grace for you, a special year for you to grow and bear fruit!

Embrace this bonus year. Be there where living waters flow and living bread is handed out. Make time to go to church, to pray, to study God's Word. Leave the rest to God! He will see to it that you bear the fruit that He requires. He will gather the crop at the appropriate time. All you have to do is to be a willing tree in the hands of the heavenly Gardener.

How Far Away?

He tends His flock like a shepherd: He gathers the
lambs in His arms and carries them close to His heart.

– Isaiah 40:11 NIV –

Are you one of those who wonder how far God is away from
you? Maybe you feel that today He is very, very far. Well, the
Bible tells you exactly how far away He is from you at this very
moment. Listen, GOD IS ONLY A PRAYER AWAY! And no
farther. He really is only a call-for-help away; no farther than
a single humble prayer asking for help. He is as close to you
as the time it takes you to speak one sentence in the name of
His Son. Yes, God is as close to you as that.

Jesus removed the distance between God and you. Now,
God is very near. You don't need binoculars or a telescope
to see His goodness. And you don't have to shout at the top
of your voice to get His attention. He is only one prayer away.
That is all! When you address Him in the name of Christ, the
last bit of distance is removed! Then you are as close to Him
as a single prayer!

I repeat: When you pray in the name of Jesus, there is no
distance between you and God. He is as close to you as that
one prayer!

Wake Up!

"The LORD your God is with you, He is mighty to save.
He will take great delight in you, He will quiet you
with His love, He will rejoice over you with singing."

– Zephaniah 3:17 NIV –

Do you live in a make-believe world? If so, open your eyes! It is time for your appointment with Destiny! Leave all your unfulfilled dreams behind, because the Lord's heavenly ladder extends down into your life today. God's plan for your life will turn into reality. As you deliberately begin to live your life in His company from now on, you'll become aware that you walk on holy ground every day. You will realize that you are in the presence of the One who holds heaven and earth in the palm of His hand. What a privilege to know that the most powerful Person in the universe accompanies you wherever you go.

Maybe you will come across a few important public figures in the course of your life, but the most important One, who is with you right now, is the living God. He is always close to you, whether you are among believers and friends, at work, or at home. Be grateful that God honors you with His personal presence! Bow down before Him. From now on invite Him every day to be the Guest of Honor in your life!

Your Life Story

Surely the LORD is in this place.

– Genesis 28:16 NLT –

Can you recall Jacob's dream (Gen. 28:10-22)? He dreamt about a ladder and saw angels climbing up and down. All of a sudden God was there, too. He promised Jacob that He would be with him. Jacob then awoke and exclaimed in shock: "Surely the Lord is in this place, and I was not aware of it" (v. 16). What a mistake not to recognize the Lord when He is with you!

Fortunately, Jacob afterwards honored the Lord by marking the spot with a rock and naming the town Bethel, the House of God. In that way a very ordinary town suddenly became the residence of God, and Jacob, in turn, became a brand-new person!

Jacob's rock proclaimed God is here. By the way, do the stories of your life also reflect the presence of God? Is your life a holy shrine to His honor? Is your life a Bethel – a house of God? Do you realize that the Holy Spirit lives within you when you bow before Jesus? Dedicate your whole life to being the living house of God. Let your every word, every deed, every thought, shout it out – God is here! Bethel!

The Master

> "No one can serve two masters. Either you
> will hate the one and love the other, or you
> will be devoted to the one and despise the
> other. You cannot serve both God and money."
>
> – Matthew 6:24 NIV –

Do you work yourself to the bone for a better future for yourself and your family? Then, let me tell you that you are bluffing yourself, for if you are a workaholic, you have become a stranger to everyone. What is the use of working yourself to death for the future while your life, here and now, is devoid of meaning? There is no guarantee on the reverse side of a banknote that reads: Possession of this note guarantees happiness. No, what one could read there instead is, "Whoever loves money never has money enough; whoever loves wealth is never satisfied with his income. This too is meaningless" (Eccles. 5:10).

There is nothing wrong with making money, but something is seriously wrong if your attitude towards money changes your role from manager to slave. The god of money does not share you with anyone. It demands your loyalty 24 hours a day. The result? It steals all your joy in life, your family, your friends ... Stop wearing yourself out for possessions, or you risk losing everything in the end! Bow before Christ instead. He is the Lord of mercy and can guarantee your true happiness and wealth!

On Your Doorstep

Let the morning bring me word of Your unfailing
love, for I have put my trust in You. Show me the
way I should go, for to You I lift up my soul.

– Psalm 143:8 NIV –

"A man can do nothing better than to eat and drink and find
satisfaction in his work. This too, I see, is from the hand of
God" (Eccles. 2:24). You will find true happiness when you
break bread with those who are close to you. The cup of your
life will run over with joy when you spend happy times with
family and friends.

The true joy of living awaits you on your doorstep each
day. All you have to do is to make each time you break bread
or visit with friends and family a festive occasion. Treat everyone sharing your meal as a special guest. Each one has come
into your life to lighten your burdens and to ease your way.

If you are far from your loved ones today, take a lesson
from the early Christians. They reserved a seat for the living
Lord at their communion table. Why don't you do that? Invite
the Lord to be the Guest at your table, even if you're only
having a simple piece of bread. There is no doubt that He will
accept your invitation to celebrate with you! He is sure to free
you from your feelings of loneliness today.

Living the Plan

"I know the plans I have for you," declares
the LORD, "plans to prosper you and not to
harm you, plans to give you hope and a future."

– Jeremiah 29:11 NIV –

When you bow before Jesus, every story of your life with a bad beginning and a dreary end is wiped out! Then you become part of a brand-new story, the master-story of God! All of a sudden, your yesterdays, todays and tomorrows are fresh and new, and eternal new life unfolds before your eyes. Yes, the complete story of your life is rewritten by only One Man.

Do you know that suddenly there will no longer be a single report in heaven containing damning evidence about your sins of yesterday, no mark of the hurt you caused a loved one or of any other personal tragedy in your life? Your name is entered only once in the books of heaven and that is in the Book of Life. It has been written in the blood of Christ. Believe it. See it. Experience it. Live it!

Jesus transforms sinners into new people, into children of God. He prepares a new road for everyone who holds on to Him as their Lord and Savior. May you once again behold Jesus, the One who changes the destiny of all for ever.

Your Facial Muscles

A cheerful heart brings a smile to your face.

– Proverbs 15:13 THE MESSAGE –

I heard about a boy once who found a dried leaf in his mother's Bible and asked her: "Mom, is this the fig leaf that Adam used in the Garden when he wanted to hide his nakedness?" Cute, not so? We should have more humor in our lives, don't you think? We should make more time for laughing and being jolly. Do we not serve a God of joy? In His kingdom joy wins. In His presence there is no place for sulking and pulling a long face (Rom. 14:17).

Perhaps we shouldn't take ourselves and others so seriously. Perhaps we should be more light-hearted about life (not that we should be frivolous!). A believer once made the remark that "God must have a very good sense of humor since He made human beings like us!" Whenever you are about to fly off the handle, ask yourself if it is really worth getting upset about. Try laughing out loud at yourself and others (or rather with others!) for a change.

God gave you many facial muscles, most of which get absolutely no exercise if you don't laugh. So, what are you waiting for?

The Voice of the Spirit

The LORD delights in every detail of their
lives. Though they stumble, they will never
fall, for the LORD holds them by the hand.

– Psalm 37:23-24 NLT –

God devised a wonderful plan to make sure that we never
forget His name. He sent the Holy Spirit to all who follow
Christ. Read Romans 8:15-16 to see how the Spirit does it:
"You received the Spirit of sonship. And by Him we cry, Abba,
Father. The Spirit Himself testifies with our spirit that we are
God's children."

Listen carefully and you will hear the Holy Spirit in your
heart calling to God lovingly and compassionately today. He
is the inner voice that calls to our wonderful heavenly Father
on our behalf! It is the task of the Holy Spirit to form an intimate, never-ending bond between you and God. He sees to
it that you are always very close to God, even when you don't
experience it!

Open your ears today and listen carefully so that you can
hear His voice deep in your heart. Hear the Spirit conversing
with God about you, calling out to the Father on your behalf.
Allow the Spirit to give you the assurance that God is your
Father, a loving Father who cares about every little detail of
your life.

Source of Joy

"Are you tired? Worn out? Burned out on religion?
Come to Me. Get away with Me and you'll recover
your life. Walk with Me and work with Me – watch
how I do it. Learn the unforced rhythms of grace."

– Matthew 11:28-29 THE MESSAGE –

Where can you find joy? In a well-stocked check account or an expensive holiday? A new house? A well-paid job? Yes, surely joy can be found in these things, but it is only temporary. So where can you find the kind of joy that lasts? Jesus promises to give lasting joy and He invites us in Matthew 11 to come to Him and experience it. His yoke is easy to carry, for He took our burdens on His shoulders when He died for us on the cross.

Too often, religious people give the impression that they are shouldering the burdens of the whole world. It shouldn't be like that. That is not what religion is about. It is about joy. How can one find the joy of Jesus? Simply by accepting gratefully the joy that He provides. And by using it and putting it to work. All you have to do is to collect your portion of heavenly joy each morning. Ask the Lord each day that you may experience His peace, and your request will be granted instantly.

God's heavenly joy can never be used up – He renews it day by day!

Name, Blame and Shame

God blesses those whose hearts are pure, for they will see God.
– Matthew 5:8 NLT –

People love to "name, blame and shame" others. They usually do it behind the backs of those they want to shame and bring into disrepute. You and I have to stop this cruel behavior. We must point out that they are transgressing the rules of Jesus in Matthew 18. There Jesus teaches that when you have something against someone else, you must always take it up personally with him or her. You do this privately, honestly, and transparently. You talk face to face, never face to back!

Before you have spoken to those who are under suspicion of wrongdoing, keep quiet. Integrity is all about the courage to look each other in the eye, never in the back! It requires face-to-face transparency. Integrity is the new game plan for all followers of Jesus, never backstabbing and shaming.

Go and learn from Jesus in Matthew 18 what the rules of the gospel are. Strictly adhere to them, otherwise your relationships will be ruined.

Doubting Thomas

"My Lord and my God!" Thomas exclaimed.
– John 20:28 NLT –

Poor Thomas – do you recall the first Sunday evening after the resurrection of Jesus when He visited His disciples, when Thomas was absent? Afterwards when Thomas heard what happened he uttered in disbelief, "Unless I see the nail marks in His hands and put my finger where the nails were, and put my hand into His side, I will not believe it" (v. 25). If you are absent when Jesus is present, you miss out on LIFE.

Fortunately Jesus specializes in giving people second chances. He cares about those who are not at peace. That is why He speaks the language of peace when they are within earshot. Eight days later, when Thomas turned up at a meeting of the disciples, Jesus arrived too. The first words that He spoke were, "Peace be with you!" (v. 26). Jesus demonstrated that the peace He offered could transform doubting Thomases in the blink of an eye when He invited Thomas to touch His wounds with his doubting fingers.

Thomas fell to the ground and called out, "My Lord and my God!" (v. 28).

Yes, skeptics gladly kneel before Christ when they experience His peace. He opens their eyes so that they recognize Him as the Lord!

Powerful Prayer

"Ask, using My name, and you will
receive, and you will have abundant joy."

– John 16:24 NLT –

Change all your prayers into regular sincere conversations with God. Choose a few Bible phrases to express your love for Him throughout the day, such as "Lord God, You are good" or "Praise the Lord." Continue doing this in times of crisis. Remind yourself in the words of the Bible that God will always be with you, and say it out loud to Him. "You shield me and keep me safe from harm because I walk close to You" or "The Lord is my Rock, my safe Haven."

Learn to use the Bible effectively by letting it become your guide in prayer also. Speak to God from His Word each day. Use the Psalms to help you share with God your own joy and sadness, your distress and pain. Be brief, sincere and to the point. Say what you have to, and say amen. Make prayer the heartbeat of your whole life before God. Continue to pray for everyone that crosses your path. Pray until heaven opens up in front of you.

Remember, the most important lesson of all is to always pray in the name of Jesus Christ.

Submit to His Will

Submit to God, and you will have
peace; then things will go well for you.

– Job 22:21 NLT –

Prayer cannot be separated from the rest of your life. There is no such thing as rattling off a few quick prayers to still your conscience while carrying on as you wish. In John 15:7-8 Jesus tells us that if we remain in Him, we will receive what we pray for. A life of obedience to God is the road to, and the result of, a life of obedient prayer. Obedience to God changes the way you pray. Your prayers do not revolve around your own selfish needs then. They don't sound like someone shopping for groceries – "pass this, give me that, do this, help me here." No, then your prayers shift the attention away from yourself to the glory of God and the coming of His kingdom.

Believe me, prayer is a serious matter! Prayer is to speak with the King of the universe. Prayer can be a wondrous adventure if you pray in submission to God's will. If you do, the floodgates of heaven will be open above you night and day, because God hears and answers prayers such as these.

Go on, knock on the doors of heaven in the wondrous name of Jesus and see what happens!

May

From the Beginning

If anyone is in Christ, he is a new creation;
the old has gone, the new has come!

– 2 Corinthians 5:17 NIV –

The basic rule of grace in the kingdom of God is: FROM THE BEGINNING, ONCE MORE! Every day with God is like a new day. He gives us a clean slate every morning! He is not able to recall our sins of the previous day if we sincerely asked for His forgiveness.

Psalm 103:12 says, "As far as the east is from the west, so far has He removed our transgressions from us." There is no place in heaven to store away the records of all the wrong we did in the past. They were tossed in the heavenly rubbish bin long ago. God does not have the time or the inclination to think back on the sins we have confessed and for which we have asked His forgiveness in the powerful name of Jesus.

God farms with grace. Forgiveness grows profusely on His heavenly farm. He forgives and forgets. God's bonus year for forgiveness, His year of second chances, has just arrived on the world market! Christ hands out this bumper crop of grace to everyone. Go on, just ask Him, and He will erase the bad records against your name in heaven forever!

Giving Time

Make the most of every chance you
get. These are desperate times!

– Ephesians 5:16 THE MESSAGE –

If you are serious about your relationship with God, then give Him one of your most prized possessions today: your time! Most Christians don't think of this when they put things on the altar for the Lord. They offer their possessions, money, self-will, and a few other things, but not many give over their daily programs to the Lord!

To live a powerful Christian life, you have to give over your watch and your precious diary into the hands of the Lord. You have to learn to synchronize your time with the time of the Lord. If not, you will spend all of your time on the wrong things.

Day-to-day faith is about surrendering your diary to the Lord each morning for Him to overwrite your priorities in heavenly ink with His heavenly ones. Your faith is truly at work when you repeat this giving-away exercise day after day and year after year.

Ephesians 5:16 tells us that we should be "making the most of every opportunity, because the days are evil." Time is precious. Each day is there for you to walk with God, but if you let it slip through your fingers you waste a precious opportunity.

Prime Time for God

Because of Christ and our faith in Him, we can now
come boldly and confidently into God's presence.

– Ephesians 3:12 NLT –

Make time somewhere during the day to switch off your cell
phone, close the door, be alone with God and read His Word.
The Lord's Word is not merely letters on paper. While you
read the Bible, the Holy Spirit is always at work burning these
letters into your heart. The heavenly seeds that He sows in
your heart while you dwell in His Word will quickly take root
in your mind, as well as on your hands and feet.

The blessings you reap if you are prepared to invest time
to seek the face of the Lord will be beyond belief, because
every time you do this you find yourself in the Holy Spirit's
sphere of power and attention. Every time you do this your
life is molded to the glory of God by the most powerful person in the universe!

There are no shortcuts on the road to spiritual success;
however, there are right roads! If you want to follow the main
road of faith, one of the most important routes to take is that
of setting aside special time for God each day. Oh yes, also
dedicate the rest of the day to God as well! Do this every day.

Focus on Jesus

Therefore, since we have been justified through faith, we
have peace with God through our Lord Jesus Christ.

– Romans 5:1 NIV –

God loves us from head to toe, despite all our spiritual weaknesses and shortcomings. Heavenly peace reins between
Him and us all who believe in Jesus Christ, even though we
sometimes make a mess of things. That is what the Bible tells
me ... and I believe it with all of my heart and soul. I believe
that God calls me His child, and that He isn't on my trail to
punish me.

Of course that doesn't mean that I have a license to do as I
please or to sin. But I know that there is permanent redemption through Jesus. In His presence I get a second chance every day, even though it may be my thousandth or millionth
second chance!

Realize that God sees all His children through the cross of
Jesus. Know that the light of the cross is the light on the road
of your life, and that it erases all those crooked roads from
the past.

Rejoice in the grace that you receive freely. Be satisfied
with what God does in your life. Allow His Spirit to root out
everything that is wrong, and keep your eyes fixed on Christ.

Filling Your Mind

Blessed are they whose ways are blameless, who walk according to the law of the LORD. Blessed are they who keep His statutes and seek Him with all their heart.

– Psalm 119:1-2 NIV –

When you travel on an overcrowded train or bus, or when you are caught in a traffic jam in your car, don't just sit there staring lifelessly into thin air. Do a valuable mind exercise instead. Think about what you read in the Bible last night. Become excited once again about the latest knock-out news you discovered in the Bible ... Also let the expression on your face show it.

In order to remember the Word of God you need to read it regularly, of course. Charge the spiritual batteries of your mind with heavenly power every single day. Let your thoughts revolve around the living words of the Bible in traffic jams, at work and at home.

Take the words of Psalm 119:97 to heart: "Oh, how I love your law! I meditate on it all day long." Wait, don't merely read these words. Live them out as well! Spiritual success is guaranteed if they spill over from your head to your hands and feet.

In His Arms

He will order His angels to protect you wherever
you go. They will hold you up with their hands
so you won't even hurt your foot on a stone.

– Psalm 91:11-12 NLT –

The well-known religious reformer Martin Luther once wrote
how his wife, Katharina, emerged from their bedroom one
morning wearing funeral clothes, and to his question "Who
has died?" she challenged him with her answer, "Your God."
She explained that this could be the only reason for his gloom.
Her words jerked Luther from his dark pit there and then.

David describes his own "dark pit experience" in Psalm
88. Listen to what he says: "I am counted among those who
go down to the pit; I am like a man without strength. I am set
apart with the dead, like the slain who lie in the grave, whom
You remember no more, who are cut off from Your care. You
have put me in the lowest pit, in the darkest depths" (vv. 4-6).
Ouch! It is no fun to plod around in a dark pit.

Are you living in a dark pit at the moment? Look around
you – even there God is at your side. He does not stand at the
top watching you struggling to get out in your own strength.
Hear the voice of the Lord right next to you in the dark. See
Him switch on a bright light of hope right there where you are.

One Day at a Time

Live happily with the woman you love through
all the meaningless days of life that God has
given you under the sun. The wife God gives
you is your reward for all your earthly toil.

– Ecclesiastes 9:9 NLT –

God takes note of what you do with today's borrowed time.
Don't wait for other people to make your life more enjoyable.
Don't think life owes you anything. If you do you are going
to sulk your life away. No, be brave! Surprise everyone. Dare
to call today a day of celebration. Choose the joy of sharing
some bread with friends. Put aside celebration time with your
children and your spouse (vv. 8:15; 9:9). Forget about an unnecessary appointment; cancel a boring meeting. Start living,
because you have only today to do it. Don't waste time. Only
if it is the will of God, will you see the sun rise tomorrow. But
that is still a day's journey away. In the meantime, live life to
the full.

God gives life in 24 hour portions of "one day at a time."
He does not guarantee the next five years of life ahead of
time. No, He gives us only today's sunshine, rain and life. At
this very moment you are experiencing your own portion of
abundant goodness from heaven. You are alive, not so? Your
heart should be full of hope and gratitude because God has
given the green light for you to be alive today.

The True Facts

"I'll be with you as you do this, day after
day after day, right up to the end of the age."

– Matthew 28:20 THE MESSAGE –

"The Lord doesn't care about me anymore. Why does He let all these terrible things happen to me?" Have you ever said words like these? Or have you thought it perhaps? Of course you are not alone if you feel like this sometimes. Many people have the same thoughts.

What are the true facts? Well, may I remind you of Jesus' last words on earth, a few minutes before His departure to heaven: He assured us that He would be with us until the end of time. Jesus will never, ever leave us – we are too precious to Him. He will accompany everyone who believes in Him to the end of the road.

Are you going to join all the grumblers of the world who complain, "No one's burden is as heavy as mine," or are you going to see the Lord who holds you safely in His hands today?

Sliding Backwards

Rather, you must grow in the grace and
knowledge of our Lord and Savior Jesus Christ.
All glory to Him, both now and forever! Amen.

– 2 Peter 3:18 NLT –

If you don't walk with Christ day after day, you fall behind.
If all your time is taken up by your busy program, and you
neglect God by putting aside special time for Him, don't be
surprised if you are half-dead spiritually. The fact is, you reap
what you sow: spiritual poverty! Learn to put your time at the
disposal of the Lord so that you can reap His blessing at the
right time.

If you want to keep pace with the daily program of heaven,
you have to make each day a special day of God. Do not put
aside only Sundays for the Lord, but make each day, from
Monday to Saturday, the special day of God. Every morning
when you wake up, thank Him for being alive. Declare this
day a day of celebration. Make an official announcement at
the doors of heaven that you are going to dedicate the full 24
hours, yes, each of the 1,440 minutes, to the Lord.

But remember, God hears you. He will take you at your
word. What He will do immediately is to overwrite all your
appointments and meetings, and your social and recreation
programs, with His heavenly program.

Good Deeds

"I'm telling the solemn truth: Whenever you did one of
these things to someone overlooked or ignored,
that was Me – you did it to Me."

– Matthew 25:40 THE MESSAGE –

Life goes by all too quickly. Do not let the few years you have
been granted slip through your fingers. Do you really gain
anything by making a lot of money but losing the very people
who are close to you? Above all, what do you gain if you are
so busy that you don't have any time for God and you lose
Him, too? Then you have literally lost everything!

Do the right thing here and now: go back to God immediately. He will receive you with open arms if you come before
Him in the name of His Son. Also, go back to your loved ones –
they will receive you as their honored guest.

Do something good for someone in the name of the Lord
today. Do not go to bed without having spoken a kind word
to someone or having performed a loving deed for someone
in need. In Matthew 10:42, Jesus gives us the assurance that
God will notice it if we give a cup of cold water to the most
insignificant of His followers to drink. The smallest gesture of
love is recorded in the most important place in the universe.

The Robber of Faith

"That is why I tell you not to worry about everyday
life – whether you have enough food and drink,
or enough clothes to wear. Isn't life more than
food, and your body more than clothing? Can all
your worries add a single moment to your life?"

– Matthew 6:25, 27 NLT –

Do you know what one of the biggest stumbling blocks is that
crosses the path of believers regularly? *Worry*! It is a robber of
faith. Worry kills our trust in God. In the parable of the sower
(Matt. 13) Jesus tells us that the seed of the Word falls in four
places. According to Him, 25% reject the gospel outright. But,
a full 75% embrace the Good News. Can you believe it? Three
out of every four people are very religious initially! Unfortunately, 50% of all those who hurriedly bow before God throw
in the towel eventually. Why? Well, there are two reasons: a)
the demands of religion, and b) worry! Those who hurriedly say
yes to God all too soon backslide into the bad habit of worrying
and running after money. Tragic, but true!

You have one of two choices – either you take God at His
word when He promises to take care of you, or you try to do
it yourself. If you carry out your daily tasks patiently, the Lord
will provide you with food at the right time. He who was there
yesterday will be at His post tomorrow and the day after that.

Two Loaves of Bread

"Therefore do not worry about tomorrow,
for tomorrow will worry about itself.
Each day has enough trouble of its own."

– Matthew 6:34 NIV –

One day, someone told me that the future looked very bleak indeed. I asked him: "What future are you talking about? The future a week from now, or the future in a year's time or in ten years' time? Because at the moment we are right in the middle of exactly that future about which we worried so much about ten years ago!" Despite that, all of us are surviving somehow! We are living last year and last week's future, here and now! Today is yesterday's tomorrow that we worried ourselves sick about. Incredible? No, it is grace! It is all thanks to God! He is true to His Word! He has cared for us exactly as He promised!

Can you recall how you worried about your future a few years back? Well, that future has arrived. Are you without food today? Not? Do you have enough warm blankets for to-night? *Yes!* Will you have enough money and supplies for the next month or so? Undoubtedly! Will you make it through the next year? Definitely! Now tell me, what are you worried about? To worry is nothing but a vote of no confidence in your heavenly Father!

Harsh Words

Remind everyone about these things, and
command them in God's presence to stop
fighting over words. Such arguments are useless,
and they can ruin those who hear them.

– 2 Timothy 2:14 NLT –

Beware of biting words; the kind that hurt others. Ban them from your lips. Train your tongue not to return evil for evil. You don't have a free pass to be rude, or to let bad language escape your lips. You don't have to be like everyone else. You are the property of the Lord. He has the exclusive rights to your life ... and that goes for your tongue, too.

Keep your cool when you get involved in an argument. Yes, you may say what you need to say, but do not change into a hooligan when you disagree with others. Make your point in a controlled and sincere manner, never with boxing gloves. This does not become children of the Lord.

"And the Lord's servant must not quarrel; instead, he must be kind to everyone, able to teach, not resentful. Those who oppose him he must gently instruct, in the hope that God will grant them repentance leading them to a knowledge of the truth" (2 Tim. 2:24-25).

Good Medicine

Watch your words and hold your tongue;
you'll save yourself a lot of grief.

– Proverbs 21:23 THE MESSAGE –

Drench your tongue with the Word of the Lord. Entrust your lips to the Holy Spirit, and your words will be edged in silver. Check your anger with gentle words. Challenge a sour face with a few friendly words. Compliment sincerely whenever necessary. Encourage others. Don't be afraid to speak your mind if others have made a mess of things, but never gossip behind someone's back. Be honest. Let your love for the Lord guide you when you reprimand wrong-doers. Sometimes you have to be strict with others as Paul instructs us when he says: "Correct, rebuke and encourage – with great patience and careful instruction. For the time will come when men will not put up with sound doctrine" (2 Tim. 4:2-3).

Of course it will take courage to swim against the tide and have God's language upon your tongue. But remember, the Rock on which you are standing is never shaken, even though you might be. Speak wisely about the Lord to others, even though you say only a few words.

Ask the Lord to load the right language onto your tongue, and leave the rest up to Him. He will turn your words into good medicine.

Don't Go AWOL

Above all else, guard your heart,
for it is the wellspring of life.

– Proverbs 4:23 NIV –

The other day someone told me about one of his colleagues who maintained that he and God had a good relationship. According to this man he liked doing sinful deeds and God liked forgiving sin. This is pure nonsense! You being a follower of Jesus Christ places you on duty for Him full-time. If you are a believer there is no such thing as "time out" to live the way you want to. If you do wrong you are going to be "AWOL" – Absent Without Leave. If you do that you are a lax disciple on point duty.

Do not give up territory to the enemy. Remain at your post, whether you are at work, among friends, in church. Even if you are the only believer among thousands – be strong! If you are with your back to the wall at work – persevere! Remember, the Lord is there with you. He will never ever leave you in the lurch. Do your point duty faithfully among people who do not kneel before God.

Remember, they take note of your example. Your actions speak louder than your words. Your fearlessness in being the Lord's anchor-person makes a deep impression on them, whether they say it or not.

Carrying the Flag

Light is shed upon the righteous and joy on
the upright in heart. Rejoice in the LORD, you
who are righteous, and praise His holy name.

– Psalm 97:11-12 NIV –

I once read a story about two armies who entered into battle in
the American War of Independence. One of the generals, realizing that his soldiers were losing badly, ordered them all to fall
back immediately. But the flag bearer, who flew the colors of
the army right at the front, refused. In haste, the general asked
a messenger to go and instruct the man to fall back immediately. But the flag bearer refused once again. Then he sent back
the following message to the general, "No, Sir, I'm not falling
back. Please instruct the soldiers to march forward to me!"

We are the flag bearers of the gospel. Often you and I find
ourselves alone on hostile territory. Perhaps we all feel like
falling back then. Don't! Instead, call fellow believers through
your actions and words to join you at the front, there where
you are on point duty for the Lord.

Plant the flag of the gospel right at the front in His honor.
Be strong for the Lord. You are never alone in any event. The
One who is stronger is with you. The Lord controls every
trench on the battlefield, each piece of ground where you may
find yourself.

Jesus' Affliction

Let us fix our eyes on Jesus, the
author and perfecter of our faith, who for
the joy set before Him endured the cross.

– Hebrews 12:2 NIV –

Jesus did not suffer on the cross to benefit Himself. Definitely not. Jesus came down from heaven for people like you and me. My only destination was death, until Jesus came and changed everything. With the blood He shed for me on Calvary, He wrote the words "paid in full" over all my sins!

Jesus' Way of the Cross is still the only Way of Life. There is no other way to God. Only the road of Jesus is the right road. His cross is the only eraser of sin. When I stand before Him with a broken heart, He erases my sin in the split of a heavenly second. He erases every fingerprint I left on sin, and every footprint I left behind on the detours of life. Christ gives me a brand-new identity; He makes me a new person from head to toe.

Calvary tells the story not only of the death of Jesus, but also of a new life for me. It is not only about suffering, but also about restoration. I took my stand at the cross of Jesus. Now I can really live for the first time! Glory to God, for the victory bells are still tolling loudly.

The Vine

"I am the vine; you are the branches. Those who
remain in Me, and I in them, will produce much
fruit. For apart from Me you can do nothing."

– John 15:5 NLT –

The scene, Luke 13:6-9: The parable of the fig tree that did not
bear fruit. The main characters: God (the Owner), Jesus (the
Gardener), and me (the tree without fruit).

The solution to not bearing any fruit: A season of grace!
Jesus undertakes to fill my life, inside and out, with heavenly water and fertilizer. He does not simply grant me a year's
grace to see what I will do with it. That would not be true
grace, because it would still leave the ball in my court. Divine
grace does not work that way. No, Jesus gives me a chance
now! He takes sole responsibility for seeing to it that I bear
fruit. Jesus puts His name in jeopardy. He takes the chance
Himself.

Do I have to do anything? Yes, I only have to be in the
vineyard! That is all. Christ looks after the rest. He does the
watering and the fertilizing. I simply have to be there in the
season of grace when He works on my life.

Where is the vineyard? The vineyard is where the Word
is. The vineyard is when I pray. The vineyard is where believers get together and spread the gospel. Be there!

Omnipotence

"And surely I am with you always, to the very end of the age."
– Matthew 28:20 NIV –

Nothing can ever separate you from God's love – not even the biggest crisis you have to face. Nothing in life is a match for the power and love of God, absolutely nothing. Paul assures us of this amazing fact in Romans 8:31-39. You are the special property of the Lord because you believe in Christ. You are so precious to Him that He carries you in the palm of His almighty hand night and day. You are never alone, not for a single moment.

Even though you may feel defenseless and weak at times, you are still a member of God's winning team. Eternity has a permanent place in your heart. You are on your way to the heavenly winning post. Keep on believing that. Do not allow your emotions to play games with you. The Lord is not far from you merely because you feel that way. The Word promises that God is always near.

Although you may feel that the prayers you send up get stuck at ceiling height, you must know that it is your feelings running away with you once again. God is omnipotent – He is with you. Believe it and be free!

His Yoke

Carefully build yourselves up in this most holy
faith by praying in the Holy Spirit, staying right
at the center of God's love, keeping your arms open
and outstretched, ready for the mercy of our Master,
Jesus Christ. This is the unending life, the real life!

– Jude 20-21 THE MESSAGE –

Are feelings of hopelessness and worry your best friends at the moment? Well, then, you are keeping the wrong company! They are going to rob you of your happiness, and of your faith. Do something about it, today. "What?" you ask? Resign from this hopeless brigade. Write a letter of resignation in which you declare that from now on you are not going to let any negative feelings or worries into your heart. If you give free entry to these feelings one more day, they are going to rob you of your faith eventually.

In the parable of the sower in Matthew 13, Jesus warns that worry is a big robber of faith. Be warned: The more you worry, the weaker your faith will be. On the other hand, the greater your faith in God, the more you trust in Him. His shoulders are broad enough to carry the cares of the whole world and to provide for everyone's needs. There is no reason why He will not carry yours. He was prepared to give up His Son to die for you, so why would He not care about every small detail of your life? Believe it.

Standing in the Wind

Pray in the Spirit at all times and on every
occasion. Stay alert and be persistent in
your prayers for all believers everywhere.

– Ephesians 6:18 NLT –

The Day of Pentecost was not windless – anything but. On that day a mighty, heavenly gale-force wind of the Spirit started blowing through our dead and dying world. When the Holy Spirit came down on that day, His wind and fire gave new life to the entire church. People who had been scared before started speaking about Christ fearlessly all of a sudden. At every turn they found their tongues had been loosened. An abundance of power was available once again – supernatural power to witness, to sing, to serve, to make miracles happen!

The heavenly Wind of the Spirit is still blowing today. His power is no less now than it was on the Day of Pentecost – only you and I restrict His power. Perhaps we no longer believe that He has remained unchanged to this day, and that He will remain so forever after. Let us ask the Spirit to fill our souls once again (Eph. 5:17). Let us spread our sails to catch the Wind, the right Wind, the Wind of heaven!

If we stand in the Wind of the Spirit, we will boldly speak about our great God. Then this broken world of ours will be full of hope again: heavenly hope!

Living Temples of God

Don't you realize that your body is the temple of
the Holy Spirit, who lives in you and was given
to you by God? You do not belong to yourself.

– 1 Corinthians 6:19 NLT –

Paul tells an unbelievable story in 1 Corinthians 6:19-20. He writes that we were bought by Jesus when we were still enslaved by sin and death. He came searching for us on the market square of sins. On that day His blood was the method of payment by which He made us His property. Isn't it unbelievable that Jesus has such abundant love for the wrong people, for sinners such as you and me? Well, that is precisely what Christ is like. That is why He buys sinners, even today. His specialty is saving the broken and the dead.

There is another important thing that Jesus did when He bought us. According to 1 Corinthians 6:19, He gave us over to the lifelong care of the Holy Spirit. There and then the Holy Spirit transformed us into temples of the living God. Now we are His final earthly home before the Second Coming. The Spirit builds living temples in honor of our Father. He transforms us into living dwellings in which God can live and work.

We have been set apart permanently to reflect God's greatness. Therefore, we have to live up to, speak up to and do up to His great name! Let's do it!

When Bad Things Happen

God is faithful; He will not let you be tempted beyond
what you can bear. But when you are tempted, He will
also provide a way out so that you can stand up under it.

– 1 Corinthians 10:13 NIV –

"This isn't fair. I have been serving the Lord for years, but now
everything in my life is going wrong. Why does God allow
this? Why doesn't He help me?" Have you heard these types
of remarks? Well, many feel this way. They think God is failing
them. Is this true? No, of course not. God doesn't take off as
soon as His children have tough hills to climb.

However, God's presence does not mean that you will experience prosperity, happiness and wealth always. He does
not guarantee that you will never be faced with dangerous
situations. God's Word promises that He will always be near,
even when you are in need. Call on Him. He will help you, but
in His own way.

Even though you may feel like you are being led like a
lamb to the slaughter and that life is knocking you down,
know that you are never alone. The hands of God your Father
enfold you. You are safe in His arms, even though you may be
bleeding. He will dress your wounds with His Spirit and fill
your life with hope and strength. He renews His true care of
you every day. The sun of His righteousness will shine on you
each day.

Too Little Too Late?

We fix our eyes not on what is seen, but
on what is unseen. For what is seen is
temporary, but what is unseen is eternal.

– 2 Corinthians 4:18 NIV –

That terrible feeling of "too little too late" often clings to you when you leave the church building after a service. Suddenly you feel as though you are the Lord's naughtiest child who can do absolutely nothing right. Well, here is some good news: Christ starts over every day with each and everyone who feels that way, including you! He promises this in this verse.

Jesus is not really as disappointed in you as others would have you believe. He is continually busy transforming you and His other children into the image of God. It happens without you even seeing it. In the same way you cannot see a tree grow, you cannot see yourself growing spiritually. But do not despair. Put your hands in the hands of the Lord and leave your spiritual growth in His care. He will let it happen. Stop focusing on all your mistakes. Place them at the feet of Christ and leave them be.

Stop thinking that you are constantly doing too little too late. To do this is to lodge a vote of no confidence in the work of the Lord. And that is not at all true.

Eyes Like Elisha

The LORD will be your confidence and
will keep your foot from being snared.

– Proverbs 3:26 NIV –

Elisha had very good eyes. He was able to see the invisible realm of God. Do you recall that night he was besieged by enemy soldiers (2 Kings 6)? His servant was petrified when he saw they were surrounded. Elisha, however, told him that their own numbers surpassed the numbers of the opposition by far. This did not make sense to his servant. His arithmetic told him that one plus one made two, and he and Elisha made only two, and they were badly outnumbered by the opposition. Then Elisha prayed to God to open the servant's eyes. All of a sudden he saw a mighty heavenly army surrounding them.

Do you have eyes like Elisha, too? Do you see God by faith, or are the problems around you the only things you see? The Almighty stays near His earthly property at all times. The superior heavenly force is on the believers' side.

However, that does not imply that we will never go through difficult times or that we will never be hurt. What it does mean is that nothing will ever be able to wrest our hands from the hands of God. We are the precious possessions of the Lord. Therefore, He is with us always.

Today

This is the day the LORD has
made; let us rejoice and be glad in it.
– Psalm 118:24 NIV –

You must make some vitally important choices again today. What are they? You must choose where to leave your finger-prints and footprints. Will your fingerprints be displayed on the same old sins and all your bad habits of yesterday again today? What about your footprints? Will they perhaps be left on the road of life where the lonely, the helpless and the hurt find themselves? Or maybe not?

It is your choice whether to touch the lives of others with the love of God, or whether to ignore them. Fortunately, you know which choices you need to make. As a follower of Jesus, the Spirit of God will speak to your heart to make the right choices today. So, what are you waiting for?

Serve the Lord today by making a deliberate choice to take someone else's burdens on your shoulders. Serve God by walking with someone for two miles instead of the one mile they've asked for. Serve Him by deciding to defend someone's integrity when others talk behind his or her back. Serve God by deciding to entrust your life to Him anew right after you have read these words.

More Than a Spectator

Live a life filled with love, following the example
of Christ. He loved us and offered Himself as
a sacrifice for us, a pleasing aroma to God.

– Ephesians 5:2 NLT –

You should do something special with the portion of life God has lent you today. Remember that you receive life only one day at a time. You don't know if you will still be here tomorrow. You are fortunate to have received today as a gift from heaven. Do something special with it. Live and use each and every second of these 24 hours to the glory of God.

Do not let worries or problems spoil your day. Erase each concern from your mind with a prayer right away. Do not allow the wrong people to pull you down into their sinful way of life. Speak only words of encouragement when others around you make nasty remarks. Share a friendly word with a colleague at work who has become a victim of grumpiness. Send an encouraging text message to a friend whom you haven't seen in a long time. Pray for someone who the Lord has placed in your thoughts.

Do not be a passive spectator of life. Play only on the playing field of the Lord today. Live with hope. Realize once more that you are the Lord's prized possession. Jesus Christ bought you with His precious blood.

It Works!

The earnest prayer of a righteous person has great power.

– James 5:16 NLT –

Prayer works. The other day I heard about a poor community in an African township that set up prayer tents. Suddenly the rate of crime in their area decreased dramatically. The chief of police asked the organizer of the prayer movement to put up more tents in areas with a high crime rate because it had such a real effect on the well-being of that community. Isn't it wonderful to hear stories like this?

Praying is speaking with God Himself. It is a personal appointment in the heavenly throne room with the King of the universe. Prayer is about being in the presence of the mighty angels of Christ, the Holy Spirit and God. That is why offering a prayer to the Father in the name of Jesus is so powerful. God is the Hearer of these prayers. He opens the heavenly gates to everyone who seeks His countenance in humility and faith.

James 4 says that we do not receive because we do not pray, and when we do pray our prayers are self-centered. These are the two big hindrances in the path of answer to prayer: not enough prayer and self-centered prayer. See to it that these hindrances are removed from your heart when you approach God.

The Speed of Prayer

"God, have mercy on me, a sinner."

– Luke 18:13 NIV –

Two of the shortest prayers in the New Testament are to be found in the Gospel of Luke. The one is in Luke 18:9-14 where the tax collector prays, "God, have mercy on me, a sinner." There and then, in a moment of heavenly grace, his prayer is answered. Jesus says that this man went home a changed person, someone whose relationship with God had been set right.

The speed of grace is always eons faster than the speed of light. It strikes you every time when you stand naked and bankrupt before God, with nothing else to offer Him than your sins and broken life. There is no speed limit to God's grace. He is always at His best when we are at our worst.

The second short prayer is in Luke 23:42 when the man on the cross next to Jesus asks, "Jesus, remember me when you come into Your kingdom." Jesus answers him, "I tell you the truth, today you will be with Me in paradise." There is no time to lose when people beg for mercy. God answers without fail and always at the speed of grace.

In Step with God

He is your example, and you must follow in His steps.

– 1 Peter 2:21 NLT –

The right question is not "What is God's will for my life?" but "What is God's will?" and how do I obey it? Did you notice the shift in emphasis? God's will is not about me. No, it is about God, 24 hours a day, seven days a week, 365 days a year. It's about His honor, His plans, His dreams, His will!

The only way my plans can synchronize with those of God is when I walk in step with Him. When my diary is replaced by the diary of the living God, and my watch is traded in for a heavenly hourglass, the right things start happening in my life. That is when God's will is done.

How does this happen on ground level in my life? Well, it all starts with prayer. Jesus taught us to pray, "Let Thy will be done!" God's will in your life is not done automatically, but you can miss out on it by being disobedient. The way to get back on track is by praying in faith, praying those getting-in-step-with-God prayers! Your life should be like clay in the hands of God every day: good quality clay that is soft and malleable.

True Life Is Really Free

Because of His great love for us, God, who
is rich in mercy, made us alive with Christ.

– Ephesians 2:4-5 NIV –

It is not thanks to you that you are a Christian today. You were stone dead and covered in sin when God bestowed mercy on you the first time. Christ gave His life for you when you were still a sinner (Rom. 5:8). Even then He loved you. Why? Well, because God is love. He has a wealth of kindness (v. 4) and is a full-time grace farmer.

God loves the wrong people – sinners! He constantly tracks His enemies in order that He can save them. That is why He took you back as His child when you were farthest away from Him. God saved you when you did not want to be saved. He was the One who softened your hard-heartedness. He was the One who delivered you to life once again.

On top of that, Christ removed your heart of stone and replaced it with a heart that loves Him. You have received the greatest heavenly gift ever – a new life, with compliments of the living God. All of that just because you bow before Jesus as your Lord. Believe this good news whole-heartedly every day and live abundantly!

June

First Aid

He has removed our sins as far
from us as the east is from the west.

– Psalm 103:12 NLT –

When sin makes you stumble, do not give up and lie down in the mess. That is exactly where the enemy wants you: wounded and without hope! No, if you have stumbled, do the following:

Confess your sin: Remember the words of 1 John 1:8-2:2 that tell us that if we confess our sins, God is faithful and just and will forgive us. His Son, Jesus Christ, is our only Advocate and Intercessor at times like these.

Accept the redemption of God: When you commit sin you must immediately confess it before God in Christ. At the same time you must know that Jesus will expiate your sins. In turn, God is a righteous Judge; He will redeem you because the sacrifice of His Son is sufficient for you and all others who approach Him with their failures and sins.

Report for duty immediately: If you place your sin in all sincerity at the feet of God, you can and must know He will grant you His divine grace for the sake of Christ. Accept His special redemption and report for duty back at the front line again.

Forgive and Forget

So what do we do? Keep on sinning so God
can keep on forgiving? I should hope not!

– Romans 6:1 The Message –

In Matthew 18 Jesus teaches us that God does not work according to a quota system for forgiveness, like Peter thought. Initially, this disciple of Jesus thought that forgiveness granted seven times was more than enough. In those days the Jews believed that three times was sufficient, so Peter thought seven times was very generous. But then Jesus surprised His disciple with the heavenly formula – 70 times seven. *Ad infinitum*. Endlessly. Constantly! God does not add up the times He has granted forgiveness. He does not keep record of the number of times you have asked His forgiveness. On the other hand, you don't have license to commit sin. Paul addresses this matter very clearly in this verse.

Grace does not give you a free pass to commit sin; on the contrary. But, if you commit sin, remember that you can be redeemed by God through Christ. Therefore, do not give up or allow yourself to be trapped in the mess you are in. At the same time, after you receive the phenomenal forgiveness of God, you should lavishly share it with others. Do not keep record of the times they have wronged you. Forgive and forget. Be finished with bitterness and reproach.

Never Too Late

The LORD will fulfill His purpose for me;
Your love, O LORD, endures forever.

– Psalm 138:8 NIV –

The other day an elderly lady told me she had been converted only recently, but that it was too late for her to do anything meaningful for the Lord. True? No, not at all! It is never too late. Ask Moses. He was a full 80 years old when the Lord decided he was ready to fulfill his life's calling to lead Israel out of Egypt.

Your every word, every action and every prayer in the service of the Lord has eternal value. Even when you give someone a cup of water to drink in the name of the Lord, it does not go unremarked in the right place in heaven (Matt. 10). When you give your last penny for the Lord, like the poor widow in Luke 21, instead of spending it on yourself, note is taken of it in the highest council chamber of the universe.

There is no age limit to being serviceable for the Lord. You don't have to be learned, great, wealthy, or whatever, either. All you have to do is to use every opportunity that comes your way through God. Transform ordinary situations into heavenly occasions to reflect the love of Christ.

Being Yourself

> "Before I formed you in the womb I knew
> you, before you were born I set you apart."
>
> – Jeremiah 1:5 NIV –

An international author recently said that when he asks people who they would like to be, 90% say they would like to be somebody else. Why are people dissatisfied with themselves? Maybe we have become victims of an artificial world where only appearance, status and money count. Your appearance, where you stay, what you do and what you drive, determine how successful you are. Everything revolves around living up to this man-made picture of happiness and prosperity.

God does not want you to become an arrogant person who is always concerned with appearance and possessions. Even less does He want you to be somebody else. Until the day that you die, you will only be you! Make peace with this fact. God thought it good to create you with your unique appearance, personality and body type. If He wanted you to be somebody else, you would have been that person, not so? Long before your birth, He planned you in detail. You are the end-product of an important planning session by God.

Thank Him for the fact that you are you! In this week, in a unique way, live according to your God-given purpose.

Never Asleep

"Watch and pray so that you will not fall into
temptation. The spirit is willing, but the body is weak."
– Matthew 26:41 NIV –

How quickly our strength wanes. Illness, worries and heavy schedules all too easily steal our life's fuel supply. Far too often we are tired, burnt out, dead beat. By the middle of the week, with the weekend hardly over, our flame burns low again. The good news is that God never becomes tired or sleepy. Psalm 121 tells us this good news. Age and illness have no effect on Him. He is never beset by boredom. Unlike we, who often doze off, God is always wide awake. When our knees buckle and our strength diminishes, God still remains strong.

More good news from Isaiah 44 is that not only is God strong when we are weak, but He renews the strength of His tired servants. He replenishes the strength of each and every one who perseveres in waiting for the Lord! That is His promise, to you too! Therefore, if you feel you are at the end of your tether, you need much more than vitamins or a weekend getaway – you need new strength that only God can provide. Knock on His heavenly door. Your portion of heavenly strength is right there waiting. Claim it in the name of Christ.

Small and LARGE

Commit everything you do to the
LORD. Trust Him, and He will help you.

– Psalm 37:5 NLT –

At times I am very aware of my weaknesses. When I trip over a stone on the road of life, I realize that I am fragile. Yes, when all is said and done, I am no more than dust and wind. Even so, this fragile old clay pot contains a precious Treasure. Truly, I am never alone. The Lord is with me because Jesus is the Lord of my life. God is my constant and only Wealth, my Gold, my Silver, my Life.

Even when I am small, God is great. When I am weak, God is infinitely strong. Every time I falter, God is my Rock. When I fall, God remains the strong One. What a miracle: small and LARGE together for ever – the weak me and Almighty God! What an act of grace to have been made a child of our heavenly Father by Christ. He is the One who catches me every time I fall. I know that God never leaves me on my own. He bends down to pick me up, exactly as Psalm 37 promises.

Therefore, I can walk straight ahead until the end because I am accompanied by the strongest One in the universe: Almighty God!

The Great Search

Because You are my helper, I sing
for joy in the shadow of Your wings.

– Psalm 63:7 NLT –

Do you sometimes long for someone so badly that it feels as if you have chest pains? Do you know that deep yearning? If you do, you will have compassion with the writer of Psalm 63 who calls out to God. He longs and thirsts for God like someone in the desert who needs water urgently. Do you know this intense thirst for God? Do you start off every morning in the desert searching for Living Water? And at night, when you lie in bed, do you long for God's strong hand on your shoulder (v. 7)? Does your inner being constantly shout for God? Then be assured that God can be found by every sincere seeker. He will quench your thirst. He will satisfy your longing. He will meet you somewhere.

No one who sincerely calls for God does so in vain. No one who seeks His company walks away empty-handed. God lets Himself be found. He does not hide. He is not busy with other more important matters when you call on Him today. Seek and you will find! That is what the Man of Nazareth said. He knows the heart of His Father best of all.

The Hairs on Your Head

"He pays even greater attention to you, down to the
last detail – even numbering the hairs on your head!"

– Matthew 10:30 THE MESSAGE –

Having read Matthew 10:30, which says that God even counts every hair on our heads, I told my baldheaded friend that he was really making the Lord's task easy. There is nothing left to count on his head!

God is so near, so intensely involved with us that He makes time to get to know the detail of our lives. So much so that He is up to date with "unimportant" detail, such as when we lose a hair. Even if you are privileged enough to have a good head of hair, how many did you lose during the night? God knows. His care is so sincere that He knows even that! How about that for attention to detail? How about that for intense awareness and priority treatment!

God takes special care of His prized earthly possessions. We, who have been bought through the blood of His Son, are His family, His handiwork, His property. That is why He nurtures and looks after us. That is why He carries and protects us. So, touch your hair (or your head!) and know that God is near. Then bow before Him in deep reverence.

A Safe Refuge

The LORD is good, a refuge in times of
trouble. He cares for those who trust in Him.

– Nahum 1:7 NIV –

Trouble! We know all about it. We experience it sometimes
in our lives. Quite often it is our best friend for too long.
Well, don't take it any longer. At the least, don't be victims
of trouble. Do not slide into a "pity me, please" attitude. Take
care that you never sing the evergreen theme song, "no one
knows the troubles I feel."

Choose to effectively and correctly handle your troubles.
Discuss them with God regularly. Pray! Seek His countenance until He opens up heaven above you. Do not let go of
His hand when you are walking in darkness. Persevere to the
end. A green pasture awaits you at the end of each trouble-
some event. That is what Psalm 23 promises. In effect, trouble
is the shortcut on the right way to where you are heading.

Fortunately, the Shepherd of your life is accompanying you
and seeing you through all your troubles while you search for
better pastures. From now on, give your troubles a hard time
when they want to rob you of your happiness. See to it that
you and the Good Shepherd, Jesus Christ, walk side-by-side
always. Note how His footprints cover all your problems.

The Little that You Have

Here is a boy with five small barley loaves and two
small fish, but how far will they go among so many?

– John 6:9 NIV –

*Of what significance can I be to God? I am too weak to really make
a difference.* Is that what you think sometimes? Well, that is
very far from the truth. The Lord does not require you to be
strong before you can start working for Him, neither does He
expect you to have all the best possible equipment at your
disposal. Everything but. Simply use that which you have already. Put that which you have at hand at the disposal of the
Lord and watch what happens!

In John 6, we read about a young boy who had five loaves
of bread and two fishes. He was only a small speck among a
crowd of people of more than five thousand who were listening to Jesus. When Jesus decided to feed everyone, that
small amount of food in His hand was more than enough
for a heavenly feast. Jesus multiplied the boy's meal and it
became enough to feed all the people.

Learn from him to give the Lord the little money, spiritual talent and commitment that you have. Then trust Him to
multiply them to bring forth a rich harvest. He will!

More Than Enough

Let us not become weary in doing good, for at the
proper time we will reap a harvest if we do not give up.

– Galatians 6:9 NIV –

Our basic needs are to have food and clothes every day. Our
foremost need is to have our dreams come true. That is what
the clever guys tell us.

Well, the Bible tells me that Christ has come to fulfill our
basic needs. John 6 says Jesus is the Bread of Life. He takes
away our hunger for ever. Christ also fulfills our foremost
needs. John 7 says that rivers of living water flow from us
when we believe in Him. He lets us experience abundance
every day. We who believe are blessed with armfuls of heavenly life of the kind that never comes to an end. Christ show-
ers us with so many blessings each day that they overflow
from our hands, feet and lips to others.

Christ is our everything! We lack for nothing. When life
is dark, He is our Light. When we are surrounded by pain
and disappointment, He is our Helper. When we feel we cannot or do not want to carry on, He is our heavenly Source
of Strength. When we are abandoned by everybody, He stays
near. When storms rage around us, He walks on the water
beside us. Truly, we have more than we need, now and for
always.

The Good Old Days

Don't long for "the good old days." This is not wise.

– Ecclesiastes 7:10 NLT –

How many of us long for the good old days? For some reason or other they always seem to be better than today. Or are they? Well, I can assure you that if we go back to those times that we idolize as the best days ever we would find fault after a short while and start longing for better days after all.

Perhaps that is why Ecclesiastes 7:10 cautions us not to think that the past is better than the present, because it is not wise to do so. If we did we would not live wisely and be fully aware of every moment we receive gracefully from God's hand.

We have only today to live life fully for the Lord and others. Yesterday is water under the bridge, and we can't be sure that we will see the light of tomorrow. But today is within our reach. Let us turn it into a festive day for the Lord.

Let us hand out cups of cool water to those who are going through difficult times. Let us be good to one another. Let us gladden the heart of the Lord today.

Precious Treasure

"Wherever your treasure is, there
the desires of your heart will also be."

– Matthew 6:21 NLT –

Everything that glitters is not gold. Sometimes the most precious treasures are not buried deep under the ground, but can be found near the surface instead. Look around – your companion, your parents and your children are the Lord's special gifts to you. They are your most precious earthly possessions. The Lord does not want you to struggle through life alone. That is why He gave you your loved ones. They are your helpers, your towers of strength, your biggest supporters, and your gold. They are the ones who constantly pray, stand by you and carry you.

What are you doing for your loved ones? Do you pray for them regularly, too? Do you set an example for them in your commitment to the Lord? Do you set aside enough time for them? Or are you always tired when you have time to devote to them? Do you constantly have the excuse of some more work to finish or two more telephone calls to make? If so, you have not really discovered God's special treasures. You are looking for gold in all the wrong places.

Look at your loved ones once more. Thank God for them and live close to them.

Run Like the Blazes

Run from all these evil things. Pursue
righteousness and a godly life, along with
faith, love, perseverance, and gentleness.

– 1 Timothy 6:11 NLT –

Can you recall the film *Forrest Gump*? He ran for all he was worth right across the USA. He told himself over and over again to just "Run, Forrest, run!" And that is exactly what he did. This is what Paul tells Timothy and all other believers to do in 1 Timothy 6:11: We all have to run. What for? No, the question should rather be from whom or from what. And the answer is, from *sin* of course! We should take care to not be in the same place at the same time as sin. If we are, we will get into trouble because sin is not something to play with.

However, to try and run away from sin is not enough. We have to run *to* someone, to Jesus Christ. Only then will we be safe, because only if we do this, sin will not be able to catch up with us and temptation will lose the race.

Which wrong things in life always get you down? Does this happen because you have not decided to run away from them? If so, today is the day to take to your heels, but then do so in the right direction. Run to the Lord. He is your safe haven.

An Actor or
the Real McCoy?

"When you give to the needy, do not let your left hand
know what your right hand is doing. Then your Father,
who sees what is done in secret, will reward you."

– Matthew 6:3-4 NIV –

Acting is the biggest industry in the world. The stars of Hollywood are the superheroes of today. They have mastered the art
of pretending. The sad thing is that pretending does not only
happen on film sets and in theatres but also in real life. Some
people pretend to be holier than a saint. The good things they
say when they move in religious circles are all an act. We call it
hypocrisy. It is a role you play on Sundays perhaps, but when
you are on your own, where no one else can see you, you show
your real colors. That is when you go off the track completely.

What about you? Are you pretending to be a believer when
it suits you, or are you the real McCoy? The proof of true faith
is whether you serve the Lord when no one is watching. Do
you do good things quietly without expecting any recognition? Jesus says in Matthew 6 that when your left hand does
not know what your right hand is doing, that is the end of
role-playing. When you serve God and worship Him when no
one is near, then that is the real thing.

Turning Words into Weapons

[Believers] must not slander anyone and
must avoid quarreling. Instead, they should
be gentle and show true humility to everyone.

– Titus 3:2 NLT –

My tongue is not mine to do with as I please. That is what the Bible says. I should not use words randomly. Words are weapons of mass destruction, or protective medicine. Depending on the mouth in which words are formed, they can be good or bad. When spoken by a fool, words are killer missiles that break and hurt others. When spoken by the wise, words are like good ointment and medicine that heals. This is what the book of Proverbs says repeatedly.

Paul says in Titus 3 that we as believers should not speak slanderous words about anyone. We should always be soft-spoken and kind. Our words may never be dangerous. They must not inflame the severe infectious situation that vile language causes in society. They must not aggravate the grave sickness that sin has brought into our world. There are enough nasty words around, too many destructive words in circulation in the world.

Let's break this evil spell by constantly speaking God-honoring language. Remind yourself to speak differently about and to people. Speak wisely, calmly and gently. Do not say and do things that will hurt others.

Are You a Worrywart?

Satisfy us in the morning with Your unfailing love,
that we may sing for joy and be glad all our days.

– Psalm 90:14 NIV –

Simplicity is one of the joys of life. It's true, isn't it? There is joy in the simple act of breaking bread with a good friend or family member. Simple joy is playing ball with your children or spending time with your family. And what a joy it is to thank the Lord for the blessing of each new day. Simplicity is being satisfied. It is saying the words of Psalm 23: "The Lord is my Shepherd; I shall not be in want."

What are you short on? Money? A better car? Different job conditions? Well, if you worry about things you lack, you will probably always be dissatisfied with what you have. Even a new car will not be enough. You will be satisfied only when you have one with a sunroof and leather seats. Or when your new training bike looks like your neighbor's.

If you worry about things you don't have, you will always want more or something different. You will always be short of something. But if you know the Lord as your Shepherd, you will truly lack nothing. You will have as much as you need.

Destined for Good Things

> We are God's masterpiece. He has created
> us anew in Christ Jesus, so we can do the
> good things He planned for us long ago.
>
> – Ephesians 2:10 NLT –

God has created us to devote our lives to doing good. That is what Paul writes in Ephesians 2:10. Did you hear? We are destined for good things and not to build castles and monuments to glorify our own names. We have been created to glorify our heavenly Father in the short time we have on earth. Therefore, we must make a difference!

We do not have to change the world. We only have to carry out the few assignments that God has in mind for us. We only have to take part in the relationships that God has planned for us and make a difference.

Well, have you discovered your call in life? Do you know what the purpose of your life is? No? Then it is high time that you start doing the right things. It is time to become part of God's plan to repair the broken world bit by bit. There are sure to be broken people around you who need a piece of bread: living bread and ordinary bread! Start there. Who knows, they have probably been destined by God to cross your path and be part of your destiny.

Counting Your Blessings

Be gentle with one another, sensitive.
Forgive one another as quickly and
thoroughly as God in Christ forgave you.

– Ephesians 4:32 THE MESSAGE –

What does your balance sheet for this year look like so far? Did you use all the chances you were given? Were you more softhearted – someone who cared more about others? Did you show more compassion; a hand more open to those in need? Was your tongue coated in silver more often than it was full of venom? Were you more faithful in prayer? Perhaps you got to know God's Word a little better? Were the lives of others enriched by your friendship? Were you a neighbor to someone whom life had knocked down? Were you the one who made a positive, heavenly difference in the lives of others?

Have you enjoyed this year so far, despite the hardship around you? Have you really noticed the sunrise and felt the wind and rain through your hair? Have you listened to the voices of children playing happily? Did you feel your minister's sermon on a Sunday morning was meant for you in particular? Did you leave church with a smile on your face because you realized God truly loves you? Well, if these moments of happiness on your balance sheet top the heartache, then it has been a good year so far.

Keeping Score

Make allowance for each other's faults, and
forgive anyone who offends you. Remember,
the Lord forgave you, so you must forgive others.

– Colossians 3:13 NLT –

Can you recall the question Peter put to Jesus in Matthew 18:21? "Lord, how many times shall I forgive my brother when he sins against me? Up to seven times?" Actually, Peter's offer was quite generous because the Jews thought forgiving someone three times was more than enough. That closed the books of forgiveness, and feelings of hate could multiply afterwards.

Jesus' reply was that seven times was not sufficient; 70 times seven would be in order. In other words, do not count the times you forgive your fellow man, for there is no end to forgiveness. Forgiveness does not work like sums of addition. The followers of Jesus do not keep record of others' mistakes, or of the times they have forgiven. They never think back on the transgressions of their friends, colleagues and family. Christians have a short-term memory when it comes to how others mess up. On the other hand, they are not blind to their own and others' flaws. However, they talk things over without being nasty about it. They never spread ugly rumors about others behind their backs. And they do not support hate speech.

gh!

ood medic

2 NIV –

June 21

ction

s by
er!

my serm
man had

...es, but
...y we want them to. Fortu-
...us. He likes all of us who bow before
...ess of what we do or fail to do.

...re His special possessions, His favorites, always (Rom.
...39). No, God does not give us a license to do wrong or to
...llow in sin, but His love for us does not depend on what we
do. He loves us in any case. His love does not see-saw – liking us today and disliking us tomorrow. No matter how deep we fall, God seeks us out every time. It is His choice. It is His divine nature.

God's love is not reactive. He does not first look at how we live and then decide whether He still likes us or not. No, God decided at the outset that those who believe in Jesus Christ are the apple of His eye. He likes us best of all His creatures. This is affirmed by the manger and the cross. God is love, and we are the objects of His affection.

ine.

ard an old man next to him st____ ___ __n. When he nudged him in the side, the drowsy ___ ___ humbled, "Sorry, dear, I'll turn over immediately." I don't know whether the elder was just making a joke, and I didn't want to ask him, but it made me realize that my sermons might be like sleeping pills to more people in the church than I would care to know.

I realized that we should not take ourselves so seriously. Perhaps we should take life more lightly (not be flippant, of course!). The facial muscles of too many church people turn to stone when they enter the church. No wonder, because many churches still have a sign out front warning: "SILENCE: CHURCH." I agree that the church is about God, but that does not mean that there is no place for humor in our religious lives.

Perhaps we should look again at the many times Jesus enjoyed the company of people and celebrated with them joyously. Let us imitate Him in that!

One by One

Never tire of doing what is right.
– 2 Thessalonians 3:13 NIV –

The right kind of impact in the world occurs at the rate of one person, one word and one action at a time. Real change is not necessarily brought about by great actions and programs. When the life of one person is filled with hope because of her or his contact with me, another brand-new row of bricks is laid on the road to heaven. The territory taken up by despair, death and hopelessness decreases by one person.

When my words and deeds bring hope to the broken and when my simple actions of compassion help heal their wounds, the world suddenly becomes more bearable, humane and safe! The sunbeams of the gospel warm our world anew.

While our world is becoming colder and more impersonal, I must be the living difference for the Lord. Everyone who comes into contact with me should have my fingerprint of compassion on their lives to show for it. Others should feel and hear the clear echo of heavenly grace in my life. One by one they should move closer to hear more about God, because my life is such a powerful reflection of His love (Matt. 5).

Success

You can make many plans, but
the LORD's purpose will prevail.

– Proverbs 19:21 NLT –

Success does not depend on the two horrible "M-things" –
money and material possessions. It is not about what you
drive, where you live or what you own. What is more, success
does not revolve around our favorite word: "mine, mine, mine."
People who are truly successful are people with integrity
(Rom. 12). These are men and women who touch the lives of
others and are a blessing to them. They make a difference to
the way others live.

Won't you please become a new trademark for excellence?
Let your love for God, your warmth and your caring be an inspiration to others! Start working on a spiritual heritage, one
through which you leave your footprints in heavenly rock and
not in sand. Do not walk over people. No, walk with them
and encourage them. Do not walk proudly in front of other
people. Walk behind them and help them when they get lost.
Do not tower above others; be a servant who looks after them
well. Let the love of the Lord spill over to them by speaking
gentle words and doing kind deeds. Make a living difference
in the lives of others. If you do, you are successful in the right
way in the eyes of the right Person.

Why So Safe?

"Walk with Me and work with Me – watch
how I do it. Learn the unforced rhythms of grace."

– Matthew 11:29 THE MESSAGE –

Orderly, structured, controlled – do these words describe your lifestyle? Do you live within a safe, highly structured routine where everyone and everything is in its right place? Wait, there is nothing wrong with a well-ordered life as such. But the question is: what do you do if an unexpected crisis descends upon you? Does the unexpected take you by complete surprise? Or is this an opportunity for growth?

Do you have the guts to see today as a clean, new page? Are you open and receptive to life's many surprises? Or is everything in your life so structured that you can even arrange your own "surprise party"? Do you still have the ability to see God's hand in a small act of kindness? Or in an unexpected smile, or a quick conversation?

Can you surprise yourself by changing your strict daily routine to visit somebody who is lonely, or to buy flowers for a loved one? Will you dare tell a colleague or a friend how God answered one of your prayers? Do you have the guts? Or do experiences like that disturb your set routines too much? Why so safe?

Use It or Lose It

Faith is being sure of what we hope
for and certain of what we do not see.

– Hebrews 11:1 NIV –

What were your resolutions for this year? Have you kept them after nearly six months have come and gone? It is quite possible that you haven't, because most people who make New Year's resolutions have forgotten them by the third week of January. However, it is not too late to begin over again. How about a new resolution to persevere on the road of God each day for the rest of the year? Remember, faith operates like the "use it, or lose it" rule in rugby. You cannot cling to last year's faith – consider it used up. Faith is about keeping at it each day. Your faith must have an impact on your life here and now, otherwise it is archive material. If it does not have a daily impact, you belong in a museum for people of obsolete faith!

Faith is entrusting Christ with your most precious possession – your life. Live your life each day in the knowledge that your faith is as alive as your most recent steps on God's road.

You must choose anew each day to follow the Lord with all of your heart. You need to decide daily to be obedient to Him in all things.

Storage Space

Love does not demand its own way. It is not
irritable, and it keeps no record of being wronged.

– 1 Corinthians 13:5 NLT –

Supermarkets normally require a vast amount of storage space
for their stock. Perhaps you, too, require a lot of storage space
in your house or apartment for food, clothes, furniture, PCs
and books. Our mind is also full of stored information. If you
are a Christian, then you definitely do not have storage space
in your mind for bad thoughts about other people!

True faith is forgetful. It has the effect of never holding
things against people. Time after time, in your head, you have
to close the little black book which records other people's
misdeeds. At the end of every day we must "delete" the negative information and transfer it to the dustbin for useless information.

In 1 Corinthians 13:5 Paul reminds us that God's people
never keep a record of wrongs. Neither should you. You are
a new person. "Remember to forget and forget to remember" when it comes to bad things. God has renewed your
thoughts, which in any event do not have enough memory or
bandwidth to store resentment or wrongs.

Your Greatest Critic

This is the day the LORD has made;
let us rejoice and be glad in it.

– Psalm 118:24 NIV –

We can be all too critical of ourselves. Far too often we only focus on our faults and failures. Yesterday's errors remove all the joy from today's sunshine. Are you perhaps too hard on yourself? Do you find it difficult to forgive? In that case, adopt Lamentations 3:22-23 as your new daily creed. These are life-changing words, born out of the dark period directly after the Babylonian exile, when the Israelites returned to a devastated Jerusalem. Listen: The Lord's kindness never fails! If He had not been merciful, we would have been destroyed. The Lord can always be trusted to show mercy each morning.

Forget about yesterday's mistakes. Know that God's love is new, every day. Today He truly makes a fresh start with you and everybody else. Today is a new day in God's kingdom. The failures of yesterday and the day before are erased by the Cross of Jesus Christ.

Notice today's new gift of heavenly mercy on your own doorstep. See God's footprints which obliterate your own. Then today's path is so much more accessible. You can make a success of every new day!

Gear Up for God

The LORD will fulfill His purpose for me;
Your love, O LORD, endures forever.

– Psalm 138:8 NIV –

Your car doesn't move when it is in neutral. Neither does your faith. You have been recreated by God to do good things for Him in the ordinary moments of your life! You can't go to heaven if you remain stationary. In fact, Paul tells us in Ephesians 2:10 that God created you to devote your life to do those good deeds for which He prepared you. Are you turning this Scripture into truth?

Every moment of your life is precious. The next hour might just be a God given opportunity in your life to do something profound in His name. During the mundane moments of your life, God sends opportunities your way.

However, no celestial warning lights are flashed. There aren't always angels who appear and shout, "Prepare yourself, God is going to start using you within 10 seconds." Instead, at the traffic light, at your desk or workplace, next to the sports field, or in class, these special moments arise out of the blue. Then you dare not act like an observer or a coward. No, then you must get into *sixth* gear for God.

Sing!

At about midnight Paul and Silas were praying and singing hymns to God, and the other prisoners were listening to them.

– Acts 16:25 NIV –

The scenario: Paul and his assistant, Silas, have just been beaten to a pulp in the city of Philippi for believing in Christ (Acts 16). Half conscious, they are thrown into the maximum security jail in Philippi.

The response: Paul and Silas start singing at midnight. They sing songs of praise – not those evergreen favorites you and I would sing, like "I am done for," but the purest songs of praise. Despite their broken bodies and without musical accompaniment, they sing, although hoarsely, the most beautiful songs of worship ever heard.

God's response: He quiets the heavens so as to hear the pure sounds. Then He stretches out His hand to touch His broken servants in Philippi. At that moment the earth shakes and the doors of the jail swing open.

Paul reports for duty again: Although the jail's doors were open, Paul did not escape. Instead, he told the warder about being saved.

The lesson: Sing! Sing songs of praise in honor of the Lord, even though it is pitch-dark around you. Even though all your prospects seem bleak – sing! Praise God, even though there may be nothing in your life to sing about.

July

Choose Joy

Whatever you do or say, do it as a representative of the
Lord Jesus, giving thanks through Him to God the Father.

– Colossians 3:17 NLT –

Maybe the problem with our plans and visions is that we
set challenges that are too difficult for ourselves. We want to
achieve the impossible. But then our spirit is broken before
we have even started. Maybe we should set smaller, more re-
alistic goals for ourselves. And the goals should also be enjoyable! This month choose to do something with your life that
will make your life and the lives of those around you happier.
Choose goals which reflect God's greatness through the ordinary things you do every day (Col. 3:17).

What about the simple decision to laugh out loud at least
once a day during the month of July? Or to drink coffee with
someone once a week? Is it too much to ask to pray for another person every day? Or to phone someone who is suffering once a week to say that you are thinking of them? Or to
secretly give extra money to somebody in need? Scatter joy
everywhere you go, God's type of joy.

You can't change the whole world and you don't have
to. But you can make your own piece of the world a happier
place. The choice is yours.

Fireproof

If you confess with your mouth that Jesus
is Lord and believe in your heart that God
raised Him from the dead, you will be saved.

– Romans 10:9 NLT –

Financial advisers regularly caution people to make the correct financial investments to ensure a safe future. Peace of mind about tomorrow ensures a better life today. Well, if you are prepared to rely on the advice of financial advisers, what about the advice of a spiritual giant like the apostle Paul? Would you rate his advice more highly than the advice of the competent people around you? Paul was privileged because he had access to the treasure house of God in heaven through prayer. And, furthermore, Paul was instructed to share God's secrets with us, free of charge!

The greatest secret which has now been revealed is that God designed an enduring insurance product which is death proof. This product was personally designed by Jesus Christ when He died on the cross for you. His instructions are simple: Confess with your mouth and believe with your heart that He is the one and only God (Acts 16; Phil. 2; Rom. 10). Then your future will be fireproof. It will also be death proof. Nothing and nobody can wrench you out of the hand of God. Therefore, you may truly live today, with great peace of mind.

Regret

When you ask, you don't get it because
your motives are all wrong – you
want only what will give you pleasure.

– James 4:3 NLT –

A few times I have stood at a death bed. No dying person has ever said to me that they regret not having worked harder, or not having made more money during their life here on earth. No, instead all would have liked to have spent more time with God and with their loved ones. A friend once was on a flight when two of the engines failed. He told me that the captain instructed the passengers at one stage to use their mobile phones and phone their loved ones. No, not their bank manager or their financial advisor. When a person's life hangs by a thread, their heart yearns for their loved ones. Then they pray. And love wins!

Let's get our priorities right while we have the time to do so. Let's walk with God. Let's join the faithful in Revelation 14:1-5 who follow Jesus everywhere He goes. Then we walk as winners on our way to the finishing line, today. Jesus walks on the road of life. When we follow Him we won't have any regrets when our last day on earth arrives. Regret is always one wasted life too late!

Start with Today

"Give us today our daily bread."

– Matthew 6:11 NIV –

Many people live in the future already. But they show up here in the present every day. In fact, they merely regard today as a fleeting moment on the road to tomorrow. Here and now is not really important. For them the meaning of life lies in tomorrow. That is a big mistake. Jesus taught us to live today, to live from here towards the future, not the other way around. In the Lord's Prayer we are taught to pray, "Give us today our daily bread," not tomorrow's bread.

In Matthew 6 we are taught not to worry today, about tomorrow's problems. Life happens today. God's grace is here today. His care, love and support as well. Tomorrow is at least a day away. A lot of water has to run into the ocean before today becomes tomorrow. What a waste of time it is if today we don't fully live to the glory of God.

What a waste to think that we are only going to get around to living to His glory tomorrow or next week. No, today is the day. Go, and receive your portion of grace from God. Give your life to Him today. Then you are living correctly!

A Divine Opportunity

"I now know beyond a shadow of a
doubt that there is no God anywhere
on earth other than the God of Israel."

– 2 Kings 5:15 THE MESSAGE –

When God called on a young Israeli slave in Naaman's household to serve Him in a foreign country, she reported for duty right there on the spot. The greatest moment in her life arrived soon afterwards when Naaman contracted leprosy. Two sentences, at exactly the right time, ensured that she become immortalized in the Bible. Her words "If only my master would see the prophet who is in Samaria! He would cure him of his leprosy" ensured that general Naaman's life changed permanently.

After Naaman was cured of his leprosy, he openly acknowledged that the God of Israel was the only God. He and his attendants had seen God's amazing power in action. Maybe the young Israelite did not know the incredible effect of her words. That does not really matter. The fruit of our work for God is not meant to be observed by us. As long as we seize every divine moment that God brings across our path, we are on track. On the day of Christ, He will show us whether we have utilized every divine moment ... or let it slip through our fingers! The choice is ours.

From the Inside Out

People judge by outward appearance,
but the LORD looks at the heart.

– 1 Samuel 16:7 NLT –

We spend most of our time getting our lives sorted out externally. Consider our domestic routines: our clothes are neatly packed in cupboards, food is stored in pantries and our cars are parked in garages. The greatest part of our time, money and energy is taken up with tangible things like clothes, cars, houses, the acquisition of possessions and our appearance.

Paul writes in 1 Corinthians 3:16 that we who believe in Christ are a temple of the Holy Spirit. We are God's new home here on earth. God does not reside in church buildings. We are His house, His spiritual temple. And yet many of our spiritual houses are derelict, because we spend too much time on our external dwellings. We believe the lie that life actually happens externally.

God teaches us that we do in fact operate differently. There is only one way to live our lives from the inside out: we must give the Holy Spirit free access to our lives, from the inside out. We must be soft clay in the Sculptor's hands so that He can decorate us with His love and mercy. Then we will live the way God wants us to.

God Knows You

You hem me in – behind and before;
You have laid Your hand upon me.

– Psalm 139:5 NIV –

You are not a biological coincidence. Psalm 139:13-14 exclaims, "For you created my inmost being; you knit me together in my mother's womb. I praise You because I am fearfully and wonderfully made; Your works are wonderful, I know that full well." God knows you inside out, from way back when. He knows more about you than you could ever know about yourself. Before your birth God already knew the path that your life would follow. "You know me inside and out, You know every bone in my body; You know exactly how I was made, bit by bit, how I was sculpted from nothing into something. Like an open book, You watched me grow from conception to birth; all the stages of my life were spread out before you, the days of my life all prepared before I'd even lived one day" (vv. 15-16).

God knows every thought that crosses your mind. He sees your whole existence in a flash, in all its dimensions. There is no part of your life that you can hide from Him. All your decisions, dreams, fears, joys – literally every millimeter of your life – are known to God. He looks right through you. Don't try to understand how it works, because it isn't possible.

Passion

"I will give you a new heart and put a new
spirit in you; I will remove from you your
heart of stone and give you a heart of flesh."

– Ezekiel 36:26 NIV –

Recently I heard two people discuss a church elder, one of
them remarking that the elder had too little passion for the
work of the Lord. This comment really got me thinking. A
church leader without passion and Christians without hearts –
how is this possible? I don't know, but it is really sad, to say
the least. Too many Christians understand the Bible intellectually, but they have not told their hearts about it. They have
the correct answers to all kinds of difficult questions, but their
faces are not radiant when they talk about God and His affairs. How sad.

The gospel requires the attention of your heart. Yes, your
head as well, but particularly your heart. If you can't testify, as
Paul did in Philippians 1:21, "For to me, living means living
for Christ, and dying is even better," then you have completely
missed the pulsating heartbeat of faith. If you are not child-
ishly excited about God and His affairs, then you lack spiritual
passion. If this is the case, you should sit in God's presence
until you experience His glory. You should leave everything
and wait upon Him until He reveals His heart to you again.

A Strong Fragrance

Thanks be to God, who always leads us in
triumphal procession in Christ and through us spreads
everywhere the fragrance of the knowledge of Him.

– 2 Corinthians 2:14 NIV –

Faith smells. And it is a strong smell. In *The Message* Paul writes, "Everywhere we go, people breathe in the exquisite fragrance. Because of Christ, we give off a sweet scent rising to God, which is recognized by those on the path of salvation – an aroma redolent with life. But those on the way to destruction treat us more like the stench from a rotting corpse." We as Christians are Christ's aroma on earth. Some people think we smell badly. Others think that we have the scent of Life. What a contrast – life and death, salvation and destruction. All of this we exude if we live close to Jesus.

It is astounding that we are God's fragrance on earth. It is so sad that some people confuse the smell we have with that of death. They can't stand us because they are enemies of the cross of Christ. Nevertheless, even though some people think we smell, it is our obligation to be Christ's aroma. We must distribute true life through our actions. How? Well, by living Christ's victory. But we must stay close to Him all the time. That is the secret. Then Christ's rejuvenating power flows through us to those who need it most today.

He Holds Me

In the same way, the Spirit helps us in our
weakness. We do not know what we ought to
pray for, but the Spirit Himself intercedes for
us with groans that words cannot express.

– Romans 8:26 NIV –

When Christ returned to heaven, He did not leave us to our own devices. He gave us the Holy Spirit in His place, as Helper, Consoler, Spiritual Assistant, Advocate, Savior, Intercessor, Builder of Temples ... Now, we are no longer alone, even if no one else is present. The Holy Spirit is our permanent companion. He is with us all the time. He raises us up when we are really down and out. He intercedes for us with the Father when we do not know how or what to pray. He keeps us on the right spiritual path to the Father's heart.

When we start losing direction, the Holy Spirit immediately comes looking for us. When we try to hide from God in the darkness of our own faults and misdemeanors, He switches on a bright spiritual light in our lives. We cannot run, we cannot hide – neither from ourselves nor from Him. The Spirit's task is to one day deliver us, safe and sound, to God the Father in His eternal heavenly dwelling (Eph. 1:13-14). This is why He consistently ensures that we stay on track. He keeps us en route to God.

Living Art

Let us then approach the throne of grace
with confidence, so that we may receive mercy
and find grace to help us in our time of need.

– Hebrews 4:16 NIV –

David states in Psalm 139 that you are a unique creation of God. The Almighty God decided that you would specifically live in these times. God sketched your life on His easel. He planned you and called you into being. And then you were born. No, you are not a coincidence. God observes your life with great interest, every day. He notes everything that you do. He hears all your words. He reads all your thoughts.

God's expectation is that you will change in order to reflect His heavenly kindness, more and more. His desire is that you will let His light shine brightly in this dark world of ours. Not only did God form you with great care, and endless love, when Jesus carried your sins on His shoulders to the cross, He remodeled you into a new person. God interceded in your life once again through Christ, because He does not want you, one of His special works of art, to go to ruin.

Give thanks to God for having created you on His easel and for re-creating you. Start achieving your unique spiritual potential.

Jesus Is the Answer

"I am the Alpha and the Omega, the First
and the Last, the Beginning and the End."

– Revelation 22:13 NIV –

"Jesus is the answer!" somebody once wrote on a wall. Some-one else wrote below it: "What is the question?" Maybe that is not such a stupid comment. Maybe we should ask the question differently. "For whom is Jesus the right answer?" Well, He is not the answer for religious people, but He is the answer for wrong people, for sinners! Jesus gives brand-new life to sinners who pitch up, bent and broken. He changes them at the speed of heavenly mercy into new persons. But for "religious"folk who think that their lives are good enough, Jesus has nothing to offer.

So, is Jesus the answer? It depends on who you ask. It depends on how great your need is. Are you desperate to sort out your affairs with God? If you are desperate to repair your relationship with God, then Jesus *is* the answer! If you have taken your sins to Him, then you will definitely know what I am talking about. But if you have not done it, then it is high time you pay Jesus a visit. He has reserved a special place for you at His feet. He will answer your most pressing questions. Just go and ask!

Setting the Pace

Let us run with endurance the race God has set
before us. We do this by keeping our eyes on Jesus,
the champion who initiates and perfects our faith.

– Hebrews 12:1-2 NLT –

In long distance races there are often "pacesetters." Pacesetters are athletes who run in the front of the pack for one or two laps, to inspire the champions to achieve better times. Normally, pacesetters retire before the end of the race. They get out of the way of the winners who break records and receive all the glory. Pacesetters are actually the unseen heroes on whose shoulders the champions stand. Maybe it is my and your calling to be spiritual pacesetters, in God's world. We should deliberately create opportunities for co-believers to run past us, to beat us. We should proactively invest in the lives of others so that they can grow past us spiritually.

When other Christians excel spiritually, we win. When we support co-believers to do things in a better way than ourselves, for God's glory, to worship better, to testify more powerfully, to teach or preach more dynamically, to be better at prayer, then Christ's message wins. In these circumstances, we contribute in a modest way to set the pace for God's athletes. The emphasis then falls in the right place, on God and on others, not on ourselves.

Not Ashamed

If anyone is in Christ, he is a new creation;
the old has gone, the new has come!

– 2 Corinthians 5:17 NIV –

I could hear the excitement in my daughter's voice when she told me that she had tickets to watch her favorite Christian band. The tickets for the show had been selling like hot cakes. My daughter just had to be there. Their music plays an important role in her spiritual formation and in her daily life. Therefore, she told everybody about it.

Her excitement made me wonder if my heart beats for Christ in the same manner as her heart beat faster when she had the opportunity of seeing her favorite Christian band performing live?

After thinking about this, the words of Paul in Romans 1:16 obtained a fresh, new meaning for me. "I am not ashamed of the gospel, because it is the power of God for the salvation of everyone who believes: first for the Jew, then for the Gentile."

How can I remain silent about the best news of the day, about the headlines for the year? How can I remain silent when Christ is the only Power in this powerless world? How can I stop rejoicing when He still changes lives?

Taste!

Taste and see that the LORD is good.
– Psalm 34:8 NIV –

"You do not want to leave too, do you?" Jesus asked the disciples after many had turned away (John 6). They had just heard that they should follow Jesus radically, but they weren't prepared to do so. They weren't prepared to eat His flesh and drink His blood, as He explained to them. The demands of discipleship were too high, and the cross they had to bear, much too heavy. Peter's answer was equally direct and straightforward: "Lord, to whom shall we go? You have the words of eternal life!" (John 6:68).

If you "taste" Jesus' words, your hunger will disappear. It is like eating eternal food. You can never go away from Him once you have swallowed His living words. It gives eternal energy, forever! But you first have to eat His words to really understand what Peter meant. How do you do that? Well, just ask Jesus to pronounce living words over you. He will do it, immediately! Then you ingest bread which will satisfy your spiritual hunger forever. You will never want to leave Jesus, because then you will die of spiritual hunger.

Before You Speak

Set a guard over my mouth, LORD;
keep watch over the door of my lips.

– Psalm 141:3 NIV –

A person thinks six times faster than he talks. Academics calculate that the typical person talks at approximately 100 words per minute, but that they think at 600 words per minute – with visuals and all! Well, if that is true, then it means that I have to be more cautious with my words – because they don't just happen automatically.

Too many dangerous words swirl around in my head before they leave my lips. For this reason I should pray Psalm 141:3 as if my life depends on it. I must beg God to place a guard in front of my mouth and allow Him to keep watch permanently over the door of my lips. Where my thoughts start I must only allow those that are good and pure. If I don't, I will think foolish thoughts. Even worse, I may speak negative words in the company of other people.

In that event, my words will become weapons of destruction and not soothing balm or good medicine. I must place my thoughts and my words, like clay, in God's hands today. Then other people will experience healing in the presence of all my words.

Get Out of the Boat

Jesus immediately said to them:
"Take courage! It is I. Don't be afraid."

– Matthew 14:27 NIV –

To walk on water is not normal. Ask Peter! You have to climb out of your boat before you can walk on water with Jesus. And that requires a fixed stare in His direction and a secure grasp of His hand. But is walking on water really as difficult as some people think. Yes and no! Yes, walking on water is difficult for those unused to doing so!

For those who never risk talking about their faith proactively, or who never stay obedient to God through thick and thin, life's storms can be devastating. But for those who time and time again risk following Jesus even in the midst of a storm, and who are not embarrassed to be carriers of the cross, sometimes they walk on water. It does not scare them. It is also not impossible.

Jesus lifts us above every storm, provided that we place our hand in His! Don't let life's storms cause you to let go of His hand. Look past your crises – look towards Him, who is greater! Walk towards Him. That is the secret.

Not for Sale

My soul finds rest in God alone; my salvation comes
from Him. He alone is my rock and my salvation.

– Psalm 62:1-2 NIV –

Two Simons ... Simon the sorcerer and Simon Peter, in the
town Samaria (Acts 8). Simon the sorcerer was known as "The
Mighty;" the other Simon as Peter, the Rock, the one upon
whose testimony Christ built His church (Matt. 16). Simon
the Powerhouse versus Simon the Rock: worldly sorcery compared to heavenly power. No contest! Simon the sorcerer was
immediately stumped when he saw how Peter communicated
the gospel to people in Samaria. The power of the Spirit that
worked through Peter changed their lives from the inside out.
Then the sorcerer tried to purchase this supernatural power.

What a mistake to think that God can be purchased with
money! The Spirit works in His own way. He is never for sale.
His power cannot be copied. Thank God, He works charitably
and completely free in the lives of those whom He changes
into temples of the Almighty. The Spirit changes ordinary
people into rocks who can bravely testify about Jesus, not into
sorcerers who try to impress with tricks.

Let Him use you as one of His rocks, so that people around
you may change in the right way, too.

Our Awesome God

"My Father, who has given them to Me, is greater than all; no one can snatch them out of My Father's hand."

– John 10:29 NIV –

A few years ago my wife and I traveled through Turkey with a wonderful group of people, where one afternoon we experienced a solar eclipse. For a few minutes the moon moved across the sun and the world around us was pitch dark. Everybody who experienced it was overwhelmed, as was I. Once again I realized just how big and mighty God is. I was in awe over His power. He has the power to push the moon quietly across the path of the sun. He can extinguish the sun when it suits Him. But the tenderness with which He guards His creation so that the planets remain in orbit day after day is too much for me to understand.

Psalm 8 cries out, "What is man that You are mindful of him?" In the greater scheme of things we are a handful of nothings, little bits of dust in life's massive machine. Yet God concerns Himself with tiny human beings like us. He creates us out of dust and He lets us live in front of Him, daily. He even loves us. God holds us, Christ's sheep, lovingly in His hands (vv. 28-30). Praise His name!

Little People

"Whoever welcomes a little child
like this in My name welcomes Me."

– Matthew 18:5 NIV –

Jesus compared His followers to little ones (Matt. 18). No, not strong ones or important ones. Not supermen with X-ray eyes that fly around from one spiritual heroic deed to the next. Not powerful lions or giant elephants. No, little ones! Leaders and followers in Jesus' group are vulnerable! Power is not their strong point, but faith is! Status and fame does not mean anything to them, but respect does! They care for each other. They constantly pray for each other, support each other; cry and laugh together. They do life together in the presence of their Father in heaven.

Jesus' little ones do not have a high opinion of themselves. They have no reason to, because they know that everything that they have is through grace. They never try to push to the front of life's queues, because it is not about them. It is only about God and His gigantic love for a world that is in ICU. Therefore they worship Jesus day and night. They talk about Him and to Him. They sing about Him. And they gladly serve those ones that He sends across their path daily.

Awe

Put yourself aside, and help others get ahead.
Don't be obsessed with getting your own advantage.
Forget yourselves long enough to lend a helping hand.

– Philippians 2:3-4 THE MESSAGE –

The world is becoming cynical. Nobody believes anything good about anybody else anymore. When somebody is successful, she or he is maligned. When somebody wins, others "steal" his or her medal by making sarcastic comments behind his or her back. Nobody is safe from the cynical comments of other people. Should we not trade in our cynical hearts for hearts full of wonder? How? Well, start by doing what Paul recommends in Philippians 2. Start by treating others as more important than you. Notice that God gives His grace in large quantities to the people at work and in the church. Remember, you are not the only person whose prayers are heard. See the beauty in friends and family despite the scars that life has inflicted on them. For a change, look past their faults; look until you see how God also blesses them with His grace.

Awe makes you smaller and others bigger. As you become smaller before God, so your cynical nature disappears. The more Christ's heartbeat echoes within you, the more you discover the beauty in others. And then you become the restorer of God's creation and not the inflictor of scars.

Against the Stream

Imitate God, therefore, in everything you
do, because you are His dear children.

– Ephesians 5:1 NLT –

"It won't work." "Don't even try." How many times have you heard statements like these when you have a dream? Don't listen to such comments. If Moses listened to all the prophets of doom on the way to the Promised Land, Israel would have collapsed into the desert sands of Egypt. If Elisha started trembling when the enemy armies surrounded the town of Dothan (2 Kings 6), like his slave did, he would have disappeared from all memory. If Paul listened to Luke and his co-workers who tried to prevent him from returning to Jerusalem (Acts 21), a large part of the Roman Empire would not have heard the good news of Christ.

If Martin Luther listened to the advice of his peers he would never have stood up against the church of his day and, in so doing, launched the Reformation. If Mother Teresa had relied on human support and finances she would never have gone to Calcutta and changed the plight of the poor and sick.

And you? Do you constantly lend your ears to a stream of pessimists, or do you listen to the calling of the Spirit within your heart?

In His Service

"Whoever wants to become great among
you must be your servant, and whoever
wants to be first must be slave of all."

– Mark 10:43 NIV –

You can place your serviette in one of two places: on your lap when you eat, or over your arm when you serve others. By the way, Jesus' favorite followers are not those being served at the table, but those serving: those who are the waiters, the slaves, the servants. That is what He says in Luke 17. His followers who make a real difference stand at the back of the queue. For Jesus first is always last and last is always first. For Him, the back is in front and the front is at the back. This sounds upside down, and it is. Being a Christian is topsy-turvy. Jesus really turned our world upside down!

Jesus does not call His "upside down" followers, lions. Instead, He calls them sheep. Not elephants, but lambs. Jesus came to earth wearing modest clothes and He spent most of His time among the "wrong" crowd of sinners: weaklings, strangers, sick people, people who had been shunned, those who were lonely, homeless and despised. In the same way, He expects us to follow in His footsteps. Therefore, Jesus' modern heroes are those who live back to front and upside down, by becoming childlike and being modest in appearance.

God Likes Me

"We believe that we are all saved the same way,
by the undeserved grace of the Lord Jesus."

– Acts 15:11 NLT –

God does not owe us anything. He is not in our service. What can we do for Him so that He owes us anything in return? In Romans 11, Paul says that God does not like us as a result of who we are. No, He loves us *despite* who we are. This is called grace, the type Paul refers to in Romans 5:

At just the right time, when we were still powerless, Christ died for the ungodly (v. 6)

God demonstrates His own love for us in this: While we were still sinners, Christ died for us (v. 8)

If, when we were God's enemies, we were reconciled to Him through the death of His Son, how much more, having been reconciled, shall we be saved through His life! (v. 10).

Powerless, sinners, enemies: that is who we were when God encountered us, by no means strong, victorious or nice! He loved us when we were knee deep in muck. Despite ourselves – that is how God likes us most! His love says so much more about Him than about us. That is what He is like. He does not owe us anything, and yet He dispenses grace to us every day.

All You Need

"My grace is enough; it's all you need."
– 2 Corinthians 12:9 THE MESSAGE –

"It's mine!" Those are the words of a two-year-old if you dare take his toy. And if you don't return it promptly, there is war, because it's "mine!" Some adults also live in this manner. Everything in the shops, every new product, has their name on it. "Mine" is what they say to themselves when they see a new car, CD, clothes, furniture, video camera, laptop or cell phone. There is no rest for their soul until that item has also become theirs. As soon as the item has been purchased, they want something else.

We live in a world which continuously creates one desire after the other. We never have enough things that can be regarded as "mine." If we don't guard against it, we can become prisoners of our desires. That is why John warns against a continuous desire for things that have to be exhibited on the "must-have" shelf (1 John).

As a believer, I often say that the Lord is my Shepherd. Well, then, I should have such a deep desire for His love and mercy that I make His love "mine" with everything that I have in me. Only then will I really have enough.

Math

If God is for us, who can be against us?

– Romans 8:31 NIV –

Are you afraid of the dark? Does that small portion of life that is yours to live every day get you down? Well, then you have to do the right thing: Pray! Ask God to open your eyes wide for a change. Start doing heavenly math. That will make you realize that ONE plus one is a winning recipe!

Take Elisha, when he was surrounded by the Arameans (2 Kings 6). The one morning his servant got up and feared for their lives. Elisha asked God to open his servant's eyes, but still he could see nothing else than the Arameans on all sides. He was paralyzed with fear.

Elisha's words, "Those who are with us are more than those who are with them," did not help. According to the servant's arithmetic, one plus one made two, and that was far less than the army that surrounded them – until God opened his eyes. Only then did the servant understand heavenly mathematics. He discovered that ONE plus one is always the majority when that ONE is God. With God on your side, you are a winner. With Him on your side, you will always be the majority.

Waiting for Instructions

"Be still, and know that I am God."

– Psalm 46:10 NIV –

Do you often feel like changing everything and everybody around you? Are you always on some or other mission? Why? Is this really God's plan for your life – to change others so that they can be better people? Do you really know what He wants you to do, or do you just decide by yourself?

If you want to be Atlas, carrying the world's misery and problems on your shoulders, I have bad news for you: You can't be everything to everybody. In the long run, you will be nothing to nobody! You do not have to change the whole world. You are not the savior of the church, or the only answer to all of mankind's problems.

Instead, you are only one person. But wait, at least you are *you*; you are one person with the spiritual potential to be yourself every day. Stop trying to be everything to the rest of the world. You might miss out on the real "you" that God created you to be. Be still in His presence until you hear where He wants you to be and what He wants you to do. Only then, show up where He wants you and wait on further spiritual instructions!

Opposites

Since we live by the Spirit, let us keep in step with the Spirit.
– Galatians 5:25 NIV –

What is the opposite of rushed? Or hasty? It's not peaceful, slow, or unhurried. Certainly not if you are walking along God's route. The opposite of all these words is: "Keeping pace with God!"

Do you live in the fast lane? If yes, you should get with it, and get into the same rhythm as God. See what His speed and rhythm is and adjust your own accordingly.

God's speed is not always the same. Sometimes you will experience a season of grace. When this happens, God wants to spoil you with His blessings. At such times peacefulness is a pre-requisite – neutral or first gear, as it were. At other times He might send you all over the place on urgent missions. This is a season of activeness and being busy. Third, fourth or fifth gear is then required.

To live in pace with God removes all frenetic urgency, ir-respective of whether you sit, stand or run with Him. If you live close to God, according to Isaiah even if others tire, you will fly on the wings of an eagle (Jer. 29:11).

Fast Enough for God

So I never lose sight of Your love, but keep
in step with You, never missing a beat.

– Psalm 26:3 THE MESSAGE –

Do you sometimes feel like pushing the cars in front of you out of the way, because you are in such a hurry? Do you always try to finish the sentences of others, because you don't have time for small talk? Does somebody who unexpectedly visits you at home disturb your routine? How impatient are you?

There is nothing wrong with being efficient and fast. Just don't be too fast for God. That's all. Remember that He created the world one day at a time. He reduced His speed from celestial speed to walking pace. Genesis 3 tells us that God actually strolled with the people that He created. Talk about a reduction in speed! The eternal God adjusted to a one-day-at-a-time speed. Why can you not achieve that, too?

Get in pace with God, one day at a time. This is the speed of God's creation, which is also His relaxation speed. At the end of the day He sat back and enjoyed His creation. Adjust to that speed. Then you are living fast enough! You will always be on time and in time for the most important things!

Carpe Diem

Satisfy us in the morning with Your unfailing love,
that we may sing for joy and be glad all our days.

– Psalm 90:14 NIV –

God likes today so much that He made it. He made it especially for us to fully enjoy! He planned it and it arrived just in time! It's only as a result of His grace that today has been added to the world's calendar. God wants us to experience today in all its splendor and beauty. We should not save our energy for tomorrow. Tomorrow is still far away. Do not do what Shirley Valentine did when she said, "I got lost in unused time!" It is terrible to get lost in that way. Too many people are lost in time. They keep waiting for better days, instead of creating something today, in God's name!

For a change, pitch up at the most important day in your own life – today! Today has the right spiritual DNA, because it was uniquely created by God. And He gave it to the occupants of this world, including you. Don't pack today away in the storage cupboard of so many other wasted, unlived days. Your daily portion of heavenly bliss awaits. Consume it and live today!

Radical

Trust in the LORD and do good.
– Psalm 37:3 NLT –

Sometimes spiritual opportunities arrive once only. Perhaps this is why the friends of the disabled man in Matthew 9 did something really radical. They decided to break down the roof of Peter's house, to lower their disabled friend down to Jesus. Talk about extreme! – tearing down a roof to get a sick friend to Jesus. Remarkable! The next day Jesus could possibly be gone and then the chance of a lifetime to bring their sick friend to Him would have disappeared.

Jesus couldn't ignore their pluck. All of a sudden they were in Jesus' personal space, in His face. That is radical faith. That is what happens when people only have one chance to change the world and to help others. Roofs have to be broken down. Appearance and etiquette are much less important than rejuvenating lives through Christ.

You have been nominated as an impact player in God's kingdom to make a difference today. Let your light shine. Leave your stamp on for all 24 hours that you have. Ensure that people who spend time with you in this time take note that you are a representative in Christ. Let your presence count!

August

God's Way

The LORD directs the steps of the godly.
He delights in every detail of their lives.

– Psalm 37:23 NLT –

Frank Sinatra sang, "I did it my way." One day I would like to sing, "I did it God's way." In fact, I want to sing it tonight, before I go to bed. I do not want to postpone my walk with God one more day. Days come and go! Opportunities abound, but sometimes days to walk with God only arrive once. There are more than enough wasted, unused days in my life. I want to stop wasting time in such a senseless way.

As Paul said in the letter to the Ephesians, I want to redeem my time. I will start by living and experiencing today (which I have received by the grace of God), in the right way. I can't afford to waste today. I want to welcome Jesus into my life today, as a special honored guest. Then I will use my time effectively.

I know that Jesus never waits until tomorrow or the next day to help. He sets His watch to the needs of broken people. His diary is overflowing with appointments with people who have sinned. That is where I want to be, with those people: radically flat-out, at top gear, at today's speed.

The Right Thing

Anyone, then, who knows the good
he ought to do and doesn't do it, sins.

– James 4:17 NIV –

Confucius once said, "To know what is right and not to do it, is the greatest deed of cowardice." James took it one step further by saying that he who knows how to do good and does not do it, sins, a contravention of God's will. James regards a life that is lived expressively as the best evidence of faith in God. Faith cannot be merely expressed by a few confessions in church, or in discussions between people about what is right and wrong. Faith must become daily experiences. Faith in God must be spoken, done, seen, heard and felt. Otherwise faith is just words in the wind, cowardice or (even worse) sin! Did you hear that?

How much of what you know is right, is demonstrated every day, in your life? Perhaps I should not ask you this question, but rather your colleagues, family, friends, a shop assistant who helped you, or the guy at the grocery store. What will they say after having been in your company? Do they experience the love of God in your life? Well, why don't you ask them?

The Price Tag

Jesus said, "I am the Road, also the Truth, also
the Life. No one gets to the Father apart from Me."

– John 14:6 THE MESSAGE –

The road to heaven has been irreparably damaged. Sin is the cause. None of us can get back to heaven on our own. Not even the nicest things that we do are sufficient or enough to create a new stairway to heaven. Every ladder that we erect is based on precarious foundations!

We need somebody to bridge this divide between God and us. If somebody does not build a path from heaven back to earth, we would be in a quandary. Somebody who is very powerful, big, strong and merciful has to help us. Fortunately there is such a person, just one – Jesus! He has already bridged the divide. Where no road existed before, He has built a road with His own life. His journey to us was the most expensive road in the universe. It opened a new road to God, a road with protection against sin and death.

If you are worried about the travel costs – Jesus has already purchased and paid for the ticket for your journey. Believe in Him as God over your life and just stay on His track daily.

The Power of His Name

Never stop praying.

– 1 Thessalonians 5:17 NLT –

Prayer should be a daily way of life for us all. Prayer is our regular, from-the-heart communication with the one and only living God. That is why Paul wrote, "Never stop praying." But remember to shoulder other people's problems when you stand in the presence of God. Place the names of the people around you before Him. You can even pray for those whom you do not know. Carry their needs to our Father in heaven; intercede for those who are suffering.

Instead of staring into space when you have stopped at an intersection, pray a sentence for the person in the vehicle next to yours. Or pray for the people sitting next to you in the bus. Maybe you are the only person who will ever pray for them. Who knows, your one-sentence-prayer could just be the missing link to open doors (in heaven or on earth) for them. Pray regularly, until the heavens open for the persons for whom you are praying. Most importantly, always remember the words of John 16:24, to pray in the name of Jesus Christ. Then mercy rains down!

Out of Control

"You will call on Me and come and pray to Me,
and I will listen to you. You will seek Me and
find Me when you seek Me with all your heart."

– Jeremiah 29:12-13 NIV –

Sometimes my prayers are nothing more than pious presentations to God of my own plans. Actually, they are disguised (or undisguised) instructions, together with all the necessary requests about precisely how and when it should happen. In fact, I am often so busy communicating my own needs to God that I forget to seek His presence unconditionally. I try, way too often, to stay in control of things, specifically through my prayers. That's a mistake! The essence of true prayer is being out of control. It means trusting God with everything. It means confessing that everything that I am and everything that I have, comes from Him.

God, and God alone, is in charge of my life. True prayer means becoming devoid of myself. My prayers should never be disguised attempts to regulate God's calendar and activities or to fill up His day with my selfish trivialities. For this reason, I submit myself, in childish belief and trust, to the will of God. For this reason, I kneel without any conditions before God, dependent and full of wonder. From now on, that is how I will live, dependent on my Father's grace! I will pray to honor Him. That's all that matters.

Faith Is ...

Faith is being sure of what we hope
for and certain of what we do not see.

– Hebrews 11:1 NIV –

Faith is:

- the certainty that Christ did everything that I could not do myself, on my behalf, to make things right between me and God.
- to expect everything from God. Faith is not something that I have in me. *My* faith is never the issue, as if it is measureable. Faith just means that I place all my trust in Christ. He makes a new life possible!
- not a manner of changing life into a safe or predictable environment. Faith does not isolate me from surprises, shocks, disappointments, unexpected happiness or uncertainty. Ask Paul, who writes in 2 Corinthians 4 that he is also perplexed sometimes.
- a lifelong adventure. Faith asks the guts to follow Jesus in a courageous way, even if you do not know where the path is taking you because you lifted His cross onto your shoulders.

Faith is the certainty of Christ and His gift of salvation, even if you are not sure of what the next 24 hours holds in store. It is the courage to trust Him today, with your life and your eternal future.

Creating Opportunities

Let us not become weary in doing good, for at the proper time we will reap a harvest if we do not give up.

– Galatians 6:9 NIV –

Many people caution you to wait for the right moment. However, the problem is that many people wait for the right opportunities until the day they die. They spend their lives waiting in vain. For them, life is like a traffic light that never changes to green. I think it works the other way around, actually. God's way is always a green traffic light. You learn what His will is while you are on the move.

Of course there is space for standing still in our spiritual lives. But faith is not one long sequence of silence, passive moments in a celestial reception. Instead, it is about the right activities. Faith happens. And it happens in real life. It means seizing every spiritual opportunity, every day, like David who accepted Goliath's challenge to Israel, as a wonderful opportunity to praise God. While the Israeli soldiers wondered how they could annihilate such a giant, David in turn wondered how he could miss such an enormous target with his five missiles! Do the same. Create opportunities to praise God, every day! Live abundantly, in praise of Him! Just do it!

Internal Radar

Set your sights on the realities of heaven, where Christ
sits in the place of honor at God's right hand. Think
about the things of heaven, not the things of earth.

– Colossians 3:1-2 NLT –

Did you know that in your brainstem there are a group of cells
that are known as the "Reticular Activating System" (RAS)?
The function of these cells is to determine which stimuli
should get priority. Test yourself – let's say that you intend to
buy a new car. Before long you will notice the kind of car you
would like to buy all around you.

In normal language we can say that these RAS cells in
our brains function as a radar system. What has this got to
do with faith? Everything! If our relationship with Jesus is really the dominant priority in our lives, then our RAS system
will be focused on seeing and creating opportunities to praise
Him. Too many Christians' radar systems are focused on other
things – money, possessions, work. God is not really the first
priority on their radar screen and they just use pious religious
language on Sundays. How do you rectify this? Deliberately
place Christ first in your thoughts. Read Romans 12:1-2 and
Colossians 3:1-2 and focus your thoughts on God's will. Then
your internal radar system will change rapidly. And when that
happens, your life comes into sync with your new priorities.

Foolishness

Everything that we have – right thinking and right
living, a clean slate and a fresh start – comes from God
by way of Jesus Christ. That's why we have the saying,
"If you're going to blow a horn, blow a trumpet for God."

– 1 Corinthians 1:30-31 THE MESSAGE –

Paul writes that the cross is foolishness to many. Have you ever considered the meaning of this Scripture? Or the meaning of his challenging words in 2 Corinthians 13, that Jesus was crucified in weakness? Foolishness and weakness – these are the words that describe the greatest and most profound act of rescue in the history of the universe. In human terms a king does not hang on a cross. And yet Jesus specifically chose this humiliating route – a choice that seems foolish to the world. In this strange way, God's power is demonstrated. When Jesus hung on the cross, powerless, an earth-shattering spiritual rescue operation took place.

Foolishness is a characteristic of the gospel. What does it tell us? At least that we should rid ourselves of our preconceived ideas about the gospel being a human success story and a magnificent display of power. It also requires us to walk the humble route with Jesus. This will not lead to our winning all the popularity contests, but it will place us on the only course with an "eternal" destination, a route following the Shepherd.

Action

Don't just listen to God's Word. You must do what
it says. Otherwise, you are only fooling yourselves.

– James 1:22-23 NLT –

Most New Year resolutions do not last long. Why? Well, scientists say that if good intentions are not converted from theory to practice within 72 hours, then they are merely a waste of time. We could just as well not have made the decision.

Therefore, the motto is ACTION! This sounds like a spiritual message too. In James 1, he says that good decisions without actions are empty. One could just as well look into a mirror and immediately forget how you look when you walk away. (This seems to be a common problem, considering how many mirrors there are in our houses and stores!)

Faith in Christ that is not converted into action is a dead faith. Let us decide here on August 10, to do the following:

- Let us commit the rest of this year to electing at least one lesson out of each sermon we hear and to implement it within 24 hours.
- Let us pray every day for at least one other person, by name.
- Let us carry at least one other person's burdens every week.

A Prayer Away

"And when you pray, do not keep on babbling like
pagans, for they think they will be heard because of
their many words. Do not be like them, for your Father
knows what you need before you ask Him."

– Matthew 6:7-8 NIV –

In his remarkable book, *Practicing the Presence of God*, written
in the 17th century, Brother Lawrence says that in the course
of the day you should pray several short, effective prayers,
rather than one long, lifeless prayer aimed at merely easing
your conscience. Jesus taught us in Matthew that God is not
impressed by a shower of words. He is not interested in long
prayers. That's not the point. Prayer never is an arm-wrestling
session with God. In any event, we do not have anything with
which to impress Him. God really needs nothing from us.

Prayer always requires faith, obedience and modesty. It
always asks that we always submit our will to His world. Do
you also want to pray effectively? Then change your prayers
into honest, open discussions with God. Also, learn to use the
Bible effectively as your most important prayer guide. Talk for
shorter periods, but more often, with God, using the prayer
guide, the Word.

Use the Psalms to assist you in communicating your joy
and sadness, your needs and pain, in your own words to God.

In His Hands

"So don't worry about tomorrow, for tomorrow will
bring its own worries. Today's trouble is enough for today."

– Matthew 6:34 NLT –

I don't know what the future holds, but I do know who holds
it! Do you believe that? If you do, you should live differently
today. Why? Because tomorrow's uncertainties cannot and
will not happen without God's knowledge. When tomorrow
arrives, He will be there. He will report for duty, just like every
other day. God will definitely be on time for tomorrow. Even
if unexpected problems arise, if bad things like illness or crime
come knocking at your door, God will not be absent. He will
not be too busy with other urgent matters.

Your life does not escape God's attention for a single moment. Did you hear: Your life will not escape His attention
ever! He didn't forget about you yesterday, it will not happen
today, and He will not forget about you in the future. God
holds you, also your times, seasons and years. Believe this,
and live with a light heart.

Live joyously in God's abundant love.

God's World View

So from now on we regard no one from a worldly
point of view ... Therefore, if anyone is in Christ, he is
a new creation; the old has gone, the new has come!

– 2 Corinthians 5:16-17 NIV –

Martin Luther said a Christian is, in the same breath, both righteous and a sinner. In ordinary language, Luther meant that you can view your faith from two vantage points – either from your own perspective, or from God's. When you look at your side of the matter, you notice all your mistakes. When you view the matter from God's perspective, you notice that He performed spiritual surgery on you some time ago to make you new and acceptable in His eyes. Read the verse again.

Before we were saved, we were sinners in God's eyes, but that era is fortunately behind us (Rom. 5:6-8). God has accepted us as His children. Jesus is our God, before whom we now kneel. And God is very happy with us. Even better, He really likes us! We are members of His new family! Royal blood courses through our veins. Believe the best news that you will hear this week, namely that Jesus' death on the cross fundamentally, dramatically and comprehensively changed the perspective from which God views all His children.

A Light Ahead

Since we have been made right in God's
sight by faith, we have peace with God because
of what Jesus Christ our Lord has done for us.

– Romans 5:1 NLT –

God loves us from head to toe, even though we have many spiritual faults. There is peace between Him and us, even if we sometimes take the wrong path. The Bible says so and I believe it with my whole heart. I believe that God calls me His child and that He is not continually trying to catch me out in order to punish me. Of course I do not have a license to remain in sin. Never. But I do know that Jesus always dispenses grace. From His spiritual home, a second chance is offered every day; even if it my thousandth second chance!

Recognize the fact that the light of the cross shines over your life travels, 24 hours a day, and that it erases all the kinks in the road. Look away from yourself. Look properly, look at God. Recognize His spiritual kindness and live! Believe in what the Bible says, "This righteousness from God comes through faith in Jesus Christ to all who believe" (Rom. 3:22). Celebrate with the Word, "Therefore, there is now no condemnation for those who are in Christ Jesus" (Rom. 8:1).

Detours

So, if you think you are standing
firm, be careful that you don't fall!

– 1 Corinthians 10:12 NIV –

"I know all the detours ... I often get distracted." Do you also say these words? Do you know from experience about straying from God's path of truth and righteousness? Are you familiar with the self-incrimination when realizing that the same old sin has you faltering again? Are you acquainted with the hurt and shame which takes hold of you when you think about the destruction when you stumbled around in the dark? If you are, then you know about falling down.

It is strange how things can derail people. As soon as you think you are on track, some terrible thing derails you. It is no wonder that Paul warned the Corinthians that they must not assume that their faith is so strong that they will never do wrong (v. 12). Sin takes hold of you at the most unexpected moments.

What can you do about this? Make mistakes in a forward-falling manner! In other words, take your sins directly to God. Of course God hates sin. It is against His will. It offends Him. And yet He invites sinners to lay their sins down in front of Him, in Jesus name. Do it now!

Dangerous Prayer

"I tell you the truth, My Father will
give you whatever you ask in My name."

– John 16:23 NIV –

Remember, every prayer that is sent to heaven in the name of Jesus Christ is a direct link with God. Never arrive alone at heaven's door. Rather knock in the name of Christ. This is what Jesus teaches us in John 16. If you rely on your own resources, you will be too weak to stand before God. When you stand before God holding the hand of Jesus Christ, He invites you in, time and time again.

Prayer is never removed from life as it happens. Put differently, we cannot whisper a quick prayer and then proceed to live as we wish. Jesus says in John 15:7-8 that we should stay attached to Him, just like the branches of a vine are attached to the stem, and then we will receive what we are praying for.

A life of obedience to God is a requirement for powerful prayer. It ensures that our prayers do not merely dwell on our own needs. Then our prayers also do not sound like shopping lists that instruct God all the time with "do this; do that; help here; give there." No, instead, the extension of His kingdom in the lives of others should be the most important matter on our prayer agenda.

Pay it Forward

"I have been a constant example of how you
can help those in need by working hard. You should
remember the words of the Lord Jesus: 'it is more
blessed to give than to receive'"

– Acts 20:35 NLT –

Give away something of yourself: a precious few seconds, a few cents, a gift, a set of clothes, a visit to someone who is lonely, a prayer, a gentle hand on someone's shoulder, a listening ear. Paul tells us that Jesus said it makes us happier to give than to receive. Believe it; do it! One of the pillars of the gospel is to give. Jesus is the perfect example of this. He gave everything. His own life was His gift to all of us.

To give brings your life in sync with the gospel. Then you live according to the basic tenets of God's kingdom. In this world everybody wants to receive as much as possible. In God's world, His people give a part of themselves. The more they give without expecting to receive something in return, the more heavenly joy streams into their world. And their dungeons become shallower.

Eventually they are only as deep as a shallow fish pond, and on a good day the dungeon disappears completely! To give genuinely is to have something of God's character. It results in experiencing abundance with God.

Overflowing

You, however, are controlled not by the sinful nature but by
the Spirit, if the Spirit of God lives in you. And if anyone does
not have the Spirit of Christ, he does not belong to Christ.

– Romans 8:9 NIV –

Do you lack spiritual power? Do you long for the experience
of God's presence in your life? Then listen to what Jesus says
in Luke 11:13 (THE MESSAGE): "If your little boy asks for a serving of fish, do you scare him with a live snake on his plate? If
your little girl asks for an egg, do you trick her with a spider?
As bad as you are, you wouldn't think of such a thing – you're
at least decent to your own children. And don't you think the
Father who conceived you in love will give the Holy Spirit
when you ask Him?"

Our heavenly Father offers the special power and guidance of the Spirit to everybody who asks for it! What are you
waiting for? Pray and receive! Open your life today to the
Spirit for a brand-new experience. He is our heavenly Father's
gift to every believer. He will guide you along the correct path,
and on no other path! He will show you where you fit in,
within the framework of God's plans. Place yourself in His
hands, like an empty vessel, and trust Him to fill you with
living water. Then you will bubble over with the right kind of
power and love!

By Your Side

"No one can snatch them away from Me, for My Father
has given them to Me, and He is more powerful than anyone
else. No one can snatch them from the Father's hand."

– John 10:28-30 NLT –

Nothing shall separate you from the love of Christ if you
know Jesus as the Lord and sole Ruler of your life. This truth
is shared by Paul in such a compelling manner in Romans
8:31-39. You are God's precious property because Christ wrote
your name in the Book of Life. Every day you, together with
all of God's children, fit neatly into the palm of His hand. You
are God's sole property, bought and sealed by His Spirit.

Even when you are weak, you are still God's property. You
are somebody with eternity in your heart. You are en route to
the winning post. Believe it. Don't ever allow your emotions
to play games with you. You are not far away from God merely
because it sometimes feels that way. The Gospels state that
God is always near.

If you think that your prayers do not rise above the roof
of your home, it is merely your emotions fooling you. God is
everywhere – all around you. Stop trying to find God in the
distance. He is close by. Believe it and be free!

A Mere Observer

Share each other's burdens, and in
this way obey the law of Christ.

– Galatians 6:2 NLT –

Are you suffering under the yoke of life's innumerous heavy burdens? Are despair and fear your closest companions? If so, you should really do something about it. "What?" you ask. Well, resign from and banish those negative emotions. Do it right away! Don't allow fear or despair to reside illegally in your heart. Also, refuse to allow a difficult work environment, loneliness or poverty to steal your freedom in Christ. Refuse to let illness and other calamities steer you off God's course.

You must do something special with this part of life that has been "lent" to you. Remember that you only have one life. Use it with wisdom! Live every aspect of it exclusively for God. Use kind words which express God's mercy to give hope to the people around you. Talk in uplifting terms when your colleagues use trite, negative or depressing language. Share a friendly smile with somebody at work, or send a supportive text message to a friend. Don't be a passive observer of life. Play on God's playing fields with love and service. Make a real difference. God's sunbeams will suddenly shine again.

The Connecting Line

To the only God our Savior be glory, majesty,
power and authority, through Jesus Christ our Lord,
before all ages, now and forevermore! Amen.

– Jude 25 NIV –

On most gravestones there are two dates – a date of birth
and a date of death. They are connected by a short line. That
short line is known as life! What happens between your date
of birth and date of death is actually what your life is all about.
You don't have any control over those two dates in your life,
but you do have control over your life in between them. You
control where it leads – to God's city or to the city of death!
Most people will not remember the dates on which your life
started and ended, but they will remember the life you lived
in between.

So, what are you doing with your life? Are you living a life
that is worthy of imitation? Are you creating happy memories
in the hearts of others? Are you leaving footprints that others
can follow and which will lead them to God? Do your fingerprints bring hope and joy to people's lives? Then people will
not just remember you with compassion, God will also know
you well. And even better, then your real life will start, on the
other side of the second date on the gravestone!

Out of Control

Sensible people control their temper; they
earn respect by overlooking wrongs.

– Proverbs 19:11 NLT –

I once read about a British pastor in his early twenties who had a congregation of more than a thousand people in London about 200 years ago. He worked himself to death to keep them happy. At the age of 29 he had a fatal heart attack. On his deathbed this talented young man said that God had given him a Bible and a horse. Now he had worked his horse to death ... what did it achieve? God needs healthy people, not people who work their horses to death and then have little energy left for His service because their health has failed.

If your life is in chaos, it is not caused by your boss, activities, schedule, diary, or your studies. You are the cause thereof. Don't point fingers elsewhere. You make that fatal decision every day to work yourself to the bone. You are not a victim or a passive observer of your busy life. You alone choose to follow that path! Nobody else forces you to damage your body.

Slow down. Realize that God is the god of your life. He will provide your needs.

Don't Be an Addict

If anyone competes as an athlete, he does not receive the victor's crown unless he competes according to the rules.

– 2 Timothy 2:5 NIV –

There is a difference between a few busy seasons in your life (which happen to all of us) and a program that is permanently filled to capacity. In everybody's life there are busy periods, but if it happens every day, then something is wrong!

Workaholism has become a socially acceptable illness – everybody does it. When do you have this terrible disease? Well, when it robs you of precious time that you should have spent with God. Or when it alienates you from your loved ones.

When you have no time left for God, for others, for yourself, or just for doing nothing, then you are addicted to your work. When you collapse dead tired into bed every evening ... just to wake up tired the next morning and begin rushing again, then you are held captive by your work.

Listen up: it is not just a bad habit to be hurried all the time, it is a sin. You are living outside God's will because you are living outside the speed limits that He determined for your body. Trust God to give you what you need daily (Matt. 6:25-34). Show that you believe it, by living at a slower pace!

Taking Responsibility

Jesus declared, "I am the Bread of Life.
Whoever comes to Me will never go hungry, and
whoever believes in Me will never be thirsty."

– John 6:35 NIV –

The other day somebody told me that he has no other choice than to work 16 hours a day. Says who? He does! Who knows, maybe you think you don't have any other choice than to live as rushed as you currently do. There has to be food on the table; the house has to be paid for ... and what about school fees, the car, retirement? In this process of running around at the speed of light you don't see God's plan for your life any longer, because you don't set aside prime time for Him.

You have changed into a full-time workaholic. You have forgotten one of the basic lessons of being a Christian, namely to ask God humbly for your daily bread (Matt. 6:9-13). You are denying your faith, through the way you live your life daily With weak excuses you flog yourself toward the hospital and the grave.

Have you forgotten that your heavenly Father wants to take care of you, and that He *will* take care of you? He knows precisely what you need (Matt. 6:25-33). Trust Him, for a change, to do exactly that.

Don't Get Stuck

The world is unprincipled. It's dog-eat-dog out there!
The world doesn't fight fair. But we don't live or
fight our battles that way – never have and never will.

– 2 Corinthians 10:3-4 THE MESSAGE –

If you are held hostage by negative thoughts, do what Paul recommends in 2 Corinthians. Take every negative thought captive that threatens to invade your thinking. Do it in the name of Christ immediately. Deliver that thought to Him and let Him deal with it. Give all other destructive thoughts to God as soon as you realize they are gathering in your heart. Be on the lookout for unwelcome thoughts that don't get caught up in hate, bitterness, lust, hopelessness, and other destructive things. Notice them in advance and stop them in the name of Christ.

Remember that no temptation that is too strong for you will ever come across your path. The Bible says this in 1 Corinthians 10:14. God never allows you to have tempting thoughts that you cannot say no to. Know that every temptation that comes across your path has been assessed in heaven before it reaches you. Therefore you can say no. You can resist every temptation in the name of Christ. Neither you nor any child of God has any excuse to succumb to temptation.

Celebration

"Be happy about it! Be very glad! For
a great reward awaits you in heaven."

– Matthew 5:12 NLT –

It seems that you can't make it through the year without hearing a few complaints about the commercialization of Sundays and other religious festivals. As far back as I can remember, religious fanatics have gone on about this. Does complaining help reduce the misuse of festive days? I doubt it. Will the exploitation of Christmas, for example, suddenly stop because some churchgoers are opposing it? Probably not! Maybe another solution? What about a more personal one? Meaning, you and I who honor Christ as our Lord should wear a permanent festival-costume this year.

Our yearlong festivities should tell of the Child in the manger who brought a new kind of peace among us. Our words, but especially our deeds of compassion towards others, should always tell of our Lord's heavenly generosity.

Then life in our area will look different 365 days a year. We decorate that little piece of world inside which we live, work and play with the right kind of joy every single day. We don't have to sing with the choir of faultfinders, criticizers, and protesters.

A Carefree Life

Always be full of joy in the Lord. I say it again – rejoice!
– Philippians 4:4 NLT –

Learn from a few important lessons from Jesus' favorite people. I refer to children, of course. Learn how to play and relax. Learn not to take yourself too seriously. Think of yourself as a child in a grown-up's body. Make time to laugh and play every day, to be careless, fun-loving and expressive. Share humorous stories. Laugh. It will add many joyful years to your life as well as life to your years.

Wouldn't it be a wonderful thing if joy, playfulness, rest and relaxation were a constant part of your life for the rest of the year? Your quality of life will change dramatically when you deliberately choose to celebrate life in the presence of our good Lord. Your relationship with Christ and others will look quite different if each of these relationships is surrounded by joy and happiness. You will discover the Lord in surprising new ways when you begin to trust Him with everything in a childlike fashion.

When you get into the rhythm of choosing day after day to live a carefree life, divine joy will be something you experience every day.

Tapping the Drum

*This will be a sign to you: You will find a baby
wrapped in cloths and lying in a manger.*

– Luke 2:12 NIV –

Do you know the "pa rum pump um pum" refrain from *The
Little Drummer Boy*? This song tells the story of a boy who
wants to play the drums with all his might for the child in the
manger.

The arrival of Jesus calls for festivity. That's what the three
wise men realized when they saw His star. Their gold, incense, and myrrh herald of the arrival of the Child of Peace
here on earth.

But the coming of Jesus is about so much more than just
presents. It's about us becoming living presents to others. Just
as Jesus came to give Himself away without any precondi-
tions, He turns us into gifts to those around us.

But there's more about the coming of Jesus that we need
to know ... if we only stand in awe at His manger, we haven't
yet walked far enough. We also need to bow down at the cross
of our Messiah. The manger calls for the cross. The gifts of the
wise men call for the gift of Jesus to us all. His own life is the
real gift. His precious life is God's ultimate gift to the whole
world.

Jesus is new life for us all. That's why we celebrate His
coming the whole year round.

Bearing the Cross

"If anyone would come after Me, he must deny
himself and take up his cross and follow Me."

– Matthew 16:24 NIV –

Gordon Wakefield writes that there can never be a hint of true Christianity without a cross – the cross of Christ that we bear, and each of us bearing our own cross. From the manger to the cross, from Bethlehem to Calvary, and from there all the way to my own life – that's the nutshell story of faith. From the cross of Jesus to the cross that I have to carry on His behalf – that's the new route that I follow.

When I become part of Jesus' story, it turns me into someone who is crucified and cross-bearing in the same instant. The story of Jesus says loud and clear that my life started over from square one.

At the manger, the cross and the empty grave I find my new identity. From there I also find the daily direction for my life. Jesus is my only compass. His arrival, His death and His resurrection are the reasons for my existence. That's why I can tap my own little drum for Him today, even while there's a heavy cross resting on my narrow shoulders. That's why I can follow Him all the way, because He sacrificed all for me as well.

"Where No Man Has Gone Before"

This is My command – be strong and courageous!
Do not be afraid or discouraged. For the LORD
your God is with you wherever you go.

– Joshua 1:9 NLT –

The Star Trek generation knows about boldly "going where no man has ever gone before." This is perhaps the cliché of all clichés. People just love this slogan. But few practice it. Few ever wander out into unchartered territory.

People love to play it safe – safe places, safe neighbors, safe jobs, safe friends, safe circumstances – that's all part and parcel of the safe package called "the good life." No wonder there are so many safe Christians and safe churches around. What a safe, boring, snoring bunch "churchianity" has turned into!

Let's boldly go places for Jesus. Follow Jesus on His terms! Follow Him into the gutters, streets, inner cities ... live for an audience of One ... even if you have to do it alone!

Past and Present

Create in me a pure heart, O God,
and renew a steadfast spirit within me.

– Psalm 51:10 NIV –

Once, I thought I had to impress other people. No longer. As a follower of Jesus, I don't want to impress, I only want to share impressive God-stories.

Once, I thought I had all the answers. No longer. As a follower of Jesus, I have more questions than answers.

Once, I had everything under control, or thought I did. No longer. As a follower of Jesus, I surrender all control to God who is in charge of everything.

Once, I enjoyed receiving more than giving. No longer. Now, as a follower of Jesus, I experience the joy of giving and sharing with people around me.

Once, nothing impressed me much. No longer. Now as a follower of Christ, I see beauty everywhere.

Once, I talked mostly about God. No longer. As a follower of Jesus, I talk more to God.

Once, I was excited about complex theological ideas. No longer. As a follower of Jesus, I am more excited about interacting with people who follow in His footsteps.

Once, people had to listen to me most of the time. No longer. As a follower of Jesus, I take more time to listen to others.

September

Wait a Minute

Their responsibility is to equip God's people to do
His work and build up the church, the body of Christ.

– Ephesians 4:12 NLT –

"Religion is just a money-making scheme." How many times have you heard expressions such as this? However, nobody complains when big businesses make excessive profits or pay their directors preposterous bonuses. I'm not trying to justify the fact that some churches or ministries have excessive funds. But to automatically think there is a problem when some churches show a healthy monthly income, while turning a blind eye to businesses who keep on feeding the monsters of capitalism and consumerism, is not the answer either.

To blindly criticize the church for not getting it right, while more than 80% of all new businesses fail within their first year of existence, is surely not the way to go. Yes, some local churches make a mess of their calling. They are stone-cold. But to generalize is dangerous. Why are we so critical of ourselves in church, but we forget to use the same yardstick when we look at other institutions in society? More often than not, I am shocked to see the poor state of leadership in many businesses – their lack of vision, team building, trust, and conflict-handling skills. Many churches get it right. They follow in the footsteps of Christ. Praise God for them!

Dare

Do everything readily and cheerfully – no bickering,
no second-guessing allowed! Go out into the world
uncorrupted, a breath of fresh air. Provide people
with a glimpse of good living and of the living God.

– Philippians 2:14-15 THE MESSAGE –

It is rather foolish to expect different results while you keep doing the same thing. Maybe you know these words. But do you believe them? Or are you a sheep? Repetition brings familiarity, and familiarity creates a feeling of security. Therefore, some people stay caught up in unhealthy situations for years. The fear of the unknown is a much greater threat to them than the fear of existing bad circumstances. It overrides the courage to explore new territory.

You will have to make a few very courageous choices if you don't want to remain a lifelong prisoner of yourself and your circumstances. You have to move forward in the name of the Lord if you want to discover new horizons. If you remain where you are now, you will never grow even one inch farther in the right direction. Listen again: If you remain where you are now, you will never grow in the right direction. The Lord created you to be a lifelong explorer. There are thousands of treasures hidden in His Word and in His world for you to discover. Consider new things. Dare to make new choices. Go and live this challenge!

Deeper into the Storm

When Jesus woke up, He rebuked the wind and the raging
waves. Suddenly the storm stopped and all was calm.

– Luke 8:24 NLT –

Paul didn't just talk about what he wanted to do for Jesus one
day. He knew daydreams wouldn't achieve anything. He had
to rock the boat. No, he had to get out of the boat to walk
the on water with Jesus. The only safe place was to wander
deeper into the storm with Christ. Risk-taking was the new
name of the game. That's why Paul refused to be a conformist.
He became ignorant to the concept "caution." It was banned
from his vocabulary forever.

No longer did Paul play according to the rules of the religious game; he made new ones. He created an entirely new
playing field. In Philippians 1:21 Paul expresses his new life
purpose in a nutshell: "Alive I'm Christ's messenger; dead I'm
his bounty" (THE MESSAGE) or, "For to me, to live is Christ and
to die is gain" (NIV). It is straight-forward, simple! No strings
attached. To live is to be in community with Christ. It is to
constantly share in His grace and oneness. Jesus is the reason
why Paul got up every morning; why he sang praises in prison
after being beaten; why he endured hardships, rejection, disappointment and suffering without giving in. Join him.

No Professionals

You are the ones chosen by God, chosen for the high
calling of priestly work, chosen to be a holy people, God's
instruments to do His work and speak out for Him, to tell
others of the night-and-day difference He made for you.

– 1 Peter 2:9-10 THE MESSAGE –

Following Christ is not intended for professionals, but rather
amateurs. Should you play around with the etymology of the
word "amateur," you will realize that it is originally associated
with words like "lover" and "suitor." Therefore only amateurs
should report for duty to God. Amateurs understand that
their service to the Lord is not something that happens part-
time or after hours. Neither are they volunteers. No, they
follow Christ full-time, constantly, over and over again, and
every single day.

Amateurs serve God full-time because they are simply
overwhelmed by His kindness. They are jubilant because, despite who and what they are, God accepts them unconditionally. No wonder that, contrary to accepted behavior, they will
choose to follow God. They help, pray, serve, seek, support,
reach out and encourage. They give themselves whole-heartedly in service to the Lord and His work. Their hearts beat
passionately. Their emotions are on a high – the real *agape*-
driven type! Their servitude flows from their hearts through
their hands, feet and lips.

God's Hope

Let us hold unswervingly to the hope we
profess, for He who promised is faithful.

– Hebrews 10:23 NIV –

Many of us read leadership books by internationally known
business gurus, or attend their seminars, as if their best-sellers
automatically turn them into the ideal role models to follow.
Do we really think that they, or the big companies of this
world, get it right all the time? Don't get me wrong, I don't
have a problem with listening to leadership specialists or
reading their books as such, but to think they have all the answers, while we in church still don't get it, is a huge mistake.

Perhaps the biggest mistake is to still use these dated cate-
gories; those "we-they," or "church-business" categorizations.
Secondly, many local churches are not doing too badly. Christ
is faithful. After 2,000 years He still looks after His interests
here on earth … including all local churches who follow the
Jesus way. No, Jesus did not give up on His people.

Through the work of the Spirit, He is in our midst. He
cares for us. He listens to our prayers. He helps us out in our
hour of need. He works through us in so many beautiful ways.
That's why the church offers real hope to the world.

Small Is the New Big

"Whoever wants to become great among you must be your servant, and whoever wants to be first must be slave of all."

– Mark 10:43-44 NIV –

"Small is the new big." Small is important. It's so important that it overtook big recently! When small is present in church, relationships are more personal. Small is also closer. Small is ... more effective. Small is face to face. Small is not as expensive. Small is faster. That's why small is the new big thing in relationships. Success and big/large/extra-large were too close for too long. Success was correlated with large numbers, huge crowds, abundant resources, colossal incomes ... those days are gone. They should never have existed in church in the first place. It's now the turn of small.

Small churches, small Bible studies, small gatherings, small services, small outreaches, small discussions, small prayers, small forms of assistance ... that's what really changes the world. Just read the Gospels again. Jesus was into small. Huge crowds, big tithes, impressive religious structures: all of that left Him cold. Jesus loved individuals. That's why He spent so much time with His group of twelve disciples or with outcasts such as Zacchaeus, the Samaritan woman, the Syro-Phoenician woman, Cleopas and his wife. Jesus was big on small. He had all the time in the world to care for individuals. He did relationships at the speed of one person at a time.

Ordinary People

Prepare your minds for action; be
self-controlled; set your hope fully on the grace
to be given you when Jesus Christ is revealed.

– 1 Peter 1:13 NIV –

Fame Lane is no longer the sole territory of big companies, large corporations or Hollywood stars. If you don't believe me, ask Funtwo, who played his guitar from his Korean bedroom to the tune of more than 70 million viewers. We live in a new world. It's flat, out of control, fast and furious. Today's heroes are ordinary people. You don't need a special costume with an "S" on your chest to make an impact.

Ordinary people change the world today. Now it's about mustard seeds, not spiritual giants and mighty believers. That's why we must take a closer look at Jesus. The real Jesus who got lost behind 2,000 years of Christian art, religious ceremonies, cathedrals and religious professionals, didn't wear special costumes or fly around in space craft. Jesus came as Himself, dressed in the clothes of slaves and outcasts. Jesus' favorite people were the lost, the downtrodden, the poor and the lonely. His "weapons" were words of grace and His healing presence. The Jesus that we need to look out for today is He who turned heaven and earth upside down by becoming a servant of all. Let's find Him. Let's follow Him.

First Line of Contact

Never be lazy, but work hard and
serve the Lord enthusiastically.

– Romans 12:11 NLT –

Recently an acquaintance of mine stopped at an accident that had just occurred and assisted one person who was seriously injured. Suddenly the man grabbed his hand and whispered, "Pray for me. I'm dying. I don't know God." My acquaintance answered, "I know a pastor who lives close by. I'll get him to pray for you." The man told the medical assistants to take care of the injured person and sped off to fetch the pastor. But he wasn't at home. He rushed back to the scene, only to hear that that the person in the accident passed away shortly after he left.

"What happened to this guy's soul?" he asked me. But his next question bowled me over. "Why aren't pastors at home when we need them?"

"Why didn't you just pray for the man?" I asked. "Me?" he asked with a shocked expression. "I'm not trained for that." "We just have to do what we have to do when the Lord calls us!" I replied. "We are heaven's first line of contact. We are on duty at all times. We don't have to know how to pray, help or care. We just have to report for duty and leave the rest in the Lord's hands."

Christian Clowns

"When you give to someone in need, don't
let your left hand know what your right hand
is doing. Give your gifts in private, and your
Father, who sees everything, will reward you."

– Matthew 6:3-4 NLT –

One of my favorite authors, Henri Nouwen, relates how he once lived in Rome for five months. What he remembered so vividly was not all the "spiritual lion tamers and trapeze artists," as he called the important church leaders in Rome, but the Christian "clowns" who unobtrusively told the true story of Christianity. It wasn't the beauty and splendor of the Vatican that caught his attention, but the simplicity of a few students from the St Egidio community in Rome who spent their time serving the homeless, drunks and prostitutes of the city. In these young people Nouwen encountered true saints who selflessly served the outcasts without expecting any recognition. These are the people who are part of the true Christian story.

We have to give up our positions as lion tamers trying to impress others with our spiritual power and wonders. It is amongst the ordinary clowns for Christ where the real difference is made and lived. Every day behind workbenches, amongst scholars, in hospitals and in churches, we have more than enough opportunity to serve unobtrusively.

Gucci to Share?

In everything set them an example by doing what is good. In your teaching show integrity, seriousness and soundness of speech that cannot be condemned.

– Titus 2:7-8 NIV –

James Twitchwell wrote a book in which he talks about the never-ending love affair that the world has with luxuries and that owning luxury items apparently brings beauty to our lives. Furthermore, it binds people from different social groupings together, according to him. Isn't it a pity that people need to justify their insatiable hunger for material possessions in such tragic ways? And yet Twitchwell writes one thing that really shook me: "If Americans can't share God, why not Gucci?" Can you believe it?

What a tragedy that in Twitchwell's opinion luxury can be regarded as more unifying than religion. This should not be true. We as believers should be a far better advertisement for God's love. We should be magnets drawing people closer to Him. As followers of Jesus we should live as servants to do all we can for others. But it is not too late to demonstrate true beauty; the kind of beauty that has lasting value. You can try to make a noticeable difference today! Be the one who shares God's love so profusely that it actually leaves people speechless. Then they don't have to be victims of earthly possessions, or a never-ending culture of consumerism.

Treasures in Heaven

"Whoever becomes simple and elemental again,
like this child, will rank high in God's kingdom."
– Matthew 18:4 THE MESSAGE –

A few years ago Arnold Schwarzenegger, the famous Hollywood star and governor of California said something more amazing than some of the "famous" expressions he is known for, like "I'll be back," or the evergreen "Hasta la vista, baby!"

He was trying to convince people that more money would not make them happier, "I now have $50 million, but I am just as happy as when I had $48 million." Absurd! But in an equally absurd world, where spending money on luxury items is more than four times higher, such statements should not surprise us.

How do we find that dividing line between "enough is enough" and "more" when we merely consider this in monetary terms? When will we learn from the book of Ecclesiastes (chapter 7) that those who regard money as everything will never have enough?

When will we start trusting in God as our heavenly Father who promises to give us everything that we need daily? Or are these nothing more than pious words from our side of the fence?

Grace Beyond the Deadline

"My grace is sufficient for you, for My
power is made perfect in weakness."

– 2 Corinthians 12:9 NIV –

I remember a particularly difficult man in my congregation while I was a minister. He didn't want to have anything to do with God. Then he became ill. After serious complications during an operation he went into a deep coma. The doctor said there was nothing they could do for him. His wife was inconsolable because she was a Christian. Every day I prayed for him at his bedside. The nurse said to me that it did not help at all, because he could not hear me.

One day, while I was praying for this man at home, I got an urgent prompting that I should immediately go to the hospital. When I got there, the nurse informed me that he was dying. Desperately, I took his hand and pleaded with Christ for mercy on his behalf. Then a miracle happened – tears started rolling down his cheeks. He didn't say a word ... only those tears. A mere five minutes later he died. Then I suddenly remembered the words of Jesus, "Today you will be with Me in paradise!" That is grace beyond the deadline!

A Walking Miracle

"The very hairs on your head are all numbered."

– Luke 12:7 NLT –

In his book *The Arithmetic of Life and Death,* George Shaffner views life from a mathematical perspective. He calculates that the mathematical possibility of inheriting 23 chromosomes from your mother is one in a million. The same applies to the 23 chromosomes you received from your father. If you multiply these two, you will come to the conclusion that the chance of you being you is one in a 100 trillion. Mind boggling! On top of that, if you remember that the same is true of your parents, as well as their parents, then even mathematics is silenced. All you can do is bow down in adoration before our great Creator God! He really cares about the detail of our lives.

As human beings we are the remarkable workmanship of God's detailed creative power. How can people so easily point fingers at Him, accusing Him of lovelessness? Shouldn't we be the accused? What will be left of us if God starts interrogating us and putting the facts on the table from His side? Let us rather humble ourselves in worship and adoration before Him.

Real Power

When I am weak, then I am strong.
– 2 Corinthians 12:10 NLT –

I never associated God's power with weakness until I had to translate 2 Corinthians into a modern-day version of the Bible a few years ago. When I read that when Christ hung on the cross in weakness, the biggest power in the universe was actually at work (chapter 13), I was blown away.

God's power in its purest form is always revealed in human weakness. This doesn't make sense to people who associate power with massive attendances and miracles. Well, it even took Paul a few prayers to come to grips with God's definition of power. Up until that point he was highly successful. But then Paul had a quarrel with a church leader in Corinth. He left the city humiliated (chapters 2 and 7). To add insult to injury, flamboyant preachers came to Corinth who were real show stoppers (chapters 10-13). Paul approached God three times in prayer to remove these afflictions.

Eventually God showed Paul that it's not about power but about grace and weakness! This simple message changed the course of Paul's entire ministry and his style of leadership forever. Hereafter, his letters are much more gentle. Learn from Paul. Learn to become weak in God's service.

Valuable Lessons

"In repentance and rest is your salvation,
in quietness and trust is your strength."

– Isaiah 30:15 NIV –

Paul discovered that God's true power is revealed in human weakness. In this paradox, the true character of God is revealed. When we are weak His glory is revealed. In order for this to happen we need to learn the following three lessons about weakness in God's presence:

Lesson one: *It is never about us*! God is always the only power supply in the church.

Lesson two: *We don't have to experience divine power before God gets to work*. He works in spite of what we see, feel or experience. We should never trust our feelings when God's presence is at stake.

Lesson three: *We'll always experience a lack of spiritual power*. There is not a single text in the Bible about people asking God to cut down on the supply of power in their lives. The constant complaint of insufficient power in the church is not necessarily a sign of small faith as people tend to think. Perhaps it serves as part of God's strategy to lead us to total dependence upon Him. The apostle Paul learned this lesson the hard way. Please learn it the easy way today.

I'm Shot

The LORD your God is gracious and merciful.
– 2 Chronicles 30:9 NLT –

In the film *Black Hawk Down,* an officer looks at a vehicle filled with wounded soldiers. Then he spots a private named Othic and orders him to drive. Othic responds, "But, I'm shot, Colonel!" Then the colonel reacts with an amazing truth: "*Everybody's shot! Drive!*" What a metaphor for our own lives.

We all get wounded sometimes. Everybody's shot, actually! But we can still drive, because *God is gracious and forgiving*. He's not like us. When He forgives us we stay forgiven. God doesn't have the time or the energy to keep on reminding us of the wrongs of yesterday or the day before. No, He already pushed them out of the way because Jesus keeps on clearing our records.

The really great news is that God doesn't have a notorious little black book tucked away somewhere in heaven to remind Him of the nasty stuff we all did somewhere in our distant, or not too distant past. That black book was torn up ages ago when Jesus pleaded our case before Him successfully! In spite of our sins, wrongdoings, etc, God takes us in His service day after day. He loves us in spite of everything we do.

Living Icons

God created human beings in His own
image. In the image of God He created
them; male and female He created them.

– Genesis 1:27 NLT –

God created us in His image. The Greek word *eikon* that the
New Testament uses for the term "image" is familiar to some
of us. The word "icon" stems from it. At least we know about
icons on our computer screens and icons in those impressive
Orthodox churches. Icons are images ... in our case, human
beings as living images of God. We are visible reflections and
representatives of the living God. This is the breaking news
right at the start of the Bible in Genesis 1. This amazing text
tells us that we share in God's divine likeness. Not even sin
destroyed all of this.

We share in God's DNA, His character, His own heart. We
humans have a common heritage as a species – we are made
in the image of God! Our abilities to learn endlessly, to feel
deeply, to live in harmony with others, to have compassion, to
love, think, rethink and to innovate, is part and parcel of the
heart of our all-loving Father. Great news, or what! That's why
Dennis Anderson said, "You cannot see faith, but you can see
the footprints of the faithful. We must leave behind 'faithful
footprints' for others to follow."

Blame Shifting

"I tell you that men will have to give account on the day
of judgment for every careless word they have spoken."

– Matthew 12:36 NIV –

After hearing the same old line for the umpteenth time that
people are tired, overworked and fed up, I catch myself actually believing some of them. Apparently, these excuses give
people a valid excuse to be rude, ill-mannered, aggressive
and insensitive. To be honest, I'm not Mr Loveable myself.
I'm probably just as unfriendly as many others around me.
I wish I could conveniently shift the blame somewhere else.
But it won't solve anything. Really, it won't!

Blame shifting doesn't work ... at least not since the beginning of time. If you don't believe me, just ask Eve and Adam.
They were the first pros who started this destructive game.
Fortunately, God didn't buy into it. God has the full picture.
He knows that our lives will have a radically different out-
come when we exercise ourselves in the spiritual discipline of
accepting responsibility for our emotions, words and deeds.
Blame shifting seems like an easy way out. It's easier to blame
the past, the present, the economy, the government or the
church than to get involved. In the end we pay a high price.
We slowly but surely disconnect from God and our true self.
What a terrible price to pay.

Who Am I?

We are God's workmanship, created in Christ Jesus.

– Ephesians 2:10 NIV –

"Who am I?" Do you ever ask yourself this question? Well, to be honest, I don't do it all that often since I made peace with the person whose body I occupy! I don't believe in introspection all that much. Years of stringent soul-searching routines, which formed part of my spiritual growth exercises, really didn't help me grow in the right direction. In the end it actually left me with more guilty feelings than ever before. It made me toxic, not healthier. It filled me with feelings of failure and doubt.

Fortunately, over the past few years I realized that I don't need to beat myself up over every negative emotion, thought or intention tucked away in the dark corners of my soul. I really found my purpose in life, namely to love Christ and serve others who cross my path. I know that I have to keep my focus on Jesus and forget about the rest.

My identity is not determined by other people's perceptions or views. I don't need to please people all the time. I only play for an audience of One. What about you? Have you sorted out your purpose in life?

Reflecting His Love

Imitate God, therefore, in everything you do,
because you are His dear children. Live a life
filled with love, following the example of Christ.

– Ephesians 5:1-2 NLT –

Do you remember the earliest term that some people used to refer to the first Christians? If you say "believers," you are not quite right. They were called "People of the Way" (Acts 9:2). The first believers were not known for what they knew, but for the way in which their lives were a testimony of their faith in Jesus. They did not have a confession of faith, but lived a life that confessed their faith. In all the right ways, their lives spoke louder than their words.

The testimony of the first Christians was a daily testimony. Others saw how they loved the Lord and one another and how they supported people in need. Their testimony was founded in a magnetic lifestyle of prayer, compassion and simplicity. That is why they were known as People of the Way – the Way of Jesus. Their faith was clearly visible in their new relationships. What a pity that today we are known more for confessions of faith on paper than for our lives filled with love for God and others. How sad that the main conversations of churches often revolve around "purity of doctrine" and not about "purity of life." Are we missing something or Someone?

Forget Un-Faith!

Believe in the Lord Jesus, and you will be saved.

– Acts 16:31 NIV –

"I don't believe in God ... " "God doesn't exist ... " How often do we hear remarks such as these! It has become fashionable for people to confess their un-faith. Hollywood actors do it; sport stars do it; business people do it, even preachers do it. Un-faith is the in-thing! People believe in un-faith to set them free from faith, or something like that. So, does this rise of un-faith mean that God is dethroned? A better question would be, was Christianity ever meant to be encapsulated in static institutions with strange rituals and professional clerics? Is this "official" face of Christianity the correct one? I don't think so.

The church is made up of people all across the globe who passionately follow Jesus. They frequently meet in church buildings, houses, offices ... They are the church because they love Jesus as Lord. They are magnetic because they care for each another and for outsiders. Their love for Christ is translated into new deeds of kindness towards friends, strangers, outcasts, sinners and foreigners. They thrive amongst un-believers. Confessions of un-faith don't startle them. They know what they know. They believe what they believe, in spite of the efforts of evangelists of un-faith who feverishly want to convert others to their faithless views.

Time Addiction

Teach us to number our days aright,
that we may gain a heart of wisdom.

– Psalm 90:12 NIV –

Time is money. There is no time for sitting around doing nothing. That is what many people believe. No wonder we are stuck with words in our vocabulary like "time wastage," "time management" and "effective time utilization." We are told that we should even save time nowadays by living more effectively?

There you have it; we are time addicts! We frequently find ourselves breaking the speed limit to each new destination in the hope of saving two or three minutes somewhere along the way. Forget about that "saved time" when we reach our destination. No, we never really save time. We only drive up our heart rates and increase our stress levels. Did you know, the Lord never created us to live like that? It is not at all part of His divine plan that you and I should break the sound barrier every day. Or is it perhaps the time barrier?

We are built for relationships. For that we need resting time and visiting time. We also need quiet time and prayer time. Not to mention times of meditation before God. Do you ever have time for this?

Reality from God's Perspective

"I have told you these things, so that in Me you may have peace. In this world you will have trouble. But take heart! I have overcome the world."

– John 16:33 NIV –

Here is an interesting question – how did the apostle Paul understand reality? Let's explore this question over the next few days by focusing on 2 Corinthians. Here we learn that God is in total control over the heavenly realm and the earthly sphere. The suffering of the righteous at the hands of the wicked, including Paul's own tribulations (2 Cor. 1) does not in any way diminish God's absolute control over reality. To the contrary, His divine power is actually revealed in the weakness of Jesus on the cross (John 13:4), but also in the ministry of His apostle (John 12:1-10). Therefore, suffering serves a divine purpose.

In an ironic way, hardships, such as those Paul endured, point to the presence of God's power. On the last day when God will visibly triumph over all powers of evil, and when His universal rule will be finally established, all the pieces of this divine plan will fall into place. God will bring a final end to the suffering of the faithful. All of this is the result of the death and resurrection of Christ. Praise His name!

A New World

Anyone who belongs to Christ has become a new
person. The old life is gone; a new life has begun!

– 2 Corinthians 5:17 NLT –

In our discussion that started yesterday on God's perspectives
on reality (2 Cor.), a second point becomes clear:

The final stage of history has already dawned on earth.
The "Messianic era" commenced when Christ brought salvation to His people. Hence, Paul's statement in 2 Corinthians
5:17 that the old *aeon* or era has passed away, the new has
come! Paul was in the privileged position to decipher history.
He had an "insider's insight" into the great cosmic drama
that was played out on the stage of history, and also in the
midst of the believers' lives in Corinth!

Thirdly, Paul knew that the present world would rapidly
pass away, soon to be replaced by a new cosmic order (2 Cor.
4:16-5:10). History is swiftly moving towards that fateful day
when evil will finally be destroyed and the righteous vindicat-
ed. This will happen on the Day of the Lord when all people
will appear before the judgment seat of Christ (2 Cor. 5:10).
The world as people know it will be transcended. From this
triumphant perspective on the Second Coming, Paul knew
that the present with all its problems and crises would work
for the future glory of the Lord (2 Cor. 6:1-13).

God's Reality

No, despite all these things, overwhelming
victory is ours through Christ, who loved us.

– Romans 8:37 NLT –

Let's continue our question from the previous two days – how did the apostle Paul understand reality in 2 Corinthians? He knew that Israel's history served as the prefiguration of the new time of the Spirit and Christ (Rom. 3:1-18). However, the time of Christ, which inaugurated God's new time of salvation, also overlaps with the works of the Evil One.

However, the god of this world, who has blinded the minds of unbelievers (Rom. 4:4), as well as those evil powers that masquerade as God's angels (Rom. 11:14), are no real threat to His power. The works of the enemy in the spiritual realm will not derail the inauguration of God's ultimate era of salvation. History has continued to run its predetermined course, in spite of various forms of evil and catastrophe, and will continue to do so until the final return of Christ.

Lastly, the present is the convergence point of God's intervention through Christ. New life is already here, but it is not yet fully revealed. Salvation is a present reality, yet all must still appear before the tribunal of Christ. But the scales have been decisively turned. The weight is now on the side of God's eternal glory!

"I Ain't Afraid of No Ghost"

God did not give us a spirit of timidity, but a
spirit of power, of love and of self-discipline.

– 2 Timothy 1:7 NIV –

You may know the song from the *Ghostbusters* movies – "I ain't afraid of no ghost." Well, we bump into ghosts all the time. We are constantly haunted by our own fears. A shocking piece of research states that the older we grow, the more our brains form synaptic links that are related to fear. Why? Is it because life is so dangerous or because people are so toxic?

Perhaps we continue to live on the fringes of our own lives ... those fringes where fear reigns unchallenged. Freedom begins when I encounter my inner fears. How? There's no quick answer. But one way is to listen to my inner self-talk. An awareness of my inner discussions will bring me into contact with my fears. Then I'll begin to see them for what they really are – pale ghosts!

God's freedom is always an inner freedom. The freedom that the Spirit brings moves me away from the fringes of my life to my inner self. His freedom lets me discover the true me. Only then will I grasp His freedom that sets people free. That's when I sing, "I ain't afraid of no ghost."

Imperfect Leaders

Work hard and become a leader.

– Proverbs 12:24 NLT –

Do you remember all those well-known leadership mantras of yesteryear, the "leadership is everything" type? Or that well-known one, "Everything rises and falls with leadership"? Perhaps leadership is somewhat overrated. Perhaps this interest in leadership is merely a baby-boomer generation thing! (I see very few leadership books from other generations.) Or perhaps the problem lies elsewhere. Perhaps the problem is our fascination with leaders, especially in church.

Good leaders, the godly sort, always make bad idols. It's as simple as that. True leaders don't like the spotlight. They don't crave attention. Yes, they have a teachable point of view, but they never mistake this fact for good leadership skills. Christ-like leaders know how to make tough calls, which often makes them unpopular with the masses. They know how to take risks which make hero worshippers very uncomfortable at times.

That's why leaders who follow in the footsteps of Jesus don't like any excessive interest in themselves or in their work for the Lord. Their one and only dream is to serve Christ and His people. True leaders are His lifelong servants.

Lukewarm

"So, because you are lukewarm – neither hot nor
cold – I am about to spit you out of My mouth."

– Revelation 3:16 NIV –

Since the time of the early church we have been stuck with human thermostats in churches all around the globe. These individuals want a safe, convenient Jesus. Therefore, they regulate the Jesus story's temperature to make Him predicable. In this process they've "domesticated" the real Jesus and His life-changing teaching about the kingdom of God. The result – we are left with a gentle Jesus, a tame Jesus, a suburban Jesus, a weird freedom-fighter Jesus, a pious Jesus, you name it ...

Ernst Kaesemann (1906-1988), the well-known German biblical scholar, provides a shocking reason for this thermostatic process that's still underway in many churches today: "People and institutions do not like to be kept continually on the alert, and they have constantly devised screens to protect themselves from too much heat."

How sad that we had to turn down the temperature of the gospel to make it more comfortable for ourselves. Let's stop this nonsense. Let's follow Jesus all the way to the cross ... with His cross on our shoulders!

Dignity

"Since you are precious and honored in My sight, and
because I love you, I will give men in exchange
for you, and people in exchange for your life."

– Isaiah 43:4 NIV –

The famous American interviewer and TV personality Larry
King once said that the words that made the biggest impression on him ever, were those of church leader Martin Luther
King, Jr. When he was refused admission to a hotel during
the days of political segregation in the USA based on his skin
color, he stood quietly in front of the hotel door. When the
hotel owner asked him what he wanted, Martin Luther King,
Jr. replied in one short sentence, "My dignity!" That was all.

Dignity is what most people today are still asking for – the
poor child in school who is overlooked by everyone; the shop
attendant and the security guard who silently go about their
work; the elderly person in the sick bay. And you and me as
well. We all want a bit of dignity and decent treatment from
other people. And that is how it should be, because the Lord
created all of us in His image.

Therefore, each one of us has value to Him. We carry eternity within us. If God values us so much, then we should also
treat one another with the necessary respect. We should be
aware of one another's dignity and respect and help defend
that dignity.

True Orthodoxy

> You yourself must be an example to them by doing
> good works of every kind. Let everything you do
> reflect the integrity and seriousness of your teaching.
>
> – Titus 2:7 NLT –

An amazing quote that really got me thinking recently comes from Peter Rollins. In his brilliant book *How (Not to) Speak of God* (2006), he writes the following: "Orthodoxy as right belief will cost us little; indeed, it will allow us to sit back with our Pharisaic doctrines, guarding the 'truth' with the purity of our interpretations. But orthodoxy, as believing the right way, as bringing love to the world around us … That will cost us everything." Wow, isn't this true? Isn't this the real problem?

How sad to think that many religious discussions, worship wars and sermons deal with propositions, dogma, beliefs, and theological issues. We have become known as believers. Nobody refers to us any longer as "people of the Way." Yes, beliefs are important. Dogma is basic to our faith.

Therefore, faith statements and confessions have immense value, but never at the expense of what I would like to call orthopraxy – lives saturated with Jesus! Then we are merely busy with religious exercises and are missing the point! We are followers of Jesus. Our lives are our strongest testimony.

October

No Sympathy

> But thanks be to God! He gives us the
> victory through our Lord Jesus Christ.
>
> – 1 Corinthians 15:57 NIV –

Many moons ago the Rolling Stones had a hit song with *Sympathy for the Devil.* Some radio stations banned the song, while many preachers warned people not to listen to it. Yes, the devil is always big news. People love to sing about him, talk about him and make jokes about him. In spite of all of this, few take him seriously.

No wonder C. S. Lewis (*The Screwtape Letters*) once wrote these famous words: "There are two equal and opposite errors into which our race can fall about devils. One is to disbelieve in their existence. The other is to believe, and to feel an excessive and unhealthy interest in them. They themselves are equally pleased with both errors."

An unhealthy interest in the devil can lead to an obsession with the occult. On the other hand, to ignore the presence of Satan leads to arrogance and a destructive belief in the power of the self. Evil is a reality, albeit in personal form, or in structures such as godless political and economical institutions. A battle is still raging for the hearts, souls and minds of people. There is a war going on! The outcome of this battle is not a secret. Jesus is the victor. He has overcome evil!

The Winning Team

With God we will gain the victory,
and He will trample down our enemies.

– Psalm 108:13 NIV –

To follow Jesus is to be on the winning side of the battle. It is to be in the presence of the One who hands out abundant life, here, now and forever. However, to be a disciple of Jesus is definitely not a walk in the park. It's no easy route.

To be a disciple of the Messiah is to live against the grain. It is to live dangerously in the storms. It is to be a living example of God's brand-new day in the kingdom. It is to know that His *shalom* is a present reality in Jesus. Actually, this is the battle cry and victory song of His followers!

Jesus is the only one strong enough to fight Satan. He already conquered the forces of darkness at Calvary. Jesus rose from the dead. He sits at the right hand of God. He has all power in heaven and on earth. Through faith in Him the Evil One is cast out! To live for God is to fight the battle the right way.

To live victoriously and beautifully for Jesus is to show no sympathy for the devil.

Carbon Footprint

By Him all things were created.

– Colossians 1:16 NIV –

Did you know that each time you switch on a light in your house, light a fire or drive your vehicle you're affecting the environment? Did you know that the way you think about the world's natural resources (water, coal, oil, fresh air, soil) is part and parcel of your faith in God? Religion is not just about God and you in isolation from the rest of His creation. God is the Creator of the entire universe, and His creation is in ruins.

Fresh water, coal and other natural resources will most definitely run out soon if we continue to use them at a rate faster than they can replenish themselves. Researchers tell us that this is already happening all around the globe.

Each person on earth has a carbon footprint. We produce carbon emissions directly or indirectly, which have a combined negative short- and long term effect on our environment. But the gospel (= good news) is that we have the capacity to make a difference. Did you know that every kilowatt hour (kWh) of electricity we choose to avoid saves over a kilogram of carbon dioxide being released into the earth's atmosphere?

Stopping the Rampage

He causes us to remember His wonderful works.
How gracious and merciful is our LORD!

– Psalm 111:4 NLT –

According to some scientists, carbon dioxide (CO_2) is the major contributor to global warming. It has led to a rise in the earth's average temperatures by nearly 33.8 °F over the past 30 years. Shocking, or what! Global warming could still raise our average temperatures by between 34.5 and 41 °F by the end of this century. Let's do something about it. Let's use less electricity. Let's use energy-saving devices and ensure the survival of God's beautiful earth for the next generation. How? Well, by becoming green and environmentally friendly.

Did you know that by installing an 11-watt compact fluorescent light in place of a normal 60-watt light, you will save 570 kWh over the lifespan of the fluorescent? This will save at least 570 kg of CO_2. God's creation is in trouble. Rivers are polluted. Clouds of smoke fill the skies. Natural forests are being destroyed.

Let's protest in the name of God. Let's stop the destruction. Let's take up our responsibility as caretakers of God's beautiful earth. Let's get it out of the intensive care unit through our prayers and our involvement in projects to protect the environment. Let's just do it!

Changing Direction

Whether you turn to the right or to the left, your ears will hear a voice behind you, saying, "This is the way; walk in it."

– Isaiah 30:21 NIV –

"Your money or you life!" "Surrender, or else ..." Many of my childhood heroes, such as Johan Wayne and Clint Eastwood, used "deep" one-liners such as these. Religious people sometimes also excel in one-liners, the "turn or burn" type.

The worst Christianized one-liner I've ever bumped into? Undoubtedly, the bumper sticker: "Ready or not, here I come – Jesus." Double ouch! The strange thing about Christian one-liners and slogans is that you often find the words "turn back" in them. "Turn back to God." "Turn back to the Bible."

It makes me wonder, why turn back? Shouldn't it rather be, "go forward," "go forward to God" or "turn forward to the Bible"? Leonard Sweet, world renowned futurist, theologian, author, speaker and the guru of those who seek God's plans in new, meaningful ways, including myself, refuses to use the term "retreat." Sweet immediately tells you that Christians never retreat. We advance. Therefore, the gatherings that he hosts at his island and mountain homes are called advances!

Christians shouldn't turn back to the Bible or the church. Then we're heading in the wrong direction. We move forward to God. We advance in His direction.

Holiness

Joyful are people of integrity, who
follow the instructions of the LORD. Joyful are those
who ... search for Him with all their hearts.

– Psalm 119:1-2 NLT –

You can't cheat your way to holiness. Recently, I attended a conference in St Antonio, Texas where the theme was "The Jesus Way." One evening I listened to one of my spiritual heroes, Eugene Peterson. In his presentation he stressed that there are no spiritual steroids for holiness. You have to live a holy life, one day at a time.

The Jesus way is not complicated. You just stay the course, day after day. You walk the walk and talk the talk every single day. There are no shortcuts, quick fixes or spiritual escape routes. To follow Jesus is a daily commitment. You must walk in the same direction, week in and week out.

Follow the Lord, in spite of all evidence pointing in the other direction. Walk behind Jesus and remain right there, even when all logic tells you to overtake Him, or to do it your own way. Never take shortcuts. You can attend all the worship experiences in the world and listen to the best sermons ever preached. But you cannot cheat your way to holiness. Follow Jesus all the way, or get left behind. Repeat this rhythm day after day. This is the holiness route. It is the simple route, the route to life.

Expect the Best

> "In everything, do to others what
> you would have them do to you."
>
> – Matthew 7:12 NIV –

We are programmed to expect the worst from others. And to keep it against them for as long as possible. When we hear a negative story about somebody, we instantly believe it until proven wrong by the facts. (And then some people still say stuff like, "Yes, but ..."). When we read an unsubstantiated gossip story about someone in a newspaper, we spread it further without thinking. When we receive a harmful text message that puts a church or one of its leaders in a bad light we forward it to our circle of friends, or tweet about it. Is this right? Heavens, no! We are called to expect the best from others at all times. And to treat them that way.

How different the texture of our lives would be if we treated others with dignity. What beautiful lives we'll lead when we start caring for others as Christ cares for them. Then we'll protect people's integrity by not believing gossip about them. Then we'll not participate in the spreading of negative stories and in keeping unhealthy perceptions alive.

Then we won't allow people to talk badly about others in our presence. We'll stop the virus by becoming the antiseptic!

Commitment

A man will leave his father and mother and be united
to his wife, and the two will become one flesh.

– Ephesians 5:31 NIV –

Far too many movies have the same recurring theme: A meets B. They fall in love ... well, sort of. But then, at the wedding ceremony, A decides not to go through with the marriage. Feelings of guilt, uncertainty, remorse and a truckload of other emotions cause A to abandon B in the presence of all the wedding guests. *Runaway Bride, Mama Mia, The Proposal,* you name it, have different takes on this theme. Are we afraid of commitment? Is marriage a fetish of some sort?

And then there's the ever-present public audience in these marriage-mania movies. They are always there to applaud the hero who gets the girl in the end. Funny how the kiss and make up scene must always takes place in front of a huge audience who must give their blessing to the final choice.

Angst about commitment is rife. But why is commitment so difficult? It shouldn't be. When A and B spend time in each other's presence and get to know each other well, they will know long before any public ceremonies whether they are meant for each other. Not so? And if they seek the face of God above all, they will have the answer.

Your Soul Mate

Marriage should be honored by all,
and the marriage bed kept pure.

– Hebrews 13:4 NIV –

Too many relationships between men and women are purely physical. They never get to know each other's hearts. After the initial flares of passion the partners discover that much more is needed to keep the relationship going. The physical stuff cannot keep a relationship strong. It works the other way round, actually – but then within the beautiful space of marriage! The secret to happiness for any relationship is to first seek your soul mate. This is a matter of prayer also. Let me rephrase: Begin your search for a soul mate by seeking the face of God long before you enter into any relationship. Never seek His face afterwards. It's always God first, all other relationships second.

Ask God to show you the right person to spend the rest of your life with. If you are married already, ask Him to open your eyes to discover the true inner beauty of your partner. Fall in love with him or her all over again. Otherwise you'll be a runaway bride or groom forever and never be content. Your marriage is God's special gift to you to fill your life with true happiness.

Just Say So!

Do not let any unwholesome talk come out of your
mouths, but only what is helpful for building others up
according to their needs, that it may benefit those who listen.

– Ephesians 4:29 NIV –

We are all builders. Some of us build thick walls of seclusion
and bitterness around ourselves. Others build bridges. Wall
builders isolate themselves from life. They lock bitterness and
hatred in their hearts that grow ever colder and harder. They
mutate into disillusioned, difficult people. What is really sad
is that people like this still hang around in churches. Not even
their faith changes their cynical disposition.

Bridge builders are open and approachable. They love to
live for God and other people. One of the most important
bridges you can ever build includes one small word. I am
referring to the word "sorry"! This is a magic word. It is like
heavenly glue that the Lord gives you to fix broken earthly relationships. It breaks down walls between people in the twin-
kling of an eye and transforms walls into bridges. Hardened
hearts are softened when a sincere apology is heard. Unfortunately, I sometimes hurt other people. But if I learn to say that
I am sorry, then I'm building in a worthy manner.

Trade in Your Troubles

Then Jesus said, "Come to Me, all of you who are weary
and carry heavy burdens, and I will give you rest."

– Matthew 11:28 NLT –

Some people are so pessimistic that they start with the obit-
uaries when they pick up a newspaper. (Maybe this image
doesn't work anymore, since death notices are currently the
headlines in our newspapers.) What a tragedy that it has become a way of life to always notice the bad things first. Listen,
there is a better way! Turn over your problems to Jesus. Stop
trying to carry your burdens on your own. Your shoulders are
not broad enough. You are going to stumble and fall.

According to Matthew 11, Jesus offers you the exchange
transaction of a lifetime. He asks you to exchange your worries and burdens for His heavenly peace. Did you hear that?
You can leave your problems with Christ in exchange for His
heavenly kindness. His shoulders are strong enough for your
distress, together with that of the rest of the world. What are
you still waiting for? Grab the opportunity of a lifetime to give
the right kind of peace permanent residence in your life.

Then all the pessimism and misery that threatens to overwhelm you will disappear like mist before the morning sun.

The Heartbeat of Life

A nap here, a nap there, a day off here, a day
off there, sit back, take it easy – do you know what
comes next? Just this: You can look forward to a
dirt-poor life, poverty your permanent houseguest!

– Proverbs 6:10-11 THE MESSAGE –

Do you sleep through your own dreams every night, or do
you experience them wide-eyed during the day? Do your
dreams ever come true? Do you already live a small part of
those plans God sowed in your heart as recently as yesterday?
Or are you still stuck amongst the hopeless, waiting for better days to descend upon you from out of the blue? Are you
actively present in every moment of your life, or are you still
planning how you are going to report for a bit of playing time
in real life? Well, then you are missing the true adventure.

Life happens one day at a time. God delivered it early this
morning with heavenly compliments right to your doorstep.
All you need to do is fill the day with all the right ingredients.
Nobody else can do it on your behalf. You must choose to love
the Lord, and to have an open heart and a merciful hand for
others. You have to decide to live the right kind of life proactively.

Dare to do this! If you put this choice off until tomorrow,
you are once again 24 hours too late.

Mistakes

Praise the LORD, O my soul, and forget not all His benefits –
who forgives all your sins and heals all your diseases.

– Psalm 103:2-3 NIV –

I am ashamed to admit that God sometimes uses my mistakes
for the good, rather than my so-called obedience. It happened
again just the other day. I lost my temper after receiving poor
service in a shop. When I walked out of there, I felt bad about
my sharp words to the shop assistant. I turned back submis-
sively to apologize. The assistant immediately asked me why I
had apologized. I shame-facedly mumbled that I was a Christian and that I had violated my life principles by speaking before considering my words. And all of a sudden this person
wanted to know more about Christianity!

It is good to know that God not only works when I think
He is working. It is just as nice knowing that the Lord does
not really need me. It is through grace alone that He uses me
with all my defects. Realizing that God loves me in spite of
myself – well, that is earth-shattering good news!

Knowing that my sins and weaknesses never restrict His
grace is also very liberating. But then I should not be content
with Him using my mistakes alone. Then I am a very poor
witness and a bad testimony for our wonderful Lord.

A Hungry World

Be an example to all believers in what you say, in the
way you live, in your love, your faith, and your purity.

– 1 Timothy 4:12 NLT –

"If you are not a good example, at least be a horrible warning!" Nowadays there are various adaptations of these words, "Don't do as I do, do as I say!" Ouch! How can I dare expect something from somebody else when I am not prepared to do it myself? That would not be right, because it would mean that I am deceitful, a warning of how others should *not* live.

If I am a follower of Jesus, He calls me every day to live and practice His kind of life filled with love and servitude. I need to model it in all I say and do. I never have the luxury of doing as I please or hiding behind my flaws and weaknesses.

No, I answer to a Lord whose burden is light. And to a Lord who isn't always ready and waiting to judge me.

True Joy

The joy of the LORD is your strength!

– Nehemiah 8:10 NLT –

Where do you find true and life-changing joy? Can you find it in a check book when can write a whole lot of zeros? Can you find it in a brand-new house? Or maybe in that dream holiday? How about a great new job opportunity? Yes, you will surely find some joy in all these things. Such things can also be blessings directly from our heavenly Father. On the other hand, all holidays come to an end, and a house ages with time.

Where do you encounter joy that is like a constant river that provides water throughout the year; the kind of joy that is not dependent on favorable external circumstances alone? Well, Jesus offers that kind of joy. He invites us to come to Him and get it for ourselves. Joy is the gift Jesus gives to His people. Go and claim your portion today. Don't hastily put it away in one of the drawers of life. Use your heavenly joy.

You can receive it every day! Every morning an updated portion of heavenly joy awaits you with your name and address on it.

Ever-Present

God is our refuge and strength,
an ever-present help in trouble.

– Psalm 46:1 NIV –

Sometimes we are in the presence of VIPs without even realizing it. Think of Jacob. Do you remember when he was fleeing from Esau and he spent one night sleeping with his head against a rock? The Lord unexpectedly appeared to Him in a dream. Afterwards, rather shocked, Jacob confessed, "The Lord is in this place, and I didn't even realize it."

The biggest mistake you could ever make is not recognizing the Lord when He is with you. That would be allowing the opportunity of a lifetime to slip through your fingers! And who knows, maybe you are going to cross paths with a few famous people this year. But the most important person of all is God Himself. You will see His heavenly fingerprints in many places around you.

Don't ignore the Lord. Don't wait until He awakens you from your dreams before you realize that He is present! Make God the Guest of Honor in your life every single day.

A High Price

"If you try to hang on to your life, you will lose it. But
if you give up your life for My sake, you will save it."

– Matthew 16:25 NLT –

You've heard of Maximilian Kolbe, the Franciscan priest who
was incarcerated in Auschwitz during the Second World War.
After an inmate escaped, as was the rule, 10 prisoners were
chosen to die in his place. One of them had a wife and children, and Kolbe volunteered to take the man's place and face
a torturous death. It took two weeks for him to die, when he
was given a lethal injection of acid.

Kolbe's actions remind me of the words of Jesus that there
is no greater love than when someone is prepared to lay down
his life for his friends!

What do we ever sacrifice for one another? Whose lives
have been enriched by us? Who knows, maybe our faith is far
too safe and boring!

Giving Life to Language

Now He uses us to spread the knowledge of
Christ everywhere, like a sweet perfume.

– 2 Corinthians 2:14 NLT –

Language is alive. Note how powerful ordinary little words like "thank you" are. Or a short sentence like "I love you!" At the same time, sharp words can cause tremendous hurt. Harsh, unkind words are like gunshots. They wound people. That is why the Bible says we should count our words before they leave our mouths.

By the way, this is not merely good advice. God made us to be able to form opinions. Our emotions are our first opinion-shapers. Some researchers believe that our emotions function up to a million times faster than our minds. When we literally count to three, our minds have kicked in. Then we can oust our emotions when they want to fire away with hasty words.

We should carefully mull over our words before they leave our lips. Once uttered, words have a life of their own. The damage they cause cannot easily be undone. Ask the Lord to review your words before they escape your mouth. Ask Him to transform them into medicine that cures. Utter words that give life and see what happens!

Getting by

"Your Father knows what you need before you ask Him."
– Matthew 6:8 NIV –

One of the greatest sources of stress to ordinary salaried people is whether their hard-earned money is going to last until the end of the month. Is this your worst headache, too? Perhaps you are feeling like the person who told me the other day, "I wish I could afford living the way I do." To millions, life is a struggle for survival. Well, I have some "irrelevant" news for you: Christ says in Matthew 6 that God provides everything His children need in life. He knows our basic needs, but more than that, He knows what we need and when we need it.

God is always on time. Why would some believers find this news irrelevant? Because they do not really believe it. They work their fingers to the bone, thinking that their survival rests with them alone. They worry, as if Jesus did not intend God's promise to apply in the third millennium. They build their own futures as if God knows nothing of tomorrow.

What about you? Is this news irrelevant to you, or do you believe it? Well, if you do, be a bit more carefree about life than you were yesterday and the day before.

The Prophet Said

The Lord always keeps His promises.
– Psalm 145:13 NLT –

Recently a businessman came to see me. He was upset. "God failed me," he told me. "I lost millions of dollars in a transaction after a Christian prophet told me to go ahead with this deal." "Why are you angry at God?" I asked. "Did you do proper research beforehand?" "Well, I did, but then a friend at our church advised me to go to a Christian prophet to make sure I was on the right track," he answered. "This prophet told me God showed her that I would succeed."

"You went to a religious fortune-teller, not to a prophet," I replied. The businessman objected angrily, "But prophets know about God's future plans." "Perhaps you should have read Deuteronomy 18 and other Bible texts about the functions of true biblical prophecy before you put your faith in today's self-appointed prophets. Prophecy is definitely not about solving personal matters or revealing future knowledge about our business deals, but about the revelation of God's plans for His people and His world," I told him.

Prophecy never sidesteps our personal responsibility. How sad that many believers refuse to accept responsibility for their personal choices. No wonder they blame their failures on someone else, or on God.

Eternal Children

Think about things that are excellent and worthy of praise.
– Philippians 4:8 NLT –

The young physicist at the Polutechnikum in Zurich should have been devastated when his dissertation was turned down. Most students give up when their professors decide their research is not good enough. But this man refused to do so. His name? Albert Einstein. Failure was not an option for him. "Long live insolence!" he cried.

Hereafter, in the Swiss city of Bern, the 26-year-old Einstein spent many hours writing three important papers that caused the biggest shifts in modern science. The reason for Einstein's success? He didn't have a big ego that craved recognition from his peers. Harvard professor Howard Gardner later said that Einstein became one of the greatest scientists of our age because of his openness, honesty, and naïveté. He remained an "eternal child."

We urgently need spiritual Einsteins who refuse to go with the religious flow. Far too many believers live mediocre lives. There are a great number of spiritual leaders occupying comfortable positions in highly predictable church environments. Far too many theologies, church programs and sermons facilitate feel-good religious experiences. No wonder Christianity has such a low impact in "the real world."

Information Overload

> Trust in the LORD with all your heart; do not
> depend on your own understanding. Seek His will in
> all you do, and He will show you which path to take.
>
> – Proverbs 3:5-6 NLT –

I was stunned when I recently read that approximately 4.4 million American children between the ages of four and seventeen have already been diagnosed with ADD (Attention Deficit Disorder) and that between 10 and 12% of boys between the ages of six and fourteen are victims of this disorder. In South Africa it is also on the increase. We live in a world where serious pressure is experienced from a very early age. Our bodies simply cannot keep up with the progress in our new world anymore. Tension, the drive for achievement and especially information overload are literally making people ill.

Speaking of information overload, in 2006, 161 billion gigabytes of information was sent across the Internet. That is three million times more than all the accumulated book knowledge throughout history, within a mere one-year period! People yearn to find sense and meaning that would bring peace to the soul. Do you also yearn for peace amidst the chaos? Well, with the Lord, the waters of rest are still flowing. His way takes you to green pastures. Embrace this knowledge with your heart ... and with your hands and feet. Join God there.

Word Count

A gentle answer turns away wrath,
but a harsh word stirs up anger.

– Proverbs 15:1 NIV –

A good friend of mine recently told me about someone who wrote the following in a letter: "Please excuse me for the fact that my letter is so long. Unfortunately, I didn't have the time to write a shorter one." True words indeed!

We are all victims of too many words. We sometimes talk, write, sing and type too much. We don't necessarily need thick writing pads or a great number of words to utter true wisdom. Short messages are often those we reflect upon the longest. Very often we find that the more words we use, the smaller the impact. (Please convey this message to those long-drawn talkers who love to take over conversations!)

Consider how many short text messages are sent with great effect every day, where 160 characters triumph. Or on Twitter, with only 140 characters. Be a counter of words from now on.

Choose your words carefully. Talk less. Practice using fewer words. Remember the warning from Proverbs that our words can be like knife stabs, or the finest silver.

Hijacked by Grace

"Prove by the way you live that you have
repented of your sins and turned to God."

– Matthew 3:8 NLT –

The young Paul was like a man possessed when he heard the
followers of Jesus claim that He was the resurrected Messiah.
No one who died on a cross could be the Messiah. It was
blasphemy! Paul persecuted the followers of Jesus with a
vengeance everywhere he went.

Then, one day, he encountered the resurrected Jesus on
the road to Damascus. This meeting altered his entire life. A
true revolutionary was born that day when Jesus and Paul met
face to face, one that redefined religion and life for millions of
people throughout history. Talk about impact!

After being "hijacked by grace", Paul's new purpose took
him on dangerous, yet highly adventurous journeys to the
farthermost corners of the world. He travelled more than
11,000 miles on foot during his various missionary journeys
across the Roman Empire. The new Paul who instantly turned
into a loyal follower of Jesus had a new vision, one that provoked, disrupted and challenged everyone and everything
around him, but one that made a huge impact, the right kind!
Perhaps we should follow suit.

Leave Haste Behind

A day is like a thousand years to the
Lord, and a thousand years is like a day.

– 2 Peter 3:8 NLT –

Being hasty is a human characteristic, not a divine one. I refer to haste. God always has time. He is never in a hurry on His way to His next appointment. Take a look at the life Jesus led on earth. He always had time, even in the face of death. When His friend Lazarus died (John 11), He was still on time! He wants us to exchange our hurried, high-octane hearts for tranquil hearts.

We should have the courage to spend time walking with God in His garden. We should once again bring His garden back to life outside the gates of Paradise. God still has so many secrets He wants to share with us here on earth; so many new joys. But then we have to take action against our hurried lives. How? Well, we have to receive medicine from the Lord for that "hurry sickness" we suffer from.

This is an illness that poisons our entire existence. Haste steals our joy. It robs us of our loved ones and of everyone that matters in our lives. What for? Only so that we can say we are the latest winners of the rat race floating trophy?

Strange but True

No prophecy in Scripture ever came from the prophet's own understanding, or from human initiative. No, those prophets were moved by the Holy Spirit, and they spoke from God.

– 2 Peter 1:20-21 NLT –

Some believers like to define their roles in God's service in terms of the prophets of the Old Testament. Strangely, they usually only use the stories of the prophets. The real day-to-day lives of the prophets never get much attention when these believers begin to define their calling or the nature of their ministries. However, to be a prophet in the tradition of a Jeremiah, Micah or Nahum, is to live against the grain. The true prophets of Israel lived on the fringes of society. They weren't the religious flavors of the day. Prophets never formed part of the mainstream religion.

To be a prophet is to see what others don't always see, to hear what others don't usually hear. But God's prophets don't just see and hear His new future; they also make known what they heard, saw and experienced. Prophets always communicate God's new day in the kingdom. They reveal God's heart. They are figures of hope with a new message of restoration. No wonder they vigorously challenge all systems, institutions, individuals, and groups that stand in the way of God's plans.

Hope Floats

Guide me in Your truth and teach me, for You are
God my Savior, and my hope is in You all day long.

– Psalm 25:5 NIV –

Good Friday is not really an appropriate name for the day
Jesus died. It is definitely not good news when someone who
came to adorn the world with so much grace had to pay for
this by death. And yet the last words of Jesus on the cross give
the right perspective to this Friday. Do you remember His
words from to the Gospel of John, "It is finished"? Without
a doubt! The price has been fully paid. The account is completely settled. The ledger between God and each person who
embraces the redemption of Jesus has been balanced.

Hope floats. Hope does not sink into the sea of hopelessness; anger does not constantly win. Grace is the new password from heaven's gates. God and people can once again
be good neighbors. Strangers and lost people may again sit
down at God's table. Death definitely does not have the final
say. Neither does all the injustice, hurt and suffering of the
life in and around you. Because today there is an empty cross
on Calvary!

Put your hand in the hand of the risen Christ and celebrate with Him at the festive table forever!

The World in His Hands

The LORD directs the steps of the godly. He delights in
every detail of their lives. Though they stumble, they
will never fall, for the LORD holds them by the hand.

– Psalm 37:23-24 NLT –

At this very moment earth is traveling through space at more
than 65,000 miles per hour, while today it will complete approximately 1, 4 million miles of its annual journey around the
son. At the same time earth is rotating around its own axle
at an astonishing 994 miles per hour. Staggering, isn't it! It
is amazing to think that God maintains everything perfectly
day after day. He is the Creator of the universe, but also the
Maintainer of the mighty and beautiful works of His hands.
Therefore you can trust God with great things.

Nothing is ever too big for Him. He balances our world
with everyone on it and everything in it. But nothing is ever
too small for Him either. The detail of your life is really of
interest to Him.

Take all your needs to Him today in prayer. Do so in the
name of Jesus. He hears you. He sees you. He cares so much
about you. The God of power is also the God of the detail of
your life. Small is never too insignificant for Him, just as nothing is ever too big.

True Identity

Therefore, there is now no condemnation
for those who are in Christ Jesus.

– Romans 8:1 NIV –

The biggest freedom on earth is being able to take off your masks in God's presence. Ask the man in Luke 18 who could only mumble one short sentence, "Have mercy on me!" Immediately he walked away a man who had been set right with God. The gospel is about what God does for free to enable you to be one with Him again, not about what you have to do to be redeemed and reunited with Him.

Freedom starts when you realize that you no longer have to try and obtain the Lord's favor. Then a whole new life opens up for you. The true key to freedom is who you are in Christ, not what you have to do for Him! To find your identity in God's free grace is still the big secret. Freedom means finding rest in the Lord, not in your spiritual attempts that keep you running around from early in the morning until late at night.

Please listen, you don't have to try and win over God's favor. He has decided to love you long ago based on who you already are in Christ.

One Step at a Time

God's way is perfect. All the LORD's promises prove true.
He is a shield to all who look to Him for protection.

– Psalm 18:30 NLT –

I admire people whose lives are so neatly organized. And those who pray and quickly receive an answer. But I have to add that I am astonished at the number of church members who think that prayer is an easy shortcut, an instant quick fix. On my side of the fence it is not that easy.

I associate myself with John Eldredge, who writes in his best-seller *Waking the Dead* that he experiences approximately 20 bright days per year when he knows exactly what God expects of him. The rest of the time God's will seems to him like driving in dense fog. Maybe you know that feeling, too. Well, then you will appreciate the words of Oswald Chambers, the missionary giant who touched so many lives: "I never see my way. I never have far-reaching plans."

Maybe God does not specialize in five- and ten-year plans. He mostly does things one day at a time, like Exodus 16 and the Lord's Prayer teaches us. Let us find His way for today, then at least we can live on course one day at a time!

Unstuff

"Whoever becomes simple and elemental again,
like this child, will rank high in God's kingdom."

– Matthew 18:4 THE MESSAGE –

Live more simply so that others can simply live. "How?" you may wonder, while considering the fact that you barely make ends meet yourself. Well, live more generously, like the Lord expects you to. You don't have to be wealthy, or have "enough" before you start sharing what you have with others. If you are in the fortunate position of being able to buy something new, like a CD, garment, TV, cell phone or treat, buy a cheaper item for a change and give the difference in the purchasing price to someone in need.

Decide when enough is really enough in your life. Ask the Lord to give you a generous heart, one that prefers giving to receiving. Also try doing a few practical things. You could, for instance, choose to have a simple meal with your friends once a month. Quietly give the money that a more expensive meal would have cost to someone who is in the Lord's service.

Live as simply as you can afford, even if you are not wealthy, so that others can at least live!

November

Carrying the Cross

Be completely humble and gentle;
be patient, bearing with one another in love.

– Ephesians 4:2 NIV –

In between all the reasons for complaining about how bad life is, you and I can choose to find our joy elsewhere. Following Jesus means having hope. Bearing His cross means being a living blessing to others.

Every day that we enjoy the privilege of living and breathing, we have the chance and honor to bear the cross of Jesus. And who knows, you and I may be the only "Bible" available to someone who finds themselves in a place of despondency. What about a gentle word of hope for them, or maybe a piece of bread to make their plight more bearable? How about a quiet prayer for a friend who is currently experiencing the sharp edge of life?

Let us carry the cross of Jesus that offers life and hope to those around us. When others start tasting and seeing life because the cross of Jesus is resting on our own shoulders, we eventually hardly even feel the weight of it anymore. The cross is only a burden when we get caught up in self-pity, or when we are not a living blessing to others.

Normal

Get insurance with GOD and do a good
deed, settle down and stick to your last.
Keep company with GOD, get in on the best.

– Psalm 37:3-4 THE MESSAGE –

I love the words of the American actress Whoopi Goldberg, "Normal is just a cycle on a washing machine." Maybe normal is precisely that – a setting on a washing machine. If we all lived and behaved like the normal person on the street, we would be in serious trouble. If we should be exactly like the "reasonable person" the judicial system talks about, we would still be caught up in "reasonability."

The world, and especially the church, desperately needs "out of the box" people, those who dance to a different beat. The ones whose lives have not fallen into a rut of predictable boredom, but who joyfully redeem every bit of time at their disposal. They are the ones who discover new horizons and conquer new heights in the name of the Lord. They inspire and infuse others to progress further and higher and more courageously on the Lord's way.

Such people regard unfamiliar territory as a challenge. They thrive on courage and risks. Hopefully you too are part of this elite group of non-conformists. People like these turn the world upside down in the name of Jesus.

Desire

Whoever finds me finds life and
receives favor from the Lord.

– Proverbs 8:35 NIV –

Robert Olsen is correct when he writes that people have a lifelong addiction to a never-ending desire for more! The popular term for this is "consumerism." According to him, it is part of human nature to constantly want more. Nobody will ever have enough. There are always more items and things to have, and we are miserable until we have it.

Many people try to find the meaning of life to escape this consumer mentality. Religion is one of the "crutches" many people try, only to discover that "it doesn't work." Of course religion does not work, at least not if you want to use it as a quick solution. One thing I discovered recently is that Jesus is not in the "quick fix" business, the way desire-driven people even in the church see it.

On the contrary, you can only follow Him on His terms. And that requires sacrifice, going the extra mile and even suffering. It requires a new you who decides to follow a new Master. But it also brings a strange new peace that will completely baffle your mind.

Modern-Day Heroes

Prophecy resulted when the Holy Spirit
prompted men and women to speak God's Word.

– 2 Peter 1:21 THE MESSAGE –

The real heroes of God in biblical times were the prophets who challenged the existing political, religious and social systems through speeches and symbolic actions. The reason – they saw and experienced God's vision for His people. The prophets just had to challenge the powers of the day to reform and rethink their present ways. No wonder God's prophets were often misunderstood, ridiculed, and dismissed as heretics. But they couldn't help themselves. They were instruments of God. They were in His service. His full-time calling on their lives surpassed their obedience to all others. They only played for an Audience of One, whatever the cost.

Modern-day prophets are urgently called for. The ones who don't settle for the same old answers in the same old safe spiritual environments. They risk their own popularity and careers to explore God's new routes of hope. They make an impact where it really counts – amongst the poor, the downtrodden, the sick and the lonely. Instead, they often opt to work amongst the poorest of the poor and sinners. Are you one of them?

Keep on Growing

Fear of the LORD is the foundation of true wisdom.
All who obey His commandments will grow in wisdom.

– Psalm 111:10 NLT –

Alvin Toffler writes, "The illiterate of the future are not those who cannot read or write, but those who cannot learn, unlearn, and relearn." What a challenge to remain inquisitive. Curiosity and inquisitiveness are precious qualities that God instilled in each one of us. Why is it that we lose it so quickly?

Why are our lives often so predictable, safe and boring? Why don't we think for ourselves? Why do pastors and ministers constantly have to think on our behalf? Why do we hide behind a few Bible verses after having "received Scripture" that causes us to refrain from seeking deeper meaning from the Word and finding the actual truths locked in the pages?

When we daily discover old and new treasures, as Jesus teaches us in Matthew 13, our lives will be one lifelong adventure. Our hearts and minds will never grow old. And we will continually be surprised by God. When we continue to learn, we will keep on growing. Dare to grow a little more in your knowledge and understanding of God today ... and see what happens!

Let's Go Fishing

"Come, follow Me," Jesus said,
"and I will make you fishers of men."

– Matthew 4:19 NIV –

I read about an American denomination that is busy raising millions of dollars to help 500 burnt-out pastors. When a clerical consultant asked their leaders why they didn't change their priorities to support the 500 most effective pastors in their denominations, the answer was rather damning: "We could never raise money for that!"

Yes, struggling congregations and clergymen need to be supported, but then it must be seen for what it is: temporary emergency assistance. When churches are artificially sustained with money, rather than empowering the growing ministries of people who want to change the world in the name of the Lord, then we are missing the point. Effectiveness in the Lord's service is all about empowering believers to spread the kingdom of the Lord in a visible way. There are more than enough new champions of faith among us in whom we should invest our prayers, involvement, time and money.

To notice them, help them and support them, is a challenge. Open your spiritual eyes for a change to see the new things that God is doing above and below the radar screens of the church. And be there!

Blessing Others

From the fullness of His grace we have
all received one blessing after another.

– John 1:16 NIV –

God favors His children with heavenly grace. But we may not keep it to ourselves. We are called to be a living blessing to others. The people Jesus cared for – the poor, the crippled, the blind and the paralyzed of Luke 14, or the captives, strangers, naked and hungry of Matthew 25 – must be on our radar screens daily. They should share in our festivities.

Did you know that a mere 42 out of every 100 people in a country such as South Africa currently have jobs? Or that, according to a recent Markinor survey, only 68 out of every 100 households have running water in their houses? Of these, only 31 have a geyser. Sixty-nine households don't enjoy the luxury of a warm shower. Meanwhile, 13 out of every 100 people in South Africa are HIV positive. While 73% say that they are Christians.

Shouldn't we as Christians have a bigger impact? Aren't we supposed to be a living blessing to those around us? If God favors us, then we should share this with one another. Otherwise we are stealing from heaven by keeping all the festive fare to ourselves!

Keeping Silent

Joyful are those who have the God of Israel as
their helper, whose hope is in the LORD their God.

– Psalm 146:5 NLT –

How can we look the other way when 30,000 people die worldwide every day due to water pollution and the serious illnesses related to it? How can we remain silent when hundreds of people are dying in Zimbabwe due to cholera? Doesn't it deeply affect us when global warming is threatening the continued existence of our planet? Can we turn a blind eye when poisonous gases are warming our atmosphere beyond its limits? Can we remain deaf when racist language dominates many of the conversations around us? Dare we keep quiet when innocent blood is shed due to senseless crimes?

Should we keep on praying when everyone around us has thrown in the towel and started following their own leads? Should we also surrender and give up hope? No, how could we? The living Lord is with us, the One who says that those who cry and grieve about all the suffering will soon be comforted (Matt. 5). We can cry, but also laugh at the same time. Therefore, our hearts are heavily burdened, but also light. Because the Lord is also present in the darkness which sometimes threatens to overwhelm us.

How Far Is God?

"My Presence will go with you, and I will give you rest."
– Exodus 33:14 NIV –

"How far from us is God really, sir?" a little girl asked me recently. "Why do you want to know?" I asked. "Well, my mom and dad say I am wasting my time praying to God because He is too far to hear," she answered.

"No, He is not far. I had a conversation with Him a few minutes ago," I immediately responded. "In fact, God is always only one prayer away." "All distance disappears in the exact place where you and I bow down before God and talk to Him in the name of Jesus. Then God is right there – a mere prayer away! We never have to shout, or use a loudspeaker to talk to Him, because He is not deaf. Neither do you have to use big and difficult words, or say long prayers. All God wants from us is sincerity. He is interested in the language of your heart. That is all."

"I agree, because I know that God is always close to me. It seems that my parents have become blind to His presence," the girl remarked with sadness in her voice, walking away.

Hard Work

Always give yourselves fully to the work of the Lord,
because you know that your labor in the Lord is not in vain.

– 1 Corinthians 15:58 NIV –

Some people complain about how hard they work. Then I say something to the effect that the license on hard work has already been snatched up by someone else. Or that hard work is not an Olympic sport that qualifies for medals. Sometimes I wonder whether some people think that hard work is somehow an achievement that earns them bonus points. Or something that others should admire you for.

I constantly remind myself of the story Jesus told in Luke 17:7-10 where He says if I have done everything for the Lord that I should have, then I don't deserve a standing ovation from Him or others. Hard work in His vineyard is a normal part of my calling. In the end, I am merely God's servant. Everything I do for God I should do diligently, without expecting any recognition. It is my life's commission to do God's will.

Hard work very often goes hand in hand with a life devoted to God. No, it is never about merit, as if the Lord should reward me if I do my share. On the contrary, it is all about gratitude on my part for the opportunity of being able to work for Him.

Investor or Consumer?

"Do not store up for yourselves treasures on earth,
where moth and rust destroy, and where thieves break in
and steal. But store up for yourselves treasures in heaven."

– Matthew 6:19-20 NIV –

There are two types of people: consumers and investors.
Consumers use up everything and everyone around them –
people, friendship, money ... you name it and they use
(abuse?) it. Consumers can never get enough of everything.
They are bottomless pits. No matter what you do for them, it
is never enough. Somewhere in the future they are going to
complain about the fact that you don't do enough for them.
After all, they believe that you and life owes them!

Alternately, there is a small group of people who live from
abundance, whom we'll call investors. They have enough,
even though they have few material possessions. They are
content. Investors have hope when the rest of the world is
hopeless. After all, they live from the Lord's abundant treasure chambers of grace. How do you change from a consumer
to an investor? Well, invest your life exclusively in God! Be
content with Him. He is more than enough. God's heavenly
treasure chambers overflow with grace, peace, freedom and
love. Become a daily partaker of His heavenly abundance.
Then you will have more than enough. Then your cup will
overflow!

Facts and Figures

"Let your light shine before men, that they may see your good deeds and praise your Father in heaven."
– Matthew 5:16 NIV –

Facts and figures impress people. When thousands of people show up to listen to a well-known preacher, many call it a roaring success. I'm not against large crowds attending religious events, but when attendance becomes the definition for success in Christianity, we are in trouble. Far too many preachers are marketed nowadays as crowd-drawing celebrities. Did we get stuck in that infamous *bodies/budget/buildings = success* syndrome? Why do we uncritically apply the rest of the world's definitions of success in church?

Perhaps I'm the only stranger in Jerusalem, but I'm convinced that Jesus focused more on reaching individuals, outcasts, marginalized people and the poor than on getting people to fill revival meetings and worship events. Success to Jesus means sowing one mustard seed at a time. And mustard seeds multiply, as Jesus teaches us in Matthew 13. The real test for kingdom growth is discipleship. Crowds and audiences don't really change the world. Yes, they fill seats. They cheer, sing, celebrate and rejoice. But the real agents of change are committed followers of Christ – the difference between fans and disciples.

Praying for Strangers

When God's people are in need, be
ready to help them. Always be eager to practice
hospitality. Bless those who persecute you.
Don't curse them; pray that God will bless them.

– Roman 12:13-14 NLT –

Do you also sometimes get dispirited when you see yet another beggar standing at the side of the road? Or maybe someone trying to sell something? Next time, do something better than just ignoring them. Pray for them! Yes, you read correctly. Pray for them. Dare to place that unknown beggar before the Lord's throne. And who knows, maybe you will be the only person who would do such an "unthinkable" thing as praying for them.

While you are being so reckless praying for people who "accidentally" cross your path, why don't you also dare to pray to God on behalf of the expressionless person in the car next to you. Or for the shop attendant or the lady at the cash register. Instead of constantly glaring at your watch and wishing it was your turn to be served, you can fill the time with short prayers for unknown people, people with real names and real faces. Who knows what God can do with such quiet prayers!

Darkness or Light?

You are a chosen people, a royal priesthood,
a holy nation, a people belonging to God, that
you may declare the praises of Him who called
you out of darkness into His wonderful light.

– 1 Peter 2:9 NIV –

Somebody said to me that the future looks rather bleak. "What future are you talking about?" I asked. "Do you mean the future in three months' time? Or the one in five years' time? We are now living the future we were so worried about five years ago!" And yet those of us who are living get by! Amazing! No, it is sheer grace! It is all thanks to God! He is really faithful! God has ensured that we made it to today! And, furthermore, He has brought the bread of mercy right to our doorstep.

Are you without bread today? *No?* Do you have enough blankets on your bed? *Yes?* Will you have enough bread to eat for the next month? Definitely! Will your health make it through today and maybe even tomorrow? Indeed! Then why are you so worried? Why do you complain that there is no future? This constitutes a motion of no confidence in your heavenly Father. He guarantees that He will give you bread for today. He, who takes care of the birds and the flowers, will care for you. His grace will be enough for you every day, yes, more than enough!

Bold Prayer

So let us come boldly to the throne of our gracious
God. There we will receive His mercy, and we
will find grace to help us when we need it most.

– Hebrews 4:16 NLT –

John Maxwell once said that the most audacious prayer the
average person prays every day is that evergreen prayer, "Lord,
bless the food that we are about to eat!" Or, like many of us
have adapted it, "Bless the hands that prepared the food." If
that has become your main prayer, then you should say the
following one as well: "Lord, help me for I know not what I
do!" Prayers are not formal recitations for the sake of some or
other tradition, or merely something I do to soothe my conscience. Prayer is a momentous matter. It involves personally
talking to the living God who holds heaven and earth in the
palm of His hand.

Ecclesiastes 4 warns us to be careful with our words in
the presence of the Lord. We have to count and consider our
words very carefully because we are speaking to the King of
the universe every time. We should know our place before
Him. Every word that comes from our lips should be sincere.

They must be chosen wisely! But it must also be bold –
meaning that they should be encompassed in faith. We should
trust God to uproot trees and plant them in the sea, as Jesus
teaches us in Luke 17.

"Mine, Mine!"

Don't forget to do good and to share with those
in need. These are the sacrifices that please God.

– Hebrews 13:16 NLT –

"Mine!" That is what little children say when you touch their toys. Some grown-ups still live like that. "Mine" is what they say to themselves when they see a new house, car, garment or gadget. There is no rest to be found until that item becomes "mine." But then a strange thing happens – shortly after "mine" has been attained, the next item appears in the shop window that must also be "mine."

We live in a world that constantly creates new needs and desires in us. If we are not careful, we can become lifelong prisoners of this kind of lifestyle. That is precisely why the Bible warns us against an insatiable desire for the things that are displayed on the "must-have" shelves of life. When we become slaves of this, it later results in us only feeling good when we receive new things. The solution to this addiction? Be content with what you have, as simple as that! Find joy in the Lord and in good relationships with those you love.

Start appreciating the little or the abundance that the Lord has gracefully bestowed upon you. Thank Him from your heart for all you have.

Sleep

"I will refresh the weary and satisfy the faint."
– Jeremiah 31:25 NIV –

Someone once told me how a pastor threw his Bible at someone who had fallen asleep in his church. "If you don't want to hear the Word at least you will feel it," he added. Maybe it was only a joke. Sleep, in fact, is a very important part of our lives. Do you sleep well? Or do your problems make you toss and turn at night? If so, the time has come for your faith in Christ to have a direct impact on your sleeping patterns.

Listen to what David says about this: "I lie down and sleep; I wake again, because the Lord sustains me" (Ps. 3:5). Rather gripping, isn't it? Trust in the Lord to deal with all your problems for a change. Then they will no longer keep you awake at night. Then you will fall asleep in the arms of the Almighty God every time.

You will no longer wake from fitful sleep in the morning; you will wake refreshed and invigorated.

Surrendering All

LORD, You are our Father. We are the clay,
You are the potter; we are all the work of Your hand.

– Isaiah 64:8 NIV –

One of my good friends told me of a very busy little boy who created havoc in a children's service. Later, he asked the little boy, "Who taught you to be so busy?" He answered as honestly as he could, "Sir, can I tell you a secret? I taught myself!" That was the most honest answer I've ever heard. Yes, it is indeed ourselves, and not always our circumstances, that make us behave the way we do. We teach ourselves every day to think, to talk and to react in certain ways.

If we don't clamp down on negative things on a regular basis, like those small bits of bitterness, anger or suspicion that all too easily find a nesting place in our hearts, before we know it we are addicted to it.

It is not necessarily the big things that derail our lives, but sometimes precisely those little things that unobtrusively get stuck in our heads. The solution? Well, we have to place our lives in God's hands today like soft clay so that He can renew us from the inside.

Auto-Pilot Mode

Live a life filled with love.
– Ephesians 5:2 NLT –

Much of our lives are spent in auto-pilot mode. We live detached lives. We constantly plan for tomorrow and save all our energy for that big somewhere on the other side of the rainbow. This auto-pilot lifestyle leads to a highly structured, "routinized"way of life. In churches you'll see this in the well-planned programs and religious events, without spontaneity or passion. Many people in church experience stagnation. They feel spiritually empty and numb as the world around them becomes more and more dull. They become bored, cynical and skeptical. Nothing excites them any longer. Not even God can surprise them because they have already planned His next renewal, revival and final return in the finest detail.

We need to attune to every moment God grants us in curiosity, openness, acceptance and love. In this way, through our constant awareness of God's graceful presence, a deep sense of compassion can be nurtured inside us through His Spirit. It will begin to flow out of us to others. The distance between God and us, and the gap between ourselves and others, will be bridged as we become more aware of God's grace.

A Living Example

> In everything set them an example by doing what is
> good. In your teaching show integrity, seriousness
> and soundness of speech that cannot be condemned.
>
> – Titus 2:7-8 NIV –

Very early on in life children learn from grown-ups that only winners really matter. First place is the most important to many parents and teachers. The academic achievers, the first team, the executive committee of learners – they usually receive most of the attention. It is really wonderful if children can develop their talents and abilities from an early age. But does the pursuit of winning place the heartbeat of a happy life before God? Aren't grown-ups perhaps guilty of placing far too much pressure on children to be mini grown-ups?

Shouldn't children learn other crucial values in life other than just winning, winning, winning? Do they often enough see how we as parents serve the Lord with commitment? Do they see every day that we have open hearts and open hands for people less fortunate? Are we living examples of forgiveness and love towards others? Who then gives us the sole right to endlessly complain about the "youth of today" or to refer to them as the "lost generation"? Maybe we deserve this title! The young ones merely learn from us how to do it the wrong way!

Divine Grace

Be kind and compassionate to one another, forgiving
each other, just as in Christ God forgave you.

– Ephesians 4:32 NIV –

The gracious heart of Jesus beats warmly for the losers of His day. Those who got a red card from the religious leaders were at the top of His gracious list.

Think about the prostitute in Luke 7. She wiped her tears from the feet of Jesus using her hair, after she burst in uninvited on a dinner where Jesus was the guest of honor. While the pious choked with indignation over the fact that Jesus forgave her sins, she heard the most beautiful words ever: "Your faith has saved you; go in peace." No wonder the religious leaders later had Him killed. They couldn't stand the fact that Jesus gave away God's kindness for free to people like her.

The grace Jesus offers isn't even cheap; it is completely free! But that is exactly what Jesus is like, even today! You are always welcome in His company, no matter how deep or far you have fallen. With Him there is always an extra portion of heavenly grace to be had! All you need to do is ask.

Into the Storm

Grace and peace to you from God
our Father and the Lord Jesus Christ.

– 1 Corinthians 1:3 NIV –

When George Bush and Tony Blair, the two most influential leaders in the world at one stage, were hot on the heels of Saddam Hussein, he was hiding in a sewer pipe in Bagdad.

When the pope and the emperor declared him to be enemy number one, Martin Luther translated the New Testament into German. That is what the heroes of the Lord do; they walk even deeper into the storm. The more fierce the battle, the more firmly they stand at their posts.

Martin Luther single-handedly faced the wandering church of his day and then chose the way of God. Contrary to everyone else, He submitted to the graceful words of the Bible. His love for God overruled his fear of people. That is why Luther nailed his 95 statements to the church door in Wittenburg, Germany, in 1517, which finally catapulted the church in a new direction.

Henceforth, grace was once again present in the church. Divine grace once again sparkled like the sun. Are you also living with God's grace? Is your faith built on Christ alone? And is the Word your only guide?

A Good Name

A good name is more desirable than great riches;
to be esteemed is better than silver or gold.

– Proverbs 22:1 NIV –

The other day I ran into a former pastor who had been falsely accused in a scandal. Out of pure frustration he later resigned. When he asked one woman why she had participated in the gossiping without ever talking to him first, she answered him with, "Well, Pastor, it was such an enjoyable story to tell. It just had to be the truth!" Can you believe it? And these are the people who should have known better and lived according to the Word!

People are sometimes prepared to rip one another to shreds without batting an eyelid. The crystal-clear biblical principle in Matthew 18, that one should rather talk to someone than about the person behind their back, is ignored in far too many religious circles.

May God keep you and me from this! May He use our words to defend the good name of other people when they are not around. May our words always frame the lives of others with honor.

The Easy Way

You must have the same attitude that Christ Jesus had.
– Philippians 2:5 NLT –

We should have the same attitude as Christ. This is what Paul writes in Philippians. He says we should look at things with a different eye; listen with a different ear; feel with a different heart; and live from a different disposition. The attitude of Jesus Christ, that sacrifices all, should reign in our lives. Every choice we make; every breath we take, every footstep and every heartbeat should be driven by self-denial and sacrifice.

The attitude of Christ is not just about questions regarding our career choice or our choice of friends. It is about matters relating to life and death. It's about radical cross bearing. You don't have the attitude of Christ merely when it comes to a few crossroad choices in your life. No, it is all about the question of whether your entire existence echoes the heartbeat of Christ every day.

Therefore, when you reach a crossroad with Christ's cross on your shoulders, the steep road is always your first choice. Because that is what Christ would have done. He would have gone deeper into the storm to find people who have gone astray.

Favor

The LORD will withhold no good thing
from those who do what is right.

– Psalm 84:11 NLT –

Let's be honest – it is wonderful to be the blue-eyed boy and to receive preferential treatment now and then. It makes you feel very special. Well, God treats all of us that way when we follow Jesus. He calls us His children. That is what Paul writes in Romans 8. We are no longer slaves who are afraid of our ill-tempered owner. We are children of the King who lives in the house of the Lord every day. He is our Father. He is close to us. In addition, He covers us with His kindness from head to toe.

God promises many times in the Bible that He will provide our daily needs. And yet most of us have cupboards overflowing with meat, vegetables and other delicacies. Not even the rising prices and high inflation have caused us to go without food or with only dry bread as a staple food. To top it all, there is more than enough food and clothing for many days to come in most of our houses.

It seems to me that the Lord is favoring us. Why then are we complaining while we enjoy so much abundance? Isn't that blatant ingratitude?

Always Near

The LORD Himself goes before you and will be
with you; He will never leave you nor forsake you.

– Deuteronomy 31:8 NIV –

There are times during your walk with the Lord that you may feel far from Him. Never forget during these "valleys" that God really is only a prayer away. Distance suddenly melts away when you call on His name. All it takes is just a little perseverance.

Isn't it remarkable to think that He has time for each one of us – for each Christian no matter who you are in the world? For Him, time changes its dimension; instantly He is there to hear your prayer, no matter how big or small. Yes, our God is omnipotent and omnipresent!

Footprints

All of you together are Christ's body,
and each of you is a part of it.

– 1 Corinthians 12:27 NLT –

Too many Christians' idea of a good life is merely the secular world view with a dash of goodness. It is just as measurable and translatable in terms of money, materialistic possessions and comfort. "I" still comes first, even though it is covered in a Christian sauce.

World-renowned church researcher George Barna recently evaluated the general behavior of Christians and non-Christians and found there was no significant difference in lifestyle. Statistics confirm that church attendance doesn't necessarily motivate people to live more like Christ. It makes people more religious, but it does not automatically make them serve Christ better!

If only 7% of people in churches find the Lord, and a full 50% admit that they do not experience the presence of God in the church, then something must be seriously wrong! These statistics emphasize the fact that we must live radically differently if we really want to make an impact as followers of Jesus. People are the body of Christ (1 Cor. 12). You and I are the church. Church happens in any place where the followers of Jesus leave footprints.

Real and Relevant

Having hope will give you courage. You
will be protected and will rest in safety.

– Job 11:18 NLT –

Recently I heard about a few residents at a retirement home
whose only income was a meager government pension. They
did not have proper food to eat. Consequently, our church
committee decided in faith to pay for the meals of 20 of these
pensioners for the next year. I was moved to tears that all
those serving on the committee were personally prepared to
help people they didn't even know.

A week or two later I received a precious note from a lady
who had been one of my teachers years ago. She wrote to say
that she was in her seventies and saw for the first time how
real and relevant the church can be, after hearing about our
involvement with these elderly people who were suffering so
much. And I know she is a very dedicated church member.

How can faith be practiced so sparsely in the church? We
constantly hear the most beautiful sermons about faith, not
to mention all the Bible studies on this topic. But where does
the average Christian ever see faith in action? And even more
importantly: where do they practice their faith? What story
does your life tell today that will fill other people with hope?

Dignity

Give to everyone what you owe them: If you
owe taxes, pay taxes; if revenue, then revenue;
if respect, then respect; if honor, then honor.

– Roman 13:7 NIV –

Pastor Semenya and his wife's nursery school for poor children is one of our church's projects. These worthy servants of the Lord do wonderful work. But financially things were really bad at one stage. Then the Lord placed them on our radar. After the church opened the hearts and wallets of family members across the globe, the nursery school was renovated; food supplies bought; their daughter's studies paid for, and Pastor Semenya even received a second-hand car via a church member who felt it was a fitting way of serving the Lord.

When my wife and the management of our congregation recently attended church there, Pastor Semenya passed a remark that touched us deeply: "Now we feel like human beings again!"

Do you treat people in a way that makes them feel human? Do you treat them with dignity when they have been robbed due to poverty and suffering? That is what Christ expects of us. Every person who crosses your path today is God's work of art. Look carefully, until you see it. Then treat them in such a way that they will realize that they are special.

Never Too Busy

In repentance and rest is your salvation,
in quietness and trust is your strength.

– Isaiah 30:15 NIV –

How many times have you phoned a call center and had to wait in a long queue? "Your call will be answered in approximately one minute and 30 seconds." Well, if you talk with the living God, you will never be told to wait your turn. You aren't told to hold because your request is being processed.

You never have to hammer on the doors of heaven to attract God's personal attention. You never have to shout to remind Him that you are there. God is never too busy to listen to any of His children. When His children wish to speak with Him He is never busy with more important matters. The Lord does not avert His eyes when we are in a crisis.

Even though it may feel as if God isn't near, *He is*! Believe in His Word and not in your feelings and changing emotions. God hears and answers. Behind the scenes things have already started happening because you are praying!

December

Radical Transformation

Guard your heart above all else, for
it determines the course of your life.

– Proverbs 4:23 NLT –

Did you know that the dominant ideas in your head determine how you live? Your beliefs about other cultures, religions, your colleagues, church and family determine your entire life. Do you really know what your own stories sound like? Take some time to consider this for a moment. But also think about the following sentence that will change your life forever if you believe it: You have to radically invite the Spirit of God into your life to transform the main stories of your life!

It doesn't help if you give your heart to the Lord, but the ideas in your head remain your own. Millions of Christians have been caught in this trap. Their thoughts are controlled by stories other than those of the Lord. They still think selfish and loveless thoughts because they don't allow the Spirit to intervene. Far too few Christians live according to a brand-new story – the story of Jesus!

His story is always one in which humility, tenderness, sacrifice and faith triumphs. The story of Jesus is radically different from the dominant themes that feature in the lives of most people. What about you? Which story triumphs in you – those you have written yourself, of those of the Spirit?

God's Protection

The LORD protects all those who love Him.

– Psalm 145:20 NLT –

There are far more Scripture verses in the Bible that say God protects us *in* danger than *from* danger. The Lord does not necessarily safeguard us from all crises, but He does guarantee His presence in the midst of every storm. God doesn't allow us to take shelter in "safe harbors" all the time.

He does not automatically guarantee safety, good weather and sunshine. He wants to teach us to walk with Christ in our storms. That is why the Bible often says that we should seek the Lord in times of affliction. He is our only rock when the storms are raging. He is our steady anchor when the winds are howling. He is present in the storm and always on duty!

When we find ourselves in a crisis, then we have to be the first line of prayer defense. We must call on the Lord, not our minister, or some or other prayer chain. It is always good if others pray for us during these times, but the Lord commands us to talk to Him during times of crisis. That is the ABC of any Storm Survival Strategy. Do it! God will give deliverance in His own way.

An Original

O Lord, You have examined my heart and know everything about me. You know when I sit down or stand up. You know my thoughts even when I'm far away.

– Psalm 139:1-3 NLT –

The Lord wants you to be yourself. He really doesn't want you to be someone else, because then you would have been that other person. As mentioned previously, a speaker recently said that when he asks people who they would like to be, more than 90% of them want to be someone else. If you spend your whole life trying to be someone else, then you are always going to be second best and not at all yourself.

Listen carefully: Until the day you die you are going to be you! Make peace with that. The Lord deemed it fit to make you, with your own unique personality, appearance and thoughts. He artistically designed you in your mother's womb, as David describes in Psalm 139. He planned your life in great detail long before you were born. You are the grand result of a divine design session.

Thank God for being you! Live your God-given potential to the full in unique ways every single day. Serve Him with your gifts, talents and personality like only you can. Only you can do that bit of work that the Lord created you for.

The Right to My Soul

Commit to the LORD whatever you
do, and your plans will succeed.

– Proverbs 16:3 NIV –

"I put my soul into my work," someone told me the other day. Well, I don't think my place of work has any right to my soul. They do have the right to a share of my time, because they buy it from me. My work can also lay claim to my loyalty. But my work cannot demand all my time and my absolute loyalty. Neither can my work determine my entire identity. I am more than my profession. I have a life after hours. I am so much more than a worker at a particular place.

No matter how good my work is for me, and how hard I work – the day that I leave or retire, I will simply be replaced by someone else! No one is indispensable. But with the Lord it is the opposite. Each one of His children is indispensable in His eyes. We are all irreplaceable. That is why only the Lord has a right to our entire lives. His wish is our command!

His dreams determine our direction and His choices are our whole lives. Therefore, we should follow Him whole-heartedly at work and also after hours.

World-Shakers

Because of Christ and our faith in Him, we can now
come boldly and confidently into God's presence.

– Ephesians 3:12 NLT –

Being mindful is not self indulgent. On the contrary, it is an inner awareness of God's amazing goodness that enhances our spiritual capacity for caring in our relationships with Him and others. We must escape our mindless routines. They often trap us in deadly habits and negative thought patterns that steal our passion and creativity. Only when we experience deep community with God through the work of His Holy Spirit, does life become more gracious and enriching.

The more we realize that we are truly filled with God's closeness through the work of the Holy Spirit, the more we become aware of His extraordinary grace and the privilege of being alive in His presence right this very moment. The more we cultivate our awareness of God's grace, the more we succeed in breaking free from our prisons of negativity and cynicism. As we experience God's peace, we begin to treat ourselves and others with more grace and dignity.

As we become more aware of God's hand in changing our world through Christ, we join His band of world-shakers who spread the good news of Christ everywhere they go.

The Naked Truth

"You will know the truth, and the truth will set you free."
– John 8:32 NLT –

Have you heard of "the naked truth"? Isn't it an interesting expression? Maybe because lies are always dressed in clothes. Or maybe because half truths love walking around in slippers. And white lies are really actually pitch black. Besides, the truth is not dressed up. It never tries to hide anything. The truth is right out in the open, visible and transparent.

People who love the truth are people after God's own heart. These are people who don't need to constantly keep track of what they had said to whom, because they know they always speak the honest, candid truth. They go to sleep peacefully each night without feeling guilty about all the truths they twisted during the course of the day to suit their needs.

Loving the truth is a very precious part of our faith. To speak, think and live the truth is the visible signature of a life of integrity before God and people. In Ephesians 6 Paul writes that the truth is the belt around our waists. It keeps our spiritual clothes in place. Is your belt properly secured today?

Friendship

Two are better than one ... if one falls
down, his friend can help him up.

– Ecclesiastes 4:9-10 NIV –

Maybe you know the expression that you should write the bad things your friends do to you in sand, but the good things they do for you should be engraved in stone. Wise words! The wind blows sand away so easily, but the wind cannot accomplish much against stone. Beware of not holding little things against your loved ones, or you may lose them. Take a back seat. Do as the Bible says: Forgive. Reach out and offer a helping hand. Be willing to start over.

When you lose a friend, you have really lost a lot. This kind of loss is immeasurable. Don't allow it to happen. A good friend is worth much more than gold. Every friend is a gift from the Lord to enrich and fulfill your life.

Never neglect your friends. Pray for them regularly and spend time with them. Make them aware that they are special and precious to you. Protect their good names and listen to their sound advice. Support and help them when they stumble and fall. Do everything in your power to be a one-of-a-kind friend.

Who Wins?

The LORD is my light and my salvation –
whom shall I fear? The LORD is the stronghold
of my life – of whom shall I be afraid?

– Psalm 27:1 NIV –

Who wins when darkness and light meet? Well, the Pharisees believed it was darkness. In biblical times, religious people were told to avoid sinners. Many churchgoers still believe this today. That is why they have so little impact for the Lord. They hide away in religious shelters and complain about the ever-increasing evil of our times.

Jesus differs radically from this fault-finding mentality. He wasn't scared of being with unclean people. Jesus wasn't afraid of sin or sickness. Learn from Jesus that light is stronger than darkness. Godliness is far more contagious than ungodliness. Paul teaches this in 1 Corinthians in terms of marriage when he says that believers should not get divorced if one's partner is not a believer. Those who should be wary are the ones who take cover in the darkness. They can only encounter God's grace when they come into contact with God's children.

The Final Score

I have fought the good fight, I have finished
the race, and I have remained faithful.

– 2 Timothy 4:7 NLT –

How about a piece of truly good news for the hopeless? Here
it is: God has already sorted out the future in its entirety. It
is not classified information. The conclusion of world history
is described quite clearly in different places throughout the
Bible. Go and read about the final scoreboard in the Word,
and then you will see: THE LORD TRIUMPHS! Nothing and
nobody can stop Him. Even as you read this, God is busy establishing His new heaven and new earth.

If you do not realize every day that the Lord is winning,
then you will be lost in hopelessness. If you forget that Christ
is waiting for you at the end of your journey on earth with a
crown of righteousness in His hand (vv. 7-8), then you will
live as pessimistically as the rest of the people around you.

God's future is unfalteringly certain. It is described in black
and white in Scripture. Your here and now and your tomorrow and the days thereafter are all in His hand. Nothing and
nobody can snatch you out of Christ's hand, He assures us
in John 10:28-30. Take this truth to heart and truly believe it.

Pious Words

Show me Your ways, O LORD teach me Your paths.
— Psalm 25:4-5 NIV —

Recently I watched a reality show about women competing for the hearts of a number of men. One lady, who wasn't chosen, said afterwards that everything happens for a reason. If Jesus wanted this guy to pick her, then He would ensure that it happened. Conversely, the woman who was chosen said that she had simply trusted in the Lord and that her dream had come true. It sounded to me like these women regarded themselves as passive victims of God's will. Had they perhaps forgotten that they had willingly entered into this show and actively taken part in it?

Paul says in 1 Corinthians 4 that we are joint managers of God's earthly household. Consequently we have to take joint responsibility for our choices. Maybe we too easily hide behind clichés like "there is a purpose to everything." Rash pronouncements about the will of God are dangerous. He is the Lord and we are only ordinary people.

We should have more respect and reverence for Him. We have to learn to count our words carefully in His presence. Perhaps we should try to be more humble when we talk about God's will.

On His Terms (part I)

You can make many plans,
but the LORD's purpose will prevail.

– Proverbs 19:21 NLT –

It's not all about you! I am referring to your faith. God does not work for you. Not even your prayers are opportunities to give Him instructions concerning what He ought to do for you and others.

Really, consider this for a change, because many people walk around sulking about God. Apparently He did not help them when He was supposed to. He didn't take the illness away or He didn't stop the crime. Neither did He put food on the table quick enough. Consequently they walk around bad-mouthing God, saying that He is not kind or that He doesn't care anymore. Well, that happens because many of us have the idea in our heads that the Lord really owes us something. We serve Him, and therefore He has to do something for us in return!

Listen, the only reason why we serve God is because He is God. He mercifully redeemed us when we were lost. He loved us while we were still His enemies. He made us His own while we were so far away from Him. That is why we serve Him. It's all about Him. We serve Him on His terms.

On His Terms (part II)

Let us run with endurance the race God has set before us.

– Hebrews 12:1 NLT –

God is not in our service; He does not work for us. We don't determine the conditions of the relationship. We should get to know God and serve Him as He reveals Himself to us in the Bible. Fortunately, our God is a merciful God. He abounds in grace and abundantly shares it with each one of us. He pours out bucketfuls of kindness over us. His rest, His peace, His joy – that is what we receive if we walk with Him.

The Lord is our only strength when we are weak. He is our resting place when we are weary. He is our Hope everything around us is hopeless. God is our shelter when we feel insecure. He is our only reason for living. He is our wealth and our rock.

The Lord is our oxygen, our breath, our entire lives. The Lord is with us in every storm. He walks with us through every dark valley and every straight road. He remains at our side until well past the finishing post.

Use It or Lose It!

Trust in the LORD with all your heart; do not depend
on your own understanding. Seek His will in all
you do, and He will show you which path to take.

– Proverbs 3:5-6 NLT –

In a certain sense, faith works like the rule in rugby that states
"use it or lose it." Yes, I know Christ has already given me
eternal life. I believe with all my heart that He will carry me
safely past the journey's end. But I also know that I can't keep
clinging to last year's used-up faith. Faith is all about how I
live for Him in the present, today.

My relationship with the Lord must have an impact on my
life today. If not, it is merely "archive material." If all I have are
just fond memories of how God used me somewhere in the
past, I am heading for the Museum of Deceased Believers!

Faith means trusting Christ every day with my most precious possession – *my life*. I have to daily live with the realiza-
tion that my faith is really only as alive and relevant as my
latest step on God's path. Faith means holding on to Christ
right now, all day long. It means looking to Him today for life,
strength, provision, mercy, compassion and His presence. It
means expecting everything from Him.

Perfect Timing

For God says, "At just the right time, I heard you.
On the day of salvation, I helped you." Indeed, the
"right time" is now. Today is the day of salvation.

– 2 Corinthians 6:2 NLT –

The Lord does two great things every day: He provides heavenly bread to all His loved ones (Exod. 16) and He also hands out brand-new life (2 Cor. 4).

God is on duty today. In fact, He reports on time for every day. Throughout the ages God has always appeared to help and assist everyone who calls Him by name. God is the God of today. God has many glorious yesterdays behind Him, and tomorrow there will be an enormous victory procession when Christ returns. But today is His day, now; it is His day for work, His day for caring, His day for sharing His mercy.

Today is the day of salvation, as Paul writes in Corinthians. He cannot wait for tomorrow as it is too far into the future. Today God wants to share His bread with you and give away abundant life. Today He wants to change the world. Today He wants to adorn your life with His heavenly grace. Are you on time for His great plans? Or are you still lingering around, lost in yesterday?

Spiritual Traffic Jams

The LORD has told you what is good, and this
is what He requires of you: to do what is right,
to love mercy, and to walk humbly with your God.

– Micah 6:8 NLT –

Nowadays you can hardly travel on a freeway without getting caught in a traffic jam, not to mention peak time, when you sit stuck behind hordes of cars. Some church members are also caught up in spiritual traffic jams. They spend their whole lives sitting at an imaginary red traffic light, waiting for the spiritual light to turn green so that they can get going for God.

Some think you have to wait for months and years for God to make His plans known to you. Until then, they sit around passively in spiritual traffic that isn't making any progress in the right direction. Such people simply talk of their intention to one day do something big for God. But they never get around to actually doing it!

Listen, God's will is a road with a green traffic light. You discover His plans while you are driving. You find God's will while you are living the right life for Him. It really doesn't help much if you are constantly stationary on the right road. Get going. Experience and do God's will today.

Making a Difference

"Not by might nor by power, but by
My Spirit," says the LORD Almighty.

– Zechariah 4:6 NIV –

Recently I learned that six out of every 10 people in Africa live under the breadline. And now, on top of that, the price of bread is going up due to the rise in wheat prices worldwide. Living under the breadline means those less fortunate than ourselves have to try and survive with less than $1 per day.

Jesus teaches me that I cannot look the other way when people around me are suffering. I cannot lessen the plight of the entire world, but I can ensure that at least one other person smiles due to the mercy of God flowing through me. I can pray for one person. I can visit or phone one person. I can be a soft pillow for one other person. I can give one person's dignity back. I can make time to ask one person how they are doing and really listen to what they have to say.

While you trust the Man from Nazareth with your life every day, He wants to entrust the needs of at least one other person to you. Are you ready? Can He trust you with one person? Or is your faith still a private matter?

Sharing Yourself

Don't forget to do good and to share with those
in need. These are the sacrifices that please God.

– Hebrews 13:16 NLT –

Relationships require far more than just exchanging information with each other. Not too long ago I had to do strategic planning with a church council. I soon realized that few people, who had been serving on the council for more than ten years, knew very much about one another. They were actually still complete strangers who merely had meetings together. And then as a team they had to make important decisions about the Lord's work!

Relationships are not merely a case of knowing all the answers to questions like what job someone does, how many children they have and where they spend their holidays. That is information. Real relationships mean sharing a part of your life with another person. No, it means sharing yourself. Real relationships happen when you and someone else start sharing the same heartbeat.

Relationships require you to be someone's tower of strength. It requires time, sacrifice and honesty. And prayer on a regular basis. Real relationships always require a lot. You have to calculate the price of friendship well, because you put your life on the line for a friend. Just ask Jesus!

December 18

Moving Forward

Your own ears will hear Him. Right behind
you a voice will say, "This is the way you
should go," whether to the right or to the left.

– Isaiah 30:21 NLT –

The other day somebody told me how a resident of a township gave directions to his home. The route was complicated. The man asked whether there was a landmark to help him know if he was on the right road. "Yes," the person replied, "when you turn left at the last turnoff and you go on another 100 meters, look in your rearview mirror. If you see a stop sign, then you know that you are on the right road." He was very serious. What a surprising way of looking at things ... and also at the right way. Sometimes you really have to look back if you want to know whether the road ahead of you is indeed the right one.

Well, the hour glass of this year is slowly but surely running out. Which correct roads do you see when you look back over the past year? What stands out as the most significant landmarks of the Lord's love and kindness? Which spiritual lessons that you learnt over the past year will be your signposts for the new road ahead? Which people served as outstanding role models for you? Whose directions are your going to follow in future? What wisdom from God's Word is going to lead you forward?

In Their Midst

As they sat down to eat, He took the bread
and blessed it. Then He broke it and gave it to
them. Suddenly, their eyes were opened, and they
recognized Him. And at that moment He disappeared!

– Luke 24:30-31 NLT –

Cleopas was upset when the women told him that they had found the grave of Jesus empty on that Sunday after the crucifixion (Luke 24:1-35). Angry and disappointed, he and his wife started back on their seven-mile journey to their home town of Emmaus in the hot desert sun. But then a man joined them. They did not recognize Jesus at first. He should have been celebrating with His angels that day because He had finally broken the gates of death. He could have been among His disciples, rejoicing in His triumph. But on the greatest Sunday ever in world history Jesus chose to walk with two doubting skeptics to their little village, eating a humble dinner with them that night.

Only once they sat at the table did their eyes open. Only after a day in His presence did Cleopas and his wife recognize the pierced hands that passed the bread to them! Jesus celebrates His triumph differently from how we do. He celebrates by lovingly walking beside people who doubt. He does this by breaking bread with them – and helping them to see.

New Humanity

For He Himself is our peace.

– Ephesians 2:14 NIV –

In Ephesians, Paul makes the point that a new form of humanity, a new Christian race took shape at the cross. In His death, Christ united both Jews and non-Jews. Later Paul makes the statement that Christ, rather than God, reconciles people to one another and to God. Obviously Paul is not contradicting himself in this regard, inasmuch as it is still God who acts in love through the Messiah, which He has appointed. Christ is the peacemaker between people of different cultures and races. The same Christ who brings peace between God and mankind (v. 16), also brings peace between man and fellow man (vv. 14-15).

The blood of Christ is the sacrifice that made Jews and non-Jews into one new person. He brought those who are far and those who are near into a new body, a new humanity, a single new person! How did Jesus unite people of different backgrounds who lived in constant opposition to one another? Paul provides the answer in Ephesians 2:14. Here he states that Christ broke down the wall, literally: the division between Jews and non-Jews. Why do we constantly rebuild these fences, then?

A Sharp Tongue

The more talk, the less truth; the wise measure their words.

– Proverbs 10:19 THE MESSAGE –

There is the saying "From your mouth to God's ears." What this means is that what we say can become a self-fulfilling prophecy. Whether positive or negative, words are given life once they leave our mouths."If you do not have anything positive to say, rather say nothing at all." These are wise words, ones we would do well to heed if we are to reflect Jesus in our own lives.

Do you remember when Isaiah told the Lord that his lips were unclean and that his words did not glorify God, a burning coal was taken from the heavenly altar and touched his mouth? His mouth was cleansed with heavenly fire.

After that he could openly share words of hope and life with others. Let your tongue also be touched by heavenly fire!

Begin Again

"All who are victorious will inherit all these blessings,
and I will be their God, and they will be My children."

– Revelation 21:7 NLT –

Imagine you got the chance to start over, what would you do differently? According to research I once read, most people would like to do something differently. What a pity that the story of our lives, of which we are the main authors, very often end up as failures. Sometimes our lives are so disordered and chaotic that we literally want to do everything over if only we had another chance.

Did you know that you really do have a chance of starting over on the Lord's terms? After all, you have the rest of the day ahead of you. It is crammed with unused hours, minutes and seconds. You have a choice – whether you are going to seize it and make the best of it to glorify the Lord, or allow the rest of the day to slip through your fingers.

Don't let today be just another 24 hours of the week. Start by making a few small changes, then progress from there.

You and I don't have to change the whole world today. We simply have to be a living blessing in the name of Jesus to those who cross our paths. That is all.

Christ in Christmas

Glory to God in highest heaven, and peace
on earth to those with whom God is pleased.

– Luke 2:14 NLT –

Christmas is nearly here. The same decorations in shops, the same types of music, gifts, lights, food, sentimental cards and advertisements are seen all around the world. And, yes, also the same complaints about the abuse of Christmas.

Many people can't wait for Christmas to either make money or to complain about it. To celebrate or not to celebrate – that is not the question! Don't be like the rest – create your own kind of celebration this Christmas. Truly make Jesus the King! Let Him be the center and the Lord of the celebration that you and your loved ones celebrate together.

Bring gifts to Jesus this year, not the other way around. During these days, let your life be the most decorated gift that testifies how wonderful and important He is. Let your relationships with others show how precious Christ is to you. Ensure that He is truly the substance of your days during this year. Let Him be the reason why you get up and go to sleep, why you care, why you love, why you live. Celebrate a new feast, a feast of life. You have all the reasons in the world to do so!

Considering Others

For to us a child is born, to us a son is given,
and the government will be on His shoulders.
And He will be called Wonderful Counselor, Mighty God,
Everlasting Father, Prince of Peace.

– Isaiah 9:6 NIV –

"Our menu for this year is Christmas lunch is bread,"is what someone tells me. "That is all we have to eat!" When I shared this with someone else, the person said,"It breaks my heart!" But when I added that I have come up with a plan to provide this person with something other than bread, and asked whether he would be prepared to get involved, I got the following answer: "Oh dear, I first have to see to it that my own family has food on the table!" Without really thinking, I replied,"That shouldn't be necessary. I saw you in the restaurant the other day, having a meal."

Forgive me; maybe I was unnecessarily frank. Or, maybe not, because Jesus taught me that when I notice real need with actual names and addresses, I cannot turn a blind eye. It is not enough to sit beside groaning festive tables and talk about the plight of others. All that matters are those small tokens of compassion – a plate of food here, a hug there. I know I cannot lighten the load of every suffering person, but neither can I look the other way. If I do, I might not see the Lord either!

Heavenly Joy

She gave birth to her first child, a son. She wrapped
Him snugly in strips of cloth and laid Him in a manger,
because there was no lodging available for them.

– Luke 2:7 NLT –

Merry Christmas! May these two words mean far more to you
than the mere fact that they sound familiar or that is seems
like the right thing to say on this day. May these two words
also bestow upon us the peace that comes from the Lord who
came to honor us with His earthly presence.

I hope these words bring you to a halt in front of the crib,
where the Christ Child first came to adorn the earth. And may
this year's Christmas move you to rest at His feet. May you
experience peace, even though strife is rampant all around
you. May you enjoy happiness, although many people know
only hatred and bitterness.

Today, tomorrow and the day after, may you experience
heavenly abundance, despite any earthly shortcoming you
may suffer. May heaven and earth rejoice with you because
you call the Child of the Crib and the Cross your Lord and
Master. May this be the main reason why this Christmas is a
merry and blessed time for you.

Relationships Are Important

The LORD has done great things
for us, and we are filled with joy.

– Psalm 126:3 NIV –

Joy comes in small portions – like that cup of coffee you share with a friend. Or in the unplanned visit with someone you meet. Life is all about relationships. Did you know that your mind was created to make decisions regarding people almost one tenth of a second faster than decisions about other things. A recent study found that when we are relaxed and not doing anything, our brain is most probably busy taking a closer look at our relationships.

The Lord created us to love. We are wired for relationships. We are designed to be able to experience deep feelings of compassion and love. Don't sacrifice this early in the new year for the sake of becoming a slave to full schedules, meetings and activities. Your faith must be relation-driven, not task-driven. Your faith is not all about the things that you do for the Lord, but also about the relationships you build.

It is about good things that you do for people with real names and addresses. Be there for the people close to you in the year ahead. But also be there for the strangers who may cross your path unexpectedly.

Taking Responsibility

"Where your treasure is, there your heart will be also."
– Matthew 6:21 NIV –

I hear you say you have no other choice but to live the hurried life you are currently living. There must be food on the table; the next house installment must be paid; groceries have to be bought; the kids' school fees are due ... Yes, that may be true, but in the meantime you may be missing God's purpose for your life because you don't allow any quality time for Him in your life. Your life is a deadly race to get everything done.

With feeble excuses to justify your flustered lifestyle, you drive yourself even further towards burnout and hopelessness day after day. It looks like you still haven't noticed that your heavenly Father is looking after you. After all these years, do you still fail to realize that He knows exactly what you need (vv. 25-33)?

Start trusting in Him from now on to provide that which He knows you need. Take note, not what you think you need, but whatever He has decided! Find rest – the right kind of rest. Don't get stuck in the same old bad habits next year by living another year beyond your own speed limit.

A Living Blessing

"Give, and you will receive. Your gift will return to you
in full – pressed down, shaken together to make room for
more, running over, and poured into your lap. The amount
you give will determine the amount you get back."

– Luke 6:38 NLT –

The hourglass is almost empty. The fuel for this year is nearly
depleted. Another successful earthly journey around the sun
is almost over. Have you been a living blessing to someone
during this past year? Have you conquered those damning
statistics that say the average church member goes through
life without ever having lead another person to Christ?

Can someone, towards the end of the year, agree that your
presence in their lives opened up a new window to God for
them? Has somebody discovered Christ as the Good Shepherd because you were walking with them in love? Well, then
it has been a phenomenal year. Nothing else measures up
against one lost sheep that has returned home, as Jesus tells
us in Luke 15. Nothing! The return of lost items is always
headline news in heaven. The safe return of every lost person
is cause for a special feast in the presence of the Father. If you
have given reason for joyous celebration in heaven due to just
a single person, then this has been the year of your life!

Eternal Compass

If the LORD delights in a man's way,
He makes his steps firm; though he stumble,
he will not fall, for the LORD upholds him with His hand.

– Psalm 37:23-24 NIV –

New Year's resolutions are so fashionable at the moment! Everyone is turning over a new leaf. Excess weight acquired during the festive season is courageously tackled and bad habits of the past year discarded. What is your great resolution for the new year? How many of the previous year's good intentions did you honor? Tragically, most people don't stick to their New Year's resolutions much longer than the third week of January. Why? Well, because any decisions that don't come from your heart will not have any long term effect.

Your convictions are like an internal compass that determines your direction in life. These convictions are the driving force that makes you get up every morning. What drives you to take on the challenges of life joyfully every day? Well, I know who gives me the strength and desire to get up every morning with hope in my heart. His name is Jesus Christ. He is the Lord. I want to make His priorities my priorities in the year to come. Whatever is important to Him will be the thing that matters most in my life during the coming year.

December 30

New Year's Plans

May He give you the desire of your
heart and make all your plans succeed.

– Psalm 20:4 NIV –

It is once again that time of the year when New Year's resolutions are made at every turn. Can you believe it! I have also made a few serious resolutions for the new year that is lurking just around the corner, such as setting aside more quiet time in my life. God doesn't compete with all the noise in and around me. I realize that I will have to hear Him on His terms in the year to come and not on mine. Consequently, I want to have more quiet time so that I may get to know the Lord better.

Another resolution – I don't want to send or answer any angry e-mails or SMSs whatsoever. It is a waste of unnecessary energy to try and reason with smart alecks, or those who are always right. Neither do I want to join the band of crazy drivers who are always speeding, only to win two minutes of time and two hours of high blood pressure as the "reward."

I want to live each day at "today speed" – one day at a time. I reckon that it is just about fast enough.

The Army of God

If you keep yourself pure, you will be a special utensil
for honorable use. Your life will be clean, and you will
be ready for the Master to use you for every good work.

– 2 Timothy 2:21 NLT –

The new year is upon us. It didn't come down on us out of the
blue. Actually we have seen it coming – ever since last year.
Only last week we were counting down the days, then the
hours, then the minutes, then the seconds. And now the new
year is upon us at last. Will it be a fresh, exciting year for you?
Are you going to be a living difference? Are you going to report for duty as a *one (wo)man army* in the name of the Lord?

It is up to you how you will live during the year that lies
ahead. Choose wisely. Every day has only 24 hours. Nobody
has ever succeeded in adding an hour to the day. Buy out the
available time in each day, as Paul suggests.

Opportunities sometimes cross your path in the most unexpected ways. Ask the Lord to make you sensitive to these
opportunities so that you will recognize them ... and seize
each one. Pray that the Lord will give you the discernment
to know in whose lives you should tarry a little longer; for
whom you should actively pray, and where you should offer
more assistance.